PENGUIN BOOKS

The Collected Plays of
GRAHAM GREENE

Graham Greene was born in 1904 and educated at Berkhamsted School, where his father was the headmaster. On coming down from Balliol College, Oxford, where he published a book of verse, he worked for four years as a sub-editor on *The Times*. He established his reputation with his fourth novel, *Stamboul Train*, which he classed as an 'entertainment' in order to distinguish it from more serious work. In 1935 he made a journey across Liberia, described in *Journey Without Maps*, and on his return was appointed film critic of the *Spectator*. In 1926 he had been received into the Roman Catholic Church and was commissioned to visit Mexico in 1938 and report on the religious persecution there. As a result he wrote *The Lawless Roads* and, later, *The Power and the Glory*.

Brighton Rock was published in 1938 and in 1940 he became literary editor of the *Spectator*. The next year he undertook work for the Foreign Office and was sent out to Sierra Leone in 1941–3. One of his major post-war novels, *The Heart of the Matter*, is set in West Africa and is considered by many to be his finest book. This was followed by *The End of the Affair*, *The Quiet American*, a story set in Vietnam, *Our Man in Havana*, and *A Burnt-Out Case*. Many of his novels have been filmed, as have two of his short stories, and *The Third Man* was written as a film treatment. His other publications include *The Pleasure Dome* (1972), *The Honorary Consul* (1973), *An Impossible Woman: The Memories of Dottoressa Moor of Capri* (edited 1975), *The Human Factor* (1978), *Doctor Fischer of Geneva or The Bomb Party* (1980), *Monsignor Quixote* (1982), *J'Accuse: The Dark Side of Nice* (1982) and *Getting to Know the General* (1984). His first volume of autobiography was *A Sort of Life* (1971), and *Ways of Escape*, a second autobiographical volume, was published in 1980.

Graham Greene has written in all some thirty novels, 'entertainments', plays, children's books, travel books, and collections of essays and short stories. He was made a Companion of Honour in 1966.

THE COLLECTED PLAYS
OF
GRAHAM GREENE

─────────── ★ ───────────

PENGUIN BOOKS

Penguin Books Ltd, Harmondsworth, Middlesex, England
Viking Penguin Inc., 40 West 23rd Street, New York, New York 10010, U.S.A.
Penguin Books Australia Ltd, Ringwood, Victoria, Australia
Penguin Books Canada Ltd, 2801 John Street, Markham, Ontario, Canada L3R 1B4
Penguin Books (N.Z.) Ltd, 182–190 Wairau Road, Auckland 10, New Zealand

The Living Room first published by William Heinemann Ltd 1953
Published in Penguin Books 1970
Acknowledgements are due to Mr Roy Campbell for permission to use
at the beginning of Act Two a passage from his translation of *The Poems
of St John of the Cross* (Harvill Press)

The Potting Shed first published by William Heinemann Ltd 1958
Published in Penguin Books 1971

The Complaisant Lover first published by William Heinemann Ltd 1959
Published in Penguin Books 1971

Carving a Statue first published by The Bodley Head 1964
Published in Penguin Books 1972

The Return of A. J. Raffles first published by The Bodley Head 1975
Published in Penguin Books 1978

The Great Jowett first published by The Bodley Head 1981

Yes and No first published by The Bodley Head 1983

For Whom the Bell Chimes first published by The Bodley Head 1983

This collection first published 1985
The performing rights in these plays are fully protected, and
permission to perform them must be obtained in advance.
Applications should be made to:
Dr Jan van Loewen
International Copyright Agency
81–3 Shaftesbury Avenue
London W1

Copyright © Graham Greene, 1953, 1958, 1959, 1964, 1975,
1981, 1983, 1985.
All rights reserved

Made and printed in Great Britain by
Cox & Wyman Ltd, Reading
Filmset in 10/12 pt Linotron Bembo by
Rowland Phototypesetting Ltd, Bury St Edmunds, Suffolk

CONTENTS

The Living Room   1

The Potting Shed   69

The Complaisant Lover   139

Carving a Statue   209

The Return of A. J. Raffles   263

The Great Jowett   327

Yes and No   355

For Whom the Bell Chimes   369

THE LIVING ROOM

★

To
Catherine with love

CHARACTERS

MARY, *the daily woman*　　MISS HELEN BROWNE

MICHAEL DENNIS　　　　　FATHER JAMES BROWNE

ROSE PEMBERTON　　　　　MRS DENNIS

MISS TERESA BROWNE

CAST

First presented on Thursday, 16 April 1953, at Wyndham's Theatre, London. With the following cast:

MARY	*Dorothy Dewhurst*
MICHAEL DENNIS	*John Robinson*
ROSE PEMBERTON	*Dorothy Tutin*
MISS TERESA BROWNE	*Mary Jerrold*
MISS HELEN BROWNE	*Violet Farebrother*
FATHER JAMES BROWNE	*Eric Portman*
MRS DENNIS	*Valerie Taylor*

The play was directed by PETER GLENVILLE

with settings by LESLIE HURRY

SCENES

Act One

Scene One   The Living Room. An afternoon in January.
Scene Two   The same. The next morning.

Act Two

Scene One   The Living Room. Three weeks later. Late
               afternoon.
Scene Two   The same. The next morning.

Act One

SCENE ONE

The Living Room. An afternoon in January.

At first sight, when the curtain rises, we are aware of something strange about the living room. The house is an ordinary Holland Park house, and there is nothing at first on which we can positively lay a finger and say, 'this is wrong', or 'this is strange'. Through a tall window at the back we see only the tops of the trees outside and the window is oddly barred up half its height. Is it that the furniture – in a fashion difficult to define – doesn't quite fit, as though it had been chosen for a larger room of a different shape? But there are many explanations for that in these days. There are two doors to the room – one is open on to the landing, the other up a small flight of stairs is closed. As the curtain rises, a bell downstairs is ringing.

[MARY *comes rapidly in. She is un-uniformed and you could not believe that those heavy, shapeless legs could belong to anyone less independent than a daily woman. She mounts the stairs to the closed door and turns the handle. It is locked.*]

MARY [*softly*]: Miss Teresa . . .

[*She listens for a moment, and then as the bell rings again, goes out to the landing and we hear her rattling down the stairs.*

Almost at the same moment we hear the sound of water pouring away from a basin in a closet, behind the second door. That for a moment seems to focus the oddness, the uneasiness of this room, for who would expect a lavatory to open immediately out of a living room as though it were – perhaps we are now reaching the heart of the problem – really a bedroom? Voices mount the stairs – a man's voice and MARY's.]

MARY: Miss Browne will be glad to see you here, Miss Rose, safe and sound.

MICHAEL: I hope she got my wire. Phew! This has been quite a climb.

MARY: It's warm for the time of year, sir.

MICHAEL: Is it? Not in the train. The heating wasn't on.

[MARY *shows in* MICHAEL DENNIS, *a man in the middle forties with a strained, rather sullen face anxious about too many things and too anxious to disguise his anxiety, and* ROSE PEMBERTON, *a girl of about twenty with a look of being not quite awake, a bewildered tousled-pillow face, a face which depends for its prettiness on youth. It will never again be quite so pretty as this year − or even this month.*]

MARY: Miss Browne will be down in a minute, sir. [*She goes out.*]

MICHAEL: Down? She must live in an attic.

[MICHAEL *and* ROSE *stand stiffly, a little apart, looking round the room.*]

Why have a living room on the third floor? Do you think it's to discourage callers? [*He moves restlessly around, but comes back to exactly the same spot, three feet away from the girl.*] What an odd room! It's the wrong shape. Do you see what I mean? Nothing quite fits. I wonder where that goes to? [*He indicates the stairs to the closet door, climbs them, and tries the handle. He returns to the same spot of carpet.*] The Browne family's skeleton? Browne with an E. Haven't you anything to say? Some joke? Something to show that we don't really care a damn?

[ROSE *shakes her head.*]

Well, I've delivered you safely. The reliable family friend. You are only twelve hours late. And we sent the right considerate telegram. The orphan is safe. But they wouldn't have worried. You were in *my* hands.

[ROSE *puts out a hand and touches him. He puts his hand over hers, holding it tightly, but they keep the same distance.*]

Be careful! You can always trust me to be very careful. I've reached the careful age. Wasn't my planning perfect? The two rooms at opposite ends of the corridor. And even the Boots was not up when our alarm went. The shoes stood on parade all down the corridor − in the correct positions.

ROSE [*imploringly*]: Do you have to? Isn't it bad enough, darling?

MICHAEL: Careful, again. Darling is a word we mustn't use. Perhaps 'dear' would be all right, from a man of my age. A

safely married man. But when I say dear, remember it means –
just that. Dear.

ROSE: We can hear anybody coming up the stairs.

[*She kisses him, and at that moment a key turns in the closet door.
They leap to their original positions as the door opens and* MISS
TERESA BROWNE *comes out – an old lady who must have passed
seventy a long while ago. She closes the door behind her.*]

Aunt Helen . . .

[TERESA BROWNE *pays not the slightest attention. She walks by
them as though they were not there and out through the door on to the
landing.*]

MICHAEL: Why did she go out like that? Why didn't she speak? Do
you think she saw us?

ROSE: No. Perhaps she heard something.

MICHAEL: There wasn't much to hear.

[TERESA *re-enters. She holds out her hand and smiles with res-
trained cordiality.*]

TERESA: My dear, you must be Rose. Mary never told me you'd
arrived.

ROSE [*kissing her*]: And you are Aunt Helen. Or do I have to call
you Great-Aunt?

TERESA: I'm Aunt Teresa, dear.

ROSE: How silly of me!

TERESA: Not silly after all these years. You were only six, weren't
you?

ROSE: Only six. This is Mr Dennis, Aunt Teresa.

TERESA: I'm interested to meet you, Mr Dennis. My poor niece
mentioned you often in her letters.

ROSE [*to* MICHAEL]: My mother.

MICHAEL: Of course. I hope you don't think, Miss Browne, that
I've let down your trust already.

TERESA: I don't know what you mean, Mr Dennis. Trust?

MICHAEL: We're twelve hours late. It seemed sensible to catch an
early morning train instead of travelling after the funeral.

TERESA: I was sorry not to be there, dear. But I couldn't leave your
uncle and your Aunt Helen. You found a room in the village, I
hope, Mr Dennis?

MICHAEL: Oh, yes. The Red Lion.

TERESA: Mass was said for your mother this morning, dear, by Father Turner.

ROSE: Oh, I'm sorry. I didn't know. I should have been there.

TERESA: We were all there – even my brother – we remembered you with her. Are you a Catholic, Mr Dennis?

MICHAEL [*abruptly*]: No.

TERESA: How odd that my niece should have left you her executor.

ROSE [*with asperity*]: Why not? My father wasn't a Catholic.

TERESA: No, dear. Poor man. Would you like a cup of tea, Mr Dennis?

MICHAEL: You mustn't bother. I only came to hand over Rose . . .

TERESA: A labourer deserves his hire. Excuse me a moment, Mr Dennis. [*She goes to the door and calls* 'Mary!' *No answer. She goes out on to the landing and calls again* 'Mary'. *From the landing*] What time is it, Mr Dennis?

MICHAEL: Just gone five.

TERESA: Mary always leaves so punctually, but she's paid till five-fifteen.

MICHAEL: I've really got to go.

TERESA: My brother always likes his cup. Mary! [*She goes downstairs.*]

MICHAEL: Well, we've broken the ice. That's not a good phrase, is it, for a pair of people skating like we are.

ROSE: Darling, what are you worrying about? Me? You don't have to. I swear it. [*With a touch of bitterness.*] I loved you the night of my mother's funeral. That's an oath, isn't it, like mixing blood. For ever and ever. Amen.

MICHAEL: Oh, it's myself I'm worrying about. I'm afraid you're going to disappear. In a wood of old people. I'm afraid I'm losing you – the minutes are hurrying. What happens tomorrow? [*He moves around the room while she stays still, at a loss, in the centre of it.*]

ROSE: You don't have to worry – You can't lose me. After all, you're the executer.

MICHAEL: You mean the executor, yes, I suppose I can always see you on business. [*Mounting the stairs.*] She came from up here.

[*He opens the closet door.*] It just doesn't make sense. The third floor. A bathroom out of the sitting-room. This must have been a bedroom.

[MISS HELEN BROWNE *enters.*]

HELEN: You're Rose?

[*They kiss.*]

My dear little sweetheart, I used to call you. And you are Mr Dennis?

[*They shake hands.*]

Oh, you wouldn't believe what a bad little sweetheart she could be sometimes.

[*She is a little younger than her sister – a fat woman, with a certain bonhomie. She can steer straight through other people's lives without noticing.*]

Teresa told me you'd arrived. She's making tea. The maid left too early, but the clock in the kitchen's fast. Rose, dear, perhaps you'd give her a hand with the bread-and-butter.

ROSE: I'm afraid I don't know where . . .

HELEN: Straight down the stairs and into the basement. You'll hear her cluttering around. [*To* MICHAEL] My poor sister's eyesight's failing. It's to be expected, of course, at seventy-eight.

ROSE [*to* MICHAEL]: I'll see you . . . ?

HELEN: Mr Dennis will stay to tea, won't you, Mr Dennis?

[ROSE *leaves the room – unwillingly.*]

I was so sorry not to have been at the church. But you do understand, don't you, I couldn't leave my brother and sister. Do sit down.

MICHAEL: I hadn't meant to stay.

HELEN: Oh, but there's so much we would like to hear. [*She sits firmly down in the most comfortable chair.*] The Brownes all have long ears, like the Flopsy Bunnies. You know the Flopsy Bunnies, Mr Dennis?

MICHAEL: I don't think I do.

HELEN: Not dear Beatrix Potter? But, of course, she was my generation. I saw her once shopping at Debenham's. Now I'd expected you – somehow – to be an older man.

MICHAEL: I'm forty-five. [*He sits unwillingly.*]

HELEN: Catholics are much too clanny sometimes, don't you think? Dear Teresa was quite surprised when my niece chose someone who wasn't a Catholic as a trustee.

MICHAEL: I was her husband's friend, you know – his pupil, too. I owe everything to him. Even my job now – at London University.

HELEN: You'll think us rather bigoted, but we never cared very much for poor John's profession. It would have been so awkward for my niece if it had been – condemned.

MICHAEL: I'm afraid you won't approve of my profession then – but I'm a mere *lecturer* in psychology. Not a professor.

HELEN: Oh well, of course, it doesn't matter about you, does it, Mr Dennis? We aren't concerned. And the will? We've had no details yet. [*Coyly*] Long ears again.

MICHAEL: Rose will have about eight hundred a year of her own at the age of twenty-five. Until then, your brother and I are trustees.

HELEN: It might have been better to have kept it in the family instead of troubling you. [*Coyly*] Now I'm being clanny too.

MICHAEL: You see, her father appointed me a trustee before he died, and Mrs Pemberton just let it stand. His friends were always her friends. I used to visit them every summer after his death.

HELEN [*sadly*]: She was the first Browne to marry a non-Catholic.

MICHAEL [*with a smile*]: The first Browne?

HELEN: The first of *our* Brownes. And you are the executor too, Mr Dennis?

MICHAEL: As I was trustee I suppose the lawyers thought it would make things go more smoothly. I shall resign as trustee as soon as the will's executed. You'll be free of me.

HELEN: Oh, but of course I didn't mean . . .

MICHAEL: I don't think I'm quite made to be a trustee, Miss Browne.

HELEN [*almost as though she had taken his point*]: We *were* a little anxious about Rose until we got your telegram.

MICHAEL: She was tired by the funeral. It would have been too much to travel all night. I thought the day train –

HELEN: Poor Rose – it must have been lonely in that house all by herself.

MICHAEL: Better than travelling, of course. [*Explaining a little too much*] I got a room at the Red Lion for myself.

HELEN: So right of you, Mr Dennis. In a village like that there'd have been a lot of silly talk if you'd stayed in the house.

MICHAEL: Even about a man of my age and a girl of hers?

HELEN [*cheerfully and inexorably*]: Human nature's such a terrible thing, Mr Dennis. Or is that very Roman of me?

MICHAEL: I haven't found it terrible. Complicated, tangled, perhaps unhappy. Needing help.

HELEN: My niece wrote in one of her last letters that you had been very helpful. We are so grateful for that. There was little we could do.

[*She notices that* MICHAEL *is a little absent. The room still puzzles him. He cannot help looking here and there, particularly at the stains on the wall.*]

[*Making conversation*] But now we can all help Rose to forget.

MICHAEL: I'm very sorry. What was that? Forget?

HELEN: Her dear mother.

MICHAEL: Is it always a good thing to forget? Of course my job is usually to teach people the importance of remembering.

HELEN: What are you staring at, Mr Dennis?

MICHAEL: Was I staring?

HELEN: I'm afraid it *is* rather a cluttered room. But you see, it's our only living room.

MICHAEL: It looks quite a big house from outside.

HELEN: A great many of the rooms are closed.

MICHAEL: War damage?

HELEN [*guardedly*]: For one reason or another.

[*As he still looks around*]

All the rooms need repapering, but one doesn't like to spend capital, does one?

[*Teresa enters, carrying a cake-stand with bread-and-butter on one level and a plum cake on another.*]

TERESA: The kettle's boiling, Helen. We shan't be a moment, Mr Dennis. Everything's set.

[*In this household she is obviously the anxious Martha; the weaker character intent on carrying out orders. The orders are first thought up somewhere else, presumably behind that mask of bonhomie her slightly younger sister presents to the world.*]

MICHAEL: It's good of you, but I hadn't meant to stay.

TERESA: Oh, but you must meet our brother.

HELEN: Don't press Mr Dennis, Teresa. He may have all sorts of things . . .

MICHAEL: Perhaps I ought to have a word with – your niece, before I go.

TERESA: With my niece? But she's . . . she's . . . dead.

HELEN [*sharply*]: He means Rose, dear.

MICHAEL: There's still a lot of business to be done. About the will. You see, the other executor is abroad.

TERESA: What a good thing you're a careful man, Mr Dennis!

MICHAEL: Am I careful?

TERESA: That's what you were telling Rose, wasn't it? 'You can always trust me,' you said, 'to be very careful.' I thought it was so sweetly put.

MICHAEL [*covering up*]: Well, an executor has to be careful – or he goes to jail.

HELEN [*defining his sphere of interest*]: You should really see my brother about all those legal things. Rose is too young to understand. Dear little sweetheart! Teresa, if Rose is tired, tell her to lie down. We can entertain Mr Dennis.

[ROSE *returns on that word, carrying the tea-things.*]

ROSE: I'm not a bit tired.

HELEN: Well then, if you'll all sit down (do take off your coat, Mr Dennis), I'll push James in. (You know he's been confined to his chair for years.) Start pouring out the tea, dear. [*She goes out.*]

TERESA [*fussing with the tea-things*]: Now find yourselves chairs. No, not that one, Rose. That's your Aunt Helen's.

[ROSE *and* MICHAEL *sit down together. They don't look at each other. Constraint keeps their eyes on a mutual object, as if it is only there, where* TERESA *deals with the tea-things, that their gaze can meet vicariously.*]

Where did you say you went to Mass today, dear?

ROSE: I didn't, Aunt Teresa.

TERESA: But it's a Holiday of Obligation, dear. Oh well, perhaps it doesn't matter if you were travelling.

ROSE: I forgot. I could have gone before the early train. But I slept so sound.

TERESA: One lump, Mr Dennis?

MICHAEL: Thank you.

TERESA: And you, Rose?

ROSE: Yes, please, Aunt.

[TERESA *is pouring out the tea as she talks.*]

TERESA: I started a novena for you as soon as I heard of your poor mother.

ROSE: Thank you, Aunt Teresa.

TERESA: I expect you'd like to go to Mass tomorrow. It's the second of nine we've arranged for her. Mary doesn't come in till eight-thirty, but we'll wake you ourselves.

ROSE: Thank you.

TERESA: Help yourself to bread-and-butter, Mr Dennis.

[ROSE *and* MICHAEL *both put out their hands, touch each other and recoil over the plate.*]

[*To* ROSE] Has Helen told you about your room?

ROSE: No, but there's no hurry.

TERESA: You see, dear, we are very cramped for space here. So many rooms are closed. We thought perhaps you wouldn't mind sleeping in here. The sofa's very comfortable. And the end lets down.

ROSE: Of course. I don't mind.

MICHAEL: I was saying to your sister, Miss Browne, that it seemed quite a large house from the street.

TERESA: Oh, it was. It was. But many rooms had to be closed.

MICHAEL: War damage?

TERESA: Not exactly.

HELEN [*outside*]: Here we are! Will somebody open the door?

[HELEN *pushes in a chair in which sits her brother,* JAMES BROWNE, *a man of about 65, with a face to which one is not sure whether nature or mutilation has lent strength. All his vitality perhaps has had to find its way above the waist. A shawl is over his legs, and he wears a scarf round his neck.*]

[*To* JAMES] James, here is Rose – and Mr Dennis, the executor.

JAMES: It's good to see you, my dear. After all these years. You've changed more than I have.

[ROSE *bends down and kisses him.*]

ROSE: How are you, Uncle?

JAMES: Pretty well, my dear. Thank God you won't play trains with my chair now! Well, Mr Dennis, I hope she hasn't been a trouble to you. We expected you last night.

MICHAEL: The morning train seemed a better idea, Mr Browne.

HELEN: *Father* Browne, Mr Dennis. My brother's . . .

MICHAEL: Of course. I'm sorry.

JAMES: Now you've seen all the family again, can you bear us, Rose? We are a bit older than we were, but we aren't so bad.

ROSE: It was good of Mother to leave me to you. I'd have been lost without you.

JAMES: The only Catholic Pemberton. But somehow I never think of you as a Pemberton.

TERESA [*handing* JAMES *a cup*]: Your tea, dear.

ROSE: Some bread-and-butter, Uncle?

JAMES: No, thank you, dear. Just the tea. I'm not an eating man.

TERESA: Oh, Rose! Such a funny thing happened last night! A lady rang up and she asked if we were the Brownes who were expecting a niece.

ROSE: Who was she?

TERESA: I've no idea. When I told her you weren't arriving till today she just rang off.

HELEN: You never told me, Teresa. What a secret little thing you are!

TERESA: I've only just remembered. [*To* ROSE] I expect it was a friend of yours who wanted to inquire.

ROSE: I can't think of anybody – in London. [*She looks at* MICHAEL *with apprehension.*]

TERESA: Oh, if it's anything important, I expect she'll ring again. Talking of important, James, Mary left a quarter of an hour early today.

HELEN: It wasn't her fault. The clock in the kitchen is always twenty minutes fast.

[*While the old people talk,* ROSE *and* MICHAEL *sit awkwardly together, saying nothing. They have no small-talk for each other.*]

TERESA: Since it's always fast she must know the real time. Will you speak to her, James? She would take it better from you. Oh . . . [*Putting her cup suddenly down, she makes for the door.*]

HELEN: Now, dear, what is it?

TERESA: If Mary left early, I don't know how the oven is.

HELEN: It can wait for a few minutes. What a little Martha you are!

TERESA: You'd be the first to complain tonight about the pie.

HELEN: Well then, let me go, dear, and I'll have only myself to blame.

TERESA: The cooking tonight is *my* responsibility. Isn't that so, James?

JAMES: It's a Thursday. Yes.

HELEN: I'll help you, dear. I can't bear to see you lifting heavy things.

[*During the argument* ROSE *and* MICHAEL *have drawn a little apart from the others.*

TERESA *leaves the room.*

HELEN *is about to follow her when she looks round and sees* MICHAEL'*s hand touching* ROSE'*s as he takes her empty cup.*]

ROSE: Thank you, dear. [*She tries to swallow the last word, but it's too late.*]

HELEN: See that Mr Dennis has a slice of my plum cake, James. [*She leaves.*]

JAMES: She has a wonderful hand with cakes, Mr Dennis.

MICHAEL: I don't think I will. I ought to be going home.

ROSE: I'm sorry.

MICHAEL: Why?

ROSE: I mean, I've been such a trouble.

MICHAEL: No trouble. But my wife gets anxious rather easily. She's – not very well. I should have gone straight home, but I thought there were things we ought to discuss – about the will.

ROSE [*anxious to ensure seeing her lover the next day*]: No, no. It can wait. Till tomorrow. You'll be coming in tomorrow? We can talk then.

MICHAEL: Of course. Any time that suits you. I'll ring you up in the morning. Have a good rest tonight.

[*They are trying to reassure each other in* FATHER BROWNE'*s presence.*]

ROSE: You've done so much for me.

MICHAEL: It's my job. I'm the executor – not the exe*cu*ter.

ROSE: It was a silly slip. I was never much good at English.

MICHAEL: As the executor and trustee [*slowly and firmly*] I'll try not to make any slips at all. Good-bye, Father Browne.

JAMES: Good-bye, Mr Dennis. We'll be seeing each other again soon, I hope.

ROSE: You put some papers down . . . over there, I think.

[*It is an excuse for them to move behind the old man's chair, out of his vision. They are afraid to kiss, but they hold each other for a moment.*]

MICHAEL: They must be in my overcoat pocket.

[*They go together to the door.*]

Don't come down. It's a long way to the hall. I'll see you tomorrow, Rose.

ROSE: Yes.

MICHAEL [*with a last look at this room which is the wrong shape*]: Good-bye. [*He goes.*]

[ROSE *follows him on to the landing. We can hear his steps on the stairs, but she still doesn't return. A pause.*]

JAMES: Come in, dear, and have another cup of tea.

ROSE [*returning*]: I don't awfully like tea.

JAMES [*guessing her thoughts*]: Yes, it's a long way down, isn't it? Only the kitchen is in the place you'd expect. In the basement. Even if you don't like tea, come in and sit down. I don't see many strangers.

ROSE: Am I a stranger?

JAMES: One can love a stranger.

ROSE: Yes. [*She comes back, but her mind is away.*] Why are so many rooms closed, Uncle?

JAMES: Have you noticed? So quickly?

ROSE: I mistook the floor just now – it's a strange house – the rooms down there seemed locked.

JAMES: I suppose I ought to tell you. But it comes from something very foolish.

ROSE: Yes?

JAMES: I wouldn't tell you if you were just staying a while. But this has got to be your home. You'll see it for yourself. You'll watch your Aunt Teresa . . . your Aunt Helen, and I suppose there's a lot to puzzle you.

ROSE: I thought it was funny the way Aunt Teresa came out of there, not paying any attention . . .

JAMES: Yes, it's funny, isn't it? Go on thinking it's funny – a bit pathetic, too. There's no harm in it. Don't let it get on your nerves. I sometimes think the young have worse nerves than we have. Age is a good drug and it doesn't lose its effect.

ROSE: But you still haven't told me.

JAMES: My dear, it's so absurd! And I should have been able to stop it. I hope you'll laugh. Please laugh – it's very funny – in its way.

ROSE: Yes?

JAMES [*nerving himself*]: You see, your Aunt Helen sleeps in the old drawing-room. Because I'm an invalid they would have insisted on the dining-room for me, but I told them they couldn't get me up and down stairs to the living room, so I have what used to be a nurse's little sitting-room here – by the night nursery – this was the night nursery in the old days. Aunt Teresa has the day nursery next to me. You see the bedrooms are all closed.

ROSE: But why?

JAMES [*slowly and reluctantly*]: They don't like using a room in which anybody has ever died.

ROSE [*not understanding*]: Died?

JAMES [*purposely light*]: It's a habit people have – in bedrooms. So the bedrooms are all shut up – except this. It's an old house, and they aren't taking any chances. They risked this one – it had been a night nursery for a long time, and children don't die very often. Anyway, they don't die of old age.

ROSE: When did it all start?

JAMES: I'm not sure. I only noticed it when our father died. It had seemed quite natural when my mother's room was shut; there was nobody else to sleep in it. I only came for the holidays, and they had no visitors. But when this [*he taps his leg*] happened and I came to live here, I noticed our father's room was closed too, and when I wanted a room on the second floor Teresa said – I think it was Teresa – 'but that was Rose's room'.

ROSE: Rose?

JAMES: Your grandmother. She was the only one of us who got married. She died here, you know, when your mother was born.

ROSE: Was that when it started?

JAMES: It may have been. Who knows when anything really starts? Perhaps it was when we were all children together in this room.

   [*A pause.*]

ROSE: It's – creepy, isn't it?

JAMES: No, no, my dear. Not creepy. I used to laugh at them and threaten to die in here. What will you do for a living room then? I'd say. But I think at the last moment they'd push me into my own room – and that could be closed afterwards.

ROSE: But I still don't understand.

JAMES: Nor do I. Perhaps it's the fear of death – of the certainty of death. They don't seriously mind accidents. They aren't so much worried about your poor mother – because she was still young. She needn't have died. It's the inevitable they hate. Of course when someone dies they'll do all the right things – they are good Catholics. They'll have Masses said – and then as quickly as possible they forget. The photographs are the first things to disappear.

ROSE: But why? why?

JAMES: You'll have to ask Dennis. He lectures and writes books and teaches psychology. I expect he'd call it an anxiety neurosis. Or something more difficult. I'm a priest and I've given up psychology. They are good people, I doubt if they've ever committed a big sin in their lives – perhaps it would have been better if they had. I used to notice, in the old days, it was often the sinners who had the biggest trust. In mercy. My sisters don't seem to have any trust. Are you afraid of death?

ROSE: I don't think so. I haven't thought.

JAMES: Of course it seems closer to them than to you.

ROSE: Are you afraid of it, Uncle?

JAMES: I used to be – twenty years ago. And then something worse happened to me. It was like God reproving me for being such a fool. When that car smash came I ceased to be any use. I am a priest who can't say Mass or hear confessions or visit the sick. I shouldn't have been afraid of dying. I should have been afraid of being useless.

ROSE: But you *are* of use to them, Uncle?

JAMES: A priest isn't intended to be just a comfort to his family. Sometimes in the morning when I am half asleep, I imagine my legs are still here. I say to myself, Oh dear, oh dear, what a day ahead! A meeting of the Knights of Saint Columba, and then the Guild of the Blessed Sacrament, a meeting of the Altar Society, and after that . . . It's strange how bored I used to be with all the running around.

ROSE: Now I'm here, can't we go out together to the river and the park?

JAMES: Yes, I'd like to now and then. But it means hiring a couple of men. It's a long way down the stairs, and I'm heavy. But I'm not going to use you, my dear. I hope soon you'll be getting married.

ROSE: There's plenty of time.

[HELEN *enters.*]

HELEN: Poor little fusspot. The oven was perfectly all right. Mary's very reliable. Has Mr Dennis gone?

JAMES: He went a few minutes ago.

HELEN: A nice man, but not much sense of humour, I'm afraid. I was telling him about the Flopsy Bunnies. He'd never heard of them.

JAMES: You mustn't be hard on him for that. I've never read *Paradise Lost.*

[TERESA *enters in a hurry.*]

TERESA: Has Mr Dennis . . . ?

HELEN: He's gone, dear.

TERESA: That lady is on the telephone again. The one who called before. She wants to talk to him.

ROSE: I have his number. [*With a trace of bitterness at the last word.*] She can get him at home.

TERESA: I said I thought I'd heard him go, and she wants to talk to you, Rose.

ROSE [*scared*]: Me?

TERESA: She says she's Mrs Dennis. Will you speak to her, dear? She's asking all sorts of questions I can't answer.

ROSE: But I don't know her. I've never even met her.

[HELEN *is listening intently*.]

JAMES: What questions, Teresa?

TERESA: She said she tried to speak to Mr Dennis last night. She wasn't well. Where do you say he stayed, dear?

ROSE: I don't know. In the village.

TERESA: And then she tried your house, and you weren't there. She sounds a little – strange. I wish you'd come, dear. She's waiting on the telephone.

JAMES: Better have a word with her.

ROSE [*desperately*]: I can't. I don't know her. Michael will be home any moment.

HELEN: Don't worry, my little sweetheart. She's tired. Such a long journey. Your Aunt Helen will take care of it for you. [*She leaves.*]

CURTAIN

SCENE TWO

The Living Room. The next morning.

[MICHAEL DENNIS *is alone. He is ill at ease. He opens a brief-case, takes out some papers and puts them back. He goes to the window and looks out.* TERESA BROWNE *enters.*]

TERESA: Good morning, Mr Dennis.

MICHAEL: Good morning. I promised yesterday I'd come in.

TERESA: We hadn't expected you quite so early.

MICHAEL: I have a lecture at eleven.

TERESA: My brother hasn't finished his breakfast. You see, my sister and I went to Mass this morning.

MICHAEL: I didn't want to bother your brother. It was really Rose I came to see.

TERESA: Oh, but Rose is out. She didn't go to Mass.

MICHAEL: I could come this afternoon. After three. I have some students at two.

TERESA: She's going out this afternoon.

MICHAEL: Well, perhaps I could look in after dinner.

TERESA: She'll be out then – so my sister says.

MICHAEL [*with sombre realization*]: And tomorrow – does Miss Browne say she'll be out then, too?

TERESA: Yes.

MICHAEL: Why?

TERESA: I suppose she knows the reason. I don't.

MICHAEL: Where is Rose?

TERESA: I don't know. I really don't, Mr Dennis. I'm never told anything in this house.

MICHAEL: I'm the executor of her mother's will – and her trustee. Your sister can't prevent my discussing matters with her.

TERESA: I've no idea what she can do and what she can't, Mr Dennis. She's a terribly determined woman. I'm her elder, but she's always had her way. Even my brother – and he's a priest . . . Do you know, Mr Dennis, she's so arranged this house that . . . that . . . [*Her eyes are on the closet.*] Well, I'm quite ashamed. I don't know what strangers think. We should have made one out of the cupboard on the landing.

MICHAEL: Suppose I just stay here till Rose comes in?

TERESA: Oh, I don't *know* that she's out. And if she's not out, she wouldn't be able to come in, would she?

MICHAEL: Miss Browne, could you take a message . . .

TERESA: I'd have to ask Helen.

MICHAEL: But I'm Rose's trustee.

TERESA: Helen thinks that was a mistake.

MICHAEL [*with anger*]: I don't care what Miss Browne thinks . . .
[HELEN *pushes* JAMES *through the door which* TERESA *has left open. She has shed her bonhomie and we can see the strong will buried in the big breasts and the stout body.*]

HELEN: Good morning, Mr Dennis. This *is* an early call.

MICHAEL [*stubbornly*]: I've come to see Rose. Good morning, Father Browne.

JAMES: I suppose I could make a joke about being pushed into this affair – if it would help.

MICHAEL: It wouldn't. When I don't know what affair . . .

HELEN: Your wife telephoned again, just after you left, Mr Dennis.

MICHAEL: I know. She told me.

HELEN: Rose is our responsibility now. So you do understand, don't you, we have to clear the matter up.

MICHAEL: What matter?

JAMES: For goodness' sake, sit down, all of you. You make me want to stand up myself.

[*They prepare to sit.*]

TERESA: Not that chair, Mr Dennis. That's Helen's.

HELEN: Teresa dear, don't you think you'd better go and keep an eye on Mary?

TERESA: It's not my turn.

HELEN: I have to have a little talk with Mr Dennis.

TERESA: But I'm the eldest.

HELEN: That's why, dear. This isn't something for *your* generation.

TERESA [*appealing*]: James – ?

JAMES: Better go, dear. There are more than enough of us as it is.

HELEN: I heard Mary on the first landing.

TERESA: She's not dusting the closed rooms, is she?

HELEN: I told her particularly not. But perhaps you had better make sure.

[TERESA *goes hurriedly out.*]

And now, James –

[JAMES *sits silent and ill at ease in his wheel-chair. A pause.*]

You promised to have a word with Mr Dennis.

JAMES [*with a helpless or perhaps appealing gesture*]: Mr Dennis is not a Catholic. I am not in the confessional. I have no authority.

HELEN: But James, a woman can hardly ask . . .

MICHAEL: This is the second time I've been on trial today. I hope I've reached the Supreme Court. You want to ask me whether Rose and I are lovers. That's it, isn't it?

HELEN: Really, Mr Dennis, we would never have put it so crudely.

MICHAEL: But I'm not a Catholic, as your brother says. I haven't

learned to talk about 'offences against purity'. In my lectures I
try to be crude – it's only another word for precise.

JAMES: Forgive me, but so far you haven't been very – precise.

MICHAEL: You said you had no authority. I agree with you. I'm
not going to answer.

HELEN: Then we can only assume the worst.

JAMES: Speak for yourself, Helen. I shall do no such thing.

HELEN: Where did you spend the night before last, Mr Dennis? It
wasn't true that you stayed in the village, was it?

MICHAEL: No.

HELEN: Why did you tell us that?

MICHAEL: I *had* booked a room.

HELEN: But when Mrs Dennis telephoned . . .

MICHAEL: Two people are on trial. I won't answer any questions –
unless Rose wants me to. I think you had better let me talk to
her.

HELEN: But you won't be able to see her again, Mr Dennis.

MICHAEL: That's melodramatic and impracticable. [*With sudden
fear*] She's not ill, is she?

JAMES: No.

MICHAEL: You are not dealing with two children, Miss Browne.

HELEN: One is a child.

MICHAEL: Legally, yes, for another year.

HELEN: I agree you are hardly a child. How many children have
you, Mr Dennis?

MICHAEL: None.

HELEN: Why do you want to see Rose again?

MICHAEL: The will . . .

JAMES: Go on being frank. I like you better that way.

MICHAEL [*stung*]: I love her. Is that frank enough for you?

HELEN: Frank? It's – it's revolting. Seducing a child at her mother's
funeral.

MICHAEL: You take your psychology out of library books, Miss
Browne.

[HELEN *begins to speak, but* JAMES *interrupts her.*]

JAMES: You've asked your questions, Helen. Now leave us alone.

HELEN: Did you hear him admit that . . .

JAMES: There's no point in anger. We only get angry because we are hurt. And our hurt is not of importance in this case. We are dealing with more important people.

HELEN: Are you calling him . . .

JAMES: Of course he's more important than we are. You and I are only capable of *self*-importance, Helen. He's still in the middle of life. He's capable of suffering.

HELEN: I wish you wouldn't preach at me, James.

JAMES: I'm sorry. Sometimes I remember I'm a priest. Please go away.

HELEN: James, will you at least promise . . .

JAMES: Helen, I can't bear your voice when it gets on one note. We are too near death, you and I . . .

HELEN: Oh, you're impossible! [*She leaves.*]

[*A pause.*]

JAMES: I knew that word would do the trick.

MICHAEL: What word?

JAMES: Death.

[*A pause.*]

What are we going to do about her?

MICHAEL: Miss Browne seems quite capable . . .

JAMES: I meant Rose. Rose knew you were married?

MICHAEL: Of course.

JAMES: You said this was your second trial today?

[MICHAEL *moves restlessly up and down the room, coming to a stop at intervals by the chair.*]

MICHAEL: When I got home last night my wife was in bed with the door locked. Like a jury after the evidence has been heard. This morning she gave me her verdict of guilty.

JAMES: Was it a just one?

MICHAEL: Do you believe in justice? [*With angry irony*] Of course. I forgot. You believe in a just God. The all-wise Judge.

JAMES: That kind of justice has nothing to do with a judge. [*He turns his head and follows* MICHAEL's *movements.*] It's a mathematical term. We talk of a just line, don't we? God's exact, that's all. He's not a judge. An absolute knowledge of every factor – the conscious and the unconscious – yes, even heredity, all your Freudian urges. That's why He's merciful.

MICHAEL [*coming to a halt by* JAMES's *chair*]: I know what I seem like to you. I *am* a middle aged man. Whose wife won't divorce him.

JAMES: That wouldn't have helped.

MICHAEL: But I mean to *marry* Rose.

JAMES: It would be better to live with her. She'd be less bound to you then.

MICHAEL: How I hate your logic.

JAMES: I sometimes hate this body cut off at the knees. But my legs won't exist however much I hate the lack of them. It's a waste of time hating facts.

MICHAEL: I believe in different facts.

[*A pause.*]

Father, we have our heretics in psychology too. I believe in the analysis of dreams, but sometimes I have had a dream so simple and brief that there seems to be nothing there to analyse – a shape, a few colours, an experience of beauty, that's all. Then I refuse to look further.

JAMES: What has that to do . . . ?

MICHAEL: Oh, I can analyse my own love. I can give you all the arguments. Pride that a girl can love me, the idea that time is hurrying to an end, the sense of final vigour which comes before old age, the fascination innocence may have when you've ceased to believe in it – it's like seeing a unicorn in Hyde Park. It's true, Father, you *can* analyse every dream, but sometimes the analysis doesn't seem to make sense. An anxiety neurosis, I say, and then the face stares back at me so young and lovely – why should I explain my love any other way?

JAMES: You don't have to convince a priest that the truth seems all wrong sometimes. I learnt that long ago in the confessional. All the same, I'd rather you were dead. Or somebody different.

MICHAEL: Different?

JAMES: Say, like your grandfather. He may have visited a brothel once in a while, when he went abroad, but he believed you only loved the person you married. He wasn't tempted to leave his wife – society was so strong – any more than you are tempted to commit murder. You may be a better man, but he caused much less trouble.

MICHAEL: It wasn't what I meant to do.

JAMES: You haven't much imagination. How can you have a love affair without trouble?

MICHAEL: I don't want a 'love affair'. I meant to break it gently to my wife — later, when there wouldn't have been any of this bitterness.

JAMES: I was wrong. You've got a great imagination. If you think you can leave a woman without bitterness.

MICHAEL: My wife and I — we haven't been lovers in a long while.

JAMES: You've been companions, haven't you?

MICHAEL: I didn't mean to hurt anyone. I had planned nothing. I hardly noticed Rose until two months ago. I came to see her mother when the doctors had diagnosed angina. She knew she might die any time, walking too far, lifting a weight. She wanted to talk about Rose. I wasn't a Catholic, but she trusted me. We both lost the man we cared for most when her husband died. Rose came into the room. I didn't bother to look up, but when she bent down to kiss her mother I smelt her hair. Then she went out of the room. She was like a landscape you see from the train, and you want to stop just there.

JAMES: Well?

MICHAEL: I pulled the communication cord.

JAMES: And there's always a fine attached.

MICHAEL: But I want to pay it. Alone. Not the others.

JAMES: Was my sister right? When you went down for the funeral, *were* you planning . . . ?

MICHAEL: Not even then. Oh, perhaps I'd be shocked too, if it weren't myself and Rose. You can't shock yourself, can you? 'The funeral bakemeats did coldly furnish forth the marriage tables.' But there hasn't been a marriage. And now there can't be. What do we do?

JAMES: You're the psychologist. Let's hear the wisdom of Freud, Jung, Adler. Haven't they all the answers you need? You can only get a priest's answer from me.

MICHAEL: I'm asking for the priest's answer. Then I'll know what I have to fight.

JAMES: There's only one answer I can give. You're doing wrong to your wife, to Rose, to yourself — and to the God you don't believe in. Go away. Don't see her, don't write to her, don't answer her letters if she writes to you. She'll have a terrible few weeks. So will you. You aren't a cruel man.

MICHAEL: And in the end . . . ?

JAMES: We have to trust God. Everything will be all right.

MICHAEL [*angrily*]: All right – what a queer idea you have of all right. I've left her. Fine. So she'll always associate love with betrayal. When she loves a man again, there'll always be *that* in her mind . . . love doesn't last. She'll grow her defence mechanisms until she dies inside them. And I'll go on as I have for the last ten years, having a woman now and then, for a night, on the sly, substitutes, living with a woman I don't desire – a hysteric. She has something real for her hysteria now, but for ten years she's invented things. Ever since our child died. Sometimes I find myself thinking she invented even that. I wasn't there.

JAMES: Can't you even find a cure for your own wife?

MICHAEL: No. Because I'm part of her insecurity. I'm inside her neurosis as I'm inside her house.

JAMES: So you'll burn down the house. For God's sake don't talk any more psychology at me. Just tell me what you want.

MICHAEL: To live with Rose. To live an ordinary quiet human life. To have a family. She can change her name to mine for convenience. For the sake of the children. So no one will know. Perhaps one day my wife will divorce me, and we can marry.

JAMES [*ironically*]: I shouldn't take the trouble. Rose wouldn't want a fake marriage.

MICHAEL: You don't know her.

JAMES: I know one side of her better than you do. You can't fob off a Catholic with a registrar's signature and call it a marriage. We do as many wrong things as you do, but we have the sense to know it. I don't say she wouldn't be happy – in a way – as long as the desire lasted. Then she'd leave you – even with the registrar's signature. I'm sorry for you, being mixed up like that, with one of us.

MICHAEL: I'll risk it.

JAMES: And your wife?

MICHAEL: A hysteric will go on with a scene until she gets what she wants. There are only two things you can do. Give her what

she wants, and that brings the next scene closer – she smells
success, like a dog a bitch. Or just walk out. She can't make a
scene alone. I've walked out for half hours long enough. I shall
walk out for good. Father, I sound cruel. I'm not. I do love her.
She's my wife. She ruined her health over the child. I want to
make her happy. I've tried to, but I can't go on. It's no good
going on – for any of us. We'll break sooner or later, and it only
prolongs the pain. What's the matter? [*He goes over to the chair.*]
      [JAMES *is trembling. His head has dropped.*]

JAMES: It's a terrible world.

MICHAEL: Can't you forget you're a priest for a while?

JAMES [*with bitter self-reproach*]: I forget it twenty-two hours a day.

MICHAEL: As a man, can you see Rose happy in this house – three
      old people and all these closed rooms? Why closed?

JAMES [*in a low, ashamed voice*]: They were afraid to live where
      anyone had died. So they closed the bedrooms.

MICHAEL [*too patly*]: So that's it. I've come across cases like that.
      Compulsive neurosis. People who won't grow up so that they
      believe they won't die.

JAMES: How you love your snap judgements, Dennis.

MICHAEL: What a household for Rose. What's going to happen
      when one of them dies – or you die? Can you see her helping to
      shift the furniture into another hiding place? Is that the life for a
      girl?

JAMES: You've got plenty of reason on your side, but –
      [*A pause.*]

MICHAEL [*he has a sense of victory*]: But what?

JAMES: God has plenty of mercy.

MICHAEL: You can't expect me to depend on that.

JAMES: I don't know that *we* do, often.

MICHAEL: It's no good asking your sister. But I ask you. Let me
      speak to her.

JAMES: Can't you let her alone for a little to make up her own
      mind?

MICHAEL: Or your sister to make it up for her?

JAMES [*his last appeal*]: You're a psychologist. You know how
      often young girls fall in love with a man your age, looking for a
      father.

MICHAEL [*defensively*]: What of it?

JAMES: Rose never knew her father.

[*He has got under* MICHAEL's *skin. His reaction is unnecessarily vehement.*]

MICHAEL: All right. I may be a father substitute. I don't care a damn, if it makes her happy. It's as good a reason for love, isn't it, as black hair or a good profile? Hair alters, a man grows a second chin. A substitute may give satisfaction for a lifetime.

JAMES: You can't think in terms of a lifetime.

MICHAEL: I might die before she got tired of me.

JAMES: You might. It's a terrible thing to have to depend on, though.

[*A bell rings below.*]

MICHAEL: Can I go and find her?

JAMES: She's not in the house. Helen saw to that.

MICHAEL: Can I wait till she returns?

JAMES: I can't turn you out, can I?

MICHAEL [*he hears footsteps on the stairs*]: That's Rose.

JAMES: It's only Mary.

MICHAEL: No. I know her step. She's coming up. Am I going to see her with your consent? Or without?

JAMES: What are you going to say to her?

MICHAEL: I'm going to ask her to pack her bag.

[ROSE *enters. She sees* MICHAEL *with surprise and pleasure.*]

ROSE: But you telephoned. They said you'd telephoned.

MICHAEL: What about?

ROSE: You couldn't come. You had to go away. For a week.

MICHAEL: I never telephoned. They didn't want me to see you.

ROSE: But that's absurd. Uncle — you weren't concerned?

JAMES: No. He wants to talk to you. You can push me out.

ROSE [*looking from one to the other*]: What's happened? What's it all about? You, both of you . . .

JAMES: He wants you to pack your bag.

ROSE [*to* MICHAEL]: You mean — go away? They know all about us? Do you want me to go away now, today? [*She speaks with excitement and no apprehension.*]

[MICHAEL *watches her with growing uneasiness. She is too young and unprepared.*]

How lucky I never unpacked the trunk. I can be ready in a few minutes. [*She turns to her uncle with sudden remorse.*] Oh, Uncle, you must think we are very wicked.

JAMES: No. Just ignorant. And innocent.

ROSE [*with pride*]: Not innocent.

JAMES: Please open the door, Rose.

ROSE: I didn't want to hurt you. It just happened this way.

JAMES: Don't worry about *me*.

ROSE: I know it's wrong, but I don't care. Uncle, we're going to be happy.

JAMES: Is he?

[ROSE *looks quickly at* MICHAEL. *He doesn't look a happy man.*]

ROSE: Darling, is anything the matter?

MICHAEL: My wife knows.

ROSE [*with the glibness and unfeelingness of youth*]: It had to happen sooner or later. Was she very angry?

MICHAEL: Not exactly angry.

ROSE: You've had an awful time.

MICHAEL: Other people are having an awful time.

ROSE: Yes, of course. It's terribly sad, but we'll be all right. You'll see. And people get over everything.

MICHAEL: She cried a great deal. I left her crying.

JAMES: Please open the door. I feel like an accomplice.

ROSE: I'm sorry, Uncle. [*She opens the door for his chair to pass.*]

JAMES: Come and see me when you've done.

ROSE: You don't think I'd go away without saying good-bye? [*Turning to* MICHAEL *after shutting the door.*] Darling, tell me what you've planned.

MICHAEL: My plans haven't been a success. My wife won't divorce me. We may never be able to marry.

ROSE [*with momentary disappointment*]: Oh! [*She sweeps her disappointment aside.*] It doesn't really matter, does it? It wouldn't have been a real marriage, anyway. And — somebody may die.

MICHAEL: You're a Catholic. I never knew any Catholics before — except your mother.

ROSE: Perhaps I'm only half one. Father wasn't.

MICHAEL: You never knew him, did you?

ROSE: No. But I've seen lots of photographs. He had a nose rather like yours.

MICHAEL [*with bitterness*]: I never noticed that.

ROSE: Shall I pack now? [*She begins to get her things together in a small suitcase while the dialogue continues.*]

MICHAEL: You don't mind – about the Church?

ROSE [*lightly as she goes to the bathroom for her spongebag and pyjamas*]: Oh, I expect it will come all right in the end. I shall make a deathbed confession and die in the odour of sanctity.

MICHAEL [*as she comes out again*]: Our children will be illegitimate.

ROSE: Bastards are the best, so Shakespeare says. [*She folds up the pyjamas and puts them in her case.*]

We did *King John* my last term at school. The nuns hurried over those bits. There was a nice phrase for bastards – 'born under the rose'. I liked Faulconbridge. Oh, what an age ago it seems –

MICHAEL: Your aunts won't let you come back here.

ROSE [*crossing to a cupboard to fetch a frock*]: Do you think I care? Darling, I can't bear this house. It gives me the creeps. Do you know why they've closed the rooms?

MICHAEL: Yes.

ROSE: I can't help wondering which of them will die where. If one of them died in here, they wouldn't have enough rooms to live in. It's really awful. Like something in Edgar Allen Poe.

MICHAEL: What a lot of books you've read.

ROSE: You aren't angry, about something, are you? I'll do anything you say. Just tell me where to go, and I'll go. Like Ruth. 'Your people shall be my people.' I suppose your people are all psychologists.

MICHAEL: Not all.

ROSE: I've read Freud in Penguin. *The Psychology of Everyday Life*.

MICHAEL: You have, have you?

ROSE: Darling, something's fretting you. You haven't fallen in love with another woman?

MICHAEL: No. I finished all that with you.

ROSE: I shall never be sure of that. You didn't waste much time with me.

MICHAEL: I haven't much time to waste.

ROSE: You are worrying, just like yesterday. What *is* the matter?

MICHAEL: Only a damned sense of responsibility. Listen, Rose, this is serious. Have you really *thought* . . . ?

ROSE: I don't *want* to think. You *know* about things, I don't. Darling, I've never been in love before. You have.

MICHAEL: Have I?

ROSE: Your wife.

MICHAEL: Oh, yes.

ROSE: You know the way around. Tell me what to do. I'll do it. I've packed my bag, but I'll unpack it if you want it a different way. I'll do anything, darling, that's easier for you. Tell me to come to Regal Court, now, this minute, and I'll come.

MICHAEL: Regal Court?

ROSE: It's where people go to make love. So everybody says. I'll go there now and come back here. I'll meet you there every day. Or I'll take my bag and go away with you – for years.

MICHAEL: Only years?

ROSE: Just say what you want. I'm awfully obedient.

MICHAEL: Dear, it's not only you and me . . . you have to think.

ROSE: Don't *make* me think. I warned you not to make me think. I don't know about things. They'll all get at me if they have a chance. They'll say, 'Did you ever consider this? Did you ever consider that?' Please don't do that to me too – not yet. Just tell me what to do.

MICHAEL: You are very dear to me.

ROSE: Of course. I know.

MICHAEL: I don't want you to make a mistake.

ROSE: A mistake wouldn't matter so much. There's plenty of time . . .

MICHAEL: 'You're not a cruel man' your uncle said to me. I don't know much about the young. I've caused a lot of trouble in the last few weeks, breaking in . . .

ROSE: And haven't I? Dear, don't worry so. Worries bring worries, my nurse used to say. Let's both give up thinking for a month, and then it will be too late.

MICHAEL: I wish I could.

ROSE: But you can.

MICHAEL: You can live in the moment because the past is so small and the future so vast. I've got a small future, I can easily imagine – even your uncle can imagine it for me. And the past is a very long time and full of things to remember.

ROSE: You weren't so horribly wise yesterday.

MICHAEL: Put up with my 'wisdom'.

ROSE: Of course. If I have to. [*Shutting her case*] Shall we go?

MICHAEL: I have to go home first – and say good-bye.

ROSE: That's hard for you.

MICHAEL [*harshly*]: Don't waste your sympathy on me. After all these years she had the right to feel secure.

ROSE: I'm sorry.

MICHAEL: Oh, it's not you I'm angry with. I'm angry with all the world who think one doesn't care . . .

ROSE: You won't let her talk you round, will you?

MICHAEL: No.

ROSE: She's had you so long. She'll have all the right words to use. I only know the wrong ones.

MICHAEL: You don't need words. You're young. And the young always win in the end. [*He draws her to him.*]

ROSE: Where shall we meet?

MICHAEL: Lancaster Gate Station, in an hour.

ROSE [*she is worried by his reserve*]: You do still want me?

MICHAEL: Yes.

ROSE: I mean, like yesterday?

MICHAEL: I still want you in just the same way.

ROSE: I wasn't much good, but I'm learning awfully fast.

MICHAEL: You've nothing to fear. [*He kisses her.*] You've got the whole future.

ROSE: I only want one as long as yours.

MICHAEL [*going*]: In an hour.

ROSE: Good-bye, my heart!

[MICHAEL *goes.*

ROSE *closes her suitcase, then goes to the window. She tries to peer out between the bars, then climbs on a chair to see better.* TERESA *enters and crosses the room to the bathroom. As the door closes* HELEN *comes in, sees the suitcase and stops.* ROSE *turns.*]

HELEN: I hope you are not opening the window, dear?

ROSE [*obeying*]: I'm sorry, Aunt Helen. [*She crosses the room and picks up her suitcase.*]

HELEN: Where are you going?

ROSE: To say good-bye to Uncle James.

　　　[HELEN *sits down heavily in a chair.*]

　　　It was very wrong of you to tell me Michael had gone away. I nearly missed him. I'll be back to say good-bye to Aunt Teresa. [*She goes out.*]

　　　[HELEN *sits silent in the chair. She puts her fingers to the corners of her eyes and gets rid of the few tears that have formed.*]

　　　[TERESA *opens the closet door and comes out.*]

HELEN [*imperiously*]: Teresa! She's going away. We've got to stop her.

　　　[TERESA *pays her no attention and tries to cross the room.* HELEN *bars her way.*]

　　　Oh, don't be absurd, Teresa. Don't keep up your tomfoolery now.

　　　[TERESA *evades her and goes out.*]

　　　Teresa!

　　　[*After a moment* TERESA *re-enters.*]

TERESA: Did you call me, Helen?

HELEN: You heard what I said – [*a sudden doubt*] – or didn't you?

TERESA: I've been in James's room. How could I hear?

HELEN [*furiously*]: You've been there – [*pointing at the closet*] – pretending not to be seen again.

TERESA: Oh no, dear, you're imagining things.

HELEN: Do you really mean to tell me . . . Are you feeling quite well, Teresa?

TERESA: I think so, Helen. Was there something you wanted to talk to me about?

HELEN: Sit down, Teresa. You know when you came in just now, you walked a little crookedly. Like ten years ago when the doctor said . . .

TERESA [*in fear*]: I don't remember what he said.

HELEN: He said you had to be very, very careful.

TERESA [*whimpering*]: I have been, Helen.

HELEN: He said . . .

TERESA [*imploring*]: I don't want to hear. I don't want to hear.

HELEN: Shall I read you some of the 'Little Flower'?

TERESA: But you only do that when I'm ill, Helen. Am I ill? Really ill? [*She sits down.*]

HELEN [*sits beside her*]: Did you feel a little faint when you got up? [TERESA *licks her lips a little with apprehension.*]

TERESA: Perhaps, Helen. For a while.

HELEN: Any headache, dear?

TERESA: I don't think so. A very little one.

HELEN: And your heart?

TERESA: It's beating rather. Helen, you don't think . . . ?

HELEN: Of course not. But we have to be very careful at our age. You'll go to bed, dear, won't you?

TERESA: But I don't want to be a trouble, Helen. It's my cooking day tomorrow. There's no one to help you in the evening when Mary leaves.

HELEN: There's Rose now, dear. Rose would help, wouldn't she? She's a good child. She wouldn't leave us if she knew we were in trouble. I'll call her now and we'll put you to bed.

TERESA: But Helen, I hate my bed. Couldn't I just rest in here?

HELEN [*lowering her voice*]: But you remember our agreement?

TERESA: I can't hear what you are saying, dear.

HELEN: You seem a little deaf this morning. Your hearing comes and goes. See if you can stand up, Teresa.

TERESA: Of course I can stand up. [*She gets to her feet with difficulty and collapses again in her chair.*]

HELEN: Come to bed, dear. Rose and I will look after you.

TERESA [*imploringly*]: Please, Helen . . .

HELEN: You've got such a pretty bedroom, dear. I tell you what. I'll send Mary to Burns Oates to get you another holy picture for that patch on the wall where Mother's portrait used to hang. Would you like another 'Little Flower'?

TERESA: I'd rather have St Vincent de Paul. But Helen . . .

HELEN: In a few days you'll be up and about again.

TERESA [*desolately*]: Days?

HELEN: Come, dear. You'll see you can't walk by yourself. Try.

TERESA: I can. I really can. [*She rises carefully to her feet and takes a step.*]

HELEN: Careful, dear. Take my arm.

TERESA: No. No.

[*With a frightened cry* TERESA *draws away and collapses on to a chair.* HELEN *goes to the door and calls* 'Rose! Rose!' *It isn't real fear in her voice.* TERESA *takes some tottering steps towards the sofa and falls on the floor. When* HELEN *turns and sees her sister, she feels panic.*]

HELEN: Teresa. Dear Teresa. Speak to me. Please. Teresa! [*She bends down and for a moment it looks as though she is going to try to drag her sister through the door. Then she runs through the door on to the landing and cries in real fear.*] Rose! Rose! Please, Rose! Help me, Rose! Help me!

CURTAIN

Act Two

SCENE ONE

The Living Room. Early evening, three weeks later.
[TERESA BROWNE *is sitting in an easy chair with a rug tucked round her knees.* FATHER BROWNE *sits beside her in his wheeled chair. He is reading aloud to her.*]

JAMES [*reading*]:
> Upon that lucky night
> In secrecy, inscrutable to sight,
> I went without discerning
> And with no other light
>
> Except for that which in my heart was burning.
> It lit and led me through
> More certain than the light of noonday clear
> To where One waited near
> Whose presence well I knew,
> There where no other presence might appear.
>
> Oh night that was my guide!
> Oh darkness dearer than the morning's pride.

[JAMES *suddenly stops.*]

TERESA: Go on a little longer. I like what you read so much better than what Helen reads. I don't understand it, but I like it. She always reads me St Theresa. She talks about *my* 'Little Flower', but it's her 'Little Flower' really.

JAMES: Helen gets confused. She thinks of us two as the old ones, but she's old too. She means no harm.

TERESA: Was I really dying the other day?

JAMES: How do I know? We are all nearly dying I hope – except Rose.

TERESA: Do you know for just a moment I didn't want to die in the day nursery where all our toys used to be. I wanted to die where everybody else had died – in a real bedroom.

JAMES: Why not?

TERESA: Oh, it was only for a moment. Then I was so frightened. More frightened than I had ever been. Helen says it was my idea first – to close all the bedrooms. I can't remember. Was it?

JAMES: You both wanted it, I think. I can't remember now. Anyway the rooms will be opened by somebody else before very long – perhaps by Rose.

TERESA: People talk about the soul, but I always think of ghosts, the dead who can't sleep. There was a story Helen told me once about lost souls . . .

JAMES [*interrupting*]: It was wrong of me to give way about those rooms. When it began it seemed silly and unimportant. Why should I fight you over a fancy? But perhaps I should have fought you. I've been very useless, Teresa. Do you know one of my 'day-dreams'? I get them again now – perhaps they belong to second childhood. I dream of helping somebody in great trouble. Saying the right word at the right time. In the old days in the confessional – once in five years perhaps – one sometimes felt one had done just that. It made the years between worth while. Now I doubt if I'd know the right word if the chance came.

TERESA: I'm afraid of dying, James, even of thinking about death. Then Rose came, and I seemed to frighten *her*. It's a nice house. We aren't bad people. I don't know why there should be so much fear around.

JAMES: Perhaps your fear frightened her. Your silly fear of death.

TERESA: Is it a silly fear, James?

JAMES: No one who believes in God should be afraid of death.

TERESA: But there's Hell, James.

JAMES: We aren't as important as that, Teresa. Mercy is what I believe in. Hell is for the great, the very great. I don't know anyone who's great enough for Hell except Satan.

TERESA: I sound a bit braver now, but it's only because I'm back here – in the living room. It was good of Helen to hide that patch in my room with a picture, but I said *not* the 'Little Flower'. Do you think Helen likes her because she died young?

Sometimes she looks at Rose in a strange way, as though she's thinking, I *may* survive even you.

JAMES: You want to rest. Shall I read a little more?

TERESA: Yes.

JAMES: St John is still talking about the dark night of the soul. It's a bit difficult to understand for me and you who've not got that far. You see it's nearness to God that withers a man up. We are all such a long comfortable distance away. He is trying to describe the black night he found himself in – a night that seemed to be without love or even the power to pray.

TERESA: I pray. Night and morning.

JAMES: Oh, I remember my baby prayers, Teresa. Our Father, Hail Mary, an act of contrition. But I can't meditate for ten minutes without my mind wandering – and as for contemplation it's a whole world away. Something I have read about in the lives of the saints. When I was working in a parish I used to tell myself I had no time for prayer. Well, I have been given twenty years and I can still only say Our Father. And do I really say that?

TERESA: I think you have got a dark night of your own, James.

JAMES: No, I'd never reach that kind of despair. I have no parish drudgery, I'm comfortable, well fed, happy with both of you. I can read you what the saints say from books, even though I can't feel with them. What's for dinner, Teresa?

TERESA: Macaroni cheese. [*Suddenly realizing he is joking*] Oh, James . . .

  [HELEN *enters*.]

HELEN: Have you heard Mary come back, dear?

JAMES: Isn't she in the kitchen?

HELEN: I sent her on an errand.

JAMES: To the shops?

HELEN: Not exactly.

JAMES: Far?

HELEN [*ambiguously*]: Oh, across the park.

TERESA: I haven't seen her since lunch.

HELEN: She went out just after lunch. I hoped she'd be back to wash up the tea-things, but I suppose I'd better do them myself.

TERESA: Rose?

HELEN: You don't expect Rose to be here, do you, dear? [*She goes out.*]

TERESA: What did she mean?

JAMES: I don't know.

TERESA: Rose was very good to me when I was ill. I'd wake up sometimes so frightened and there she'd be, dozing in the chair by my bed. I remember when I was a child, before Helen was born, Mother used to give me a nightlight because I was so afraid. It made a sound like someone breathing quietly. Like Rose asleep.

JAMES: She's a kind child.

TERESA: Except at the beginning. She was very harsh to me at the beginning. I wonder why.

JAMES: It doesn't matter now.

TERESA: Just before I was ill, I remember Helen saying something to me about Rose going away. Where would she go to? Running away, I think she said. But why should she run away from us? Is that fear again?

JAMES: Don't worry. She's still here.

TERESA: People don't tell me things. And there's such a lot I don't understand.

JAMES: Don't try. It's much better to believe only what we see, and not ask questions. Leave questions to the psychologists. 'Is this really so?' they ask you. 'Do you really think that or just think that you think' . . .

[*They neither of them have heard the footsteps on the stairs.*]

MARY [*outside*]: But, Miss Rose . . . Please, Miss Rose.

ROSE: Come along in here.

MARY: I had my orders, Miss Rose.

ROSE: I know what your orders were.

[*The door is flung open and* ROSE *pushes* MARY *in ahead of her.* ROSE *has changed since we last saw her. She is angry now, but it isn't that. Three weeks ago she was a muddled, enthusiastic, excitable child. She looks several years older now. She isn't quite as pretty as she was. Disappointments, decisions and frustrations have filled the weeks and she has had time to think. Perhaps that's the biggest change.*]

ROSE: Go on. Tell your story.

MARY: But, Miss Rose . . .

ROSE: Oh, your employer isn't here, is she? [*She goes to the door and calls out.*] Aunt Helen! Aunt Helen!

TERESA: She's in the kitchen, Rose.

ROSE: She'll be up soon. Now her spy's returned.

MARY: Please, Miss Rose . . .

ROSE: Were you all in on this?

JAMES: We don't even know what *this* is.

ROSE: I'm sorry. I might have guessed it was *her* work. She hates me.

JAMES: Nonsense.

ROSE: And I know why. Love is normal. Love is being born and growing older and having children and dying. She can't bear that. She wants to build a wall of closed rooms – and in the middle there's this *living* room. Nobody will ever die here. Perpetual motion. Nobody will ever be born here. That's risky. I can camp here all night because I'm young and there's no danger, but a man mustn't come and see me here because life might not stand still. We might make love and that means getting older, running risks – in your precious museum piece of a room. Period 1902.

[HELEN *has entered during the last line.*]

HELEN: What's that about 1902, little sweet – ? [*She sees* MARY.] Mary, what are you doing here?

ROSE: I brought her up with me. I wanted to hear her report too.

HELEN: What report, dear?

ROSE: The report on my movements, of course. How I arrived at Regal Court at two-forty-five and left at five-fifteen. How she recognized no one else who entered – because he'd got there first.

HELEN: Mary, you'd better go.

ROSE: I want to hear the report.

HELEN: Go, Mary.

[MARY *leaves.*
A *pause.*]

I can't think what you are talking about.

ROSE: Oh yes, you can. And now I'll give you all the details Mary doesn't know. Michael was there at half-past two – before me and Mary. I got there at three and I dressed again at five. She couldn't tell you that, could she? And we didn't make love all that time. Because people can't. And we'd been there three or four times every week for three weeks. Ever since you stopped my running away for good. [*Bitterly*.] With your great need of help. You could have done without me all right – if Mary's time had not been taken up this way.

JAMES: Is it true, Helen?

HELEN: Oh, yes, it's true – in a way. I wanted to know where she went off to nearly every afternoon. I suspected this.

JAMES: Why?

[TERESA *has been quietly crying*.]

HELEN: Stop snivelling, Teresa.

JAMES: I said why?

HELEN: She's our responsibility. It was my duty to clear this thing up. You're so weak, you threw them together. She told you she was going away with him. It's a mortal sin.

JAMES: How do you know?

HELEN: Because he's a married man, of course.

JAMES: Do you think you know a mortal sin when you see it? You're wiser than the Church then.

HELEN: Have some common sense.

JAMES: Yes: if you would have some charity.

HELEN: James, you're a fool.

JAMES: I see what's in front of my eyes. God doesn't require me to do more –

HELEN: You've heard her – bragging. They'd have been living together now, day in day out, if I hadn't stopped them.

JAMES [*sharply*]: Stopped them?

ROSE: Of course we'd have been together. Of course we'd have been lovers. Oh, you talk a lot about mortal sin. Why didn't you let me go? Is this any better? Afternoons at Regal Court.

HELEN: It *is* better. It will soon come to an end – this way.

ROSE: Love ending is a good thing, isn't it? To you.

HELEN: This sort of love.

ROSE: What's the difference between this sort of love and any other? Would making love feel any different if he hadn't got a wife? [*She answers her own question in a lower voice*] Only happier.

JAMES [*who has been waiting his opportunity*]: You said you stopped them?

HELEN: Yes. I'm not ashamed of it. I've kept her in the Church, haven't I? She can go to confession now any time she likes.

ROSE: And do it again, and go to confession, and do it again? Do you call that better than having children, living together till we die . . .

HELEN: In mortal sin.

ROSE: God's got more sense. And mercy.

HELEN: And it's another sin to trust too much to His mercy.

ROSE: Oh, they have a name for that too. I know it. The nuns taught it me. It's called presumption. Well, I'm damned well going to presume.

JAMES [*to* HELEN]: What do you mean, you stopped them?

HELEN: Teresa wasn't ill.

ROSE: Not ill? She was in a faint on the floor.

HELEN: I told her she was ill. She believed it.

ROSE [*turning quietly away*]: Oh.
　　　[*A long silence.*]

HELEN [*defensively*]: I had to act quickly, James.

JAMES: I'd think you were a very wicked woman if you weren't such a fool.

TERESA: I don't understand what you are all talking about.

JAMES [*to* HELEN, *bitterly*]: Perhaps *you* can explain it to her, *I* can't. Teresa, dear, go to your room with Helen. You've been up long enough.

TERESA: Are you trying to get rid of me, James?

JAMES: Yes, dear, I am. Take my book. I want a word with Rose alone.
　　　[TERESA *begins to cross the room. Near the door she pauses.*]

TERESA: Aren't you coming, Helen?

HELEN [*to* JAMES]: I don't trust you. I'm staying.

JAMES: If you want to, you will. I know that. Rose, *you* see Teresa to her room.
　　　[ROSE *takes* TERESA *by the arm and leads her through the door.*]

TERESA [*as she goes, with a note of appeal, like a child*]: You'll come and say good-night, James?

JAMES: It's early. I'll come and read to you till you feel sleepy. I'll come before dinner.

[ROSE *and* TERESA *go out.*]

JAMES [*to* HELEN]: You might have killed Teresa.

HELEN: I only told her she didn't look well. I'd no intention . . .

JAMES: You've told us clearly enough what you intended.

HELEN: I wish the girl had never come here.

JAMES: Oh, so do I, so do I. We've ruined her between us.

HELEN: Us? We aren't to blame. That man with all his wickedness . . .

JAMES: Don't blame him. Blame our dead goodness. Holy books, holy pictures, a subscription to the Altar Society. Do you think, if she had come into a house where there was love, she wouldn't have hesitated, thought twice, talked to us . . .

HELEN: And why didn't she?

JAMES: Because there was fear, not love, in this house. If we had asked her for a sacrifice, what would we have offered? Pious platitudes.

HELEN: Speak for yourself, James.

JAMES: I do. Goodness that sits and talks piously and decays all the time.

HELEN: He seduced her.

JAMES: It's a silly word, but what if he did? God sometimes diverts the act, but the pious talk He seems to leave like the tares, useless.

[ROSE *enters.*]

ROSE [*defiantly*]: Well?

JAMES [*to* HELEN]: You'd better apologize to her.

HELEN: Apologize?

JAMES [*to* ROSE]: She had no right to have you followed.

HELEN: She's in our care. She lied to us.

ROSE: You lied to me.

HELEN: There are lies and lies.

JAMES: There needn't be any more. God forgive me, but you bore me, Helen. Please go away.

HELEN: I'm going to stay here.

JAMES: I know I'm your brother, but I'm still a priest. I've asked you to go.

[HELEN *makes for the door, but she flings back one more insult.*]

HELEN: Oh, the Church is well rid of a useless priest like you, James. [*She goes and the door closes.*]

[*Silence.*]

ROSE [*defiantly*]: You know what this means?

[*No answer.*]

If Aunt Teresa's well, I'm free. I can go with him. We are just where we were.

JAMES: Are you?

ROSE: We haven't tired of each other, if that's what you mean. [*Defiantly*] We love each other more. We know each other properly now.

JAMES: I'm glad the hours in Regal Court were so rewarding.

ROSE [*her voice breaking*]: Don't laugh at me. Please don't laugh at me.

JAMES: I don't feel like laughing.

ROSE: Uncle, it isn't wonderful at all. It's sad, sad. [*Sitting on the floor by his chair*] I'm tired. I don't know what to do.

JAMES: How is he standing it?

ROSE: We both stand it when we are together. We are happy at half-past two, we are still happy at three o'clock. Then we sometimes sleep a bit. It's not so bad at four o'clock, but then we hear the quarter strike and all the sadness starts. Every day at a quarter-past four. We behave awfully sensibly when five o'clock comes. There's a beastly little French gilt clock on the mantelpiece. One day I'm going to smash its pretty face. I oughtn't to tell you all this.

JAMES: I want to hear. People don't talk to priests much – except in formulas, in that coffin-shaped box of ours.

ROSE: 'Since my last confession three weeks ago I've committed adultery twenty-seven times.' That's what Aunt Helen would like me to say, and, Father, it doesn't mean a thing. We are supposed to be talking to God, aren't we, through you, and God knows all about the clock on the mantelpiece. I don't want to confess. I want to say, 'Dear God. Give us more love. Give us a life together. Don't let it be just Regal Court over and over again.' Do you understand?

JAMES: A little. All I can.

ROSE: What are we to do?

JAMES: My dear . . .

ROSE [*interrupting him*]: I'm not asking you as a priest, I know *that* answer. But I can't believe it's true what Aunt Helen says, that God would rather have Regal Court and saying good-bye three times a week than – the other thing.

JAMES: What?

ROSE: Oh, peace and children and getting older. Outside the Church.

JAMES: You wouldn't be happy . . .

ROSE: Oh yes, I would. Don't make any mistake about that, Father. I could live a lifetime without the sacraments. That wouldn't hurt – but a lifetime, without him . . .

JAMES: One gets over a separation. Time passes.

ROSE: You have to live through it first though. You have to dream at night you are together and wake up in the morning alone, and count the hours till bed again.

JAMES [*sadly and with amazement*]: What a lot of growing up you've done in three weeks.

ROSE: Do you think if I left Michael I could really love a God who demanded all that pain before He'd give Himself . . .

JAMES: You simplify too much.

ROSE: But it's a simple situation, Father. There's nothing complicated about this – love affair. I'm not a case history.

JAMES: The trouble is you don't trust God enough. He would make things so much easier for you if you would shut your eyes and leave it to Him.

[ROSE'*s face hardens during this speech. She will not be persuaded.*]

ROSE: Would He? It's not the way He always works. Look round the world nowadays. He seems to want heroes and I'm not a hero. I'm a coward. I can't bear too much pain. There are a lot of us like that, Father. When I betray Him, I'm not doing any worse than Peter, am I? God died for the cowards too.

[*A bell rings below.*]

JAMES: He made them into heroes, even Peter.

ROSE: Oh, we read about God's successes. We don't read about

His failures. His happy failures. Who just don't care much about Him, and go on living quietly all the same.

JAMES: One has to deserve to be a failure.

ROSE: But, Uncle, I don't want to try, I'm a coward. I just want a bit of ordinary human comfort. Not formulas. 'Love God. Trust God. Everything will be all right one day.' Uncle, please say something that's not Catholic.

[HELEN *enters hurriedly*.]

HELEN: There's someone downstairs to see you, Rose.

JAMES: Who?

HELEN: Mrs Dennis.

JAMES: What does she want? [*With suspicion*] Who brought her here?

HELEN [*with a suspicion of secret triumph*]: I've told you – she wants to see Rose.

[ROSE *turns away with a movement of panic.*
A pause.]

JAMES: Is this your work again, Helen? Tell her Rose is sick, not here. Tell her anything, but get rid of her.

HELEN: She has a right . . .

JAMES: This child has had enough to stand.

HELEN [*scornfully*]: Child?

JAMES: Yes. Child.

[ROSE *suddenly turns back to them.*]

ROSE: I'm here, aren't I? What are you waiting for? Tell her to come up. [*She crosses to the door and pulls it open.*]

[HELEN *passes quickly through and is heard calling to* MARY *to show* MRS DENNIS *up.*]

JAMES [*unwilling to go*]: Can you stand it?

ROSE: I've been standing the thought of her, haven't I, all these weeks.

[JAMES *stops his chair by the door and appeals again.*]

JAMES: Call me if you need me. I'll be in my room.

[ROSE *obstinately makes no reply and* JAMES *leaves.*

ROSE *stands alone, facing the door as* MARY *shows* MRS DENNIS *in and hurriedly closes the door on her.* MRS DENNIS *is a woman of about forty-five, with prematurely grey hair and a strained neurotic but determined face. She comes in and looks uneasily about her as though the strangeness of this living room communicated itself even to her.*]

MRS DENNIS: Is Michael here?

ROSE: No. Did you expect him to be?

MRS DENNIS: He said he was at a lecture, but I never know now. You're Rose, aren't you?

ROSE: You're his wife, aren't you?

MRS DENNIS: I read one of your letters. It fell out of his dressing-gown pocket.

ROSE: Yes?

MRS DENNIS: He's always been silly that way – keeping letters.

ROSE: Is that what you've come to tell me? Was it worth climbing all those stairs?

MRS DENNIS [*maliciously*]: I thought your letter so touching. You trust him so much.

ROSE: Yes. I do.

MRS DENNIS: You shouldn't, you know, but of course you can't know, he wouldn't tell you. But there's always been trouble with his students. Reading Freud together, I suppose. The third year we were married – just after our baby died – I could have divorced him.

ROSE: Why didn't you?

MRS DENNIS [*fiercely*]: Because he's happier with me. He'll always be happier with me. I'd forgive him anything. Would you?

ROSE: No. Because I love him. I wouldn't want to hold him prisoner with forgiveness. I wouldn't want to hold him a minute if he wanted to be somewhere else.

MRS DENNIS: He only *thinks* that.

ROSE: He has a right to think. He has a right to think wrong.

MRS DENNIS: If he really loved you, he'd have left me.

ROSE: He meant to. Three weeks ago.

MRS DENNIS: But he's still here.

ROSE: Because I wouldn't go.

MRS DENNIS: Why?

ROSE: I was caught like him. By pity [*savagely*] – He pities you.

MRS DENNIS [*maliciously*]: It didn't feel like pity – last night.

ROSE [*crying out in pain*]: I don't believe you.

MRS DENNIS: If I'm ready to share him, what right . . .

ROSE: You're lying. You know you are lying. What have you come here for? You're just lying to break me. You're wicked.

MRS DENNIS: Wicked's an odd word from you. I *am* his wife.

ROSE: You can stay his wife. I only want to be his mistress.

[MRS DENNIS *suddenly crumbles. She drops into a chair and begins to weep.* ROSE *watches her for a moment, but she cannot remain indifferent.*]

I'm sorry. [*With a gesture of despair.*] Oh, it's all such a mess.

MRS DENNIS: Please don't take him away.

ROSE: What can I do? I love him. I love him terribly.

MRS DENNIS: But I love him too. I only want him near me still. It doesn't hurt you.

ROSE [*bitterly*]: Doesn't it?

MRS DENNIS: I was lying. We haven't – been together like that for years.

ROSE: Oh, love isn't all making love. I'd sometimes give that up, to be together. At meals. Come into a house where he is. Sit silent with a book in the same room.

MRS DENNIS [*hysterically*]: When are you going? I know you are planning to go. Don't torture me. Tell me.

ROSE: I don't know.

MRS DENNIS: You're young. You can find any number of men. Please let him alone. [*Spacing her words.*] I can't live without him.

[ROSE *watches her hysteria grow. She is trapped and horrified.*]

I'll die if he leaves me. I'll kill myself.

ROSE: No. No. You never will.

MRS DENNIS: I will. I know what you're thinking – after that, I could marry him.

ROSE: Please . . .

MRS DENNIS: Go away from him. Please. Go somewhere he won't find you. You're young. You'll get over it. The young always do.

ROSE: But I don't want to get over it.

MRS DENNIS: I'm ill. Can't you wait? Just wait six months and see. Six months isn't long. [*With almost a cry.*] You haven't any right to hurt me like this. [*She gets up and comes across the floor to* ROSE.] No right. [*Suddenly she strikes* ROSE *in the face, but immediately she*

*has struck she goes down on her knees and starts beating the table with
her fists.*] You made me do that. You made me. I want to die. I
want to die. I want to die.

[ROSE *stands helplessly above her as* MRS DENNIS *beats the table.
She doesn't know what to do.*]

He wants me to die too. You all want me to die.

ROSE: No. No. [*In a moan of despair*] We only want to be happy.

MRS DENNIS: If he runs away, I shall go mad. [*She gets clumsily to
her feet. The paroxysm is over. She sits down in a chair again.*] Please
will you get me some water?

[ROSE *goes to the closet door. As she enters the closet,* MRS DENNIS
*hurriedly gets up and finds her bag which she had laid on the table. A
tap runs. She takes a bottle out of her bag and unscrews the top. As*
ROSE *comes in again she conceals the bottle in her palm. She takes
the glass of water.*]

MRS DENNIS: Could you turn out that light, dear? It's so strong.

[ROSE *turns away to find the switch.* MRS DENNIS *begins to pour
some tablets into her hand. She does it slowly with the obvious
purpose that she shall be seen when* ROSE *turns. When* ROSE *sees
what she is at, she runs to her and snatches the bottle which she
throws into a corner of the room.*]

[*Hysterically*] Why did you do that? I can buy more.

ROSE: Buy them then. You're just blackmailing me.

[*She hears the sound of feet coming rapidly up the stairs and runs to
the door.*]

Michael, for God's sake.

[MICHAEL *enters.*]

Michael.

MICHAEL [*looking at his wife*]: I heard she was here.

ROSE [*breaking down*]: She tried to kill herself.

MICHAEL: Oh no, she didn't. I know that trick of hers. [*To his
wife*] You promised you wouldn't do that again. It does no
good, dear.

MRS DENNIS: Don't call me dear.

MICHAEL: You are dear. I call you what you are.

[ROSE *watches. She is distressed, puzzled. She hasn't yet grown up
enough to realize that there are many ways of love.*]

MRS DENNIS: But you are going to leave me?

MICHAEL: Yes.

MRS DENNIS: Oh, you've said it now. You've said it. You've never *said* it before.

MICHAEL: I've been weak. I know. I've made matters worse. I'm supposed to know about people's minds, but when it comes to the point I behave like everyone else.

MRS DENNIS: She's too young for you, Michael.

MICHAEL [*with bitterness*]: I'm making her older already.

MRS DENNIS: What happens to me, Michael? There isn't even a child.

MICHAEL: You'll settle down. You have friends. After a little while [*he is almost pleading his own cause with her*] surely we can see each other.

[ROSE *turns sharply away. She can't bear any longer the sight of them together. They are unmistakably man and wife.*]

MRS DENNIS: If you go away, you'll never see me again. You won't know what's happening to me. You won't know if I'm ill or well. I'm not going to have you come and watch my tears.

MICHAEL: But I want you to be happy. We haven't been happy. Long before I met Rose . . .

MRS DENNIS: You talk so much about happiness. No. I wasn't happy. Do you think I'm going to be more happy without you? Happiness isn't everything, is it? Do you often come across someone happy at your lectures? I don't want to be alone, Michael. I'm afraid of being alone. Michael, for God's sake . . . I forgot. You don't believe in God. Only *she* does.

[ROSE *can stand it no more. She comes back into the fight.*]

ROSE: Stop. Please stop. You are making it so complicated. Both of you.

[*They both turn and look at her. It's as if she were the outsider. She looks from one to the other.*]

We love each other, Mrs Dennis. It's as simple as that. This happens every day, doesn't it? You read it in the papers. People can't all behave like this. There are four hundred divorces a month.

MICHAEL: Then there are hundreds of suffering people.

ROSE: But, darling, *you* aren't going to suffer, are you? You want to live with me. You want to go away. You don't want to stay with her. We are going to be happy.

MRS DENNIS: You see – *she* doesn't suffer.

MICHAEL [*turning on her angrily*]: She doesn't shout it aloud, that's all. She doesn't use it as a weapon. [*Lowering his voice*] I'm sorry. I'm shouting too. This is making us all hysterical.

MRS DENNIS: You won't have to be hysterical any more. [*She gets up.*] You can go home. [*She catches on the word.*] I mean to the house – and pack. I won't be there. I'll keep out of the way till you've gone. [*She walks to the door.*] You can sleep there tonight. I won't be there. [*She goes.*]

[ROSE *holds out a hand to* MICHAEL, *but he doesn't see it. He is staring at the door.*]

MICHAEL [*to himself*]: God knows what she'll do.

[*He leaves the room, and we hear him calling to her from the head of the stairs – it is the first time we have heard her first name.*]

[*Outside, calling*] Marion! Marion!

[ROSE *listens with her hand still held out. Then she lets it fall to her side.*]

MICHAEL [*outside*]: Marion! [*He comes slowly back into the room – talking more to himself than to* ROSE, *to keep his courage up.*] She won't do anything. People who talk about suicide never do anything.

[*A pause.*]

Do they?

ROSE: No. What are *we* going to do, Michael?

[*He doesn't hear her. His eyes are on the door.*]

Michael! Michael!

MICHAEL: Yes?

ROSE: What are we going to do, Michael?

MICHAEL [*with unhappy bitterness*]: Oh, we are going to be happy.

ROSE: Are *you*?

MICHAEL: Of course. And you. We'll both get over this. [*Still with bitterness against himself*] It's easy to get over other people's pain. I know. I deal with it all day long. Pain is my profession.

ROSE: Did you mean what you said to her? That we are going away?

MICHAEL: Did I tell her that? Oh yes, she made me angry.

ROSE: Didn't you mean it?

MICHAEL: Of course. As soon as your aunt's better. We always said so.

ROSE: She's better now. I'm free.

MICHAEL [*slowly*]: Then – of course – we can go.

ROSE: When? Now? Tomorrow?

[MICHAEL *hesitates very slightly.*]

MICHAEL: The day after. You see – I must find out how she is.

ROSE: I wish you didn't love her so.

MICHAEL: My dear, my dear – there's no need of jealousy.

ROSE: I'm not jealous. I hate to see you suffer. That's all.

MICHAEL: We'll be all right – the day after tomorrow. [*He kisses her and goes to the door.*]

ROSE [*anxious, not knowing what to say, in a schoolgirl accent*]: À bientôt.

MICHAEL [*his mind still on his wife*]: I wish I knew where she'd gone. She hasn't many friends. [*He goes out.*]

[ROSE, *at that last phrase, puts her hand over her mouth. As soon as she hears his feet on the stairs she sits miserably down, her hand still clamped over her mouth, as though that can stop tears. The sound of* HELEN'*s voice and the grind of the chair wheels drives her to her feet.* HELEN *pushes in her brother in his chair.*]

HELEN: When are you leaving? It's convenient to know.

ROSE [*the phrase sounds weak even to her*]: The day after tomorrow.

HELEN [*to her brother*]: Don't forget you've promised to read to Teresa.

JAMES: I won't forget. But there's something you've forgotten.

[HELEN *hesitates, then goes to* ROSE *and kisses her cheek.* HELEN *leaves.*

ROSE *feels the place as though she were feeling a roughness of the skin. A long pause.*]

Can I help at all?

ROSE [*as though to herself*]: I told him not to make me think. I warned him not to.

[FATHER BROWNE *sits hunched in his chair saying nothing.*]

If we'd gone that day we'd have been happy. I don't think unless people make me. I can't think about people I don't know. She was just a name, that's all. And then she comes here and beats her fists on the table and cries in the chair. I saw them together. They are *married*, Uncle. I never knew they were married. Oh, he'd told me they were, but I hadn't seen them, had I? It was only like something in a book, but now I've seen them together. I've seen him touch her arm. Uncle, what am I to do? [*She flings herself on the ground beside him.*] Tell me what to do, Father!

JAMES: When you say 'Father', you seem to lock my mouth. There are only hard things to say.

ROSE: I only want somebody to say, 'Do this, do that.' I only want somebody to say, 'Go here, go there.' I don't want to think any more.

JAMES: And if I say, 'Leave him' . . .

ROSE: I couldn't bear the pain.

JAMES: Then you'd better go with him, if you're as weak as that.

ROSE: But I can't bear hers, either.

JAMES: You're such a child. You expect too much. In a case like yours we always have to choose between suffering our own pain or suffering other people's. We can't *not* suffer.

ROSE: But there *are* happy people. People run away all the time and are happy. I've read about them.

JAMES: I've read about them too. And the fairy stories which say, 'They lived happily ever afterwards.'

ROSE: But it *can* be true.

JAMES: Perhaps – for fools. My dear, you're neither of you fools. He spends his time dissecting human motives. He knows his own selfishness, just in the same way as you know your own guilt. A psychologist and a Catholic, you can't fool yourselves – except for two hours in Regal Court.

ROSE: I can. I can.

JAMES: You've got a lifetime to fool yourself in. It's a long time, to keep forgetting that poor hysterical woman who has a right to need him.

ROSE [*crying out with pain*]: Oh!

[*The door opens and* TERESA *enters in her dressing-gown.* ROSE, *with her hand over her mouth, follows with her eyes.* TERESA, *paying no attention to them, goes to the closet. As the door closes,*

ROSE *sobs on her uncle's knee. He tries to soothe her with his hand. She raises her head.*]

It's horrible, horrible, horrible!

JAMES: I hoped you'd go on thinking it was funny.

ROSE: I can't go on living here with them. Like this. In a room where nobody has died. Uncle, please tell me to go. Tell me I'm right to go. Don't give me a *Catholic* reason. Help me. Please help me.

JAMES: I want to help you. I want to be of use. I would want it if it were the last thing in life I could have. But when I talk my tongue is heavy with the Penny Catechism.

ROSE: Can't you give me anything to hope for?

JAMES: Oh, hope! That's a different matter. There's always hope.

ROSE: Hope of what?

JAMES: Of getting over it. Forgetting him.

[ROSE *jumps to her feet and swings away from him. He is struggling for words but can find none – except formulae.*]

Dear, there's always the Mass. It's there to help. Your Rosary, you've got a Rosary, haven't you? Perhaps Our Lady . . . prayer.

ROSE [*with hatred and contempt*]: Prayer!

JAMES: Rose . . . please . . . [*He is afraid of what she may say and desperately seeking for the right words, but still he can't find them.*] Just wait . . .

ROSE: You tell me if I go with him he'll be unhappy for a lifetime. If I stay here, I'll have nothing but that closet and this – living room. And you tell me there's hope and I can pray. Who to? Don't talk to me about God or the saints. I don't believe in your God who took away your legs and wants to take away Michael. I don't believe in your Church and your Holy Mother of God. I don't believe. I don't believe.

[JAMES *holds out a hand to her, but she draws away from it.*]

I wish to God I didn't feel so lonely.

[HELEN *enters. She takes the scene coldly in.*]

HELEN It's nearly dinner time. Teresa's been asking for you, and I've got to lay the table here.

JAMES: Couldn't we tonight – use another room?

HELEN: You know very well there isn't another room.

[*She takes his chair and pushes him to the door. He makes no further protest. He feels too old and broken.*

To ROSE]: If you'll start laying, I'll be with you in a moment.

[HELEN *pushes* JAMES *out.*

ROSE *is alone.*]

ROSE: I don't believe. I don't believe. [*She drags herself across the room. She sees the bottle and kneels down and picks it up. Then desperately she goes towards the closet door and calls.*] Aunt Teresa! Dear Aunt Teresa . . .

[*The closet door opens and* TERESA *comes out. She moves across the room, ignoring* ROSE, *as is her custom.*]

Please, Aunt Teresa . . .

[*For a moment the old fuddled brain seems to take in the appeal. She half turns to* ROSE, *then walks on to the door.*]

For God's sake, speak to me, Aunt Teresa! It's Rose!

[TERESA *goes out and shuts the door behind her.*

ROSE *sinks hopelessly down on the landing outside the closet door.*]

Won't somebody help me?

[*She begins to shake the tablets out of the bottle. When she has them all in her hand, she makes an attempt to pray, but she can't remember the words.*]

Our Father who art . . . who art . . .

[*Suddenly she plunges into a childish prayer quite mechanically and without thinking of what she's saying, looking at the tablets in her hand.*]

Bless Mother, Nanny and Sister Marie-Louise, and please God don't let school start again ever.

CURTAIN

SCENE TWO

The Living Room. Next morning.

[*A lot of bedding is piled on the floor.* FATHER JAMES BROWNE *sits in his chair and* MICHAEL DENNIS *has his back turned to him and is staring through the window.* MARY, *the daily woman, is dragging a heavy chair towards the door.*]

MARY [*pausing*]: 'Miss Helen,' I said, 'it's time you let things rest where they rightly belong.' 'Mary,' she said, 'you are paid by the hour for your services and not for your advice.'

JAMES: Do you want help with that chair?

MARY: I'd rather not, sir. Let each stick to his own job, or more harm's done. [*She gets the chair almost to the door, and turns again. To* JAMES] I wish I'd said to her, 'Miss Helen, I'm paid for housework,' before ever I went watching that poor girl.

JAMES: There are a terrible lot of vain wishes about the house today.

MARY: I'm forgetting the bedding. [*She piles the bedding on the chair.*] It's an awful waste of space. Will they let me keep the empty trunks in here, do you think? And where will you be eating your meals now? It seems a shame to me in a house as big as this there shouldn't be one living room for all of you.

[HELEN *enters during her speech.*]

HELEN: You are taking a long time, Mary.

[MICHAEL *moves from the window and* HELEN *sees him.*]

I didn't know Mr Dennis was here.

[MARY *leaves.*]

MICHAEL: I came to see her. You hadn't even the mercy to warn me she was dead.

HELEN: But you're not one of the family. [*She picks up a chair.*]

MICHAEL: For somebody so frightened of death you've done a lot of harm.

HELEN [*carefully ignoring* MICHAEL]: James, if we use Teresa's room as a bed-sitting-room – it's large enough – we shan't have to move you at all.

JAMES: I'm not interested today in where I sleep.

HELEN: If you were a woman you'd realize that life has to go on.

MICHAEL: Rose was a woman, and she had a different idea.

[HELEN *puts down the chair.*]

HELEN: Why are you blaming me for this? If anyone's guilty, it's you. [*To* MICHAEL] It's you who've been killing her – all these weeks at Regal Court. Killing her conscience, so in the end she did – that.

MICHAEL [*accusingly to* HELEN]: If you hadn't brought my wife here, there'd have been no sleeping pills.

JAMES: There would have been a window, a Tube train. It won't help her to choose who's guilty. [*To* MICHAEL] And you are not supposed to believe in guilt.

HELEN: I *know* the guilty one.

MICHAEL [*breaking out*]: You do, do you. Look in your damned neurotic heart . . .

JAMES: I thought Freud said there was no such thing as guilt . . .

MICHAEL: For God's sake, don't talk psychology at me today. Psychology wasn't any use to her. Books, lectures, analysis of dreams. Oh, I knew the hell of a lot, didn't I, about the human mind – [*Turning away*] She lay on this floor.

JAMES: And our hearts say guilty.

MICHAEL: Yes. Guilty.

HELEN: Mine doesn't.

MICHAEL: Then why don't you sleep in this room? You're innocent. All right then. What are you afraid of?

JAMES: Yes, what are you afraid of, Helen?

HELEN: [*startled*]: You know we agreed . . .

JAMES: Agreed?

HELEN: I couldn't frighten Teresa like that. You know how she feels. We can't go against Teresa – she's so old. I'm not afraid, but Teresa . . .

JAMES: It's Teresa, is it?

HELEN: Of course it's Teresa. No one should sleep in this room, James.

JAMES: Even me?

HELEN [*fearfully*]: It's all decided, James. Teresa's bedroom will be the living room too. Mary's preparing it now. You know what a lovely room it is, James. Plenty of space. [*Puts the chair outside the door and returns.*] It's time to close this room.

JAMES: You can leave us, Helen, and see about your business.

[HELEN *hesitates, with her eye on* MICHAEL.]

The room won't harm him and me for the little time we'll be here.

[HELEN *makes to reply, but instead she picks up a small chair and goes out.*

A pause.]

MICHAEL: Three weeks ago Rose and I came into this room together. A lover and his inexperienced mistress. [*As though defending himself*] You can't believe how happy she was that day.

JAMES: She grew up quickly.

MICHAEL: Did she talk to you last night?

JAMES: Yes.

MICHAEL: Why did she do it?

JAMES: She was afraid of pain. Your pain, her pain, your wife's pain.

MICHAEL: It was my wife who rang me here just now. She'd heard. God knows how. She was – terribly – sympathetic.

JAMES: What will you do?

MICHAEL: Go on living with her. If you can call it living. It's a funny thing. I'm supposed to be a psychologist and I've ruined two people's minds.

JAMES: Psychology may teach you to know a mind. It doesn't teach you to love.

MICHAEL: I did love her.

JAMES: Oh yes, I know. And I thought I loved her too. But none of us loves enough. Perhaps the saints. Perhaps not even them. Dennis, I've got to tell somebody this. You *may* understand. It's your job to understand.

MICHAEL [*bitterly*]: My job –

JAMES: For more than twenty years I've been a useless priest. I had a real vocation for the priesthood – perhaps you'd explain it in terms of a father complex. Never mind now. I'm not laughing at you. To me it was a real vocation. And for twenty years it's been imprisoned in this chair – the desire to help. You have it too in your way, and it would still be there if you lost your sight and speech. Last night God gave me my chance. He flung this child, here, at my knees, asking for help, asking for hope. That's what she said, 'Can't you give me anything to hope for?' I said to God, 'Put words into my mouth,' but He's given me twenty years in this chair with nothing to do but prepare for such a moment, so why should He interfere? And all I said was, 'You can pray.' If I'd ever really known what prayer was, I would only have had to touch her to give her peace. 'Prayer,' she said. She almost spat the word.

MICHAEL: I went away to look for my wife. I was frightened about *her*. What do we do now? Is everything going to be the same as before?

JAMES: Three old people have lost a living room, that's all. A psychologist with a sick wife. She's fallen like a stone into a pond.

MICHAEL: Can you believe in a God who lets that happen?

JAMES: Yes.

MICHAEL: It's a senseless creed.

JAMES: It seems that sometimes.

MICHAEL: And cruel.

JAMES: There's one thing I remember from the seminary. I've forgotten nearly all the things they taught me, even the arguments for the existence of God. It comes from some book of devotion. 'The more our senses are revolted, uncertain and in despair, the more surely Faith says: "This is God: all goes well."'

MICHAEL: 'All goes well.' Do you really feel that?

JAMES: My senses don't feel it. They feel nothing but revolt, uncertainty, despair. But I know it – at the back of my mind. It's my weakness that cries out.

MICHAEL: I can't believe in a God who doesn't pity weakness.

JAMES [*imploringly*]: I wish you'd leave Him alone today. Don't talk of Him with such hatred even if you don't believe in Him. If He exists, He loved her too, and saw her take the senseless drink. And you don't know and I don't know the amount of love and pity He's spending on her now.

MICHAEL [*bitterly*]: A little late.

JAMES [*pleading*]: I wish you could understand that today it's only your pain speaking. All right, that's natural. Let it speak. Let it have its silly way. There's a man down the road dying of cancer. His pain is speaking too. Of course we are in pain. Do you want to be the only exception in a world of pain?

MICHAEL: And *you* believe God made the world like that.

JAMES: Yes. And I believe He shared its pain. But He didn't only make the world – He made eternity. Suffering is a problem to us, but it doesn't seem a big problem to the woman when she has borne her child. Death is our child, we have to go through pain to bear our death. I'm crying out with the pain like you. But Rose – she's free, she's borne her child.

MICHAEL: You talk as if she were alive. [*Rounding suddenly on* JAMES] Oh yes, your Church teaches she's alive all right. She teaches she's damned – damned with my wife's sleeping pills.

JAMES: We aren't as stupid as you think us. Nobody claims we can know what she thought at the end. Only God was with her at the end.

MICHAEL: You said yourself she almost spat the word 'prayer'.

JAMES: It may not have been her last word, and even if it were, *you* ought to know you can't tell love from hate sometimes.

MICHAEL: Oh, she wasn't complicated. There was no neurosis about her. No middle-aged conflicts. She was young and simple, that's all. And she cared no more about your Church than I do.

JAMES: Do you really think you'd have loved her if she'd been as simple as all that? Oh no, you're a man with a vocation too. You loved the tension in her. Don't shake your head at me. You loved her just because she was capable of despair. So did I. Some of us are too small to contain that terrible tide – she wasn't, and we loved her for that.

MICHAEL [*bitterly*]: A stone in a pond.

[*The door opens and* TERESA *enters. The old lady is staggering under a load of bedding that she planks down on the sofa.*]

JAMES: What is it, Teresa?

TERESA: My room can be the living room. I shall sleep here.

[HELEN'*s voice is heard outside.*]

HELEN [*voice outside*]: Teresa. Where are you, Teresa?

[HELEN *follows her sister into the room. She is too agitated to pay any attention to* MICHAEL.]

HELEN: Teresa, are you ill again? What are you doing? Whose bedding is that? Everything's arranged.

TERESA: I'm sleeping here. [*Begins sorting out the bedding.*]

HELEN: Here? James, tell her she can't. She doesn't understand what she's doing. She can't sleep here. I won't allow her to sleep here. We all agreed. Please, James, say something to her.

[TERESA *continues unperturbed, and* JAMES *watches the two women from his chair while* MICHAEL *turns from the window to watch also.*]

HELEN [*she is in a panic now*]: Teresa! Dear Teresa! You can't! She died in here. In this room, Teresa! [*Tries to snatch the clothes off the couch again, kneeling beside it.*]

JAMES: Stop it, Helen. We've had enough of this foolishness. God isn't unmerciful like a woman can be. You've been afraid too long. It's time for you to rest, my darling. It's time for you to rest.

[HELEN *collapses suddenly across the bed crying like a child back in the nursery.* TERESA *is the strong one now, she sits beside her, smooths her hair and talks to her in the nursery language of an elder sister.*]

TERESA: Tears, tears, tears – they are only good to water cabbages. It's all nonsense, my dear. Why shouldn't I sleep here? We're not afraid of the child. And there'd be no better room for me to fall asleep in for ever than the room where Rose died.

[*She is still comforting* HELEN *as the curtain falls.*]

CURTAIN

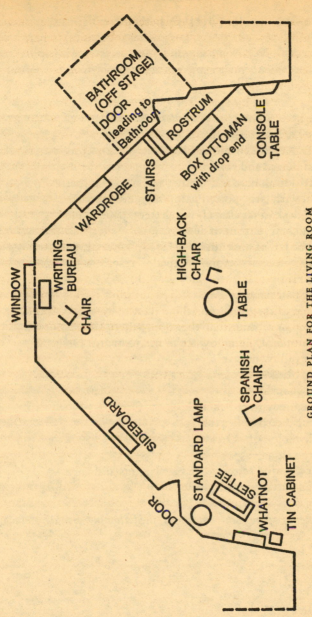

GROUND PLAN FOR THE LIVING ROOM

PROPERTY PLOT

Act One

Settee D.R. with cushions
Lamp standard and shade
Sideboard with blue and white vase, white statuette
Pedestal with large potted palm, above sideboard
Writing desk: on it china bowl, letters, papers, etc.
Upright chair in front of desk
Wardrobe left of desk. In it:
     large piece of cretonne draped to resemble clothes bag
     two slips
     one pair pants
     three pairs of stockings
     one pair of shoes
Box ottoman, D.L. below stairs and rostrum. On it:
     one pillow in case
     one blanket
Spanish chair D.R.
Round table with red chenille cloth, C.
High-backed chair L. table
Console table D.L. On it:
     large china vase
Whatnot behind settee, with bowls, jugs and vases
Dark red curtains in window

If the interior of the bathroom is seen, the following should be on view:

Bath
Geyser
Basin
Towel rail
Lavatory pedestal

Bath mat, towels, spongebag, tumbler, pyjamas hanging on hook
   behind door

Personal props:

Wicker work–basket containing wool, several bills
One book – Poems of St John of the Cross
One suitcase
One copy of *The Lady* magazine
One pair of scissors
One copy of *The Times* newspaper
Brief-case
Small pillow in case
Knitted rug
Small bottle containing 'sleeping pills'
Wheelchair with dark grey rug, and ashtray on arm
Tea tray. On it:
      teapot with tea
      sugar basin with loaf sugar and tongs
      milk jug with milk
      five cups and saucers and spoons
Three-tier cake stand. On it:
      plate of bread and butter (top)
      plate of fruit cake (middle)

Effects:

Bell
Door slam

Property changes:

ACT ONE, SCENE ONE:
Remove: Cake stand, tea tray, bedding
Set: Suitcase upstage of wardrobe. *The Lady*, scissors and *The Times* on centre table. Spanish chair slightly more upstage

ACT TWO, SCENE ONE:

Remove: *The Lady*, scissors and *The Times*

Set: High-backed chair to R. of table. Table move a little L. Book
    of poems on table. Wheelchair L. of ottoman
    Reset bedding on ottoman *plus* two sheets

ACT TWO, SCENE TWO:

Remove: Sideboard, desk, pedestal and palm, table, settee, lamp
    standard, curtains, loose cover from ottoman, sleeping
    pills, vase from console table

Set: Spanish chair well down R. High-backed chair down R. Piles
    of bedding

THE POTTING SHED

★

AUTHOR'S NOTE

The Potting Shed was produced in New York in 1957 with a different third Act which appears in the American edition of the play. For the English production we have reverted to the last Act as it was originally written and this is the only version authorized for Great Britain.

CHARACTERS

(in order of appearance)

DR FREDERICK BASTON, *an old friend and fellow-worker of H. C. Callifer. Age early 60s.*

ANNE CALLIFER, *daughter of John Callifer. Age 13.*

SARA CALLIFER, *former wife of James Callifer. Age about 36.*

MRS CALLIFER, *H. C. Callifer's wife. Mother of John and James. Age about 70.*

JOHN CALLIFER, *the father of Anne. Age about 48.*

JAMES CALLIFER, *the ex-husband of Sara, brother of John. Age about 44.*

DR KREUZER, *aged anything between 50 and 60.*

CORNER, *James Callifer's fellow-lodger. Age about 30.*

MRS POTTER, *aged about 75.*

MISS CONNOLLY, *housekeeper to Father William Callifer. Aged about 55.*

FATHER WILLIAM CALLIFER, *aged about 60, uncle of John and James and brother of H. C. Callifer.*

CAST

The Potting Shed was first produced in London on 5 February 1958 at the Globe Theatre by H. M. Tennent Ltd and Donmar Productions Ltd with the following cast:

DR FREDERICK BASTON	*Walter Hudd*
ANNE CALLIFER	*Sarah Long*
SARA CALLIFER	*Irene Worth*
MRS CALLIFER	*Gwen Ffrangçon-Davies*
JOHN CALLIFER	*Lockwood West*
JAMES CALLIFER	*John Gielgud*
DR KREUZER	*Peter Illing*
CORNER	*William Peacock*
MRS POTTER	*Dorothy Dewhurst*
MISS CONNOLLY	*Aithna Gover*
FATHER WILLIAM CALLIFER	*Redmond Phillips*

The Play directed by MICHAEL MACOWAN

with Settings by PAUL MAYO

SCENES

Act One

Scene One   The living-room of the Callifers' house. 'Wild
            Grove', in what was once the country. An afternoon
            in March.
Scene Two   The same. Evening, a few days later.

Act Two

Scene One   James Callifer's lodgings in Nottingham. Four weeks
            later.
Scene Two   Father William Callifer's presbytery, somewhere in
            East Anglia. A few days later.

Act Three

The living-room of 'Wild Grove'.

Act One

SCENE ONE

It is the living-room of 'Wild Grove' one autumn afternoon. If one were to describe the room in terms of its owner, H. C. Callifer, a high-minded rather pedantic room and a little outmoded. There are a lot of books but they look even from a distance dull and heavy books. One might have taken them for works of theology if one was unaware of H. C. Callifer's reputation. Alas! how much of the world, after a period when Callifer was classed with Wynwood Read and 'The Cosmic Fallacy' with 'The Martyrdom of Man', has become unaware of that reputation. The world has changed around this room, this house. When Callifer first built 'Wild Grove', planning it with the woman he loved, those factory chimneys which now appear in the distance through the garden-window did not exist. There was a grove – perhaps there was even a wildness in Callifer himself, but more than forty years have passed since then. The Grove has become a grave and in the best bedroom upstairs, H. C. Callifer is dying. Throughout the scene that follows till the very end we hear at times the footsteps of those above; conversations are interrupted while the quality of the footsteps is, as it were, assessed.

When the curtain rises there is only one occupant of the living-room – a man twenty years junior to Callifer himself, but twenty years at this period of life have ceased to count. DR FREDERICK BASTON *is now well past sixty though he was once Callifer's youngest and cleverest disciple. His reputation grew with Callifer's, but he was never a rival. If Callifer had died at sixty,* BASTON *would have written his biography and carried on his work, but when the tide of the world's favour receded from Callifer, it receded from* BASTON *too. They are part of the same beach. Will any publisher now be sufficiently interested to commission a biography?*

A tired fussy figure, worrying too much about details, BASTON *is seated on the sofa correcting some sheets of manuscript.*

BASTON: It needed courage in those days to meet the opposition of the churches, the vested interests of superstition. [*The sound of the words does not satisfy him and he repeats the sentence, substituting* 'challenge' *for* 'opposition'. *Satisfied he rises and continues his rehearsal.*]

Callifer's greatest book was of course *The Cosmic Fallacy*, but those who were closest to him knew what store he set by that charming, pathetic and charitable study of Jesus Christ, the first-century religious leader, *He Was a Man*. He was a man. We can say that too, in a different sense, of Callifer. Those of us who loved him most, his wife, his sons – [*He corrects his page.*] his son, his oldest friend and disciple, repeat with sorrow, 'He was a man.' We would be unworthy of him – [*He reaches the mirror and against his will his finger goes up and squeezes a stye on his lid: a pause: he turns to pace again.*]

    [A GIRL *of thirteen comes through the garden-window unnoticed and watches him.*]

– unworthy of him, if, if – [*He consults his pages, looks around, picks up an ash-tray from a table.*] we did not recognize that these ashes that at his request I now resign to the river and the fields and the earth he loved – [*He makes a motion with his ash-tray.*] are all that remains. . . . [*Back again while the* GIRL *observes him.*] Now that the immense spaces of the empty universe, of uninhabited planets and cooling stellar systems have taken the place of the Christian God, we have Callifer to thank for a human life worthy of courageous Man. To the Christian superstition of eternal life, he bravely countered with the truth, Eternal Death.

    [*The* GIRL *interrupts, interested, matter-of-fact.*]

ANNE: Has Grandfather died, Dr Baston?

BASTON [*put out*]: I'm sorry – didn't hear . . . where did you come from?

ANNE: The garden.

BASTON: Playing?

ANNE: Would you mind being careful what questions you ask me?

BASTON: Why?

ANNE: There you go again. You see, I've made a vow that for one month I'll speak the exact truth. A lunar month, not a calendar. There are still eighteen days to go.

BASTON: What happens afterwards?

ANNE: I shall tell lies again like everybody else. Is Grandfather dead yet?

BASTON: He's making a wonderful fight.

ANNE: So would you, wouldn't you? It can't be very nice, being dead. Is Granny with him?

BASTON: Yes. And your father. And the doctor, of course.

ANNE: Will he last the night, do you think?

BASTON: So *you* ask questions too.

ANNE: Only when I really want to know the answer. Practical questions. That was another vow of mine. Only I'm keeping that vow for ever.

BASTON: Who did you vow to?

ANNE: To the inevitability of evolution and the sacredness of man.

BASTON: It sounds a big vow.

ANNE: I got it from an essay of Grandfather's, *The Credo of Septic*.

BASTON: Sceptic.

ANNE: Sceptic. You know, I liked what you said just now about uninhabited planets.

BASTON: I can see you're a real Callifer.

ANNE: Sometimes I wish this planet was uninhabited too. No human beings, only hills and rivers and sky.

BASTON: I rather like human beings.

ANNE: I don't. They are so untidy. Stomach-aches, colds in the head, spots –

[BASTON *automatically puts up his hand to his stye.*]

Aunt Sara's in the garden, snivelling in a deck-chair.

BASTON: What a hard child you are.

ANNE: It's no good being mushy, is it? It's the truth that matters. And she *is* snivelling.

BASTON: You could have said 'crying'.

ANNE: But crying's quite a different thing.

BASTON: I expect she's very fond of your grandfather.

ANNE: Perhaps. Or she may be snivelling for lost love, though it's not likely after all these years. I call her Aunt Sara, but strictly speaking I shouldn't, should I, not after she divorced Uncle.

BASTON: A courtesy title.

ANNE: I don't understand why she comes here, and not Uncle James.

BASTON [*uneasily*]: I suppose he was too busy to come. Or perhaps his paper couldn't spare him. And it's a long way from Nottingham.

ANNE: My school is further than Nottingham. They fetched *me*.

BASTON: I expect there was some reason.

ANNE: They never told him Grandfather was dying.

BASTON: Nonsense.

ANNE: But I *know*. They gave me the telegrams to take to the post office. There was one to you and one to Father, even one to her, but not to him. Is he a criminal? That's a practical question.

BASTON: Of course he isn't.

ANNE: Or wicked?

BASTON: No, no.

ANNE: Or mad?

BASTON: Of course not.

ANNE [*a pause for thought*]: Then I was quite right to do what I did.

BASTON: What did you do?

ANNE: I sent him a telegram myself.

BASTON [*in a shocked voice*]: That was very, very wrong of you.

ANNE: Why?

BASTON: To upset everybody at a time like this. With your grandfather dying upstairs.

ANNE: Is Uncle a hunchback? Has he got a face of horror?

BASTON: You're a silly interfering little girl. I only hope he has the sense not to come. I shall have to warn your grandmother.

ANNE [*pondering the word*]: Warn . . . ?

BASTON: He's not wanted here. Nobody wants him here.

ANNE [*going thoughtfully to the window*]: I see. I'm sorry.

> [*She goes out through the french windows, passing* SARA *as she does so.*
>
>> SARA *is a woman of about thirty-six, good-looking, but carrying with her a sense of disappointment and drift.*]

BASTON [*holding out his sheaf of papers*]: She's made me forget every word. [*He lays the papers on a table.*]

SARA: Is he dead?

BASTON: No. They'll call us at the end. Do you know what that child has done? She's sent for James.

SARA: Poor James. But is that so awful? He's got the right, hasn't he . . . ?

BASTON: And that old man has the right to die in peace.

SARA: Sometimes the dying want to forgive.

BASTON [*evasively*]: Oh, I don't think there's anything to forgive.

SARA: It will be strange seeing James after all these years. What does a man become when a wife leaves him on his own? He ate salt on his bread and he used to take tea not coffee for breakfast. Those are the things one remembers. [*A pause.*] Why did they always hate him so? I don't.

BASTON [*hedging*]: It's not hate. They never got along, that's all. Even when he was a boy . . .

SARA: I would have loved a child of mine whatever he did. [*A pause.*] Do you know, they only got fond of me after the divorce? They wrote to me so kindly then. But as long as James and I were together I was infectious. A mother generally defends her son, doesn't she? – but when I divorced him, I won his mother's approval.

BASTON: I shan't tell Mrs Callifer yet. Perhaps he'll have the sense to keep away. For your sake too, it would be painful . . .

SARA: Would it? I suppose so. It's very bitter when a man leaves you for nothing. I wouldn't have minded so much if he'd been in love with another woman. I could bear being beaten by someone younger, someone lovely. But I was beaten by a bed-sitting room in Nottingham. That's all he left me for.

BASTON: I remember your house at Richmond. It was very beautiful.

SARA: But he wouldn't live in it. [*Bitterly.*] It contained *me*.

BASTON: I never understood it. He always seemed so fond of you.

SARA: Do you know what it's like being married to a sleep-walker?

BASTON: I don't know anything about marriage. I never had the nerve to commit it.

[*The door opens and* MRS CALLIFER *enters – a handsome upright figure in spite of her seventy years.*]

BASTON: How is he?

MRS CALLIFER: He's sleeping again. He was conscious for nearly five minutes. I almost hoped.

BASTON: You ought to rest, Mary. Let Sara or me . . .

MRS CALLIFER: I'll rest when it's over.

BASTON: You're killing yourself.

MRS CALLIFER: Oh no, Fred, don't worry. That would be too good. [*A pause.*] Next week we would have had our golden wedding.

> [*She goes over to a table where* BASTON *has laid down his papers. Before he can interfere she has picked one up. He waits with a look of embarrassed shame.*]

It reads very well, Fred. 'Cooling stellar systems'.

BASTON: Those are *his* words.

MRS CALLIFER: We had a royalty statement last week. They only send them once a year now. They'd sold three copies of *The Cosmic Fallacy* for export.

BASTON: Anyway it's in print still.

MRS CALLIFER: Oh yes. At that rate it will be in print longer than we shall be. Christianity is the fashion now.

BASTON: A passing fashion.

MRS CALLIFER: Of course. But how he hates those sentimental myths, virgin births, crucified Gods. [*She is thinking of something else, and talks to distract herself.*] Just now, from Henry's room, I thought I heard a dog barking. Did you?

BASTON: No. Perhaps a stray . . .

MRS CALLIFER: I must remember to look at the wire netting on the gate. We had a lot of trouble once with dogs, messing up the flower-beds.

SARA [*with a smile*]: I have one now, but I never bring it.

MRS CALLIFER: You think I'm very fussy, but you know it's not old age. I've always detested dogs, haven't I, Fred?

BASTON: Always.

MRS CALLIFER: Parodies of men and women. I hate parodies. We both always hated parodies. Where's John?

BASTON: I thought he was with you.

SARA: He went to the post office.

MRS CALLIFER: I hope he won't be long. [*She tries to talk very detachedly and sensibly, but she can't prevent her restless movements and the quick changes of subject that show her mind is elsewhere.*] It was good of you to do the flowers, Sara. Very nicely, too. Perhaps a little modern. I'm surprised *The Times* hasn't rung up.

SARA [*comfortingly*]: The *Rationalist Review* was on the telephone an hour ago. A Mr Minster. He was very concerned.

MRS CALLIFER [*dismissing the comfort*]: We never thought very highly of Mr Minster. Where is Anne?

SARA: In the garden.

MRS CALLIFER: If he becomes conscious it will be the last time. I do want him to see all the faces he loved. You, Fred, especially. [*But this statement is too near the emotion she is trying to suppress.*] It was good of you to come at once, take all this trouble. You know I tried to persuade him to alter his will – about the ceremony. The River Wandle is not how he remembers it. Too much pollution from the dye factory, and the housing development has ruined the fields.

BASTON: John and I found a spot where you can only just see the chimneys . . .

MRS CALLIFER: Well, of course it doesn't matter, does it? It's just a gesture, scattering ashes. People are so sentimental sometimes – about death – wishing to be buried together.

SARA [*breaking the silence*]: I really believe I did hear a dog.

MRS CALLIFER: I thought I'd have Mrs Bentham in to make new slip-covers. These are really too old. [*She desperately slides across the surface of the unfamiliar new life of a widow.*]
  Do you really have to go next week, Sara?

SARA: Oh, I could always make an excuse.

MRS CALLIFER: I thought if you could stay a few more days – we might hire a car and go to the spring flower show at Weston. I missed it last year when Henry was ill.

SARA: Of course I'll stay.
  [ANNE *comes quietly and rather secretively in through the window. She slides to a chair and takes the first book to hand.*]

MRS CALLIFER: I do wish John would come back. I'd better get some patterns to show Mrs Bentham.

SARA: I'll write for you.

MRS CALLIFER: Why, Anne, I didn't see you come in. Where have
    you been?

ANNE [*carefully*]: In the garden.

BASTON [*trying to be breezy*]: Playing?

ANNE [*gives him a withering look – questions again*]: No.

SARA: Anne, that's not the way to speak to Dr Baston. He only
    wanted to know what you were doing.

    [ANNE *scowls into her book.*]

MRS CALLIFER: You haven't been picking the daffodils, dear, have
    you?

ANNE: No, Granny. [*She takes the book and tries to escape, but
    something in her manner attracts attention.*]

MRS CALLIFER: Where have you been, dear?

ANNE: It's not fair all of you asking questions. I told you my vow.
    You oughtn't to ask any questions till the vow's over.

MRS CALLIFER: All the same, I *am* asking, Anne.

ANNE [*sullenly*]: I've been to the potting shed.

    [*A pause.*]

MRS CALLIFER: Oh. [*A pause.*] Why the potting shed? You know I
    don't like you going there. The gardener's complained of you
    knocking over the seedlings.

ANNE: I didn't touch them.

SARA: What were you doing?

ANNE: Oh, if you've got to know, I was shutting up a secret
    dog.

BASTON: A secret dog?

SARA: Then we did hear a bark.

MRS CALLIFER: Do you mean a stray dog?

ANNE: No. A secret dog.

MRS CALLIFER: But you know I won't have dogs here. Who does
    it belong to?

ANNE: A man.

SARA: What man?

ANNE: He's come to see Grandfather.

SARA: I said – what man?

ANNE: Well, if you must know, your ex-husband.

MRS CALLIFER: James?

ANNE: Yes.

MRS CALLIFER: Did you know about this, Sara?

BASTON: Anne sent him a telegram.

MRS CALLIFER: Where is he?

ANNE: I don't know. I told him you didn't like dogs. He'd forgotten. So he asked where he could put it, and I told him the potting shed. I said I'd show him the way, but he said I could do it for him. When I looked back, he'd gone. We'd meant to keep it a dark secret, but you would ask questions.

[JOHN, *the eldest son, Anne's father, enters through the left door. He is correctly dressed. He will only, in the event, need a black tie to be prepared for the funeral.*]

JOHN: Mother, do you know who's here?

MRS CALLIFER: James.

JOHN: He's in the hall.

MRS CALLIFER: If he's here, well – of course – naturally – he's welcome.

[JAMES *enters through the left door. He is five years younger than John, who must be nearly fifty, but in some ways he looks the elder. Life hasn't dealt with him so well: he appears nervous and ill at ease, a stranger in his parents' house. His clothes are less new and less suitable.*]

How are you, James? I'm glad you could come.

[*He kisses her cheek awkwardly. Then he sees* SARA.]

JAMES: Sara – [*He makes an odd movement of apology.*] I didn't mean to be a nuisance. I just thought if Father . . .

MRS CALLIFER: Of course you're not a nuisance. We telegraphed for you.

[ANNE *looks up at this lie.*]

JAMES: Anne telegraphed for me. [*Nodding at* ANNE.]

MRS CALLIFER: I told her to, James.

[ANNE, *with a flurry of anger, goes back into the garden.*]

JAMES: I see.

MRS CALLIFER: This is Frederick Baston, James. You remember Dr Baston . . .

JAMES: It's so many years . . .

[*They shake hands with constraint.*]

How's Father?

MRS CALLIFER: It will be any moment now.

JAMES: Can I see him?

MRS CALLIFER: Better not – at present. He's unconscious.

[*There is a pause. He stands there as though surrounded by strangers as ill-at-ease as himself. Then* SARA *breaks the circle and goes to his side.*]

SARA: How are you, James?

JAMES: Oh well, very well, Sara. And you . . . ?

SARA: Oh, I'm well, too.

JOHN: How's the paper, old man?

JAMES: That's well. And the bank?

JOHN: Oh – flourishing.

BASTON: How's the weather up north?

JAMES: It was raining when I left.

[*A pause.*]

MRS CALLIFER: I must go to Henry.

[*She leaves the room.*]

SARA: Well, let's sit down.

JOHN: If you don't mind, I want to have a word with Fred – about the ceremony.

JAMES: The ceremony! What a cold word.

[JOHN *and* BASTON *leave.*]

SARA: Dr Baston is reading an oration. [*She points to the table.*] There it is.

JAMES: My mother didn't even let me know.

SARA: You heard what she said.

JAMES: It wasn't true. I had the true story from Anne. I was to be left out. Why? One's father's death is usually supposed to be important.

SARA: Perhaps it's not very important if you believe in nothing afterwards. Or do you? I ought to know. We were married for five years, but it's the tea you had for breakfast I remember. You liked it strong. Otherwise you said you couldn't taste it. Does your landlady make good tea?

JAMES: I suppose so. Sara, what's wrong with me? Why do they keep me away? I wasn't much of a husband to you, I know, but I wasn't bad, was I?

SARA: No. You weren't bad, James. It was just you weren't interested. You pretended very well and very kindly. Even in bed you pretended. I used to think there was another woman somewhere. Someone like the tea, strong enough for you to taste. You couldn't taste me. What do you think about when you are alone?

JAMES: Think about?

SARA: I used to imagine you were thinking of someone else. But when you went away – there was nobody. How bored you must have been with me.

JAMES: No, I wasn't bored. I knew I made you unhappy. There seemed no point in going on. I wish you had married again, Sara. John's a born widower, but you . . .

SARA: I took a lover after you went. He didn't pretend. And then one night I woke and saw him sleeping beside me, content – and I remembered you with your eyes open, thinking of something else, and I didn't want him any more. I didn't love him any more.

JAMES: What's the good of talking importantly about love? It doesn't last like a book or a tune. It goes out with the breath, and we can always snuff that out, can't we? We're not worth loving.

SARA: Then nothing is.

JAMES: And I love nothing.

SARA [bitterly]: You do indeed. In the night you'd wake loving Nothing. You went looking for Nothing everywhere. When you came in at night I could see you had been with Nothing all day. I was jealous of Nothing as though it was a woman; and now you sleep with Nothing every night. Oh hell, give me a cigarette.

JAMES: I don't smoke. [Pause.] Sara, what's wrong with me?

SARA: You're not alive. Sometimes I wanted to make you angry or sorry, to hurt you. But you never felt pain. Why did you marry me?

[JAMES makes a gesture.]

I believe it was curiosity to see if you could feel. You didn't feel.

JAMES: I thought if I saw my father now, at the end, he'd tell me. Tell me what's wrong.

SARA: I thought I knew what it was.

JAMES: Yes?

SARA: When your mother heard about the telegram she was afraid.

JAMES: Afraid of what I'd do?

SARA: Afraid of what you are.

JAMES: A middle-aged newspaper man. I go to the office at four and usually get away by one in the morning. I sleep till nine – I mean, I stay in bed. I take the dog for a walk in the park and have a meal with Corner.

SARA: Corner?

JAMES: He shares my lodgings – a reporter on the *Journal*. My landlady has a penchant for tinned salmon. My dog likes it, but it often makes him sick. He's not a very good dog – parents unknown.

SARA: You shouldn't have brought him here. Your mother hates dogs.

JAMES: Yes, I know. I forgot. You see, our acquaintance has not been very continuous.

SARA: Don't be bitter. She's very unhappy now.

JAMES: I'm not bitter. I want to know, that's all. What's your earliest memory, Sara?

SARA: Driving a goat-cart.

JAMES: I can remember nothing. Absolutely nothing. Until I was ill, just before they sent me away to school at fourteen. Lying in bed with a sore throat. A light was burning, and a nurse – a very kind nurse – was bringing me soup. I thought she was an angel – I'd seen a picture of one once, I suppose, in a shop.

SARA: I'd come and live with you at Nottingham if you wanted me.

JAMES: What about the house in Richmond?

SARA: I'd sell it. I only came here because I thought I'd see you. But I didn't dare to ask why you weren't here. [*A slight pause.*] You know, I love you, James.

JAMES: Sara –

[*He comes behind her and puts his hands over her eyes.*]

I could always talk to you better in the dark. Sara, I simply don't know what love is. What is it?

SARA: It's what I feel now.

JAMES: But if I took my hands away and we saw each other, I'd see – a want. Isn't there a love that just exists and doesn't want? [*He takes away his hands.*] My father's dying. He has nothing to hope for, any more, for ever. When he looks at me, don't you think I might see – just love? No claim, no hope, no want. Whiskey taken neat.

SARA: The strong taste.

JAMES: Yes.

[*The noise of feet on the ceiling above.*]

Listen. Perhaps he's woken up. I haven't seen him for fifteen years, Sara. Perhaps he'll speak.

[*He moves a little towards the door.* MRS CALLIFER's *voice calls from the stairs:* 'John! Fred!' *The noise of quick footsteps, and then* MRS CALLIFER *enters.*]

MRS CALLIFER: Where's Anne?

SARA: In the garden.

MRS CALLIFER: Please fetch her quickly.

[SARA *goes out into the garden.*]

JAMES: Father?

MRS CALLIFER: Yes.

JAMES: Can I go up?

MRS CALLIFER: Please wait. The nurse has to let me know.

JAMES: There's not much time, is there?

MRS CALLIFER: He mustn't have a shock – now.

[SARA *comes in with* ANNE.]

Go upstairs quickly, dear. Both of you.

[*She steps aside for them and they go out.*]

JAMES: I thought we had to wait for the nurse?

MRS CALLIFER [*slowly, bracing herself for the plain truth*]: James, I don't want you to see him.

JAMES: But why? I've come for that.

MRS CALLIFER: I didn't send the telegram.

JAMES: I know. I'm going to see him, though.

[*He moves towards the open door, but* MRS CALLIFER *shuts it and stands with her fingers on the handle.*]

MRS CALLIFER: I don't want to be harsh. That's why I meant to let you know afterwards. But he's got to die in peace.

JAMES: Why should I destroy his peace?

MRS CALLIFER: I love him, James. I want so much to see the last of him. Promise me you won't move from here.

JAMES: No. [*He shakes his head.*]

MRS CALLIFER: Then I stay. [*She leans wearily against the door.*]

JAMES: Mother, if you love me . . .

MRS CALLIFER: I love him more.

JAMES: Give me one reason.

[*She doesn't answer, but she is crying.*]

All right. You've won, Mother. I promise not to come.

[*As she goes through the door, the curtain begins slowly to fall on him alone, facing the door. He raises his head a little as though trying to hear the sounds overhead.*]

CURTAIN

SCENE TWO

Late evening, some days later.

[BASTON, JOHN *and* JAMES *are drinking whiskey in a group round a table on which a number of manuscripts and books are piled.* JOHN *is going through them.* SARA *and* ANNE *sit on the other side of the room reading, but in* ANNE'*s case the reading is an excuse for sitting up and listening.*]

JOHN: Look at this. Strange the things he kept – an invitation to a college dinner in 1912.

[*He drops it into a waste-paper basket.*]

Do you know what all these books are? Old visitors' books.

JAMES [*ironically*]: Perhaps he thought the signatures might become valuable.

JOHN [*taking him seriously*]: I hadn't thought of that. Wells came several times. And there is Bertrand Russell for lunch. Do you think I ought to keep them?

JAMES: No. [*He takes one at random and opens it.*] Ah, here is Dr Baston's autograph.

BASTON: You'll find me on a lot of pages, I'm afraid.

JAMES: August 3–8, 1919. Do you remember that visit?

BASTON: As a matter of fact, I do. The first summer after the war. It was beautiful weather. We played cricket in the Long Meadow. You children too.

JAMES: I don't remember. [*But he is trying hard.*]

BASTON: It was before they built the dye factory. You could understand then why the house was called 'Wild Grove'. There was a wood of beech and wild nut-trees where the housing development is. I remember I hit a six into the River Wandle.

JAMES: I must have been nearly eight that summer. [*He sits with the book on his knees, thinking.*]

　　[JOHN *discards more papers into the waste-paper basket.*]

SARA [*closing her book*]: I think I'll go to bed. Are you coming, Anne?

ANNE: No, I want to finish the chapter.

SARA: It's long past your bedtime.

BASTON: It was so hot we all played in bathing-drawers. What happy times those were!

ANNE: I won't be long, Aunt Sara.

SARA [*pauses by the men as she goes out*]: I thought your oration was spoken very well, Dr Baston.

BASTON: Thank you, my dear.

SARA: Are you really going tomorrow, James?

JAMES: Yes, I have to.

SARA: I'll see you in the morning?

JAMES: I'm leaving very early.

SARA: I'll get up. [*She touches his arm with her hand.*] Good night, dear.

JAMES: Good night, Sara.

　　[*He stares down at the visitors' book without looking up. She goes slowly out.*]

BASTON: I was reminded of that game this afternoon during the ceremony. We were in the same field. You children called your father the demon bowler. He bowled underarm, but very fast.

JOHN: Yes, I remember. With a tennis ball!

JAMES [*a pause*]: I don't remember.

JOHN: Poor Father! Here are the expenses of a holiday in France in

1910. Bottle of red wine, 1 fr. 50 centimes. Filed for future reference.

JAMES [*opening another of the books*]: 1925 – that was the year I was ill, the year I went away to school. Who's William Callifer?

BASTON: Don't you even remember your own uncle?

JAMES: No. Didn't he get a telegram either – or is he dead?

[ANNE *looks sharply up*.]

JOHN: Father never had much to do with him.

JAMES [*turning the pages*]: He was here for three days that autumn.

BASTON: It was the last time. He behaved rather badly.

JOHN: It was bad enough to have a convert in the family – but when he became a priest . . .

JAMES: I'm glad I'm not the only pariah among the Callifers.

[*He puts the book down*.]

JOHN: Bertrand Russell again. I hope he was worth his meal-ticket.

[ANNE *closes her book and comes over*.]

BASTON: How are the vows, Anne?

ANNE [*she pointedly ignores so silly a question*]: Uncle James, if I put out some water in the hall, will you take it to the potting shed?

JAMES [*uneasy*]: The potting shed?

ANNE: To your dog, stupid.

JAMES: Couldn't you do it for me? You've been looking after him.

ANNE: I think Spot would prefer you, after what happened this afternoon. If I go now, he'll think he's still in disgrace. Granny was so angry.

JAMES: But I don't know where it is, Anne.

ANNE: You've seen me going there often enough. Down the path by the laurels. You can't miss it. Good night, Daddy. [*She kisses her father*.] Good night, Dr Baston. [*Stiffly*.]

BASTON: Good night, Anne. [*Sententiously*.] It's a good thing when a sad day ends.

ANNE: Oh, it wasn't all sad, was it? I thought it was awfully funny when Spot came bounding along looking for Uncle James, and you dropped the ashes.

BASTON: It wasn't very nice for your grandmother. It spoiled the ceremony.

ANNE: You were just saying: 'I now consign to the river . . .' You could have altered it quickly and said: 'I now consign to Long Meadow.'

JOHN: Do go to bed, Anne.

ANNE [*pauses at the door*]: You won't forget the water, Uncle James?

[*He shakes his head.* ANNE *leaves.*]

BASTON: How heartless children are.

JOHN: Oh, I don't think she meant it that way. She was being practical that's all. Her mother was the same. Help yourselves to whiskey.

BASTON: Thanks. It *was* unfortunate you brought that dog.

JAMES: I know. I forgot.

[*They help themselves.*]

Was Mother asleep when you went upstairs?

JOHN: She seemed to be.

JAMES: You'll say good-bye for me, won't you?—say I'm sorry I—butted in.

BASTON: You exaggerate.

JAMES: Do I?

[*A pause while he looks at the visitors' book again.*]

Fancy a Callifer being a priest.

BASTON: As a priest he isn't exactly a success.

JAMES: People believe, don't they, some of them, that the spirits of the dead will pass over a glass of wine, rippling the surface. [*He regards his whiskey.*] Will whiskey do? Can you invoke the dead with whiskey?

JOHN: What nonsense you talk, James.

BASTON [*dryly*]: It's the method your uncle is said to use.

JAMES: You mean he drinks?

BASTON: Inordinately.

JAMES: How unlike a Callifer. Well, I'm going to bed.

BASTON: Don't forget the dog.

JAMES: Oh, the dog. [*Something disturbs him.*] Surely he can do without water just tonight. [*He goes to the garden-window and looks out at the dark.*] He's asleep. And it's late. It will do in the morning.

JOHN: So long as he doesn't wake Mother with his howling.

JAMES: Couldn't you do it, John? It's very dark outside. You know the way.

JOHN: And be bitten at the end of it? Look after your own dog, James.

JAMES: I've forgotten where the potting shed is.

JOHN: Anne told you. Down the laurel walk. You can't miss it. And there's a flashlight on the hall table.

[*A distant howl.*]

BASTON: Listen. He *is* howling.

JOHN: You'd better let him out and keep him in your room.

[*Another howl.*]

Oh, for God's sake, James, do something. He'll keep everybody awake.

[JAMES *goes unwillingly out to the hall. A door closes.*]

BASTON: He hasn't changed. Always difficult.

JOHN: Do you think I ought to look through all these books, Fred?

BASTON: I wouldn't bother. They wouldn't fetch much . . .

JOHN: We did have some interesting visitors. How do you pronounce CZECHWYICZ?

BASTON: Oh, that was the Polish delegation. A disappointing lot. Very unsound on evolution.

[MRS CALLIFER *enters. She is in her dressing-gown.*]

MRS CALLIFER: I didn't mean to interrupt . . .

JOHN: Can't you sleep, Mother?

MRS CALLIFER: I did, for a little. Has James gone to bed?

JOHN: Yes. And we are just going. [*He drops the books into the basket.*] Try to sleep.

MRS CALLIFER: A book will help. [*Sadly.*] You've done a lot of tidying already, John. You and Fred have been very helpful. [*She goes over to the bookcase and picks almost at random.*] Perhaps this will send me to sleep. Oh, I'm sorry, it's one of yours, Fred. [*She opens it and reads the dedication.*] 'To Henry Callifer, a great leader and a great friend.' Strange that doesn't sound true any longer.

BASTON: I don't follow you.

MRS CALLIFER: How could you, Fred? But for nearly fifty years I've looked after his laundry. I've seen to his household. I've paid attention to his – allergies. He wasn't a leader. I can see that now. He was someone I protected. And now I'm unemployed. Please go to bed, both of you, and leave me alone.

JOHN [*standing up*]: You have your family, Mother.

MRS CALLIFER: You don't need protection, John. You're like me, a professional protector. It wasn't what I intended to be. But men either form us with their strength, or they form us with their weakness. They never let us be.

BASTON: Mary, you mustn't . . .

MRS CALLIFER: Poor James had to suffer. We did him a great wrong, Henry and I. Why shouldn't he know – as much as we know?

BASTON: It would be a mistake. After all these years. And what *do* we know?

JOHN: You've never told me anything.

MRS CALLIFER [*ignoring him*]: I don't want your empty spaces, Fred. I don't want anything except Henry. Henry alive. Somehow. Somewhere.

BASTON [*with a gesture of comfort*]: Mary . . .

MRS CALLIFER: I've often talked so harshly of him to you, and yet I loved him.

BASTON: So did I.

MRS CALLIFER: Please, John, both of you, go away. I'll be all right when I'm alone. But I'm not strong enough yet for sympathy.

JOHN: Come up soon, Mother.

MRS CALLIFER: In a little while. But it's such a large room. I'll move into Sara's when she goes. Good night, my dear.

[*She kisses* JOHN *on the cheek.*]

JOHN [*leaving*]: Good night, Mother.

MRS CALLIFER: Good night, Fred.

[*She lifts her cheek for him to kiss.*]

BASTON: You'll call me if there's anything . . .

MRS CALLIFER: Of course. You must look after that stye, Fred. You've been squeezing it again. And you a doctor.

BASTON [*absent-mindedly, at the door*]: I'll look in at Henry . . . [*He stops, aghast at what he's said.*]

MRS CALLIFER: Don't worry, Fred. We'll all make that mistake for a while. Today when I was ordering lunch I said, 'Not french beans.' He always hated them. Now we can have them every day.

BASTON: Mistakes like that are a kind of immortality. You remember Samuel Butler's sonnet:

> 'Yet meet we shall, and part, and meet again,
> Where dead men meet, on lips of living men.'

As long as there are you and I – and his books.

MRS CALLIFER: Yes, three copies for export. There was once a Callifer Club, do you remember?

BASTON: Yes. Mary, I was going to write to Macmillan's and suggest a biography, an intimate biography with letters . . .

MRS CALLIFER: Don't, Fred. Wait until a publisher writes to you. I'd rather hope than collect polite refusals.

BASTON: As you wish. But when he had his first bad illness, they did suggest . . .

MRS CALLIFER: That was thirty years ago. Your oration will do just as well, Fred, for those who are interested. I'll have it printed. For private distribution. Do you think two hundred copies? There may be still some members of the club . . . It was very dear and generous of you. If only that wretched dog hadn't . . . Oh, well. I'll read myself to sleep with your book, Fred. Good night.

BASTON: Good night, Mary.

MRS CALLIFER: Turn out the light, dear, as you go. [*He goes out.*]
[*And* MRS CALLIFER *sits in a straight arm-chair under a reading lamp. She begins to read, but she can't concentrate, and almost at once she puts the book down. The door to the garden opens and closes and she turns with a wild movement, as though she expected to see someone. Then, with knowledge of the truth, and with the despair of it, she whispers, 'Henry . . .' The french window opens and* JAMES *enters. There is a tenseness in his manner, an impression of fear, and he carries a bowl of water. He sees his mother and stands awkwardly like a boy caught in an absurd action.*]

MRS CALLIFER [*peering into the shadows*]: Is that you, James?

JAMES: Yes, Mother.

MRS CALLIFER: I thought you were in bed. What's that you've got in your hand, dear?

[*It's as if in this half-darkness they have both shed thirty years. A middle-aged mother is talking to her half-grown son. They have different interests, but they are gentle and kind to each other.*]

JAMES: A bowl of water – for the dog.

MRS CALLIFER: Oh. [*It's too late at night to be unkind about the animal.*]

JAMES: I started to take it to him. But, Mother . . .

MRS CALLIFER: Yes, dear?

JAMES: I was too frightened.

MRS CALLIFER: Why frightened? Was it the darkness, dear?

JAMES: No. I don't mind the dark.

MRS CALLIFER: Then what was it?

[*He puts the bowl down and comes slowly towards her ring of lamplight.*]

Tell me what happened, dear.

JAMES: I didn't want to go. I was frightened before I left the house, just as though I knew someone was waiting for me, among the laurels, on the path to the potting shed.

[MRS CALLIFER *makes a movement which might be one of fear or tenderness.*]

MRS CALLIFER: My poor James.

[*He sits down, like a child, on the floor at her feet.*]

JAMES: Mother, I'm sorry. About the dog and coming here. Disturbing you.

[*She pats his shoulder. It's almost as though the constraint between them were at last breaking down.*]

MRS CALLIFER: My dear, don't worry. You're my son, James.

JAMES: Yes. I'm your son, Mother. Will you tell me, please, now – now my father's not here – what's wrong?

MRS CALLIFER: Wrong?

JAMES: Wrong with me. So that you were afraid to see me. Oh, except between trains at Nottingham when you were taking Anne to school. Do you remember when we met that time for tea at the Kardomah? I made you meet me. But I still hoped that in a way you would be glad to see me. And then I walked in from the street, and you sat there waiting, hard and afraid. Afraid of me. We talked about what the weather had been like here. And then you said you had to catch your train. What did I do, Mother, all those years ago, that was so horrible?

MRS CALLIFER: You are imagining things.

JAMES: No. Mother, there's usually a moment when parents begin to speak the truth to their children. It's been a long time delayed in our case.

MRS CALLIFER: There never is such a moment. First the children are too young, and then the parents are too old for truth. I'm too old, James. Please.

JAMES: Then there is a truth.

MRS CALLIFER: You'll have to go somewhere else to find it.

JAMES: I've looked for it already in some strange places.

MRS CALLIFER: Yes?

JAMES: Once a week I go to a doctor and he injects me with methedrine, and I talk and talk.

MRS CALLIFER: What good does that do?

JAMES: None yet. I tell him how my marriage broke and about my childhood, all I can remember. How my parents avoided me. Don't we have to learn love from our parents, like we learn to walk? You taught me to walk, but I've no idea what love is.

MRS CALLIFER: You are wrong, James. You had love, so much love, my dear, until . . . [She stops.]

JAMES: Until what?

MRS CALLIFER: I'm very tired, James. Please don't ask me tonight.

JAMES: I'll be gone tomorrow.

MRS CALLIFER: We shouldn't have buried it; but now it's been buried such a long time, I don't know what it would look like.

JAMES: Mother, please. Shut your eyes and think I'm your child. There's something I don't understand, and I fear it, and I've come running.

MRS CALLIFER: I've got to protect Henry.

JAMES: He's dead.

MRS CALLIFER [with a moan of pain]: Can't I be loyal to him for a few hours?

JAMES: It won't affect him.

MRS CALLIFER: How do we know?

JAMES: I don't. I thought you did. [He scrambles to his feet; his appeal is over and the bitterness returns.] Don't worry. I won't ask you again. I dreamed for a moment you were my mother and I was your child, and I went to my mother with my fear. For now, I thought, my father isn't here to be protected. Doesn't a child deserve protection too?

[MRS CALLIFER's *head is bowed, and she is crying.*]

I pretended to myself you were a mother like other mothers, and I was a child like any other child. Somebody you can comfort so easily, saying, 'They are only shadows,' and lighting a lamp, or giving him a toy spade to dig with . . .

MRS CALLIFER [*with an elderly whimper of pain*]: Oh, do you remember that toy spade? You were only six.

JAMES [*in excitement*]: What do you mean?

MRS CALLIFER: We can be hurt by such silly things. You spoke as though you never liked that spade, but you were so happy with it . . .

JAMES [*almost with fear*]: I've never remembered anything as far back as that before. [*It is as though at last a whole world of memory is at the door of the mind.*]

MRS CALLIFER: Let me go now.

[*He makes no move to stop her.*]

We can talk again – one day. Good-bye. [*She kisses his cheek.*] I don't suppose I shall be up when you go. [*She goes out.*]

[*And* JAMES *makes no reply – he is staring at a toy spade that has swum up from the unknown past.*]

The door opens, and ANNE *comes in in her dressing-gown. He doesn't see her. A long pause.*]

ANNE: Hullo.

JAMES [*turns quickly*]: What do you want?

ANNE: That's an awfully difficult question to answer.

JAMES: What have you been doing out there?

ANNE: Listening.

JAMES: That's very wrong.

ANNE: Don't you ever do anything that's wrong?

JAMES: Yes, and sometimes I can't even remember what.

ANNE: Are uncles prohibited?

JAMES: . . . ?

ANNE: As husbands?

JAMES: Yes.

ANNE: It's a pity. We'd get on very well together. You see, I don't know what love is, either.

JAMES: You certainly have been listening.

ANNE: I'm curious by nature. I'd make a good detective. I mean – when the vow is finished. You can't expect a detective to tell the truth.

JAMES: Why were you listening?

ANNE: I was on the prowl and I heard voices. There's an awful lot to be found out everywhere.

JAMES: Everywhere?

ANNE: I'm frightened of the laurel walk, too. After dark. That's why I wouldn't take the water to Spot. I kept on thinking, 'Out, out, damned spot.' Because if there were ghosts, the potting shed might be haunted . . .

[JAMES's *attention is caught.*]

. . . and you can't be quite certain of anything, can you?

JAMES: Why – the potting shed?

ANNE: Something awful happened there once.

JAMES: How do you know?

ANNE: I heard the gardener talking one day to a man who'd come for seedlings. He was talking about Potter, the gardener they used to have here years ago. He said, 'I always thought Mr Callifer was pleased when old Potter passed on.' He meant died, you know. The other man said why, and Willis – he's the gardener now – said, 'I reckon it was because he was here when that thing happened. He saw it all. Right here. Something shocking it was.' I don't like the smell of mould, do you?

JAMES [*letting it sink in*]: Something shocking . . .

ANNE: I expect they hushed it up, but that's why I thought, 'Out, damned spot.'

JAMES: I don't believe you.

ANNE: You must. Because of my vow.

JAMES: But it needn't have anything to do with me. I couldn't have done anything very terrible. Not at that age.

ANNE: He said, 'Poor Master James.'

JAMES: I remember nothing. Nothing. I don't look like someone who'd do anything shocking, do I?

ANNE [*remembering her vow, she looks at him carefully before replying*]:
No. You don't look like that, but I don't suppose people
usually do. Everything is possible, isn't it?

CURTAIN

Act Two

SCENE ONE

A month has passed. This is the living-room of JAMES CALLIFER'S *lodgings at Nottingham. The furniture is his landlady's, and could belong to nobody but a landlady: the bobbed fringes of the sage-green tablecloth, the sideboard with a mirror, the glass biscuit-box with a silver top, the Marcus Stone engravings.*

The door of the living-room is open, and voices can be heard outside. CORNER *enters followed by* DR KREUZER. KREUZER *is an elderly man with a tough kindly face, obviously in a state of anxiety.* CORNER *is in the early thirties . . . thin and nervous, a heavy smoker.* KREUZER *wears an overcoat.* CORNER *is obviously at home. He clears newspapers from a chair for* KREUZER.

CORNER: Come in, Dr Kreuzer. Callifer's spoken of you many a time.

KREUZER: You're Mr Corner, aren't you? He's spoken of you, too. The only real reporter the *Journal* has, he says.

CORNER: He doesn't say it to me. Sit down and wait, Dr Kreuzer. He must be back soon.

KREUZER: Haven't you seen him this morning?

CORNER: Not since breakfast. He said he had an appointment with you and methedrine. Sounds like a girl.

KREUZER: Not unlike, Mr Corner. It makes a shy man talk. Callifer left me two hours ago. I must get hold of him. Have you a phone here?

CORNER: I wouldn't use it if I were you. It's a party line. Unless it's an emergency. Is it?

KREUZER: I don't know. I wish I did.

CORNER: What's happened?

KREUZER: He took something from my desk which I need back.

CORNER: Stole it?

KREUZER: No, no. It was my fault. A patient doesn't steal.

    [KREUZER *can't keep still.*]

CORNER: What's wrong with him, doctor?

KREUZER: I don't know.

CORNER: We all have moods.

KREUZER: Some moods are blacker than others.

CORNER: But he's good at his job. Or he wouldn't have stayed five years on the *Journal.*

KREUZER [*hardly listening*]: When he takes a walk, where does he go?

CORNER: He used to go along the Trent when he had the dog. Or down to the goose market.

KREUZER: Hasn't he got the dog still?

CORNER: It ran away.

KREUZER: I'm sorry.

CORNER: He didn't seem to mind.

KREUZER: I wonder why he didn't tell me about it?

CORNER: Perhaps it wasn't important enough.

KREUZER: You live with him, Mr Corner. What is important to him?

CORNER: I wouldn't know.

    [*The door opens and* JAMES *enters. He is still in an exalted state from the methedrine.*]

JAMES: Well, well – so you've hunted me down to my digs, Dr Kreuzer. Digs – the word sounds like an animal's hole, doesn't it?

KREUZER: I wanted to see the kind of place you live in. It's a bit anonymous.

JAMES: A lodging for the night. The slow dark hours. For me and my colleague, Corner. I'm glad you've met Corner. You read him every day. [*He picks up one of the newspapers.*] Listen to this – 'Councillor Worm's Tour in Europe'. 'Councillor Worm, who has just returned from a visit to Paris and Le Touquet, reports that the French feel deeply.' The text is Corner's. The headlines are mine. I wanted to call it 'a worm's-eye view', but the chief sub-editor is against jocularity on the *Journal.*

CORNER: There's a telegram for you on the mantelpiece. He's

always like this, doctor, after he's seen you. She seems to be a nice girl, methedrine.

KREUZER: She can let a man down, too.

JAMES [*reading telegram*]: It's from my mother. I suppose she's fetching Anne from school. It's just as I told you. This is the way she always visits me. Between trains. Lucky, Nottingham is a junction. In the summer term I never see her: I suppose there's a better connection.

KREUZER: You're still excited, Callifer.

JAMES: Well, I've remembered something, haven't I? Did you ever have a toy spade, Corner? Doctor, are all your patients as anxious as I am to be cured?

KREUZER: They don't come until they want it enough.

JAMES: You should try him, Corner. You might stop throwing away half-smoked cigarettes at three and eleven a packet. It might lend colour to your reports of council meetings. A jab in the arm, a little nausea for a few seconds and then – a desire to talk till the cows come home. What time do cows come home, Corner?

CORNER: It depends what you mean by cows. Callifer, if your mum's coming I'm going to my room. She always makes me feel like an office-boy. Good-bye, Dr Kreuzer.

KREUZER: Good-bye, Mr Corner.

CORNER: I'll come for a shot in the arm myself one day.

[CORNER *leaves. There is a short silence.*]

KREUZER: It's not only the methedrine which is exciting you.

JAMES: Why are you really here, doctor?

KREUZER: I have a sense that I failed you today.

JAMES: You? Why?

KREUZER: You came to me with a kind of hope.

JAMES: I went away with a kind of hope, too.

KREUZER: We are not in my consulting-room now. Perhaps you can talk to me more easily here.

JAMES: I've talked myself dry. Six months of talking. It hasn't got us far. Perhaps what I really need is action.

KREUZER: What action? What's that you're playing with?

JAMES: A toy. Something I picked up. We've been talking about childhood so long, you mustn't mind if I start playing with toys again. Not a spade this time. We've exhausted the spade.

KREUZER: Oh no, we haven't. You brought it up – and there we stopped. You had an important engagement. Don't you remember?

JAMES: There's no point in the spade. Every child has one. Or so I've read. I've read a lot about childhood. It helped to fill the gap.

KREUZER: How?

JAMES: I built up an imaginary childhood. That plot of garden. Seed envelopes with coloured pictures that one bought in shops. But there were more important seeds, doctor, not in packets. Seeds in old cardboard boxes. One stole them from the gardener and planted them in the ground and one never knew what flowers or vegetable would grow. The boxes lay on the earth in the potting shed. [*He stops abruptly.*]

KREUZER: Go on.

JAMES: I can't. [*He gets up.*] It's too hot in here.

KREUZER: Sit down. I'll open the window.

[*He opens the window behind* JAMES's *head and shivers slightly in the cold air.* JAMES *remains standing.*]

In what book did you read about the potting shed?

JAMES [*agitated*]: I don't know. I can't remember.

KREUZER: Perhaps it was a real potting shed.

JAMES: Yes. A real potting shed. And a month ago I began to walk down the laurel path towards it. It was dark. I was carrying water for my dog. And I didn't have the courage even to come within sight of the door. Father, can't you tell me . . .

KREUZER: You called me Father.

JAMES: So I did. But he's dead, and he'll never tell me now.

KREUZER: Relax. Try not to worry. Talk about something else. Forget the potting shed.

JAMES: I had. All those years. [*He sits.*] But you can't forget for ever what exists. Sooner or later, a smell, a touch . . . our footsteps make such a pattern over the world in forty years, they'd have to tread the same path again sooner or later. Wouldn't they, doctor?

KREUZER: I believe there's nothing human which can't somehow with patience be recalled.

JAMES: And do you believe in anything that isn't human?

KREUZER: No, I don't believe. Sometimes I doubt my disbelief.

JAMES: What could have happened that was so terrible it wiped out all memory? I was a boy, doctor. What a boy can do is very limited.

KREUZER: Perhaps it was something done to you.

JAMES: Then why the disgrace? Oh, I know some parents make a fuss about the little sexual games children play. Not my parents, though. It can't have been anything like that. They were never worried by anything human.

KREUZER: That word human again.

JAMES: Well, God was taboo. My father had killed that superstition for his generation. Poor Father! I'm glad he didn't realize how it was beginning to return. Like memory. We were not allowed ghost stories, either. Do you believe in ghosts, doctor?

KREUZER: No.

JAMES: Or the soul?

KREUZER: I've never understood what the word means.

JAMES: If I had a child, I wouldn't forbid it fairy stories. They might develop the sense of hope. If a pumpkin can turn into a coach, even this dreary room, that tablecloth, those awful ornaments, could be a palace, with limitless corridors.

KREUZER: Did you ever want a child?

JAMES: No. I didn't want to create new convicts for a prison. To have a child you need hope.

KREUZER: There seems to be plenty of hope, then, around us. Judging by the birth rate.

JAMES: There should be another word for that simple sort of hope.

KREUZER: It's enough for most of us.

JAMES: Doctor, I'm not sneering. I want it to be enough for me too. Why isn't it? What happened to me – in that shed?

KREUZER: For six months now I've been trying to find out, and you haven't given me a clue.

JAMES [*pleading for hope*]: I was beginning to remember.

KREUZER: Yes. Outside the door. But what happened when the

door shut behind you? Was there a lock? A bolt? A catch? Answer me quickly.

JAMES [*in a low voice*]: I can't remember.

KREUZER: Were you alone?

JAMES: I don't know.

KREUZER: Think aloud. Invent. Tell a story – any story – a fairy story. Whatever comes into your head.

[JAMES *puts his head in his hands*.]

You've seen many other sheds like that, haven't you, besides the one you fear so. Describe them to me. Anything. The spades leaning against the wall. The smell of mould.

[*A pause, while* JAMES *tries to remember, to invent*.]

JAMES: It's as if there were only one place like that in the world. The walk was called the dark walk. The door was never painted.

KREUZER: Are you inventing?

JAMES: I think so. I don't know. I kept my spade in there, with the real spades. In that way it seemed to be no longer a toy. But that was years before. Something made a pattern on the path as I walked, like a snake crawling beside me.

KREUZER: A snake?

JAMES: No, not a snake. I don't know. When I came in sight of the door my heart was beating. I stopped to get my breath. My head was aching too, but I wasn't unhappy any more. Just frightened.

KREUZER: You'd been unhappy?

[JAMES *pays no attention to the question*.]

Was somebody waiting for you?

JAMES: Yes, or something. I don't know. I can't remember. That damned door shuts it all out. [*Despairingly*.] Doctor, we can go on for a lifetime like this, I'll never get through that door.

KREUZER: And when you came out again?

JAMES: I don't believe I ever came out. Sometimes I think I'm still lying there.

KREUZER: Lying?

JAMES: Oh, it was only the first word that came. I'm tired, doctor, and my mother will be here any moment now.

KREUZER: You are frightened of making an effort to remember. I can't cure you. Perhaps there's nothing to cure.

JAMES: What do you mean?

KREUZER: I can only cure the irrational, the exaggerated, the abnormal. If a man is melancholy because he's lost his leg, I'm not called in. He has good reason.

JAMES: You think I may have reason?

KREUZER: Yes. But what happened inside the door to give you the reason – the mind boggles at that.

JAMES: So we give up? Right. It was my last fling, too.

KREUZER [apprehensively and sharply]: Don't be a bigger coward than you need be.

JAMES: Trying to make me angry, doctor? You can't. My plan needs courage.

KREUZER: I was just talking, Callifer, to make *you* talk. I never give a patient up.

JAMES: Has no one given you up?

KREUZER [after a pause, unwillingly]: Yes, one.

JAMES: He got tired of it?

KREUZER: Yes.

JAMES: Did he find another cure?

KREUZER: Not what I can admit is a cure. Perhaps this may interest you. He killed himself.

JAMES: Oh. [The words have struck home.]

KREUZER: He was my son.

JAMES: I'm sorry.

KREUZER: He wouldn't be treated by anyone else. I tried to make him, but he was afraid. He was never afraid of me. I had to go and tell his mother. We hadn't met for years. She took it badly.

JAMES: How long ago?

KREUZER: Ten years. I swore then I'd never leave a case unfinished. Even if a patient tried to give me up. They often do.

[Somewhere below the front door-bell rings.]

JAMES: My mother, Doctor Kreuzer.

KREUZER: Before I go – [He holds out his hand.]

JAMES: I don't understand.

KREUZER: You acted very quickly. I suppose it was when I turned to telephone. I forgot to examine my desk before you left. My tablets, please.

JAMES: Suppose I won't give them to you.

KREUZER: It's not very important. I'm trying to save you from a stomach-ache, that's all. They're not poisonous.

JAMES: Then why did you follow me here?

KREUZER: I couldn't allow a patient to leave me ever again in that state of mind.

[*The door opens and* CORNER *lets in* MRS CALLIFER.]

CORNER: Here's your mother, Callifer. [*He goes.*]

[JAMES *hands the bottle to* KREUZER.]

MRS CALLIFER: James . . . Is Anne here?

JAMES: No, Mother.

MRS CALLIFER: I lost her at the barrier. I'm sorry, James, interrupting . . .

JAMES: No, we've finished. Quite finished. This is Dr Kreuzer, Mother.

[*They shake hands.*]

MRS CALLIFER: He's not ill, is he, doctor?

JAMES: He's not that kind of doctor. He makes me talk, that's all.

MRS CALLIFER: Is that supposed to be a good thing nowadays?

KREUZER [*picking up his case*]: Your generation believed in letting sleeping dogs lie, Mrs Callifer.

MRS CALLIFER: Was that so wrong?

KREUZER: You were clever at keeping them asleep, but sometimes they wake up your children.

MRS CALLIFER [*to* JAMES]: Do you think I ought to go back to the station?

JAMES: Anne's old enough. She'll find her way.

MRS CALLIFER: I can't think how I lost her. She went ahead while I collected the luggage. She said she'd wait at the barrier.

KREUZER: Well, good-bye, Callifer. Same time next week?

JAMES: It's no use, doctor. We've failed.

KREUZER: I told you. I never give up.

JAMES [*seeking an excuse*]: I'm sorry, but I can't afford to play at this any longer.

KREUZER: There'll be no charge.

[MRS CALLIFER *can feel the conflict between the two men, though she cannot understand it.*]

MRS CALLIFER: If it's a question of money . . .

KREUZER: It isn't. It's a question of courage.

JAMES: No. Only a question of hope.

KREUZER: Callifer, I've had this conversation before with some-one else. I beg you . . .

JAMES: I shall do nothing foolishly. I'm quite calm. You can feel my pulse. [*He holds out his hand.*]

KREUZER [*turning hopelessly away and picking up his bag*]: It would be useless. I should feel only the methedrine. Mrs Callifer, if only you would help him . . .

JAMES: Look, I don't want my mother troubled.

KREUZER: I thought you didn't know what love was? Very well, then, but I'll phone you in the morning. Good-bye, Mrs Callifer. [*He goes out.*]

JAMES: He's a good man.

MRS CALLIFER: What were you talking about before I came?

JAMES: A potting shed where something happened. Mother, why did you leave my uncle out as well as me when my father was dying?

MRS CALLIFER: There had been a quarrel years ago.

JAMES [*sits down at his desk*]: I can't remember his face.

MRS CALLIFER: Don't try, James. He belongs to the past. Like your father and me. Old years are like old people. You should let them get weaker and weaker. Age is not pretty or graceful except in books. Leave old years alone, James.

JAMES: They won't leave me alone.

[*A noise on the stairs.*]

Oh, I think the truant has turned up.

[*The door opens and* ANNE *comes in. She is in her school uniform. She tries to slip in with a certain unobtrusiveness.*]

ANNE: Good afternoon, Uncle James.

JAMES: Hello, Anne.

ANNE: Where's Spot?

MRS CALLIFER: Where have you been, Anne? You said you'd wait at the barrier.

ANNE: I did.

MRS CALLIFER: You weren't there. I looked for you.

ANNE: Somebody told me you were waiting outside. So I went outside and I didn't find you, and then I took the wrong bus.

MRS CALLIFER: Where have you been, Anne?

ANNE: I told you. Nowhere.

MRS CALLIFER: What have you been doing?

ANNE: Nothing.

JAMES: Nothing and nowhere. It's the Callifer touch.

MRS CALLIFER: I thought you were such a truthful girl.

ANNE: Oh, that was weeks ago. My vow is over. I can tell as many lies as I want to now.

MRS CALLIFER: But you oughtn't to want to.

ANNE: You have to, if people ask too many questions, or if you want to lure somebody to a certain house at a certain hour . . .

MRS CALLIFER: What on earth are you talking about now?

ANNE: I can tell Uncle James. I can't tell you.

MRS CALLIFER: Why not?

ANNE: You have grandmother eyes.

JAMES: What are they?

ANNE: Old and upright.

JAMES: And mine?

ANNE: Oh, your eyes don't say anything. They just look away. Some people's eyes are always saying 'Cleanliness is next to godliness' or 'Virtus laudata crescit'.

JAMES: 'Virtus . . .'?

ANNE: It's the school motto. 'Virtue grows by praise', and whenever they say anything nice they expect the virtue to grow. Automatically. Like watering radishes.

MRS CALLIFER: Anne, I asked you . . .

ANNE: Where *is* Spot, Uncle?

JAMES: He ran away.

ANNE: There ought to be paw prints as well as finger prints.

MRS CALLIFER: She's talking a lot of nonsense to hide something.

ANNE: Where did you see Spot last, Uncle?

JAMES: I don't know. He was a very quiet dog. I hardly knew when he was there.

ANNE: You could advertise.

JAMES: I expect he's happier where he is.

MRS CALLIFER: Can't you see the child's play-acting? Anne, what have you been up to?

ANNE: Didn't I tell you that I'd make a good detective? When my vow was over. Any moment now you'll hear a ring and that will be the answer to all the trouble.

JAMES: Who's going to ring, Anne?

ANNE: Mrs Potter.

JAMES: Who's Mrs Potter?

ANNE: Potter's wife. Yesterday I sent her a telegram.

JAMES: It's quite a habit of yours.

ANNE: Well, you came, didn't you, when I telegraphed? And so, I expect, will Mrs Potter.

MRS CALLIFER: We are on our way to 'Wild Grove', Anne. We have to catch a train. In three quarters of an hour.

ANNE: 'Wild Grove' can wait. I've just sent them a telegram too, that you'd been detained on urgent business. The real detective work came first, finding out that Mrs Potter hadn't passed on. And where she lived, and when I found that out, everything was easy. Even the telegram. Of course she had quite a journey. We may have to wait for hours and hours, but it will be worth it, won't it, because she'll tell us what Potter saw.

JAMES: I'm just beginning to understand.

MRS CALLIFER: What's the child done?

JAMES: Perhaps what Dr Kreuzer couldn't do.

[*A bell rings.*]

ANNE: There, I told you.

[*Pause while they listen.*]

MRS CALLIFER: But Potter's dead.

ANNE: This is Mrs Potter.

MRS CALLIFER: What did you put in the telegram?

ANNE: 'Dying. You can relieve a mind in torment. Come tea-time. Saturday.' I signed it Callifer.

MRS CALLIFER: Anne!

ANNE: Well, we are dying, aren't we, all of us?

[*The bell rings again.*]

ANNE: Shall I go?

JAMES: No.

ANNE [*her hand on* JAMES'S]: Your hand, Uncle. You're afraid.

JAMES: No, no. It's the methedrine.

ANNE: I'll answer the door.

MRS CALLIFER: No.

ANNE: I will.

JAMES: Stop where you are.

ANNE: You *are* afraid.

JAMES: That's what Dr Kreuzer said.

[*The bell rings a third time, impatiently.*]

Don't be so impatient. Can't you wait a few seconds longer on the doorstep? You've been waiting for thirty years.

[*A long pause. No further ring.*]

ANNE: She's gone. We'll never know now.

[*The door opens and* CORNER *enters.*]

CORNER: There's a woman at the door, Callifer. She says . . .

MRS CALLIFER: Please tell her there's no one at home.

CORNER: She says she has an urgent telegram. From you, Callifer.

MRS CALLIFER: Please tell her it was a mistake, Mr Corner. A child's silly prank. Here, give her this for her fare.

JAMES: No. Ask her to come in.

MRS CALLIFER: You'll only hear a lot of nonsense. Fairy stories, James. [*She is between him and the door.*] Mr Corner, my son's excited by his treatment. Send her away.

[CORNER *hesitates.*]

He's not in a fit state.

JAMES: She's come to see me, Corner. Not my mother. I'll fetch her if you won't.

[CORNER *looks at the two of them, shrugs and goes out.*]

Mother, you stood in front of a door like this once before. But not again.

MRS CALLIFER: What's the use, James? She wasn't there. She's only heard stories, exaggerated stories, Potter's stories. She knows nothing.

JAMES: Then tell me yourself. All you know. In your words. Before she comes. I'll send her away if you'll tell. Mother, it's you or Mrs Potter.

[*A small white-haired scared* WOMAN *enters. She is over seventy years old, and her face is wrinkled and country-like. She gives a frightened little nod and beck towards* MRS CALLIFER.]

MRS POTTER: You won't remember me, ma'am.

MRS CALLIFER: Oh yes, I remember you very well.

JAMES: I'm Mr Callifer.

MRS POTTER: I was expecting a sick gentleman from the telegram. Are you Master John?

JAMES: No, I'm James.

MRS POTTER [*uneasily*]: Oh.

JAMES: Come in, sit down, Mrs Potter.

[*She sits defensively on the very edge of the chair, looking nervously at* MRS CALLIFER.]

I want to ask you some questions, Mrs Potter. There's something I have to find out.

MRS POTTER: What sort of questions, Master James?

JAMES: Do you remember the summer of 1925?

MRS POTTER: All summers seem alike to me now, sir. Only warmer in those days.

JAMES: This was a different summer from all the others. Do you remember my uncle, Father Callifer?

MRS POTTER: Oh yes, sir, a fine young man. You and he were very close. That is, before . . .

JAMES: Before?

MRS POTTER [*evasively*]: There's always trouble in families, sir.

JAMES: Mrs Potter, one day that summer your husband went to the potting shed and found somebody, something, there.

[*A pause.* MRS POTTER *stares at her hands.*]

It was something that shocked him very much. He wouldn't have kept it dark from you, would he?

MRS POTTER: Potter and me never had secrets.

JAMES: What did he tell you?

MRS POTTER: It's a long, long time ago, sir.

JAMES: But you remember it.

MRS POTTER: Potter said don't tell a soul, and I never have. For your poor dad's sake.

JAMES: My father's dead. You can tell me now.

MRS POTTER [*pleading*]: But you know, sir, already. What's the good of raking around?

JAMES: I've forgotten everything that happened that day.

MRS POTTER: You couldn't, sir, no . . . [*She stops again.*]

JAMES: Mrs Potter, I didn't send you that telegram, but my mind *is* in torment. I've *got* to know.

MRS POTTER: Ask your mother. Me, I'm only Potter's wife. Potter's widow. What'd *I* know about it?

JAMES: Well, Mother?

   [*His mother turns away.*]

You see, my mother won't tell me. You are the last chance I have, Mrs Potter. If you owe anything to us . . .

MRS POTTER: I owe everything to the Callifers. But if your mother doesn't want you to know . . .

JAMES: Weren't we friends in those days, Mrs Potter?

MRS POTTER: You was always my favourite, Master James. It wasn't any fault of yours what happened. You were a dear boy to me. If your father had let you alone . . .

JAMES: I haven't asked you for anything in thirty years, but I'm begging you now . . .

   [MRS POTTER *looks at* MRS CALLIFER.]

MRS POTTER: But your mother . . .

MRS CALLIFER: All right. I'll tell you. You had an accident in the potting shed.

JAMES: An accident?

MRS CALLIFER: You slipped and fell. You were unconscious when Potter found you. And afterwards . . . it made you strange.

JAMES: Mad?

MRS CALLIFER: Not exactly mad. You didn't get on with your father. Family life wasn't good for you.

JAMES: Is that all?

MRS CALLIFER: All except Potter's fairy stories.

JAMES: Then I want the fairy stories.

MRS POTTER: They weren't fairy stories, Mrs Callifer. Potter was no liar. Your husband knew that. That's why he sent him away.

MRS CALLIFER: He was too old for the work. My husband gave him a good pension.

MRS POTTER: Oh, it was a good pension, but his heart was in his garden and it killed him.

MRS CALLIFER: He spread stories.

MRS POTTER: It was the truth.

MRS CALLIFER: How could it be?

MRS POTTER: It's not the first time. There was Lazarus. They buried *him*.

ANNE: Who was Lazarus?

MRS CALLIFER: Someone in a book.

MRS POTTER [*angrily*]: A book you Callifers aren't allowed to read. All right. I'll tell you how it was, Master James. It was dinner-time. Potter was late. Near two o'clock. I knew something was wrong as soon as he came in. He had his coffin face. It was bad for Potter because he found you first.

JAMES: He found me?

MRS POTTER: He lifted you down, poor boy.

JAMES: Lifted me . . .

MRS POTTER: You were hanging there, sir. You'd used a cord from the play-room. He cut you down.

JAMES: Was I –

MRS POTTER: There wasn't any life in you, sir.

MRS CALLIFER: No! [*She makes a motion of protest.*]

MRS POTTER: Forgive me, ma'am, but it's what Potter said.

JAMES [*as though it were a real question, and that he half expects the answer to be No*]: But I am here? This is my room.

MRS POTTER: Potter did all he could. He was a great swimmer once, sir, and he knew all about artificial respirationing. It wasn't any use he said. Your heart was stopped. He was always a truthful man.

JAMES: Last week I cut my hand. It bled.

MRS POTTER: Potter left the door open, and he looked up and saw your uncle was there. 'Master James has killed himself,' Potter said. You were stretched out there on the ground and you had no more breath, Potter said, than a dead fish.

MRS CALLIFER: James, it was all a mistake. You don't take this seriously, James?

JAMES: What's your story, Mother? You've kept it dark a long while.

MRS CALLIFER: There was no story to tell. We didn't want you to remember how foolish you'd been. You were in a coma from shock. When the doctor came he revived you.

MRS POTTER: Not the doctor. Potter left you with your uncle, Master James.

MRS CALLIFER: Potter did better than he knew. Perhaps he did save your life.

MRS POTTER: Potter never thought that. He was beyond human aid, Potter said.

JAMES: Mother, where's my uncle now? [*Pause.*] You may as well tell me.

MRS CALLIFER: Even if I knew where he was I wouldn't tell you. What use could he be to you in the state you'd find him in?

JAMES: Mother, you can't hush *him* up. There are directories where one can find a priest's address.

ANNE [*coming forward*]: I'll find it for you.

   [*They all turn and look at her.*]

It will be a lot easier than finding Mrs Potter.

JAMES: No! Leave this to me.

CURTAIN

SCENE TWO

Evening. The sitting-room in FATHER CALLIFER's *presbytery in an East Anglian town. There is something in its homelessness that reminds us of* JAMES CALLIFER's *lodgings in Nottingham. Only instead of pictures by Marcus Stone there are a hideous Sacred Heart, a dreary print of a Mother and Child belonging to Raphael's most sugary period. There is a crucifix on the dresser instead of a biscuit-box. One feels that all has been inherited from another priest. They are part of a second-hand uniform. There are two doors, one opening on another part of the house, the other into a little drab hall.*

   There are the remains of an evening meal on a tray on the table in the sitting-room. A bottle of cheap altar wine is all but finished.

   [MISS CONNOLLY, *Father Callifer's housekeeper, has just let a man into the hall. He wears a raincoat over his shoulders. In the half-dark, for the only light comes from the street outside, we do not at first recognize* JAMES CALLIFER. MISS CONNOLLY *is a hard-*

*faced woman of over fifty. She has known many other priests in her
time and has learnt only too well to distinguish between the office
and the man.*]

MISS CONNOLLY: For what would you be wanting the Father at
this hour? There's proper times for confession. They are on the
church-board. It is confession?

JAMES: No.

MISS CONNOLLY: Instruction? I doubt if he's in a fit state after his
supper. He's easily tired.

JAMES: So I've heard.

MISS CONNOLLY: You shouldn't believe all you hear. Where do
you come from?

JAMES: A long way. Just tell him . . .

MISS CONNOLLY: I can't let you have a light. The bulb's burned
out and I haven't a spare one in the house.

JAMES: I don't mind the darkness.

MISS CONNOLLY: I promise nothing, mind. You should have
come in the morning. He's best after breakfast.

JAMES: I won't be here. I'm only passing through.

MISS CONNOLLY: Then what kind of instructions are you
expecting?

JAMES: Instruction was *your* word.
    [*She goes out impatiently, shutting the door behind her, crosses the
    sitting-room and goes out by the other door. Now we can hardly
    make out* JAMES *at all. He sits quietly until the others return. We
    hear their voices first on the stairs outside the sitting-room, or rather*
    MISS CONNOLLY's *voice.*]

MISS CONNOLLY [*voice*]: And when can I find you capable?
Answer me that.
    [FATHER CALLIFER *enters, followed by* MISS CONNOLLY. *He has
    a stubbly worn face with bloodshot eyes: a dirty wisp of a Roman
    collar has been made by twisting and folding a handkerchief round
    the top of his shirt.*]
I'm waiting for an answer.
    [*The* PRIEST *goes to the mantelpiece and places his hands on it as
    though for support. He has his back to* MISS CONNOLLY *and the
    audience.*]

They'd have written to the Bishop long before this if I'd let them. [*A pause.*] Don't think they haven't learnt what happened in your last parish and the one before that. If I hadn't begged them time and again to give you a chance if only for my sake . . .

CALLIFER [*not turning*]: Your sake?

MISS CONNOLLY: I've been the priest's housekeeper here for twenty years and never had a breath of scandal before. But unless you give me your solemn honest-to-God promise you'll keep off the liquor I'll not be preventing them any longer writing to the Bishop.

CALLIFER [*swinging suddenly round*]: Do you think I'd mind that? Let them take away my faculties. Don't threaten a convict with the loss of his chains.

MISS CONNOLLY: Speak lower if you don't want to advertise your shame to a stranger.

CALLIFER: Go and fetch the man whoever he is.

MISS CONNOLLY: I'm going to have my say first. Here they want a priest with the faith in him. Don't turn away and pretend you don't understand.

CALLIFER: Fetch him in, I say.

MISS CONNOLLY: You and I have got to have this out once and for all. [*With a slight softening.*] It's for your sake I'm speaking.

CALLIFER: I say Mass every Sunday at eight-thirty and on week-days at seven for those who care to come. There aren't many of them. What else do you want of me?

MISS CONNOLLY: Oh, you stand at the altar all right, gabbling your way through as quickly as possible to get at your break-fast. But you don't believe a word you are saying.

CALLIFER: How do you know?

MISS CONNOLLY: In a life like mine you get an ear for such things.

CALLIFER: Yes, I suppose so.

MISS CONNOLLY: You should have heard poor Father Murphy and the beautiful voice he had. He wouldn't have read other men's sermons because he had no thoughts of his own.

CALLIFER: I can tell he never preached to you on charity.

MISS CONNOLLY: I found your new hiding-place this morning.

[CALLIFER *turns his back on her and moves away.*]

[*More gently.*] Father, what kind of a priest are you?

CALLIFER: A priest who does his job. I say Mass, I hear confessions, if anyone has a stomach-ache in the night, don't I go to him? Who has ever asked for me and I haven't come?

MISS CONNOLLY: Miss Alexander.

CALLIFER [*slowly with shame*]: Yes, you would remind me of that.

MISS CONNOLLY: I couldn't wake you. I had to say next day you were sick. Sick!

CALLIFER: Miss Connolly, you've looked after a lot of priests. You take it as your right to speak your mind to them. And me – You expect me to serve you, all of you, every day for twenty-four hours. I mustn't be a man. I must be a priest. And in return after Mass you give me coffee and eggs (in all these years you've never learnt how to make coffee) and you make my bed. You keep my two rooms clean – or nearly. [*He runs his finger along the mantelpiece.*] I don't ask you for any more than you are paid to do.

MISS CONNOLLY: The people here have a right to a priest with the faith.

CALLIFER: Faith. They want a play-actor. They want snow-white hair, high collars, clean vestments (who pays the cleaner? – not their sixpences), and they want a voice that's never husky with the boredom of saying the same words day after day. All right. Let them write to the Bishop. Do you think I want to get up every morning at six in time to make my meditation before Mass? Meditation on what? The reason why I'm going on with this slave-labour? They give prisoners useless tasks, don't they, digging pits and filling them up again. Like mine.

MISS CONNOLLY: Speak low. You don't understand what you are saying, Father.

CALLIFER: Father! I hate the word. I had a brother who believed in nothing, and for thirty years now I have believed in nothing too. A father belongs to his children until they grow up and he's free of them. But these people will never grow up. They die children and leave children behind them. I'm condemned to being a Father for life.

MISS CONNOLLY: I've never heard such words before out of a priest's mouth.

[*A pause.*]

CALLIFER: You wouldn't have heard them now, if the bottle you found hadn't been empty.

MISS CONNOLLY: They say your breath smells in the confessional.

CALLIFER: And so do theirs. Of worse things. I'd rather smell of whiskey than bad teeth.

MISS CONNOLLY: You're full of it now.

CALLIFER: Oh no, I'm empty. Quite empty.

[*The door from the hall opens and* JAMES CALLIFER *enters.*]
Who are you?

JAMES: Your nephew. If you are Father Callifer.

CALLIFER: My nephew? [*Pulling himself together.*] Well, well, it's long since I've seen any of the family. I wouldn't have kept you waiting if I'd known. I thought you were just . . . well . . . You should have warned me you were coming. Miss Connolly . . .

MISS CONNOLLY: I can get the guest-room ready right away.

JAMES: I'm not staying. I was only passing and I thought . . .

CALLIFER: The nearest town where you'll be comfortable is Wisbech. That's twenty miles away. You'd do much better to stay the night here.

MISS CONNOLLY: The sheets are ready aired.

CALLIFER [*he is unused to being a host: nobody has stayed in this house for years*]: Have you dined? It would be no trouble, would it, Miss Connolly, you could . . . ?

MISS CONNOLLY: There's a couple of chops for tomorrow's lunch. It won't take a minute . . .

CALLIFER: Where are my manners? I forgot to introduce the two of you. This is my housekeeper, Miss Connolly. My nephew, John.

JAMES [*who does not correct him*]: How do you do, Miss Connolly? I had food on the way. I just wanted to see you, have a word with you after all these years. Perhaps a drink.

CALLIFER [*watching* MISS CONNOLLY]: Of course you must have a drink. While Miss Connolly is getting your room ready. Sit down, my dear fellow, sit down. *That's* the only comfortable chair. Now, Miss Connolly, what have we in the house?

MISS CONNOLLY [*grudgingly*]: There's a bit of sherry.

CALLIFER: Not at this hour.

MISS CONNOLLY: Maybe I can find some altar wine.

CALLIFER: Do. And bring a jug of water.

MISS CONNOLLY [*suspiciously*]: What would you be wanting the water for?

CALLIFER: To temper the wine, Miss Connolly.

[MISS CONNOLLY *goes out*.]

A good woman – in her way. And how's the bank?

JAMES: I work on a newspaper.

CALLIFER: Oh, I was thinking . . . but I haven't kept up. Were you at your poor father's funeral?

JAMES: Yes, but I wasn't invited.

CALLIFER: Nor was I, but you . . . [*He looks at him sharply.*]

JAMES: For the same reason. I'm James, Uncle, not John. A strange meeting, isn't it – the first since that potting shed.

[*At this moment* MISS CONNOLLY *enters with a tray. She puts it on the table.*]

MISS CONNOLLY: Is there anything else you'll be wanting?

CALLIFER: No. You can go to bed. I'll show my nephew to his room.

[*She leaves.*]

So you are James.

JAMES: Yes.

CALLIFER: I wish you hadn't come.

JAMES: Why?

CALLIFER: We were very close once. Do you remember?

JAMES: No.

CALLIFER: I'm glad. You won't find me so changed then.

JAMES: I couldn't help hearing just now . . . you didn't lower your voice.

CALLIFER: That's honest anyway. So we needn't pretend. You'll have some whiskey? A reunion like this demands . . . [*He doesn't wait for an answer, but goes to his bookcase and draws out the second volume of the 'Catholic Encyclopaedia'. Behind it is a full bottle.*] Volume 2, Assi to Bro. I can't offer you soda. She'd notice if I kept soda in the house. [*He pours out two very large glasses and drinks deeply of his own.*] Welcome to my home. Rather different from 'Wild Grove', isn't it? But then your father and I followed different ways. They say you can tell a man's character from his furnishings.

[JAMES *looks around.*]

Yes, you can see mine standing all round you for yourself. What sort of rooms have you got, I wonder? They'll have told you at 'Wild Grove' that I'm over fond of this. [*He raises his glass.*] But I do my job. Nobody can deny I do my job. Look at the pictures, the books. I keep up appearances, don't I? We are intelligent men, you and I. Look at that picture of the Sacred Heart. A Christmas card made out of a medical text-book. [*He takes another long drink of whiskey.*] Does John drink?

JAMES: A glass of wine with his meals.

CALLIFER: A lucky man. How does it go? 'They scoff at scars who never felt a wound.'

JAMES: What's your wound. Uncle?

CALLIFER: My wound? Nothing serious. It's a difficult thing, though, practising a faith, day in day out, when you don't believe one jot of it. Do you know that at night I still pray – to nothing, to that. [*He indicates the crucifix with his glass.*] I was teaching you to believe in that when your father interfered. How right he was.

JAMES: Right?

CALLIFER: He was a very clever man. Older and cleverer than I was. He took everything I told you and made fun of it. He made me a laughing stock before you. I had taught you about the Virgin birth and he cured you with physiology.

JAMES: Was that why I tried to kill myself?

CALLIFER: So you know about that, do you? He was a bit too rough. A child can't stand confusion. [*A pause.*] Fill your glass. We have to get through this bottle by twelve.

JAMES: Why by twelve?

CALLIFER: I have to say Mass in the morning. I abide by the rules. It's the least I can do.

JAMES: For whom?

CALLIFER: For myself. [*He gives an unhappy laugh.*] I caught you there. You thought you had squeezed out a small drop of faith. But there isn't one drop.

[MISS CONNOLLY *enters. She has an old-fashioned kitchen alarm clock in her hand.*]

MISS CONNOLLY [*harshly*]: I've set the alarm for six. [*She sees what they are drinking.*] So that's why you asked for the water. Where had you got that hidden?

JAMES: I brought it.

MISS CONNOLLY: I try so hard to keep him off the drink, and now you are sending him drunk to bed.

JAMES: I'm sorry. I needed the drink more than he did.

MISS CONNOLLY [*her harshness gone as she looks at the old man drooping in his chair*]: You'll see he goes up to bed soon, won't you; he has to wake early. He works hard in his way. Do you know what he called himself just now? A convict. He said he was in prison. I'm the warder, I suppose. He hasn't any love or gratitude in him for all the years he's been looked after.

JAMES: It's a terrible thing to have nothing in you.

MISS CONNOLLY: And I'd give my life for him. [*She goes out.*]

CALLIFER [*rousing himself*]: I've made her angry again. What were we talking about? Where's the point? I think I'll go to bed.

JAMES: Have you really forgotten what happened?

CALLIFER: I've forgotten nothing. I don't like to remember, that's all. It was a terrible day for everybody. I was very angry with your father for the way he treated you. Of course he had reason, but it was a shocking thing for a boy to be brought to hang himself.

JAMES: What happened when you found me? I wasn't – dead, was I?

CALLIFER: How could you have been dead? It was a coma. Just a coma. The doctor said so.

JAMES: Did the doctor bring me to?

CALLIFER: Oh no. You were awake before he came.

JAMES: It isn't possible, is it, I mean – what Potter thought?

CALLIFER: How could it be? If you were dead, it would have been a miracle, and if it were a miracle God would exist. That hideous picture there would have a meaning. But if God existed, why should he take away his faith from me? I've served him well. I go on serving him. The saints have dark nights, but not for thirty years. They have moments when they remember what it felt like to believe. [*Pause.*] You shouldn't have come.

JAMES: Tell me what you remember.

CALLIFER: The shed and you lying there and Potter struggling with your arms.

JAMES: And then?

CALLIFER: I prayed. I was a model priest, you see, with all the beliefs and conventions. Besides, I loved you. Yes, I remember now, how I loved you. I couldn't have a child and I suppose you took his place. When I had you on my knees I remember a terrible pain – here. So terrible I don't think I could go through it again. It was just as though I was the one who was strangled – I could feel the cord round my neck. I couldn't breathe, I couldn't speak. I had to pray in my mind, and then your breath came back, and it was just as though I had died instead. So I went away to bury myself in rooms like this.

JAMES: What did you pray?

CALLIFER: It's so long ago.

JAMES: Try to remember.

CALLIFER: What difference would it make to you?

JAMES: I've been close to despair too.

CALLIFER: What made you remember me?

JAMES: Potter's widow.

CALLIFER: Is he dead? Poor fellow. And so you came to me? Do I look as though I could be of any use to anyone at all? [*Pause.*] It was an awful moment finding you dead in that way.

JAMES: Dead?

CALLIFER: I mean you seemed to me dead.

JAMES: What did you do?

CALLIFER: I'd have given my life for you – but what could I do? I could only pray. I suppose I offered something in return. Something I valued – not spirits then. I really thought I loved God in those days. I said, 'Let him live, God. I love him. Let him live. I will give you anything if you will let him live.' But what had I got to give him? I was a poor man. I said, 'Take away what I love most. Take . . . take . . .' [*He can't remember.*]

JAMES: 'Take away my faith, but let him live'?

CALLIFER: Did you hear me?

JAMES: Yes. You were speaking a long way off and I came towards you through a cave of darkness. I didn't want to come. I struggled not to come. But something pushed me to you.

CALLIFER: Something?

JAMES: Or somebody.

[CALLIFER *begins to weep*.]

Uncle, can I help?

CALLIFER: I even forgot what I said to Him, until you came.

JAMES: Do you really believe . . . ?

CALLIFER: He answered my prayer, didn't he? He took my offer. Look around you. Look at this room. It makes sense, doesn't it, now. You must forgive me. I'm tired and a little drunk. I haven't thought about that day for thirty years. Will you see me to my room? It's dark on the landing. [*He gets up and then pauses and looks up at the hideous picture*.] I thought I had lost Him for ever.

CURTAIN

Act Three

The living-room at 'Wild Grove'.
A few days later. Night.
JOHN *is there,* KREUZER, BASTON, SARA *and* MRS CALLIFER.
They are sitting grouped together with something of the air of a board meeting.

BASTON: Pass me the cigarettes, will you?
   [*Everyone is waiting for someone else to speak.*]
JOHN: Light?
BASTON: Thanks.
JOHN: Sara?
SARA: No thanks.
JOHN: Can I get anybody a drink? Dr Kreuzer?
KREUZER: Thank you, no.
BASTON: It's nearly morning and no one has spoken frankly yet.
  You've brought Dr Kreuzer a long way for nothing.
JOHN: Well, it's not an easy subject, one's got to break the ice.
MRS CALLIFER: You were always a bit heavy on your feet, John.
JOHN: Mother, I'm trying . . .
MRS CALLIFER: You are used to Board Meetings, I'm not, and I'm
  not clear about the agenda.
BASTON: The agenda as I see it . . .
  [*He becomes aware of* MRS CALLIFER'*s exaggerated expectancy and*
  falls silent.]
MRS CALLIFER [*over-sweetly*]: Yes, Fred . . . ?
BASTON: There's only one thing on the agenda. The insanity of
  your son.
MRS CALLIFER: Thank you, Fred. Now surely somebody can
  speak.
JOHN: Is Anne . . . ?
MRS CALLIFER: Safely in bed.
JOHN: I thought I heard someone on the stairs.

SARA: Imagination. I locked James in. He was asleep when I turned the key. I felt as though . . . as though I were cuckolding him.

JOHN: It was necessary.

SARA: But I'd like to unlock the door before he wakes. So that he won't know.

JOHN: I'm afraid – what we've got to face . . . [*He stops again.*]

MRS CALLIFER: For goodness' sake, John, face it then.

JOHN: He's my brother. You both forget I'm concerned too.

MRS CALLIFER: Say what's on your mind then.

JOHN: I think Fred and Dr Kreuzer have got to decide whether we can ever unlock that door again.

[*A pause.* SARA *reacts.*]

MRS CALLIFER: I've never believed in captivity – even for animals. Fred, don't you remember that letter we all signed . . .

BASTON: Mary, this is different. This is for his good.

MRS CALLIFER: I've heard people defend zoos in just the same way. The animals are freed from starvation and fear. Oh yes, I know all those answers. Don't hand them out to me, Fred. We fought in the same causes.

BASTON: And sometimes we were wrong. Sometimes we were too general and too emotional. We must avoid sentimentality.

MRS CALLIFER: That's what we always call a sentiment we don't share, isn't it? I'm his mother, Fred.

BASTON: Mary, let's just deal with the facts. At fourteen he tried to kill himself. Since then he's suffered from all kinds of delusions: melancholia, a sense of persecution. He's even hinted at suicide again. Dr Kreuzer has told us so. And now this fantastic, monstrous idea of his. He should have compulsory treatment.

KREUZER: He was having it voluntarily.

BASTON: I don't believe in these Central European methods with drugs . . . I'm not saying anything against you, Dr Kreuzer, but you failed. He abandons his treatment, off he goes to his uncle. We don't know what happened between them, but we do know he came down here with this *idée fixe* that he had been 'raised from the dead' at fourteen by the prayers of William Callifer.

MRS CALLIFER: There was someone else who believed that.

BASTON: Oh yes, your gardener. A man who could barely write his name.

MRS CALLIFER: I didn't mean him.

BASTON: Even his uncle, when he recovered his senses . . .

MRS CALLIFER: I meant my husband, Fred.

BASTON: Mary, that's nonsense. You know it's nonsense.

MRS CALLIFER: Oh no, it isn't. Why do you think I was afraid to let James see him when he was dying? Henry was a fraud.

BASTON: You appal me. You don't know what you are saying. I always thought you loved him.

MRS CALLIFER: One can love a fraud. Perhaps it's easier than loving rectitude. All his life he'd written on the necessity of proof. Proof. And then a proof was pushed under his nose, at the bottom of his own garden, in the potting shed.

BASTON: But you didn't believe . . .

MRS CALLIFER: No, I didn't. It was a long time before I realized just how much he did. Fred, I saw his face. We always knew each other's thoughts. I could hear him saying to himself, 'Must I recall all those books and start again?' But I was trained to my job. I began to protect him. My husband, not my son.

BASTON: He never said anything which could remotely . . .

MRS CALLIFER: He never said anything to anyone. But, Fred, he never published another book.

BASTON: *He Was A Man*.

MRS CALLIFER: That was in proof already.

[*Pause.*]

KREUZER: Dr Baston, why did you call me in? Surely there was another doctor you could have fetched – the doctor who was here when it happened.

BASTON: I was that doctor.

KREUZER: I see.

BASTON: I assure you there was nothing abnormal . . .

KREUZER: You used massage?

BASTON: There was no question of massage. It was too late.

KREUZER: Too late?

BASTON: I mean he was conscious when I arrived.

KREUZER: Oh, I see.

BASTON: The layman can't recognize death. He thinks because a glass doesn't fog or a leaf on the lips move . . .

KREUZER: They tried that?

BASTON: If such a test for death were infallible, and it never could be, even then I wouldn't accept a miracle. I would simply say we had to re-define our terms – the concepts life and death.

MRS CALLIFER: Henry told himself that too. The trouble was he didn't believe the argument.

KREUZER: Did you write up the case – in the medical journals?

BASTON: How could I? I only had Potter's word. An ignorant gardener. And a priest's. I wouldn't take a priest's word on that subject.

KREUZER: Fair enough.

MRS CALLIFER: Would you have taken Henry's?

JOHN: Mother, we are off the point. What we've got to decide is quite simple. Should James go into – a home? After all this business, I consider it's our duty . . .

MRS CALLIFER: Duty. For his own good. All the old words we used to expose. What does Sara say?

[A pause.]

SARA [dropping her head]: You're his mother. I'm – nothing.

BASTON: I want you to sign the certificate with me, Dr Kreuzer.

KREUZER: I'm not satisfied, Dr Baston.

BASTON: How many times do your patients have to attempt suicide before you are ready to certify them?

KREUZER: An attempted suicide is not necessarily serious. Only the suicides that succeed. [He looks down at his hands.]

BASTON: Not serious. You astonish me, Dr Kreuzer.

KREUZER: People play-act – to others, to themselves. The majority of attempted suicides never meant to succeed.

BASTON: But sometimes, Dr Kreuzer, people may succeed through inexperience.

KREUZER: You can hardly gain experience in killing yourself, Dr Baston.

BASTON: You know very well what I mean. Things may go wrong – a man may stumble on the right number of pills.

KREUZER: Very seldom. We all have great unconscious wisdom.

BASTON: He succeeded the first time.

KREUZER: He what, Dr Baston?

BASTON [*embarrassed*]: I mean he would have succeeded if the gardener had not found him. [*Running hastily on.*] You are taking a great responsibility, Dr Kreuzer, if you don't sign with me. He's your patient. Coroners are apt to take a harsh view of psychiatrists whose patients kill themselves. Has it never happened to you?

KREUZER: Yes. Once.

JOHN: Dr Kreuzer, aren't we really supporting your view? After all, we don't live in an age of Victorian lunatic asylums, cruel warders, strait jackets –

KREUZER: Are you sure?

JOHN: If he is certified, he'll be forced to complete his treatment. With you, Dr Kreuzer.

KREUZER [*to* BASTON]: No patient can be forced. We can only persuade. Just why do you want him put away? Perhaps you want to forget him as his father did?

BASTON: How dare you?

KREUZER: Anger is always an interesting symptom.

BASTON: I was appealing to you for the sake of those who love him – his mother . . .

MRS CALLIFER: Leave me out, Fred. If I'm asked I shall say he's as sane as the rest of us. If that counts at all.

[*The door opens and* JAMES *enters. A kind of guilty silence falls over the group.*]

SARA: I thought you were asleep.

JAMES: The sound of the key turning woke me. I'm a very light sleeper.

SARA [*brazening it out*]: How did you get out?

JAMES: You forget Anne's room is next mine. Every detective knows the Morse Code. Dot dot dot, dash dash dash, dot dot dot. That's an S.O.S.

[*A pause.*]

[*He looks round them*]: There was some confusion at first. She had mislaid her code and thought I was signalling 'Proceed straight to nearest port'.

[*Another pause.*]

Well, what have you decided?

[*There is something carefree in his attitude, like someone who has survived a serious illness. He has not been offended by the locking of the door.*]

I don't suppose you want my opinion, but you know, I've never felt saner in my life.

JOHN: Threatening to kill yourself – that wasn't very sane.

JAMES: Oh, that. That belongs to the past. It won't happen again.

JOHN: Don't you think a period of rest – with really first-class treatment –

JAMES: I don't need it any longer. The gap's filled. I know what happened.

JOHN: What do you know?

JAMES: That I killed myself in the potting shed.

BASTON [*impatiently*]: And you say you are sane.

JAMES: Do you think everyone who believes in a God is mad?

JOHN: Why should He do a miracle for you?

JAMES: If I knew I wouldn't believe in Him. I couldn't believe in a God I could understand.

BASTON: The asylums are full of people who think God chose them specially.

JOHN: Did Uncle William talk you into this?

JAMES: He thought like all of you it was a mistake. It was the only belief he had left. He had become a real Callifer – for my sake. Only the Callifers have usually not taken to the bottle.

JOHN: Then why can't you take his word? He was there, with you. [*With a sneer.*] Praying away.

JAMES: I saw the result. I thought like you that it must be all a fairy tale, but then I saw his room. Have you ever seen a room from which faith has gone? A room without faith – oh that can be pretty and full of flowers, you can fill it with Regency furniture and the best modern pictures. But a room from which faith has gone is quite different. Like a marriage from which love has gone, and all that's left are habits and pet names and sentimental objects, picked up on beaches and in foreign towns that don't mean anything any more. And patience, patience everywhere like a fog.

SARA: Like our marriage?

JAMES: No. We were like the room without faith. We hadn't lost anything valuable.

SARA: You are very cruel, James.

JAMES: I don't mean to be. I had no idea what love was in those days.

SARA: Why did you come back here?

JAMES: To see you, Sara, but last night they told me you had gone.

SARA [*to* MRS CALLIFER]: Did you . . . ?

MRS CALLIFER: It was Dr Baston. He wanted his talk first.

JAMES: Don't you think it's my turn now, Dr Baston? I want to be alone with Sara.

BASTON: I won't take the responsibility.

MRS CALLIFER: Then I will.

BASTON: He's in no state . . .

MRS CALLIFER [*as she leaves*]: You've been very loyal to Henry, Fred. It's James's turn now.

JAMES: John?

JOHN: I'm trying to do the best for everyone – Mother as well as you.

KREUZER [*taking* JOHN's *arm*]: Let's have a word together.

[*He leads him out.* BASTON *holds his ground.*]

JAMES [*to* SARA]: This time I haven't brought a dog to interrupt Dr Baston's speech.

[BASTON *goes angrily out.*]

SARA [*nervously, playing for time*]: Did Spot ever come back?

JAMES: No. Someone brought an impostor to me. The spot was on the wrong side.

[*He advances towards* SARA, *but she retreats from him.*]

You don't have to be afraid of me. I'm the one who's afraid. [*Looking at his hand.*] My hand's trembling. Strange. It didn't tremble the first time.

SARA: What first time?

JAMES: The first time I proposed to you. Things weren't important to me then. I can't even remember the name of the restaurant. Or the words I used. But this time coming down I counted every stair – there are nineteen of them, and there's a picture askew above the twelfth. I stopped to set it right. That gave me time to think.

SARA: Think what?

JAMES: Think of what I'd say – I love you, Sara.

SARA: Just because you believe Potter's story?

JAMES: Yes.

SARA: That God answered that prayer?

JAMES: Yes.

SARA: But what do you want?

JAMES: I want to marry you.

SARA: It didn't work the first time.

JAMES: I was the wrong man to make a death-bed marriage. Nothing mattered because everything would be over soon. We were all going to be dead as last year's dog. Now when I look at you, I see someone who will never die for ever.

SARA: A curious snobbery.

JAMES: The strong taste. Sara, you never believed I wanted you, and you were right. Your kiss was always a question and I hadn't got an answer. I couldn't love you any more than you can love a tree, a glass of wine, a cat.

SARA: People love cats.

JAMES: Do they? Then they don't know the meaning of the word.
   [*Again she backs away.*]

SARA [*hastily*]: No, please don't move. Look at me.
   [*Slowly.*] Yes, I used to see Nothing there. I was a fool. I hated Nothing.

JAMES: Can we try again?

SARA: I remember the same words, but I spoke them. And you wouldn't listen.

JAMES: Poetic justice.

SARA: I don't want justice. But don't you understand, James, this belief of yours is worse than nothing. It's sent you too far away. I don't belong to your world of God and prayer.

JAMES: Oh, prayer. I don't want to pray. Something happened to me, that's all, like a street accident. I don't want God. I don't love God. But He's there – it's no good pretending. He's in my lungs like air.

SARA: He's not mine. I'm sorry, James. You believe in God and life eternal. But I don't want to be that important. I wasn't kissing God when I was kissing you. I was only saying, 'I have remembered to order the steaks. And I know you don't like water-cress. And I'll be here tonight, and next night, and the night after' . . . I don't want eternity. I hate big things – Everest and the Empire State Building.

JAMES: Everest exists.

SARA: Then I wish you'd brought something back to prove it. Like the lover in the story – one out-of-season flower.

[SARA *goes to the door.*]

JAMES: Sara, don't go.

SARA: We've said all there is to say.

JAMES: Not all.

SARA: Let me go.

[SARA *leaves and* MRS CALLIFER *comes in through the garden door.*]

MRS CALLIFER: I went into the garden for a breath of air. It will be light soon.

JAMES: I'm sorry, Mother. A miracle in the family is worse than a Borstal case.

MRS CALLIFER: You've no proof, have you, James?

JAMES: Not the kind Baston needs. But don't tell a man who has just seen a ghost that he has no proof. I've seen that room. I've seen my uncle. I don't need any other proof of God than the lack of Him there. I've seen the mark of His footsteps going away.

MRS CALLIFER: It's a cruel God you believe in.

JAMES: Perhaps He had no choice.

MRS CALLIFER: A God who can't choose?

JAMES: God is conditioned, isn't He? If He's all-powerful, He can't weaken. If He knows everything, He can't forget. If He's love, He can't hate. Perhaps if someone asks with enough love, He has to give.

MRS CALLIFER: People are asking all the time.

JAMES: Are they? It needs a lot of belief. And a lot of love.

MRS CALLIFER: But your uncle doesn't believe.

JAMES: Oh yes, he does. I left him praying.

MRS CALLIFER: Is he happy?

JAMES: He wanted more than I could give him. Don't you remember anything, he said, can't you tell me that it's all true – the Trinity, the Resurrection, the Virgin birth. I suppose if he'd been a Buddhist he would have wanted news of Buddha. But I'd brought nothing back. Not one flower.

[*Pause.*]

MRS CALLIFER: What are you going to do, James?

JAMES: Marry Sara, I hope. I'm going to start a long courtship. Flowers, chocolates.

MRS CALLIFER: She's not very good with flowers. It will take time.

JAMES: Time's not important. Time's for a time.

MRS CALLIFER: A long time in my case. And time is all I know.

JAMES: I move my hand. It moves in space and time. When there's no time there'll be no movement any more. When we think, we think one thing after another. Time, again. When there's no time we shan't think any more.

MRS CALLIFER: A frightening world.

JAMES: I've been there and I'm not frightened.

MRS CALLIFER: All the same don't talk to Sara about eternity. Give her time, give us all time. You mustn't mind our anger – you've spoilt our certainties . . .

JAMES: I thought you had none.

MRS CALLIFER: Oh, the Callifers knew everything. It was all right to doubt the existence of God as your grandfather did in the time of Darwin. Doubt – that was human liberty. But my generation, we didn't doubt, we knew. I don't believe in this miracle – but I'm not sure any longer. We are none of us sure. When you aren't sure you are alive.

[SARA *enters. She hesitates.* JAMES *doesn't hear her.*]

SARA: Have you seen Anne?

MRS CALLIFER: What?

SARA: She's not in her room.

JAMES: Try the larder.

SARA: It was the first place I looked.

JAMES: Perhaps she's on the prowl again.

SARA: I'd better try the garden.

MRS CALLIFER: Take my coat.

[SARA *picks the coat from the table.*]

JAMES: You sounded so final just now.

SARA: I just wanted to get away. I wanted to cry for five minutes, that's all.

JAMES: Yes, you have been crying.

[JAMES *puts the coat over her shoulder.*]

SARA: Your hand's still trembling.

JAMES: You know the reason.

[*They go out into the garden.*

MRS CALLIFER *is for a moment alone. Then someone knocks on the door.*]

MRS CALLIFER: Come in.

[KREUZER *enters.*]

KREUZER: Well, Dr Baston has unwillingly accepted my view.

MRS CALLIFER: That James is sane?

KREUZER: That an illusion can help to cure.

MRS CALLIFER: Oh, Dr Kreuzer. Dr Kreuzer. How you have it both ways.

KREUZER: I saw you from the window just now coming back from the garden.

MRS CALLIFER: Yes. I went to the potting shed. I've never been there since it happened.

KREUZER: What did you do there?

MRS CALLIFER: I went in. The door wasn't locked. I wasn't frightened. There was nothing ghostly there. The ground wasn't holy. There were no voices and whispers and messages. Only the boxes of seeds and the gardening tools and some broken flower pots and an old bulb catalogue. It wasn't important any more, and I thought perhaps even miracles are ordinary. What do you think, doctor?

KREUZER: I don't much care one way or the other.

MRS CALLIFER: Was that why you weren't angry like the others? What a family for you to find yourself in, Dr Kreuzer. Poor Fred. He's very cross. He fears I've been converted to miracles.

KREUZER: Have you?

MRS CALLIFER: No. [*She begins to straighten the room.*] But haven't you any set ideas you want destroyed, Dr Kreuzer?

KREUZER: I hope not. I would rather think one thing one day and another the next. If we don't kill any possibility, perhaps we'll die without a ghost haunting us.

MRS CALLIFER: I thought you wanted the truth. You are a scientist.

KREUZER: I only want a relative truth to make life tolerable.

MRS CALLIFER: That's not very brave, is it?

KREUZER: Courage can be a very difficult neurosis.

[MRS CALLIFER *draws back the curtain. It is broad daylight now. In the window-seat* ANNE *lies asleep with the window open behind her.*]

MRS CALLIFER: The detective asleep at her post.

KREUZER: One of the brave ones who believe they can find the truth.

ANNE [*stretching and yawning*]: Oh, I've had such a funny dream. I was going down the path to the potting shed and there was a lion there fast asleep.

KREUZER: What did you do?

ANNE: I woke it up.

MRS CALLIFER: Did it eat you?

ANNE: No, it licked my hand.

CURTAIN

THE COMPLAISANT LOVER

★

A Comedy

CHARACTERS

(in order of appearance)

VICTOR RHODES   MARY RHODES
WILLIAM HOWARD   ROBIN RHODES
CLIVE ROOT   A HOTEL VALET
ANN HOWARD   DR VAN DROOG
MARGARET HOWARD

CAST

The *Complaisant Lover*, produced by Sir John Gielgud, with scenery by Carl Toms, was first presented at the Globe Theatre, London, on 18 June 1959, with the following cast:

VICTOR RHODES	*Ralph Richardson*
WILLIAM HOWARD	*Lockwood West*
CLIVE ROOT	*Paul Scofield*
ANN HOWARD	*Polly Adams*
MARGARET HOWARD	*Madge Compton*
MARY RHODES	*Phyllis Calvert*
ROBIN RHODES	*Hugh James*
A HOTEL VALET	*Gerald Flood*
DR VAN DROOG	*Oliver Burt*

SCENES

Act One

Scene One	A cutlet with the Rhodes.
Scene Two	Amsterdam: the end of a holiday.

Act Two

Scene One	Home again with Rhodes. Nine days later.
Scene Two	The same, after an interval of a few hours.

Act One

SCENE ONE

The living-room of a house in North London. It is designed to serve as both dining-room and drawing-room, the walls slanting in the centre towards the footlights and back again, so as to form an inner room rather than an alcove, where the men in the party now in progress are sitting over the wine. There is a sideboard and upstage from the sideboard a door. The men are in dinner jackets.

At the back of the living-room tall windows open on to a small garden, but the curtains are drawn. A door opposite the dining-room leads to the hall and stairs.

The host, VICTOR RHODES, *is a man in his middle forties. He has a plump round face, now a little flushed with wine, an air of happiness and good-nature. Throughout the scene we are a little haunted by the thought that we have encountered him somewhere before; his anecdotes, of which he has so many, have surely at one time fallen into our own ears. He is on his feet half-way between sideboard and table.*

On the right of his empty chair sits WILLIAM HOWARD, *a local bank manager, a man in his late fifties. The third man, the youngest there, is in his late thirties, with sullen good looks and an air of being intellectually a little more interesting than his companions. He runs, as we soon learn, a local antiquarian bookshop: his name is* CLIVE ROOT, *but the profession of* VICTOR RHODES — *and it is perhaps a professional air which we are trying to identify — remains unknown until later in the scene.*

The women are upstairs, but they will soon drift down to the drawing-room. There is MRS HOWARD, *a woman in her early fifties, quiet and kindly; her daughter* ANN, *a girl of nineteen, pretty and immature, and* MARY RHODES, *a woman in the middle thirties, who moves quickly, nervously, with unconscious beauty.*

When the curtain rises only the men are there. From the attitude of the men VICTOR *is obviously concluding a long address.*

VICTOR: Off on the wrong foot, arse over tip, and there I was looking up at the stars – I mean Oxford Circus. And what did my wife say – 'That word in nine letters was escalator.' Ha ha ha. If there's one thing I thank God for, Mr Root, it's a sense of humour. I've attained a certain position in life. There are not many men in my profession I would acknowledge as my masters, but I would sacrifice all that – this house and garden, that chair you are sitting on, Mr Root – it cost me no mean figure at Christie's, I like beautiful things around me – what was I saying, William?

HOWARD: You were telling Mr Root and me about your sense of humour.

VICTOR: That's right. A sense of humour is more important than a balance at the bank – whatever William may say.

HOWARD: I don't say anything, Victor, you never let me.

VICTOR: Ah-ha, William has a sense of humour too, you see. Perhaps it's not so important in a bank manager as in a man of my profession, but it's not our professions that I have in mind. Mr Root, you are looking tonight at a very rare phenomenon – two men who are happily married. And why are we happily married?

HOWARD: Because we happen to like our wives.

VICTOR: That's not enough. It's because we've got a sense of humour. A sense of humour means a happy marriage.

CLIVE: Is it as simple as that, Mr Rhodes?

VICTOR: I can assure you there are very few situations in life that a joke won't ease.

HOWARD: You were going to let us have some port, Victor.

VICTOR: Port? [*He looks at the decanter.*] Oh yes. [*He sits down.*] You, William?

HOWARD: Thanks. You, Mr Root?

CLIVE: Thanks.

VICTOR: Do you know how this business of passing the port clockwise originated?

HOWARD: Yes, Victor. I learnt it from you. Last week.

VICTOR [*unabashed*]: Ha, ha, that's good. I'll remember that to tell my victims.

HOWARD: How are the second-hand books, Root?

VICTOR: You ought to call them antiquarian, William. It's more expensive. Do you know the first thing Dr Fuchs found in the Antarctic?

HOWARD [*wearily*]: No, Victor.

VICTOR: A second-hand Penguin.

[*He looks from one to the other, but nobody laughs.*]

CLIVE: The second-hand books would gather a lot more dust, Mr Howard, if it wasn't for your daughter.

HOWARD: I never thought of Ann as a great reader.

[ANN *has come down first of the women. She stands a moment as though listening and then picks up a magazine.*]

CLIVE: Her interests are specialized. The early Western. We are talking of you, Ann.

ANN: Only Zane Greys.

VICTOR: Not highbrow, anyway. She's too pretty, William, to be highbrow.

CLIVE [*who obviously has some hidden antipathy to* RHODES]: Brows are a matter of opinion, Mr Rhodes. The early Zane Greys cost quite a lot already and they are a good investment.

VICTOR: Investment? That's an idea. A man says to me – they often do if I give them the chance, 'I'm buying tobacco now for a rise. What do you say?' And now of course I'll tell him 'Put your money into Zane Greys'.

CLIVE: You'd be giving perfectly good advice. Unless someone discovers that books are a cause of cancer.

HOWARD: At the bank I tell my customers, 'hold on to gold'.

VICTOR: Send the port round again, Root.

[MRS HOWARD *has come down closely followed by* MARY RHODES.]

MARY: She *will* bring in the coffee before I ring. I suppose it's nearly cold.

MRS HOWARD [*feeling the pot*]: Oh no.

MARY [*with her eyes on the other part of the room*]: I wish you'd pour out.

MRS HOWARD: Of course I will. Sugar?

MARY: Please.

ANN: Oh, Mother – not in mine.

MRS HOWARD: I forgot she's on a diet. Look up what time the

Larkins are on, dear. Your father won't want to miss them. [*Handing* MARY *her cup.*] Thank God I'm past dieting. I've got my man.

MARY: We both have, haven't we? [*She takes her cup and goes to watch the men.*]

[*Her husband has at last found his chance.* CLIVE *looks up and sees her. They watch each other while* VICTOR *talks.*]

VICTOR: Now take that chap Farquhar I told you about last week.

MARY [*to* MRS HOWARD]: We have them for better, for worse.

HOWARD: Why should we, Victor?

VICTOR [*quite unthrown*]: Take him anyway. Most interesting man. He's put his little all into potatoes. He was telling me yesterday that they're growing a new kind which will be pale mauve in colour.

HOWARD: Why?

VICTOR: The ladies will like it. Pretty on the plate. It's the same with oranges. A man in the fruit trade told me you can't sell a green orange. Tastes just the same, but you can't sell them. In South Africa they pass them through gas chambers to make them orange.

MRS HOWARD: Really!

HOWARD [*trying to switch him*]: Could I have a last glass of port, Victor?

VICTOR: Of course, William. Not me though. You, Mr Root? You have strong young teeth.

CLIVE: What have teeth got to do with it?

VICTOR: Too much wine causes acidity. Acidity causes tartar. Tartar . . .

[MARY *turns away and goes back to* MRS HOWARD.]

CLIVE: I'll have another glass. There are worse things than tartar.

VICTOR: Such as . . . ?

CLIVE: The worms that eat my stock. They're like some people, Mr Rhodes. You can only tell where they have been by the holes they leave behind.

VICTOR: I'm rather a specialist in holes myself.

CLIVE: I thought perhaps you were.

VICTOR: Here's a riddle for you. What kind of thing is it we prefer with holes in it?

HOWARD: Gruyère.

VICTOR: You're the first person to guess.

HOWARD: You told it to me, Victor, a month ago.

VICTOR: It comes of knowing so many people. One forgets to whom one has told what. Believe me, I've told a man his own life history before now.

HOWARD: We believe you.

VICTOR: For goodness sake, Root. Your cigar. It's burning the cloth.

[CLIVE *snatches up a cigar butt and finds it to be only a trick one, the glowing end formed of red paper.*]

CLIVE: I'm so sorry. Mrs Rhodes . . .

HOWARD: It's only a fake. Never mind, Root.

VICTOR: You should have seen his face.

MARY: You have to pass an initiation–ceremony in this house.

CLIVE: I used to be very fond of these tricks – when I was a child.

VICTOR: You aren't offended, old chap, are you?

CLIVE: No. Interested, that's all. Jokes like this must be a compensation for something. When we are children we're powerless, and these jokes make us feel superior to our dictators. But now we're grown up, there are no dictators – except employers, I suppose.

HOWARD: I'm the only one here who has an employer – if you can call Head Office that.

VICTOR: I just think jokes like that are funny. I don't see why you have to analyse everything.

CLIVE: You should read Freud on the nature of a joke.

VICTOR: Oh, I suppose he sees sex in it. Sex everywhere. [*He holds up the cigar butt vertically.*] Can you see any sex in that, William?

HOWARD: Well, frankly, Victor, yes, I can.

[VICTOR *looks at the cigar butt and drops it hastily.*]

VICTOR: It's time we joined the ladies. Anybody want to wash? The plants can do with a shower. No?

[*They move into the other section of the room.*

MARY *watches* CLIVE *come in, and so does* ANN. CLIVE's *eyes are on* MARY.]

MRS HOWARD: If you'd stayed tippling much longer you'd have been late for the Larkins.

HOWARD: My wife always pretends it's I who must see them.

MARY [*to* CLIVE]: Was the port all right? I went to the Army and Navy for it myself.

CLIVE: It was very good, and the cigar butt was very good too. Did that come from the Army and Navy?

MARY: Oh, he has a lot of little tricks like that. He's very fond of bleeding fingers and flies on lumps of sugar.

[MRS HOWARD *is pouring coffee again and* VICTOR *is carrying round cups.*]

VICTOR: Sugar, Mr Root?

CLIVE: No thanks.

[MARY *raises her eyebrows and* CLIVE *shakes his head.* VICTOR *has passed on.*]

He would hardly try to catch me twice in one evening. It would be a bit conspicuous.

VICTOR: Why are we all standing around, William? Here, Root, you'll find this chair comfortable.

[*As* CLIVE *goes towards the chair,* MARY *gets there first and, lifting the cushion, removes a small flat cushion.*]

Mary, what a spoil sport you are.

MARY [*to* CLIVE]: This plays Auld Lang Syne. If Victor had disliked you, he has another that cries like a baby and says Mama.

VICTOR: My wife doesn't approve of my jokes, Root, but I have the support of my children.

CLIVE: How old are your children?

VICTOR: Sally's fifteen – she's away at school, and Robin's twelve. At the moment he's passionately in love with Ann here. He'll be down in a minute. It's only the tele that could have kept him away so long.

HOWARD: Has he proposed yet, Ann?

ANN: No. Unless you count giving me a stuffed mouse. He's stuffed it himself – very badly.

HOWARD: He's scientific, is he, like his father?

VICTOR: Oh, Robin and I understand each other. We speak the same language.

MARY: Give him a smile, Ann, when he comes in. The mouse meant a lot. I can never understand why people laugh at children's love. Love's painful at any age.

VICTOR: Oh come, Mary. I don't find it painful.

[MARY *turns abruptly away and becomes aware of the way in which* ANN *is watching* CLIVE. *She looks quickly back at* CLIVE, *but* CLIVE *is unaware of* ANN.]

MRS HOWARD: Don't forget the Larkins.

VICTOR: There's time for more coffee first. You can trust me. I've never missed the Larkins yet. Do you know Lord Binlow? He likes them too.

HOWARD: The old Liberal? Is he a friend of yours?

VICTOR: Oh, he comes in regularly every three months. An affable old thing. I have to gag him or we'd never get our business done. He told me the Prime Minister can't understand the jokes. They're too quick for him — like the Russians.

[ROBIN RHODES *comes in in a dressing-gown.*]

ROBIN: Father, only three minutes for the show.

VICTOR: Manners, Robin, manners. Don't you see who's here?

[ROBIN *looks across at* ANN.]

ROBIN: Oh yes, I do.

[ANN *works up a smile for him which immediately raises his spirits.*]

Good evening, Mrs Howard, Mr Howard. Good evening, Mr . . .

MARY: This is Mr Root, Robin. He has the bookshop near the heath.

VICTOR: The root of all evil. [*He looks hopefully round, but no one laughs except* ROBIN.]

ROBIN: That's frightfully good. [*He realizes no one else has laughed.*] Isn't it?

HOWARD: Your father has a great sense of humour.

ANN: Have you been stuffing any more mice, Robin?

ROBIN: Oh no, I only did the one. I shan't do any more. It's not very well stuffed, I'm afraid.

ANN: It was sweet of you to give me your only one.

ROBIN: I'm afraid it's a bit ragged. It'll fall to pieces pretty soon, but then just throw it away.

ANN: I'll keep it in memory.

ROBIN: You could keep an ear perhaps. That would be quite clean and it wouldn't take up any room. Come on, it's time for the Larkins.

CLIVE [*catching* MARY'*s eye*]: I'm like the Prime Minister. I think I'll stay behind with the coffee.

[MARY *is about to speak when* ANN *speaks first.*]

ANN: I'll keep you company, Clive. I don't want to see it either.

[MARY *hesitates, then leads the way out.*]

VICTOR [*to* HOWARD *as he goes*]: We stow the tele away in the old nursery. Mary can't bear that eye watching her. Guilty conscience, you know.

MRS HOWARD [*as she goes*]: I wish we had a spare room for ours, but there's only the cellar.

HOWARD: Can't use that. Door opening and shutting all the time. Upset the wine.

[*They have all gone.*]

ANN: Would you like some more coffee, Clive?

CLIVE [*looking at the books on the shelf*]: No thanks. It'll keep me awake.

ANN: Are you a bad sleeper?

CLIVE: Sometimes.

ANN: I can let you have some awfully good pills.

CLIVE: Surely you don't take pills. At your age.

ANN: How I hate that phrase.

CLIVE: What phrase?

ANN: 'At your age.' They say 'Do you still read Westerns at your age?' As though nineteen was middle aged, and then when I have a benzedrine at breakfast . . .

CLIVE: Benzedrine!

ANN: There you are. 'Benzedrine at your age,' you were going to say, and this time nineteen means something in the nursery.

CLIVE: Why do you take benzedrine?

ANN: I'm dieting. To get rid of this and this. They call it puppy-fat. Sometimes I want to scream at them – nineteen is a woman. I could have had a child of six by now.

CLIVE: Six?

ANN: Yes, six. I'm one of the early ones. I'm not a puppy, Clive.

CLIVE [*at the shelves*]: Why do you read Zane Grey?

ANN: Because England's so damnably small. I can't walk to your shop without seeing four people I know. We all sit around and eye each other like suspects in a detective-story. Is Zane Grey less worth reading than Agatha Christie?

CLIVE: No.

ANN: Sometimes I think I'd marry anyone who wanted to get away. Not necessarily marry either. I'm such a bitch, Clive, I have to make an effort even to smile at that little brat with his dried mouse.

CLIVE: Robin's not a bad child, is he?

ANN: They think it funny and rather charming that he's in love with me – and rather a compliment to me. It's all very whimsical because we are both children and we don't know what love really is.

CLIVE: Do you?

ANN: Yes.

CLIVE: Poor you.

ANN: You sound as if you don't much like it either.

CLIVE: No, I don't.

ANN: Clive, let's go away together.

CLIVE: Go away?

ANN: For a time. It needn't be always if you don't like me. It could be a trial-week.

CLIVE: Ann dear, you aren't in love with me.

ANN: How do you know?

[CLIVE *makes a gesture.*]

You mean *you* are not in love with me. I know that. It doesn't matter so much, does it? There's always lust.

CLIVE: That's not a word Zane Grey uses.

ANN: I don't get everything out of books, Clive. I've got eyes and a body under this puppy-fat.

CLIVE: You aren't fat, Ann. You're very pretty.

ANN: As pretty as the girls in Curzon Street?

CLIVE: I don't go to bed with the girls in Curzon Street.

ANN: Never?

CLIVE: I've done it. Two or three times I suppose. When I've been fed up and alone.

ANN: You aren't alone now?

CLIVE: Yes. I'm very alone.

ANN: Well, then, why go to Curzon Street when there's me?

CLIVE: Lust isn't very strong, Ann, unless there's love too. Curzon Street takes only half an hour. And there are twenty-four hours in a day.

ANN: We have things in common. Books.

CLIVE: *Riders of the Purple Sage* is a subject we might exhaust.

ANN: How cold and beastly you are.

CLIVE: Only sensible.

ANN: You'll be able to boast now, won't you, that you've had an immoral proposal from a girl of nineteen.

CLIVE: I'm not the boasting kind. I've been trained in a different school, Ann. You see, the first woman I loved was happily married.

ANN: Have you loved a lot of people?

CLIVE: Only four. It's not a high score at thirty-eight.

ANN: What happened to them, Clive?

CLIVE: In the end the husbands won.

ANN: Were they all married?

CLIVE: Yes.

ANN: Why do you choose married women?

CLIVE: I don't know. Perhaps I fall in love with experience.

ANN: One has to begin.

CLIVE: Perhaps I don't care for innocence. Perhaps I'm trying to repeat that first time. Perhaps it's envy of other men, and I want to prove myself better than they are. I don't know, Ann. But it's the school I've been brought up in. There are no girls of nineteen in my school. We don't throw the school cap over the windmill, and there are no lessons in 'all for love and the world well lost'.

ANN: You don't sound so happy in your school.

CLIVE: I hate the lessons, but I'm very good at them.

ANN: What lessons, Clive?

CLIVE: Oh, how to make a husband like you. How to stay in the same house as the two of them and not to mind that, when night comes, she'll pay you a short visit if the coast is clear and he'll sleep away the whole night beside her. Then, of course, there are all kinds of elementary lessons. On passports, hotel-registers, and on times when it's necessary to take adjoining rooms. And how to postpone discovery in spite of those kind mutual friends whom you always meet at unlikely little hotels in the Midlands.

ANN: Does the husband always discover?

CLIVE: They always have. And then the worst lessons begin.

ANN: You mean – about divorce?

CLIVE: No. I've heard about divorce. I've never encountered it. In my case the husbands have always been complaisant. You see, they love their wives too much to leave them, so they say. I seem to have always had an eye for very lovable women.

ANN: I suppose I'm terribly young, Clive, but I don't understand.

CLIVE: And people would call me a cad for telling you.

ANN: I have to learn.

CLIVE: Don't marry an Englishman, Ann. Englishmen prefer their friends and their clubs to their wives, but they have great staying power and a great sense of duty. The lover relieves them of their duty. And then you see without that – trouble, a beautiful brother–and–sister relationship can develop. It's very touching. And so damned boring for the lover.

ANN: Are you in love now?

CLIVE: Yes.

ANN: And that's how it is?

CLIVE: I tell myself it can't happen that way again. I'll see that it won't happen that way.

ANN: You want to marry her?

CLIVE: Yes.

ANN: I wish you wouldn't tell her – whoever she is – about me.

CLIVE: I'll try not to. But, Ann, when you're in love, you don't have secrets.

ANN: I've proved that, haven't I? I'd better go and look at the tele after all. Are you coming, Clive?

CLIVE: No. His Master's Voice is bad enough. I can't bear His Master's Eye.

[MARY enters.]

MARY: You two still talking away?

ANN: About Zane Grey. You know it's my only subject, Mary.

[*She leaves.*]

MARY: She's upset. Why did she stay behind, Clive?

CLIVE: Oh, you know what the young are like. A crisis.

MARY: Still worried about her puppy-fat?

CLIVE: Yes.

MARY: I wish I was her age.

CLIVE: I don't.

MARY: What do you think of Victor?

CLIVE: He's been very kind to me.

MARY: Why shouldn't he be? He has no suspicion.

CLIVE: Are you sure? I thought that cigar . . .

MARY: I know Victor.

CLIVE: Yes. Of course. I forgot that.

MARY: It was sweet of you to come.

CLIVE: I didn't want to.

MARY: It was necessary, Clive. If we are to see more of each other. Now he knows you, he won't worry.

CLIVE: That's kind of him.

MARY: He *is* kind, Clive. Why don't you like him?

CLIVE: Perhaps he'll grow on me in time. With his anecdotes. He has a great many.

MARY: They come his way.

CLIVE: He reminded me of my dentist. I'm sorry. Forgive me, Mary.

MARY: Why should I? He *is* a dentist.

CLIVE: Oh. You never told me that.

MARY: We haven't spoken of him much, have we? He's not been your favourite subject these few weeks. And it's not exactly a glamorous profession.

CLIVE: Who cares?

MARY: I didn't want you to laugh at him, that's all.

CLIVE: Are you so fond of him?

MARY: Yes. [*Pause.*]

CLIVE: When are we going to get some time together, Mary?

MARY: I only missed one day with you this week.

CLIVE: You know what I mean by time.

MARY: Dear, I promise. Sometime, somehow. But it's difficult. It wouldn't be safe in England.

CLIVE: I don't want to be safe.

MARY: But . . .

CLIVE: All right. We can go abroad.

MARY: I've spent my hundred pounds with the children.

CLIVE: So have I. But there are ways. I can fix it. Couldn't we . . . next week . . .

MARY: Sally comes back next week for half-term. I have to be here. Then there's a Dental Association dinner, and Victor would think it odd if I was away. I always go with him.

CLIVE: After that . . .

MARY: Robin's got to have three teeth out. Don't look angry. Even a dentist's child has tooth-trouble. And I have to take him.

CLIVE: Doesn't your husband pull them out?

MARY: Of course he doesn't.

CLIVE: Surely you could change that appointment?

MARY: You don't know how difficult appointments are. We'd have to wait a month for another.

CLIVE: And then, I suppose, it's almost time for Sally to come home again.

MARY: You shouldn't have chosen a woman with a family, Clive. My job is full time just as yours is. You can't pack up and go away whenever you like either.

CLIVE: All the same I'd do it if you asked me to.

MARY [sharply]: Perhaps children are more important than second-hand books. [Pause.] Clive, don't let's get angry with each other – not tonight. It's been so good seeing you here. In my home. It's as though our life together were really beginning.

CLIVE: Cosy evenings with the dentist!

MARY: Are you going to use that against me now? What's wrong with being a dentist? It's more useful than selling Zane Greys to teenagers.

CLIVE: The teenager asked me to go away with her.

MARY: Ann!

CLIVE: Any time I liked. For as long as I liked.

MARY: What did you say?

CLIVE: Naturally I refused the invitation.

MARY: Poor Ann.

CLIVE: I also promised, if I could, to keep it secret. What liars and cheats love makes of us.

MARY: You should have said yes. There wouldn't be any complications with Ann. She wouldn't have to write postcards home and buy presents for the children. She wouldn't remember suddenly in the middle of dinner that she'd forgotten to buy a pair of football boots. She's free. Do you think I don't envy her? I even envy her virginity.

CLIVE: That's not important.

MARY: Oh yes, it is. Men are jealous of a past if there's nothing else to be jealous of. You need your bloody sign.

CLIVE: I need a few weeks' peace of mind. If you're with me, I can sleep because you are not with him.

MARY: I've told you over and over again – I've promised you – we haven't slept together for five years. But I have no sign to prove it.

CLIVE: After a dental dinner and a drink or two things happen . . .

MARY: When that dies out, Clive, it doesn't come back. And sooner or later it always dies. Even for us it would die in time. It dies quicker in a marriage, that's all. It's killed by the children, by the chars who give notice, by the price of meat.

CLIVE: If only you had separate rooms.

MARY: The space between the beds is just as wide as a passage.

CLIVE: When he wakes up you're the first thing he sees. I envy that.

MARY: I'm up first. Clive, I'd move into the spare room, but he'd notice it. Sometimes bed-time is the only chance we have to talk. Dentists are very busy men.

CLIVE: I need a chance too.

MARY: What you and I talk about is so different. With Victor I talk about Sally's room which needs re-painting. Can we postpone it till the autumn? Her school-report says she has a talent for music. Ought she to have extra lessons in the holidays? And then there's the dinner which went wrong. Too much garlic in the salad and the potatoes were under-cooked. Clive, that's the sort of talk that kills desire. Only kindness grows in that soil.

CLIVE: A lot of kindness.

MARY: Yes.

[ROBIN's *voice calling*: 'Mother. Mother.']

The show must be over.

CLIVE: So we can't be together because of the dental dinner? Is Victor speaking on the problems of tartar? Do you dance with the other dentists?

MARY: Clive, what makes you rough tonight?

CLIVE: Perhaps a trick cigar.

MARY: Or refusing an invitation to an adventure?

[ROBIN's *voice nearer*: 'Mother. Mother.']

CLIVE: I want one week with you—I might be able to persuade you then.

MARY: Persuade me of what?

CLIVE: To marry me.

MARY: Yes. It's possible.

CLIVE: Or he might discover where we'd been.

MARY: Yes.

CLIVE: He'd divorce you, wouldn't he, if he knew?

MARY: How can I tell?

CLIVE: Or would you tell him how sorry you were and ask to be taken back to the twin bed?

MARY: I'd never say I was sorry. I love you, Clive.

[ROBIN *enters as they move towards each other.*

MARY *is quick to adapt her words, quicker than* CLIVE *could ever have been.*]

MARY: I really do love you for all the trouble you take to find Ann and me the cheapest books. We've ruined you between the two of us.

ROBIN: Mother, the tele's terrible tonight. Father says it's the X-ray next door.

MARY: That's your father's joke, dear. Mr Saunders wouldn't have a patient at this hour.

ROBIN: He says Mr Saunders works twenty-four hours a day because his patients are so rich. He won't take National Health.

MARY: Where are the others, Robin?

ROBIN: Oh, listening to something political.

MARY: Have you finished your homework, dear?

ROBIN: I can finish it in the morning.

MARY: Then be off to bed now. It's late.

ROBIN: You won't forget to say good night?

MARY: No.

ROBIN: Do you think . . . ?

MARY: It's too late to think. Off with you.

ROBIN: What does sesquioxide mean? It's in my French dictionary.

MARY: I don't know. What does the dictionary say it is in English?

ROBIN: It says in English it's sesquioxide.

[ROBIN *goes out again.*]

MARY: He and Victor have a lot in common. You see what I mean now, don't you? A moment ago I could have slept with you on the sofa. I don't mean sleep. I wanted to touch you. I wanted your mouth. Now . . . homework, Mr Saunders's X-rays, tucking a child up in bed. Don't let's have a family, Clive, whatever happens.

CLIVE: I'd have liked your child.

MARY: That's what you think now. But love and marriage don't go together. Not our kind of love. Please, Clive, be patient. You don't believe how much I long to say 'All right, nothing else matters, we'll go away tomorrow, the first plane anywhere. I won't think about Robin or Victor or Sally's music-lessons. I'll only think about me. Me.'

CLIVE: Not me?

MARY: We'd be too close to know which was which.

CLIVE: Mary, come back to me tonight.

MARY: I can't. How can I?

CLIVE: Say you are taking the dog for a walk.

MARY: There is no dog. Only a cat. And cats take their own walks.

[*The door opens and* ANN *comes in. She realizes for the first time with whom* CLIVE *is in love.*]

ANN: I'm sorry. I didn't mean . . .

MARY: We were only talking about dogs and cats and who likes which.

ANN: The tele was in bad form tonight.

MARY: So Robin told us.

ANN [*with relief*]: Oh, has he been here?

MARY: Yes. Surely he said good night to you?

[*Voices outside and the* HOWARDS *and* VICTOR *enter.*]

VICTOR: One for the road. I insist. While I call a taxi.

MRS HOWARD: We'll walk home. It's a fine night. Don't you agree, William?

HOWARD: Yes. Good for Ann's dieting, too.

VICTOR: All the more time for a Scotch.

MRS HOWARD: Not for me.

MARY: Nor me.

[VICTOR *fetches the whisky from the sideboard on the dining side of the room. He can be seen pouring out and arranging the glasses on a tray. He shifts the position of one glass. There is something a little too studied about the arranging.*]

CLIVE [*to* ANN]: I'll walk back with you if I may.

MARY [*quickly*]: There's no need for you to go yet. It's only half-past ten.

CLIVE: I have to be up very early. I've got to finish cataloguing.

MARY: Surely you can choose your own time for that.

CLIVE: You wouldn't understand how important a bookseller's catalogue is.

ANN: It must be like writing a novel.

[VICTOR *returns with a tray of whisky.*]

CLIVE: Yes, I think it is. One has to know what to put in and what to leave out.

ANN: I'd love to see how you do it.

CLIVE [*his eye on* MARY *but his speech to* ANN]: Come in tomorrow morning and I'll show you. You could help me a lot if it would amuse you.

ANN: I'd love to help you.

VICTOR: Take your glass, William.

[HOWARD *takes a quick look at the tray, takes two glasses and hands one to* CLIVE.

VICTOR'*s face shows dismay. He puts the tray down but doesn't take the third glass.*]

HOWARD: Here, Root.

CLIVE: Thanks.

HOWARD: Your health, Victor. An excellent whisky. Why aren't you drinking?

VICTOR [*picking up the third glass*]: I'll join you in a moment. Got to say good night to Robin.

[VICTOR *starts, glass in hand, towards the sideboard, but* HOWARD *pursues him.*]

HOWARD: And health to our lovely hostess, Victor. You'll join us in that, surely.

VICTOR: I seem to have drowned this whisky. I'll get myself another.

HOWARD: I said a health to Mary, Victor. You can't refuse that. Drink up like a man.

[VICTOR *is cornered. He puts the glass to his mouth, but it is a trick dribbling-glass and the whisky pours down his jacket.*]

HOWARD: Hoist with your own petard.

CLIVE: A dribbling-glass now!

[*Everyone laughs except* MARY *and* CLIVE *who watches her.*]

HOWARD: He meant that for you, Root. Have you ever thought of trying one of those glasses on a patient, Victor? It might make him laugh in the chair.

VICTOR: It's not my lucky evening. I think you and Mary conspired . . . [*Goes to the sideboard and pours himself another drink. Over his shoulder*] The fact is I'm not appreciated, Root. Except by my son.

MARY: Won't the whisky stain?

VICTOR: There wasn't enough whisky in it, Mary. You know I wouldn't waste my good Black Label. Well, here's to the whole pack of you, laughing hyenas though you are. This one is an honest drink. I remember Lord Caton saying once, 'I don't like that pink stuff you put in my glass. Why don't you give me a whisky? Alcohol kills germs.' I said, 'Lord Caton, I've seen many people cock-eyed from whisky, but I've never known any cocci or streptococci, or even staphylococci killed by alcohol yet.' Come along, one more for the road, both of you.

HOWARD: Not me. We've got to keep your hand steady for the sake of your patients. Come on, Margaret.

MRS HOWARD: It's been a lovely evening. We were so glad, too, to have a chance of meeting Mr Root. [*To* CLIVE.] Ann has talked about you so much.

CLIVE [*as* ANN *holds out her hand*]: You forget. I'm coming with you.

ANN: Good night, Mrs Rhodes. Thank you so much.

VICTOR: Coats this way. [*He leads the way out.*]

HOWARD: Victor's in good form. A cutlet with us next time, Mary.

CLIVE: Good night, Mrs Rhodes, and thank you.

MARY: We'll see you again soon?

CLIVE: I may be going abroad for a while.

MARY: I'll drop in tomorrow morning.

[*Only* ANN *is left in the doorway. She watches them.*]

CLIVE: Not in the morning. I'm cataloguing with Ann.

MARY: Oh yes. I forgot.

[*She watches him follow* ANN *out. She stands listening to the sound of good nights. A door closes. She goes to the window, and drawing the curtains apart, watches her guests depart – one of her guests at any rate. A key turns in the lock outside and then a bolt is thrust home.* VICTOR *is securing the house for the night.*

He comes in.]

VICTOR: Window locked?

MARY: Yes.

VICTOR: I think they enjoyed themselves.

MARY: Yes.

VICTOR: I liked your young friend, Root.

MARY: I'm glad.

VICTOR: So did Ann, I think. Ha, ha.

[VICTOR *collects the glasses and carries them into the other half of the room.*]

They'd make a good couple.

MARY: He's nearly twenty years older.

VICTOR: Well, I'm more than ten years older than you are. A difference like that gives a marriage stability. [*He goes to the window.*] This window's not locked. Are you sure yours are?

MARY: Yes.

[*He comes and tests them all the same.*]

VICTOR: Now did I, or did I not, lock the back-door?

MARY: What are you afraid for, Victor? There's no old family silver.

VICTOR: Well, there's always a little cash lying around. And there's your fur coat.

MARY: The insurance is worth more than my old mink.

VICTOR: It's the idea of the thing, I suppose. [*He yawns and sits down on the sofa.*]

MARY: Tired?

VICTOR: A bit. [*Pause.*] You think I'm too careful about the house. But I'm not so careful as my father used to be. He always locked the inside doors too. Even the lavatory. He really believed it was all part of the Church of England because of that piece in the church-service. You know – a strong man keeps his house.

MARY: There's something too about moths.

VICTOR: Oh, mothballs are your province. But I always believe that wearing clothes instead of storing them keeps the moths away.

MARY: I expect you're right.

VICTOR: The same applies to teeth.

MARY: How interesting.

VICTOR: Mary, is something wrong?

MARY: What could be? I clean my teeth twice a day.

VICTOR: I didn't mean your teeth.

MARY: I thought that was your chief interest.

VICTOR: Yes. After my family. Is that wrong?

   [*She doesn't reply.*]

You weren't ashamed of marrying a dentist sixteen years ago.

MARY: I'm not ashamed, Victor. Not of you.

VICTOR: But people are. I don't know why. My patients don't ask us to dinner. Yet they ask their doctor. Though he deals in more ignoble parts of the body than I do.

MARY: I told you I'm not ashamed.

VICTOR: I wonder how many doctors could say they were as trained as I am. I have to know surgery, radiology, prosthesis . . .

MARY: What's prosthesis?

VICTOR: It's too late to tell you now.

MARY: It *is* late. Is your first appointment at nine?

VICTOR: Nine-thirty. There was a time, Mary, when you were interested in what I did.

MARY: Of course I'm interested.

VICTOR: Admit you aren't. There's nothing wrong in that. If those two young ones marry, you can be sure Ann won't be so interested in the bookshop after a few years. It's human nature, Mary. I used to enjoy shopping with you. I don't now. I get impatient when you can't decide about the new curtains. I feel out of place among the shop-assistants – as you would feel in my surgery in town. We have different professions, Mary. For a year or two we want to share them, but we can't. I'm not a mother and you aren't a dentist. That's not a tragedy.

MARY: Who's talking about a tragedy?

VICTOR: It's not enough to break a marriage.

MARY: Of course not. Who said it was? What's the matter, Victor?

VICTOR: I've felt for the last month that you were unhappy. And now I've drunk enough to talk. We don't talk often.

MARY: I've been a little tired, that's all. The spring. It's always tiring.

VICTOR: You need a holiday without the children. While Sally's away.

MARY: It's difficult. There's half-term. And Robin's teeth.

VICTOR: We are both working too hard. We ought to go off somewhere – by ourselves. You and I haven't had a holiday together for a long time.

MARY [*flatly*]: We haven't, have we?

VICTOR: The sooner the better for both of us. If only for a week. Suppose after Sally goes back . . .

MARY [*quickly*]: There's the Dental Association dinner.

VICTOR: Oh yes. I'd forgotten. [*Doubtfully, asking her advice.*] I could miss it, couldn't I?

MARY: You never have.

VICTOR: I mustn't get too set in my ways.

MARY: It's the only time in the year you can meet Baxter and Saville.

VICTOR: A wife comes before old friends. You don't look well, Mary.

MARY: Suppose I went off for a few days on my own.

VICTOR [*with a cheerful laugh*]: You'd be bored to death.

MARY: How do you know?

VICTOR: Well, I mean it's so unlike you.

MARY: I could go with someone.

VICTOR: Who?

MARY: Oh, somebody's sure to be free.

VICTOR: But you said just now how difficult it was to get away.

MARY: You don't need me at the dinner.

VICTOR: You always come.

MARY: I have old friends as well as you.

VICTOR: I offered not to go. Mary, it looks very much . . .

MARY: Yes?

VICTOR: As though you'd rather have a holiday without me.

MARY: That's stupid, Victor.

VICTOR: Then why shouldn't we both leave out the dinner?

MARY: You'd miss it, that's why. And when I'm tired like this I'm no companion, Victor.

VICTOR: Where did you think of going?

MARY: I don't know. Somewhere abroad – somewhere quiet. I could go with Jane. She never spends her allowance. We could manage on it for a week.

VICTOR: Have I ever met Jane?

MARY [*lying hard*]: I think once.

VICTOR: I have an idea. [*He takes out his notebook to examine the dates.*] You could go away with what's-her-name – Jane – immediately after half-term, and then four days later I'd join you – after the dinner. Then I'd have both, the dinner and the holiday with you. Perhaps we could even get rid of Jane.

MARY [*desperately seeking a solution*]: It doesn't seem fair to Jane. To come all that way . . .

VICTOR: What way?

MARY: From Northumberland.

VICTOR: Well then, why not take our holiday in Northumberland?

MARY: But I want sun, Victor, sun. We have enough rain here. And think how dreary it would be for Jane.

VICTOR: When did I meet Jane?

MARY: When we were married, I think. She never comes to London.

VICTOR: Just stays there in the rain? What's her other name?

MARY [*the first word that comes*]: Crane.

VICTOR: Jane Crane stays in the rain. She sounds a bit lowering as a companion.

MARY: It wouldn't be much fun for you with her there.

VICTOR: Oh, I don't know. She'd be a companion for you while I was busy.

MARY: Busy at what?

VICTOR: That's another bright idea of mine. I've always wanted to see the Dutch dental hospitals. So you and Jane could go to Amsterdam.

MARY: It rains in Amsterdam.

VICTOR: Nonsense. It's called the Venice of the north.

MARY: I think that's Stockholm.

VICTOR: Well, let's go to Stockholm then. Swedish dentistry is just as interesting, and there's a special Scandinavian allowance for tourists.

MARY: I'd thought of some little place in the south. In the sun.

VICTOR: Oh no, that wouldn't do at all. It would have to be a city because then I can get a business allowance. The three of us can't enjoy ourselves on Jane's hundred pounds.

MARY: I hadn't thought there would be three of us.

VICTOR: Be sensible, Mary. You'd be bored to death alone with Jane. You haven't seen her for years. So you say. You might not even like each other now. Early friends drop out like – like milk teeth.

MARY: Please – do you have to bring dentistry into everything?

VICTOR: You're behaving in a very odd way, Mary. Here I am proposing a holiday, trying to make the whole thing fun for you, and one would almost think I was forcing you to go away. Stockholm is one of the beauties of the north. There are lots of people who'd give their . . . [*He hesitates.*]

MARY: Eye teeth to see it.

VICTOR: The town hall is famous. And the glass.

MARY: The Royal Family is the most democratic in Europe. Please, Victor, if it has to be a city I'd rather go to Amsterdam.

VICTOR: Right. It was my first choice too. Now let's look at dates. Sally goes back on the twelfth. There's no reason why you and Jane shouldn't leave on the thirteenth. My dinner's on the sixteenth. I could join you on the seventeenth.

MARY: Leave one day, Victor, for a hangover. You won't be in bed till two.

VICTOR: Right. Then I'll join you on the eighteenth. When does Robin have his teeth out?

MARY: Not till the twenty-fifth.

VICTOR: Splendid. We'll get a whole week together. And Jane may not want to stay as long as that.

MARY: I don't suppose she will. But there's Robin. We can't leave him all alone.

VICTOR: He can go to his aunt. Now don't think about it any more. My secretary can book the plane and the hotel rooms – the Amstel is the best. Is Jane a Miss or a Mrs?

MARY [*hesitating*]: Miss. Why?

VICTOR: The air-company will want details of the names.

MARY [*seeing the complications ahead*]: I'd rather go by boat. The sea air . . .

VICTOR: Two-berth cabin then?

MARY: Leave out the cabin. It's expensive.

VICTOR: Dear Mary, I hope I can still afford a cabin for my wife. Would you rather have two singles?

MARY: But, Victor, would you mind very much if I paid for myself – just this time?

VICTOR: But why?

MARY: I want it to be my present for Jane. She's not well off.

VICTOR: You know you'll be short before the end of the month.

MARY: If I am, then I'll come to you.

[*The sound of* ROBIN *crying:* 'Mother, Mother, Mother.']
[*Wearily.*] I forgot to say good night.

VICTOR: Time for all of us to say good night.

MARY: You use the bathroom first. I want to write to Jane.

VICTOR: Why not wait till morning?

[ROBIN's *voice:* 'Mother, Mother, Mother.']

MARY [*shouts*]: I'm coming, Robin. [*To* VICTOR.] I want to write while the idea's fresh. I won't be long.

[MARY *goes out.* VICTOR *looks around to see that everything is tidy. He straightens the cushions. As he does this to one of the chairs he remembers the musical box, and fetches it from where* MARY *had put it; he slips it again under the cushions.*

He sits down for a moment to try it out, a blissful look upon his

*face, and lets it play two bars. Then he gets up and puts out the light
and goes into the other half of the room.*

*There he locks the whisky in the sideboard cupboard. He turns
out the lights there too and goes.*

Pause and then MARY *enters.*

*She goes to a telephone and dials a number. After a while a voice
answers.*]

MARY: Clive. Are you alone? . . . I'm coming away with you,
Clive . . . I only mean a holiday. Could you leave on the
thirteenth? . . . No, we can't go there, it's too far for a short
holiday, Clive . . . But I can only manage four days. I'm sorry,
but that's how things are. And, Clive, it's got to be Amsterdam
. . . I can't tell you why now. It just has to be, Clive. It's the
Venice of the north . . . All right. If you don't want four days
alone with me in Amsterdam, just say so. We can call it off . . .
If it does rain, Clive, what does it matter? We'll just stay in bed,
drinking Bols, whatever that is . . . Oh, he's quite happy about
it. He thinks I'm going with someone called Jane Crane . . .
No, she doesn't exist . . . The name just came into my head . . .
What do you mean, 'Jane, Jane, tall as a crane'? Why do you all
have to make up verses about her? . . . I don't care if Edith
Sitwell wrote them. I can't alter Jane's name now . . . Clive,
will you do the bookings? I'll pay you back, next month when
my allowance comes in. Any hotel but the Amstel . . . I know
it's the best, but someone I know is arriving there on the
eighteenth. I don't want them mixed up . . . You are happy,
darling? . . . Yes, I am . . . No, we won't buy diamonds . . .
Did you say herrings? *Raw* herrings? . . . Oh, but I think raw
herrings sound fascinating, and anything may happen, Clive,
anything. Even in Amsterdam.

[*The* CURTAIN FALLS *as she talks.*]

SCENE TWO

A hotel bedroom in Amsterdam. Two single beds have been pushed together to make a double. They are unmade. The room is that of a medium-priced hotel: a desk, one easy chair, a tall looking-glass in the wardrobe door, a door leading to the bathroom. The room is in the confusion of packing up. One man's incredibly shabby suitcase is already locked and ready by the door; two women's cases – very decorative – lie open in a froth of tissue paper beside the bed. The bathroom door is open and MARY *speaks from inside to* CLIVE, *who is sitting glumly on the bed in his shirt-sleeves.*

MARY'S VOICE: You haven't packed your face-cloth.

CLIVE: Never mind.

MARY'S VOICE: And there's a packet of razor blades here.

CLIVE: Let the valet have them.

MARY'S VOICE: Darling, do you always scatter your belongings over the globe like this?

CLIVE: How damnably cheerful you sound.

> [MARY *comes to the door of the bathroom, her hands full of plastic pots and tubes. She is still in her dressing-gown.*]

MARY: I've been happy, that's why. Haven't you?

CLIVE: Yes, in a way.

MARY: Is that all?

CLIVE: The first day I was happy. Even the second. Yesterday was not so good.

MARY: I loved yesterday.

CLIVE: The shadow of today was over it. But I didn't know then what a shadow. Mary, why didn't you tell me about Victor before we came away?

MARY: I was afraid you wouldn't come.

CLIVE: You could have told me yesterday.

MARY: And spoilt it all. All the lying late in bed, the wine we drank at lunch, even that silly film we saw . . .

CLIVE: Yes, you were happy, and all the time you were deceiving me.

MARY: I've been happy deceiving Victor too, haven't I? You didn't mind me being happy doing that.

CLIVE: I understood our relationship was rather different.

MARY: Do you think I like packing up and going off to the Amstel to meet Victor?

CLIVE: He gets a whole week of you. I had three days.

MARY: It was the only way I could manage anything at all.

CLIVE: He fixed our holiday. Why didn't he fix our room at the Amstel too?

MARY: I told him Jane wanted somewhere small and quiet.

CLIVE: So he had our address all the time?

MARY: Something might have happened to the children. I had to be available.

CLIVE: Of course your room at the Amstel will be a much nicer one than this.

MARY: I've booked two single rooms, Clive.

CLIVE: And tonight I suppose you'll take him to that little restaurant by the canal . . . and that bar . . .

MARY: I won't take him anywhere we've been together.

CLIVE: There aren't so many good restaurants in Amsterdam and Victor likes his food.

MARY: Darling, what's the great difference? If I weren't meeting him at the Amstel, I'd be meeting him at home tonight. I'm just meeting him, Clive, as one meets a kind relation and talks about the family.

CLIVE: This was our life here. We haven't had a very long one. Three days of birth, growing up, and I suppose this is age. Why had he got to butt into *our* life?

MARY: Some people might say you'd butted into his.

CLIVE: Oh, don't be so damnably fair minded. Not today.

MARY [*on her knees by a suitcase*]: Clive, help me with this case.

CLIVE [*not looking at her*]: What's wrong with the bloody case?

MARY: I can't make the key turn.

CLIVE: I suppose you've busted the lock.

MARY: Won't you help?

CLIVE: Why should I help you to go away from me? [*All the same he joins her.*] You shouldn't buy cases for looks. You ought to buy them for wear.

MARY: Yours hasn't worn so well.

CLIVE [*struggling with the key*]: Anyway I don't go in for fancy monograms. M.R. for Mary Rhodes.

MARY: It could stand for Mary Root too.

> [*There is a ring at the door.*]

Come in. Entrez. Whatever you call it.

> [*The* HOTEL VALET *enters.*]

VALET: Are your bags ready, Madam?

MARY: I won't be a minute.

CLIVE [*pointing to his case*]: You can take that – the shabby one.

> [*The* VALET *leaves with* CLIVE's *suitcase.*]

MARY: It's no use. The lock *is* broken.

CLIVE: I'll get you a strap.

MARY: Have you time before the plane?

CLIVE: I don't have to report for an hour. When do you have to report?

MARY: He's on the midday plane.

CLIVE: We may pass each other at the airport. Don't worry. I'll be ready to hide my face behind a newspaper.

MARY: You needn't. He wouldn't think there was anything wrong.

CLIVE: Is he as dumb as that?

MARY: It's not dumbness. When a man doesn't want a woman any more, he can't imagine anyone else desiring her – that's all.

> [CLIVE *gets up.*]

CLIVE: I'll go and buy the strap.

> [MARY *remains squatting by the suitcase.*]

Aren't you going to kiss me? For being obedient.

MARY: This isn't good-bye. Even at the air-terminus it won't be good-bye. Clive, we're going to be together again. Over and over again. For years.

CLIVE: Are you sure?

MARY: Even if you told me you didn't want to go on, I wouldn't believe you. I have my proofs, Clive.

CLIVE: Where are they?

MARY: I can't show them to you now.

> [*Pause.*]

CLIVE: I'll be back as quickly as I can.

> [*When* CLIVE *has gone* MARY *busies herself packing again. Then she goes to the telephone.*]

MARY: Reception please.

[*There is a ring at the door.*]

Entrez. Reception? This is room 121. Will you have my bill ready, please?

[*The door of the bedroom opens.* MARY *has her back to it as she telephones.*

The VALET *stands on one side to admit* VICTOR *who is followed by a man in a continental suit.*]

Yes. We're checking out in a few minutes. [*Over her shoulder to the* VALET, *her hand over the receiver.*] You can't take my bags yet. I'm waiting for a strap. [*To the Reception.*] Yes. We had breakfast this morning.

[*The* VALET *leaves.*]

VICTOR: Guess who's here!

MARY: Victor!

VICTOR: I thought you'd be surprised.

MARY: What are you doing here?

VICTOR: I was very careful at the dinner. I didn't have a hangover and I caught the night boat.

MARY: Why didn't you go to the Amstel?

VICTOR: I did, but you hadn't arrived. Anyway, it's such a huge place, Mary. I thought it'd be more fun being here. And Jane will be happier not moving.

MARY: Jane's gone home.

VICTOR: Oh fine. Of course I'm sorry to have missed her.

MARY: You wouldn't be comfortable here, Victor. And I don't think they've got another room. Jane's was taken at once.

VICTOR: Oh, this is quite big enough for two. A fine big bed.

MARY: It's not really a double bed. I don't know why they arranged it this way. There's a nasty crack in the middle.

VICTOR: Oh well, we only need to pull the beds apart. Bathroom through there? [*He is already taking control of the room.*] Separate toilet – that's nice. What's the coffee like?

MARY [*weakly*]: Good.

VICTOR: And the rolls?

MARY: They're good too.

VICTOR: Raw herrings. And cheese for breakfast. How it all comes back.

MARY: Comes back?

VICTOR: I used to know Amsterdam well when I was a student. I'll show you spots you won't have found with Jane. [*He sits on the bed and bumps up and down.*] Good mattress too. This is much more sympathetic than the Amstel.

[*The* STRANGER *coughs.*]

MARY [*helplessly*]: Who's this man, Victor? Your bodyguard?

VICTOR: Oh, stupid of me. He was at the dinner. Dr van Droog – my wife.

DR VAN DROOG [*bows, and says something rapidly in Dutch*]: Buitengewoon aangenaam met Uw charmante echtgenote te ontmoeten.

MARY: Dinner?

VICTOR: The dental dinner. We travelled across together. Dr van Droog is one of the biggest manufacturers of dental instruments in Holland. The trouble is he doesn't speak any English.

MARY: You must have had a very gay dinner. But why bring him here?

VICTOR: He's staying here.

MARY: You don't mean with us?

VICTOR: No, no. He always stays here on his way to The Hague.

VAN DROOG: Het was my zeer aangenaam Uw echtgenoot te ontmoeten, en in elk gewal wat hartelijkheid te kunnen uitwisselen, daar wij bij gebrek aan een gemeenschappelijke taal helaas niet van gedachten kunnen wisselen.

MARY: What's he saying?

VICTOR: I don't fully understand.

VAN DROOG: Het was mij een eer de gast te zijn van de Dental Association of Great Britain.

VICTOR: It may be important. Ring for the valet.

MARY: The valet? [*She rings obediently.*]

VICTOR: To translate of course.

VAN DROOG: Neemt U my niet kwalyk dat ik geen Engels ken.

[*A ring at the door.*]

VICTOR: Entrez.

[*The* VALET *enters and goes for the bags.*]

[*Now in charge of the situation.*] No. Not the bags. I want you to translate what this gentleman has to say.

VALET [*in Dutch*]: Hy wil dat ik het vertaal, Mynherr.

VAN DROOG [*rapidly*]: Zeg aan Mijnheer, dat het mij zeer aangenaam is, met zijn vrouw kennis te maken.

VALET: He says it is a great pleasure, sir, to him to have met your
wife. [*To* DR VAN DROOG.] Waar ontmoette U de vrouw van
deze heer?

VICTOR: What are you saying?

VALET: I am asking him, sir, where he had the pleasure of meeting
your wife.

VICTOR: Here, of course. Where do you think? This is my wife.

VALET [*looking at* MARY *reproachfully*]: I see. I did not understand. I
am sorry.

VAN DROOG: Wilt U aan Mevrouw zeggen dat ofschoon, ik geen
Engles spreek, ik er veel van kan verstaan, als men langzaam
sprekt.

VALET: He wants me to tell your wife that though he cannot speak
English he can understand a lot if you speak very slowly.

MARY: That's certainly going to be fun. Victor, would you mind
going away for a few minutes – to the bar, anywhere, with Dr
van Droog. I have to get dressed and go and find a strap for my
bag.

VICTOR: There's no hurry for that now. We're staying here.

VAN DROOG: Het zou mij een groot genoegen doen, als Mijnheer
en Mevrouw Rhodes mijn gasten willen zijn in mijn fabriek in
den Haag. Het is een zeer moderne fabriek, en ik heb een nieuw
ontwerp voor een dril, die beter is dan de Duitse.

VALET: The gentleman says he would be delighted if the two of
you would be his guests at his factory at The Hague. He says it
is very up to date and he has a new – [*the* VALET *hesitates, not
knowing the word in English*] – a new, better than the German, a
new . . .

VICTOR: New what?

[*The* VALET *puts his finger in his mouth and imitates the sound of a
drill.*]

MARY: Vivid. Only you left out the spasm of pain. Victor, please
go. Just for a few minutes while I get dressed. [*She is watching
the door anxiously*.]

VICTOR: A moment, and I'll get rid of him for you. Must be
polite. [*To the* VALET.] Will you explain to Dr van Droog that

we shall be delighted to visit his factory. I am looking particularly for some new instruments for gingivectomy.

VALET: For what, sir?

VICTOR: For gingivectomy.

MARY: I'm not going to stand here in my dressing-gown, half naked, while you discuss ginger-something with Dr – Dr –

VALET: I do not know the word in Dutch, sir.

MARY: Take him away, Victor, or I'll push him out.

[MARY *makes a gesture with her hand, but* DR VAN DROOG *seizes it and holds her firmly while he makes her a speech in Dutch.*]

VAN DROOG: Ik ben zo verheugd dat U myn uitnodiging aangenomen heeft. Myn collega's en ik zien Uw bezoek met ongeduld tegemoet.

[*In the middle of the speech the door opens and* CLIVE *enters.* MARY *has her back turned while she listens to* DR VAN DROOG. VICTOR *sits on the bed facing the door. He smiles brightly at* CLIVE.]

VICTOR: How are you, Root? Nice to see you.

[MARY *turns quickly, but even more disconcerted than* MARY *is the* VALET.]

CLIVE [*awkwardly*]: I didn't know you were here.

VICTOR: Just moved in.

CLIVE: I thought you were going to the Amstel.

VICTOR: It's better here. There's a sort of holiday feeling about this place. What are you doing in Amsterdam?

CLIVE: I was getting a strap. For this suitcase.

MARY [*coming to the rescue*]: Clive's been buying books. It was such a surprise when Jane and I ran into him. He's been very kind to Jane.

VICTOR: This is Dr van Droog, a neighbour of ours at home, Mr Clive Root. [*To the* VALET.] Go on. Translate.

VALET [*translating unwillingly*]: Dit is onze buurman in Engeland.

[DR VAN DROOG *bows and replies in Dutch.*]

VAN DROOG: Zeer aangenaam, U te ontmoeten. Ik hoop dat U de professor en zyn echtgenote wilt vergezellen naar den Haag om myn fabriek van tandeheelkundige instrumenten te bezichtigen.

VALET [*wearily*]: Dr van Droog welcomes you to the city of

Amsterdam and hopes you will accompany the Professor and his wife to The Hague to see over his manufactory of dental appliances.

VICTOR: Good idea, Root. Come along with us.

CLIVE: I'm leaving today.

VICTOR: The books can wait. Stay and keep my wife company while I'm doing the clinics. Know Amsterdam well?

CLIVE: My first visit.

VICTOR: I'll show you around then. There's a little restaurant – by the canal – if it's still there . . .

CLIVE [*watching* MARY]: It's still there. I know the one you mean.

VICTOR: They used to do wonderful chickens on a spit.

CLIVE: The spit still turns.

VICTOR: Talking of spit . . . [*To the* VALET.] Ask Dr van Droog what one has to pay here for absorbent wools. By the gross of course.

VALET: Please I do not know the Dutch . . . please . . .

CLIVE [*to* MARY]: I hope this strap will do. [*He drops it on the suitcase and prepares to go.*]

MARY: Where are you going?

CLIVE: Home.

MARY: You don't have to be at the airport yet. There were those books we had to talk about.

VICTOR: Oh, if you're going to talk about books I'm off. With Dr van Droog.

[VICTOR *takes* DR VAN DROOG's *arm, but* DR VAN DROOG *begins to talk rapidly again in Dutch.*]

VAN DROOG: Bent U ooit in India geweest?

VALET [*patiently*]: Dr van Droog wants to know whether you have ever visited India.

CLIVE: No. I haven't. Why?

VALET [*to* DR VAN DROOG]: Neen.

VAN DROOG [*to* VALET]: Zeg aan Mynheer dat zyn voornaam my interesseert. Is hy misschien een afstammeling van de be-roemde Robert Clive?

VALET [*to* CLIVE]: Dr van Droog is interested in your pre-name. He thinks you are perhaps an ancestor of the great Robert Clive.

VICTOR: Descendant.

CLIVE: No.

VALET [*to* DR VAN DROOG]: Neen.

MARY: Victor. Please, Victor.

[VICTOR *at last succeeds in getting* DR VAN DROOG *through the door.*]

VICTOR: We'll be waiting in the bar. Don't be long. [*He goes.*]

[*The* VALET *follows and closes the door.*]

CLIVE: Who in God's name is that man?

MARY: Why *are* you called Clive?

CLIVE: My father was a great admirer of his. To the point of imitation.

MARY: Imitation?

CLIVE: He shot himself. Like Clive. From a sense of failure. It's not a bad reason. So now the family is reunited – here. Has Victor decided on which side of the bed he is going to sleep?

MARY: I've got to dress. [*Breaks away and goes to the bathroom.*]

CLIVE: He likes to give the final turn of the screw, doesn't he? He's not satisfied with moving into our room and our bed. He has to make it a cheap farce with his Dutch manufacturer of dental instruments. We aren't allowed a tragedy nowadays without a banana-skin to slip on and make it funny. But it hurts just the same.

MARY [*coming to the door without her dressing-gown*]: What? What were you saying about banana-skin?

CLIVE: Nothing that mattered. It can hurt just as much as the great Clive's bullet, that's all.

MARY: What's banana-skin got to do with it?

CLIVE: Oh, forget the banana-skin. It's Victor. Victor coming here. Where we made love.

MARY: That's not Victor's fault. He doesn't know.

CLIVE: Doesn't he? I *happen* to be in Amsterdam – I *happen* to walk into your bedroom before you are dressed. But oh, no, Victor's a damned wise monkey. He sees no evil, thinks no evil.

MARY: That's not a bad quality.

CLIVE: You always leap to his defence, don't you? If you love him so much, why did you come away with me?

MARY: There are different kinds of love.

CLIVE: Oh yes, the higher and the lower. And I'm the lower.

MARY: I didn't say so. Clive, how many times do I have to swear to you that Victor and I aren't lovers? We aren't man and wife in that way. Why won't you believe me?

CLIVE: Go and look in the glass before you put your frock on. Then you'll know why. I'll never believe you, Mary, until you sleep beside me every night.

MARY: You haven't children.

CLIVE: A loveless marriage isn't good for children, so the *Sunday Mirror* says.

MARY: But you see, Clive, this isn't a loveless marriage.

CLIVE: Yes, I do see.

[MARY *goes back into the bathroom to put on her frock.*
CLIVE *takes a small package out of his pocket and puts it on the dressing-table. He is moving to the door when* MARY *calls to him.*]

MARY'S VOICE: What are you doing, Clive?

CLIVE: Catching my plane.

[MARY *comes back with her frock on.*]

MARY: Why don't you stay as Victor asked?

CLIVE: Good God, do you really expect me to take the next-door room . . . ?

MARY: Victor's going to be busy all day.

CLIVE: Mary, you're either the most immoral woman I've ever known – or the most innocent.

[MARY *takes up the package.*]

MARY: What's this, Clive?

CLIVE: A present I meant to give you when we got past the Customs.

MARY [*excited and beginning to unwrap it*]: Clive!

CLIVE: You'll have to take it through yourself now – or get Victor to hide it among the absorbent wool rolls.

MARY [*opens a box*]: Ear-rings. But they're diamonds, Clive.

CLIVE: This is the city for diamonds.

MARY: You can't possibly afford . . .

CLIVE: They're the profit on one fine copy of Redoute's *Lilies*.

MARY: But the currency . . . This couldn't have come out of your £100.

CLIVE: There are always ways. I went to a little man in Knights-bridge. There are quacks nowadays for every known disease – even for a collapsed currency. The currency quacks are especially smart. They have deep carpets and the receptionists are sexy and frankly impertinent because they think you may be a film-magnate.

MARY: Why a film-magnate?

CLIVE: All film-magnates suffer from collapsed currencies. It's rather like visiting a fashionable abortionist.

MARY: You could go to prison for this.

CLIVE: So could he. Everything is on trust between two crooks. No letters. No cheques. Just cash and guarded telephone calls naming no names. Of course this was a very small transaction. He wouldn't have bothered with it if I hadn't had a good introduction.

MARY: Who from?

CLIVE: A film-magnate who happens to read books. Erotica, of course.

MARY: Clive, they're lovely. But I don't need presents from you.

CLIVE: I would rather have given you a plain gold ring.

MARY: You know I want the plain gold ring.

CLIVE: I wish you would show it in the usual simple way.

MARY: What's that?

CLIVE: Leave your husband and marry your lover.

MARY: Do you call that simple?

CLIVE: Hundreds of people do it every year.

MARY: Perhaps they're tougher than I am then. I've known you for less than two months, and I've known Victor for sixteen years. He's never been unkind even when I've run up bills. He's a good father. The children love him. Particularly Robin. It wasn't his fault we stopped – sleeping together. I warned you before, Clive – marriage kills that.

CLIVE: It can't go on like this, Mary. Odd days arranged by Victor. You have to choose.

MARY: And if I won't choose?

CLIVE: I'll leave you.

MARY: Do you mean that?

CLIVE: Yes.

MARY: And go off with that little bitch from the bank?

CLIVE: Perhaps. I hadn't thought of it.

MARY: You're so free, aren't you? You don't have to choose. You don't have to go to someone you love and say, 'I'm leaving you. After sixteen years I'm leaving you for a man I've slept with for a month. You'll have to see to things for yourself – the dentist for Robin and writing to Matron about Sally, booking rooms for the seaside in August and getting all those damned little objects for the stockings in time for Christmas.' I'm married, Clive. You aren't. You are a foreigner. Even when I sleep with you you are a foreigner.

CLIVE: If we were married . . .

MARY: You don't want that sort of marriage and I don't. You only marry that way once, and you've never tried.

CLIVE: Oh yes, I've tried.

MARY: You want to be a lover with a licence, that's all. All right. You win. I'll leave Victor, but not just yet, Clive. Not before Christmas. Please not before Christmas. Be patient until January, Clive.

CLIVE: I'd wait for longer than that if you'd promise . . .

MARY: Couldn't we wait till he finds out? He's sure to find out sooner or later.

CLIVE: He has a wonderful capacity for not noticing.

MARY: If he found out he wouldn't want me to stay, would he? There wouldn't be a struggle, or a choice. He'd throw me out. Say you'll wait till then, Clive.

CLIVE: Just now you only asked me to wait till January.

MARY: Perhaps he'll find out long before then.

CLIVE [an idea has been born]: It's possible.

MARY: Just give me time. You gave me the ear-rings. Give me time too. Till he finds out.

CLIVE: Till he finds out.

MARY: I must go down, Clive. It's all right, isn't it, now?

CLIVE: Yes, it's all right.

MARY: And we'll see each other next week?

CLIVE: Of course. Won't you put on your ear-rings?

MARY: I'd better not. Not just yet. He might notice.

CLIVE: I see. Good-bye, Mary.

MARY: Until next week?

CLIVE: Until next week.

MARY: Aren't you coming down?

CLIVE: I'd rather not see Victor for a while if you don't mind.

MARY: He'll think it odd your staying up here.

CLIVE: Tell him I asked if I could use your desk to write a letter. I shan't be here long.

MARY: Au revoir, darling. [*She touches the bed with her hand as she leaves.*]

[CLIVE *waits a moment and then goes to the desk and takes out notepaper and envelope. He unscrews his pen and on the point of writing stops and rings the bell.*

After a pause the VALET *enters.*]

VALET: Yes, sir? Can I take the bags now?

CLIVE: No. The lady is staying here. Do you want to earn 50 guilder?

VALET: Well, sir, naturally, but . . .

CLIVE: You have only to write a letter for me. I'll dictate it.

VALET: What kind of letter, sir?

CLIVE: Shall we say 100 guilder and no questions?

VALET: As you please, sir.

CLIVE: Then sit down.

[*The* VALET *sits.*]

Here is a pen. Begin 'Dear Mr Rhodes' – no, make it Dear Sir. 'I am the valet who looked after you in room 121.' Got that?

VALET: Yes, sir.

CLIVE: 'I am sorry to see a gentleman like you so sadly deceived.'

VALET: How do you spell 'deceived', sir?

CLIVE: Spell it any way you like. It will look more convincing.

VALET [*spelling out*]: D-e-s-s-e-v-e-d.

CLIVE: Good enough. 'A beautiful woman your wife . . .'

[*The door opens and* VICTOR *enters. The* VALET *looks nervously up, and stands. He is completely confused.*]

VICTOR: Mary here?

CLIVE: She went down to find you. I asked if I could use your desk – and your valet.

VICTOR: Why the valet?

CLIVE: I have to write a bread-and-butter letter in Dutch.

VICTOR: Well, make yourself at home, old chap. Make yourself at home.

CLIVE: Thank you.

VICTOR: Carry on. Don't mind me. Just going to wash.

[VICTOR *goes to the bathroom and begins running water. It has a proprietary sound which infuriates* CLIVE.]

CLIVE [*to* VALET]: Sit down.

[*The poor man is hopelessly confused but he obeys.*]

'I have so much enjoyed my stay with you.'

[VALET *hesitates.*]

Go on. 'The windmills were just as I'd always imagined them.'

[*The* VALET *writes.* VICTOR *emerges, drying his hands.*]

VICTOR: Just going to take my wife shopping. I've managed to lose Dr van Droog. See you in London.

CLIVE: Give Mary my love.

VICTOR: Right you are. [VICTOR *pauses at the bed and picks up the bed-clothes.*]

Can't say I like sleeping under these. I like good English blankets. Good-bye, Root.

CLIVE: Good-bye.

[VICTOR *leaves.*

CLIVE *turns to the* VALET.]

Go on now with the letter. 'I am sorry to see . . .' No, we've done that. 'I feel that it is my duty to tell you . . . that before your arrival . . . your wife was sharing room 121 . . . for four days . . . with the gentleman who went out to buy a strap. They had behaved very intimately together . . . and I am quite ready to be a witness in any proceedings . . .'

[*The* VALET *looks up.*]

Spell it how you like . . . 'that you may wish to take. Your humble servant . . .' Now sign it, and post it a week today.

VALET: Shall I read it to you, sir?

CLIVE: No. I don't want any more to do with the beastly thing. Address the envelope to Victor Rhodes, Esq., 18 South Heath Lane, London, N.W., England.

[DR VAN DROOG *puts his head inside the door and speaks in Dutch.*]

VAN DROOG: Het spyt my ik ben Mr en Mrs Rhodes kwytger-aakt?

VALET [*getting to his feet*]: He wishes to know where is Mr and Mrs Rhodes. I do not know who he is. I do not know who they are. I do not know who you are. I do not understand this. [*Indicating the letter.*] I do not understand one damned thing.

Act Two

SCENE ONE

The same scene as Act One, Scene One, about five-thirty of a warm sunny evening.

The sitting-room is empty, but glasses for cocktails have been laid out on the dining-room table.

ROBIN's voice calling: 'Mother, Mother.'

MARY enters the dining-room carrying bottles. She is wearing the new ear-rings. The voice goes on calling 'Mother', but she pays no attention, counting and marshalling the glasses: it is the eternal background noise of her life at home.

ROBIN enters the drawing-room through the garden-window, then shouts again.

ROBIN: Mother.

MARY: If you want to speak to me come where you don't have to shout.

ROBIN [*between the rooms*]: What's the capital of Madagascar?

MARY: Antananarivo.

ROBIN: Thanks. What's a prime number?

MARY: A number that you can't divide into equal parts.

ROBIN: Thanks. What's Tio Pepe?

MARY [*looking at the bottle in her hand*]: Sherry.

ROBIN: Tio means ten in Swedish.

MARY: Thanks.

ROBIN: There's a stamp I haven't got on one of Father's letters.

MARY: What kind?

ROBIN: Dutch. A new issue.

MARY: I suppose that will be from Dr van Droog. I wonder who we can get to translate it.

ROBIN: Can I peel the stamp off? It's on the hall-table.

MARY: Not until your father's opened the letter.

ROBIN: Who's coming to the party?

MARY: Mr Root and the Howards – the Morgans, the Forsters I think. I can't remember.

ROBIN: Is Ann coming?

MARY: I suppose so.

ROBIN: Do you think she'd like an electronic eye? I made one yesterday.

MARY: It would be an improvement on a stuffed mouse. Help me carry in some of these glasses, and I want to shift some tables into the garden. We've got to spread the party. Don't take too many at a time.

[ROBIN *follows her into the sitting-room, carrying glasses.*
   During the ensuing dialogue they also carry one or two small tables through the garden-windows.]

ROBIN: Is Jane Crane coming?

MARY: No. Why?

ROBIN: It'd be just interesting to see her. None of us have.

MARY: She went straight home by train.

ROBIN: Jane Crane went home by train. She'll never be seen here ever again.

MARY: Why does everybody have to make up rhymes about her? It's quite an ordinary name, isn't it?

ROBIN: Not a *very* ordinary name. Did she like Amsterdam?

MARY: Of course. Why?

ROBIN: What did you do all day?

MARY: Why we – we looked at museums and things.

ROBIN: That sounds pretty dreary. You must have been glad when Father came.

MARY: Of course.

ROBIN: Did Father like Jane Crane?

MARY: They never met.

ROBIN: She *is* a mystery woman, isn't she? Nobody's met her except you.

MARY: And Mr Root.

ROBIN: Oh, was he in Amsterdam too?

MARY: Yes.

ROBIN: Ann's got a crush on him.

MARY: How do you know?

ROBIN: I saw them on the heath while you were away. They looked as if they were in an about-to-take-hands condition. It would be terrible, wouldn't it, if they married.

MARY: For goodness sake stop talking about things you don't understand.

[VICTOR *enters. He carries the afternoon post in his hand.*]

VICTOR: Sorry I'm too late to help. Who's coming?

MARY: The usual people. Had a bad afternoon?

VICTOR: Four fillings, three scalings and one extraction.

ROBIN: Did you use gas?

VICTOR: Pentothal. [*He sits heavily down on the sofa.*] The new girl makes everything twice as long. She has no sense of order.

ROBIN: What kind of fillings were they, Father?

MARY: Don't worry your father. He's tired. Have you done your homework?

VICTOR: One porcelain and three amalgams.

ROBIN: Don't you ever use gold now?

VICTOR: Thank God, gold foil is out of fashion. It took five times as long.

ROBIN: Why?

MARY: Robin, I said homework.

ROBIN [*disgruntled*]: Oh, all right.

[ROBIN *goes.*]

MARY: He's at a tiresome age.

VICTOR: Oh, I think he was really interested. It would be amusing, wouldn't it, to have a dentist son.

MARY: Would it?

VICTOR: I could take him into partnership before I retired.

MARY: And you could consult each other at meals.

VICTOR: Yes. [*He notices the irony too late.*] What's wrong, Mary?

MARY: Nothing. Read your mail.

[*During the ensuing dialogue* MARY *moves the glasses and bottles between the two sections of the room and the garden.*]

VICTOR: There's nothing interesting. Two bills. Three catalogues and a letter from Dr van Droog.

MARY: It *is* from Dr van Droog?

VICTOR: It must be. He's the only man I know in Holland.

MARY: Robin wants the stamp.

VICTOR: He could have taken it.

MARY: I told him not to, until you'd read the letter.

VICTOR: Not much good reading. It'd be double-Dutch to me. [*He opens one of the catalogues.*]

MARY: That was a terrible day at The Hague. Except for the Bols. I drank four glasses. I simply had to.

VICTOR: I don't know. It wasn't so bad, was it? The supersonic drill was interesting. True, I didn't take to it much. That jet of water playing on the patient's tooth to keep it cool – I'd be afraid of not seeing the way and cutting the nerve.

MARY: Victor, can't you leave dentistry behind in the surgery just for a little?

VICTOR: I'm sorry, Mary. You see, it's my life. [*He opens another catalogue.*] Even my letters are dental. What does a dentist do when he retires? He can hardly write his memoirs. The patients wouldn't like it.

MARY: He has to fall back on a hobby like other people.

VICTOR: You don't much care for my hobby, do you? You know that shop in Oxford Street. I saw a wonderful rat there the other day. Beautifully made, real craftsmanship. You make it lurk in the shadows of the room. [*He throws down the catalogue.*] Oh God, I'm feeling tired today. Well, here's for Dr van Droog. Why are there so many g's in the Dutch language? [*Opens the letter with the Dutch stamp.*]

[MARY *goes into the dining-room and begins to decant some whisky.* VICTOR *puts the letter on his knee, then picks it up and reads it again.*]

MARY [*from the other room*]: Why don't you go to bed? I'll tell them the truth and say you're tired. When they've gone I'll bring you up a tray. It's a cold meal anyway.

[VICTOR, *with sudden decision, tears the letter in two and drops it on the sofa.*]

What about it, dear?

VICTOR: No. I'll stay.

[*Pause.*]

MARY [*from the other room*]: Did you remember to write to Sally for her birthday?

VICTOR: Yes.

MARY [*from the other room*]: We've only got one bottle of sherry, but the men will take whisky, won't they, or Martinis. Let me make the Martinis if you're tired.

[MARY *comes into the living-room with a cocktail shaker.*] Poor dear. You do look all in.

VICTOR: Is Root coming?

MARY: Yes, I think so. Why? He was so kind, you know, to Jane. Took her round to museums and art-galleries – all the places that bore me. We need more ash-trays. [*She is quite unconscious of the situation and the effect of her words on* VICTOR.] Did I tell you I got a letter from Jane this morning? She's so sorry that she missed you in Amsterdam. Now there she is, back in the frozen north. She's quite a hermit, but perhaps she'll come to London after Christmas and then you'll meet her.

VICTOR [*who can bear no more*]: It seems unlikely.

MARY: Unlikely?

VICTOR: Mary, was Root sleeping with you in Amsterdam?

[*A long pause.*]

MARY: Yes.

VICTOR: It was stupid of me not to guess. You married a stupid man.

MARY: You aren't stupid, Victor. I was beastly and clever with my lies. I hated them.

VICTOR: I suppose I ought to be glad the lies are over, but I'm not. I just don't know how to take the truth.

MARY: How did you find out?

VICTOR: This letter. From the valet in the hotel.

MARY: The valet!

VICTOR: A bit sordid, isn't it?

MARY: You tore it up.

VICTOR: I thought for a moment I could pretend it hadn't come. But I'm not strong enough. And what's the use of my lying too?

MARY: Let me see it.

VICTOR: I'll read it to you if you like. It's in English. [*He puts the two pieces of the letter together.*] 'Dear sir, I am the valet who looked after you in room 121.' You remember the man. He translated for Dr van Droog. 'I am sorry to see a gentleman like

you so sadly deceived.' His spelling is not very good. 'A
beautiful woman your wife . . .'

MARY: What a foul letter.

VICTOR: It gets a bit confused here. I don't know what he means.
He writes, 'I have so much enjoyed my stay with you. The
windmills were just as I always imagined them.'

MARY: He must be mad.

VICTOR: What difference does it make? You said you slept with
Root. He goes on, 'I feel it is my duty to tell you that before
your arrival your wife was sharing room 121.' I don't have to
read any more, do I?

MARY: No.

VICTOR: Are those his ear-rings you are wearing?

MARY: Yes.

VICTOR: An expensive present. I couldn't buy you much on my
£10 a day allowance. He seems to know the ropes better than I
do.

MARY: He went to a black marketeer in Knightsbridge. A currency specialist.

VICTOR: It's the only romantic thing a man can do in these days,
risk prison for a woman. I can't even do that. I'm a father. I can
only give you a scarf with a map of Amsterdam on it. They
look as though they're good diamonds.

MARY: You talk as though he bought me.

VICTOR: He did buy you. He bought you with novelty, anecdotes
you hadn't heard before, books instead of teeth. I know what
you think of my job. You didn't feel that way when we started.
You used to talk quite poetically about dentistry. Only you
called it 'curing pain'.

MARY: You are causing it now.

VICTOR: Me causing it? I remember a poem by Swinburne about a
woman who loved a leper and washed his sores with her hair. Is
it so much more difficult to love a dentist?

MARY: There never was such a woman. Or if there was it didn't
happen that way. The sores would have got on her nerves very
soon.

VICTOR: Like my dentist's chair?

MARY: Like your rat and your burning cigar and your dribbling-glass. Victor, I'm sorry. I don't want to be angry. I don't know why I am. It's you who ought to be angry.

VICTOR: I was angry just now, but I couldn't keep it up. What are you going to do?

MARY: I wasn't planning to do anything until you found out.

VICTOR [*getting up from the sofa*]: I wish I hadn't. Oh, how I wish I hadn't. If that damned valet hadn't written . . . Does Root want to marry you?

MARY: Yes.

VICTOR: Do you want to marry him?

MARY: I want to be with him, when I can, as much as I can.

VICTOR: That wasn't what I asked.

MARY: I never thought about marriage until he talked about it.

VICTOR: Don't think about it now. Mary, marriage isn't the answer. First editions can be just as boring in time as dentist's drills. He'll have his hobbies too and you won't care for them in a year or two. The trouble about marriage is, it's a damned boring condition even with a lover.

MARY: I didn't know you'd been bored too.

VICTOR: I can put up with any amount of boredom because I love you. It's the way of life that's boring, not you. Do you think I'm never bored with people's teeth? One has to put up with it. Boredom is not a good reason for changing a profession or a marriage.

MARY: We haven't been married properly for years.

VICTOR: Oh yes, we have. Marriage is living in the same house with someone you love. I never stopped loving you – I only stopped giving you pleasure. And when that happened I didn't want you any more. I wasn't going to use you like a pick-up in the park.

MARY: How did you know that?

VICTOR: You were always very quiet when we made love, but you had one habit you didn't know yourself. In the old days just before going to sleep, if you had been satisfied, you would touch my face and say 'thank you'. And then a time came when I realized that for months you had said nothing. You had only touched my face. [*In sudden pain.*] Do you say thank you to Root?

MARY: I don't know. Perhaps.

VICTOR: You are always so damnably honest – that's the awful thing about you.

MARY: What do you want me to say, Victor?

VICTOR: I want you to make absurd promises, to say you'll give him up, I want you to lie to me, but it never even occurs to you to pretend. You never pretended even in bed. It was thank you or nothing.

MARY: I never knew you noticed so much.

VICTOR: I'm not more stupid than other men.

MARY: You are talking to me as though I was a woman, and not just your wife. Do I have to sleep with another man before you do that?

[ROBIN's VOICE *with its maddening wail:* 'Mother, Mother.']

VICTOR: You'd better go to him.

MARY: I promised nothing.

VICTOR: I meant Robin.

MARY: He can wait. He only wants help with his homework.

VICTOR: We are all of us asking you for help, aren't we? Poor Mary.

[ROBIN's VOICE: 'Mother. Mother.']

How I wish all those people weren't coming.

MARY: It's too late to stop them now. It's a wonder the Howards aren't here already. They're always so punctual.

VICTOR: Mary, what do I say to Root? How do I behave in front of them? They don't know, but he does. How does a cuckold meet a lover the first time? It's funny how even now I depend on your advice.

MARY: I can't advise you.

VICTOR: You chose the furniture, you chose my shirts and my ties. I bring you patterns of my suits. You've always chosen for me. I'm lost when I'm not in my surgery. Mary, I can't live in a surgery.

[ROBIN's VOICE: 'Mother. Mother.']

MARY: I'll have to go. He won't stop until I do.

VICTOR: Mary, please stay with me.

MARY: Don't make me choose. I can't choose.

[ROBIN's VOICE: 'Mother.']

I'll have to go.

[*As* MARY *passes him* VICTOR *clutches her arm.*]

VICTOR: Have I got to meet him?

MARY: I can't put him off now.

VICTOR: I'm just not accustomed . . . I need you, Mary.

MARY: So does he.

VICTOR: He hasn't sixteen years of habit behind him.

[MARY *goes,* VICTOR *stands for a moment, then without thinking what he is doing he collapses on to the musical chair and puts his face in his hands.*

The chair starts playing 'Auld Lang Syne', but VICTOR *doesn't hear. He is crying behind his hands.*

As the music grinds to a close MARY *returns.*]

MARY: What on earth . . . ?

[*The music stops.*

MARY *goes to him and tries to pull his hands away, but he is ashamed of his tears.*]

Victor, please, Victor. Be angry. I'm an unfaithful wife. Victor. [*She kneels beside him.*] You have to divorce me. Please do something, Victor. I can't.

VICTOR [*taking his hands from his face*]: I'm sorry. The new girl, she's so careless. No oil of cloves. No guttapercha. It's been a bad day at the surgery. Just give me time to think.

[*The front door bell rings and* MARY *rises to her feet to go and greet her guests. The first to enter is* CLIVE. VICTOR *rises reluctantly. Both are at a loss.*]

CLIVE: Good evening.

VICTOR: Good evening.

CLIVE: I hope you had a good time in Amsterdam.

[*A pause.*]

VICTOR [*pulling himself together*]: Oh, for me, you know, it wasn't altogether a holiday. Work. There's always work. Sit down. Would you like a whisky or shall I mix you a dry Martini? I make good dry Martinis.

[*The bell is ringing again as*

THE CURTAIN FALLS]

SCENE TWO

The same scene about two hours later.

During the progress of the scene the light changes from late afternoon sun to dusk.

VICTOR sits at the dining-room table alone with an empty glass in front of him.

ROBIN comes in from the garden carrying some orange-squash at the bottom of a glass. He is about to go into the dining-room when he sees his father. He studies him from a distance, then turns back into the drawing-room.

MARY comes in from the hall.

MARY: Have you seen your father?

ROBIN [*he hardly hesitates*]: No.

MARY: The Morgans were looking for him to say good-bye. And now the Forsters are going. If you see him ask him to come outside. Tell him the party's nearly over.

ROBIN: OK.

MARY: And please, for heaven's sake, don't say OK again or I shall scream. [*She goes into the garden.*]

[*ROBIN goes back to the point where he can watch his father. Presently he speaks.*]

ROBIN: Father.

VICTOR: What is it?

ROBIN: They've run out of soda-water in the garden. Can I find some?

VICTOR: Of course.

[*ROBIN comes into the dining-room and opens the sideboard to find the syphon. When he finds it he syphons some soda into his orange-squash.*]

ROBIN: Mother's looking for you.

VICTOR: Yes?

ROBIN: I didn't tell her you were here.

VICTOR: Why? I'm not in hiding.

ROBIN: She said I was to tell you the party's nearly over.

VICTOR: Thank God for that.

ROBIN: Yes. It's not a very good party, is it, as parties go?

VICTOR: No?

ROBIN: There's a sort of mood around.

VICTOR: What kind of mood?

ROBIN: Like the last act in *Macbeth*. 'Tomorrow and tomorrow and tomorrow.'

VICTOR: Couldn't you be a bit more precise?

ROBIN: Everybody seems to be expecting something – something like the wood coming to Dunsinane.

VICTOR: You seem to know *Macbeth* very well.

ROBIN: Yes. I'm acting the Second Murderer at the end of term. But I may be the First Murderer yet because the First Murderer's got mumps.

VICTOR: Tell your mother I'll be out in a minute or two.

ROBIN: I needn't say I found you if you'd rather not. Why don't you go to the nursery? Nobody's going to use the tele. The programme's awful today. I'll bring you up a drink and some sandwiches.

VICTOR: I told you I'm not in hiding. And this isn't *Macbeth*. Please go and find your mother, Robin. I want to talk to her alone.

ROBIN: Today everybody wants to talk to everybody alone. Ann's following Mr Root like a hungry jackal, and Mr Root's dodging about trying to see Mother like a . . .

VICTOR: I don't want to know what Mr Root's like.

ROBIN [*sadly*]: I'm the only one nobody wants to be alone with. Not even Ann.

[*He is going out when* VICTOR *calls him back.*]

VICTOR: Robin. Come here, old chap.

[ROBIN *approaches.*]

I want to talk to you. [*He doesn't know what to say.*]

ROBIN: Yes?

VICTOR: Do you know a boy at your school called Adams?

ROBIN: Yes. He's got a gold plate in his mouth.

VICTOR: I put it in. Do you know him well?

ROBIN: Oh, pretty well.

VICTOR: Do you know about his family?

ROBIN: Oh yes, his father ran away with a girl who works in the Zoo.

VICTOR: Does he mind much?

ROBIN: Not very much. He said it was more fun in the old days.

VICTOR: Weren't there quarrels?

ROBIN: Oh, that was part of the fun. He said you never knew what was going to happen next. It's very quiet now, he says.

[*Pause.*]

VICTOR: Does he see his father?

ROBIN: He goes to a theatre with him every hols and he stays with him for two weeks in the summer. But he feels rather flat about that because the girl from the Zoo's never there. She used to look after Pets' Corner and he's passionately interested in pandas.

VICTOR: But he's quite happy – on the whole?

ROBIN: Not at the moment. He had a rat that died.

[*Pause.*]

VICTOR: The other day – you know that shop in Oxford Street – I saw a wonderful rat made of plastic.

ROBIN: Oh good. Did you buy it?

VICTOR: No. Your mother's a bit tired of my jokes.

ROBIN: I'm not. Wouldn't it be grand to have enough money to buy the whole stock? A different catch every day of the week for a year.

VICTOR: I think if I did that your mother would leave me.

ROBIN: Oh well, I expect we'd manage somehow together. Do you mind me saying OK?

VICTOR: I suppose in time I'd get tired of it too. Go and find your mother.

[MARY *has entered with the* HOWARDS *during the last of this dialogue.*]

MARY: Oh, Victor, that's where you've been hiding.

VICTOR: Not hiding.

MARY: The Forsters and Morgans went without saying good-bye, and here are William and Margaret. They're leaving too.

MRS HOWARD: It's been a lovely party. The sun's come out specially for you.

HOWARD: A change after last week. Record rainfall for the month. But of course you missed that.

VICTOR: It rained in Amsterdam too.

MARY: Robin, go and tell Ann her mother's leaving.

ROBIN: Where is she?

MRS HOWARD: She's by the rockery with Mr Root.

   [ROBIN *leaves*.]

HOWARD: You look all in, Victor. Never known you so quiet.

MARY: He's had a hard day.

HOWARD: Raking in the shekels. Lucky for you people aren't all like me. No trouble with *my* teeth. Every one false.

VICTOR: Then you ought to be careful of the gums.

HOWARD: He's always got an answer, hasn't he?

MARY [*covering for* VICTOR]: There's a new assistant. She's a bit careless. There's nothing more tiring than training a new girl.

MRS HOWARD: We won't wait for Ann, dear. Tell her we've gone on.

HOWARD: I don't know what she finds to say to that young man.

MRS HOWARD: I expect much the same as what I said to you. Years ago.

MARY: He's not so young. I'd like to see Ann with someone more her own age. He's too old for her. [*Her anxiety shows a little too much*.]

VICTOR [*with controlled anger*]: It's no concern of ours.

MRS HOWARD [*making peace*]: What lovely ear-rings, Mary. I've been admiring them all the evening. Did Victor give them to you?

MARY [*with the slightest hesitation*]: Yes.

HOWARD [*to* MRS HOWARD]: That's what comes of being a dentist. If I gave you diamonds I'd be suspected of embezzlement.

MRS HOWARD: If you gave me diamonds nobody would believe it. They'd think I had a lover.

HOWARD: Now we know why you chose Amsterdam, Victor. How did you work the currency, old fox?

VICTOR [*he can stand no more*]: I worked no currency. I'm not a black marketeer, William.

   [*He walks from the dining-room.*
     An embarrassed silence.]

HOWARD: Well, I am sorry. I never meant . . .

MARY: Nor did he. He's tired and worried, that's all.

HOWARD: I never thought I'd see Victor unable to take a joke. Do you remember a few weeks ago how he had to drink from his own dribbling-glass . . .

MRS HOWARD: We aren't always in the mood for jokes, William. Come along, dear, or you won't get any dinner.

HOWARD [*as they move out*]: You will tell him, won't you, that I never meant . . .

MARY [*going towards the door with them*]: Of course. Don't worry.

MRS HOWARD: Don't come, Mary. We'll let ourselves out.

> [*They leave.*
>
> MARY *goes immediately to the dining-room door and calls* 'Victor'. *A pause and she calls again* 'Victor.'
>
> CLIVE *followed by* ANN *comes from the garden.*]

CLIVE: He went to the garage.

MARY: Garage?

CLIVE: He said something about going for a drive.

MARY: How odd. He doesn't like driving. He never drives himself if he can help it.

CLIVE: Is something wrong?

MARY: Yes. [*She looks at* ANN.] He had bad news today. A letter from Holland.

CLIVE: I see.

MARY: Are you sure you do?

CLIVE: Yes.

MARY: How can you possibly know what was in the letter?

CLIVE: I can guess. Was he angry?

MARY: Not angry. If you want to know, he wept. I've never seen him weep before.

CLIVE: Ann, you'd better go home.

ANN: Why? I know what you're talking about.

CLIVE: Oh no, you don't. Even Mary doesn't.

MARY: What do you mean?

CLIVE: Christmas was too far off, Mary. I couldn't wait so long. I dictated the letter.

MARY: You . . . ?

CLIVE: I borrowed your room for the purpose. Don't you remember?

MARY: What a bastard you are.

ANN: Don't call him that.

MARY: Oh, go home, Ann. Please.

ANN: Why should I? This concerns me too.

MARY: How can it?

ANN: I happen to love Clive.

MARY: Love? My dear, that's a thing one can sometimes say after bed, but never before.

ANN: How I hate your experience.

MARY: Aren't you looking for it? Go and find it with someone of your own age. Clive's too used for you.

CLIVE: Mary!

MARY [*to* CLIVE]: Aren't you? Even I didn't expect this last clever stroke of yours. An anonymous letter to a husband. He's lived with wives too long, Ann. He's learned too many tricks.

ANN: You drove him to it.

MARY: If you took Clive on, you'd have to learn to love where you don't trust. Better wait a while. You'll be riper for him in a few years after you've been married too.

ANN [*to* CLIVE]: She calls you too used. Look at her. Can't you see what she's like now?

CLIVE: I see somebody I love and want, that's all.

MARY: You read too much Zane Grey, Ann. Clive isn't one of your great open spaces. He's more like an overcrowded town. Only I happen to love overcrowded towns. I like a tenement life. I'd be bored with prairies, and the only animal I love has got two backs, not four hooves. Call it *nostalgie de la boue* if you like.

ANN: I call it dirt. I'm free. I want to marry Clive.

MARY: Marriage is not all that clean.

[ANN *is crying.*]

Do you want a handkerchief?

[ROBIN *appears unnoticed from the garden.*]

ANN: Not one of yours.

[ANN *takes a handkerchief from her bag and accidentally drops a glass object that breaks.*

CLIVE *is going to stoop for it when she stops him.*]

Don't bother. It's only some nonsense her child gave me.

[ROBIN *comes forward and picks up the pieces in silence.*]

I'm sorry, Robin. I didn't mean . . .

[ROBIN *doesn't reply, but after gathering up the pieces, makes for the door.*]

Give them to me. I can stick them together again.

ROBIN: It doesn't matter. It didn't work anyway.

MARY: Where are you going?

ROBIN: To bed.

MARY: Where's your father?

ROBIN: In the garage.

MARY: Is he still there?

ROBIN: I heard him start the car, but he didn't come out.

[ROBIN *leaves the room.*

There is a pause. The thought of suicide has come to all three of them, but no one likes to speak first.]

CLIVE: I expect he's just fooling about with the engine. Cleaning it or something.

MARY: He never has before.

CLIVE: Would you like me to go and find him?

MARY: No, I'll go. [*But she doesn't move either.*] He wouldn't, would he, do anything silly?

CLIVE: Of course he wouldn't.

ANN: What are we standing here for? Somebody's got to go and see.

[*She starts for the garden.* CLIVE *goes after her and takes her arm.*]

CLIVE: Not you, Ann.

[*She pulls away from him, then stops in the window looking at something outside.*

VICTOR *enters.*

A pause.]

VICTOR: Hullo. What is it?

MARY: Where have you been?

VICTOR: In the garage. There are only two places where a man can be alone in his own house.

[*Another pause.*]

CLIVE [*to* ANN]: I'll see you down the street.

[ANN *says nothing. They walk to the door.*]

MARY: I'm sorry, Ann.

ANN: That seems to be the signature-tune today.

CLIVE [*at the door*]: I shall come back.

[CLIVE *and* ANN *leave.*]

MARY: You scared us. We half thought . . . Robin heard the engine running.

VICTOR: Yes?

MARY: Of course, I knew you wouldn't do anything silly really.

VICTOR: Silly is the operative word. I only wanted to be alone, so I sat in the car. Then I remembered something I had read in the papers. I turned the engine on. I shut the garage doors. But the word 'silly' came to my mind too, and the headline in the newspaper: 'Love Tragedy in West Drayton.' This isn't West Drayton, but the district is wrong for tragedy too.

MARY: How could you even have thought . . .

VICTOR: It's unfair, isn't it, that we're only dressed for a domestic comedy. A suicide looks better in a toga, and carbon monoxide poisoning is not exactly a Roman death. I thought of Macbeth.

MARY: Why Macbeth?

VICTOR: 'The way to dusty death.' Robin hopes to play the First Murderer at the end of term.

[*Pause.*]

MARY: What do you want me to do, Victor?

VICTOR: If I asked you to give him up, would you do it?

MARY: No.

VICTOR: I understand how you feel. You see I don't know how to give you up either.

MARY: Somebody has got to do something.

VICTOR: That's what I thought when I went out to the garage. But why should I be the one who acts? There are three of us.

MARY: Clive acted. He wrote that letter.

VICTOR: Clive wrote it?

MARY: I mean he dictated it to the valet.

VICTOR: Then why on earth did he write all that about windmills?

MARY: I didn't ask him. I'm sorry, Victor. It was a monstrous thing to do.

VICTOR: I dare say in his place I might have done the same. If I'd thought of it.

MARY: You wouldn't have. You are a good man. Victor, be glad you aren't married to a good woman. The good are horribly hard to leave.

[*Pause.*]

VICTOR: Does anybody have to leave? I can forget the letter, Mary. Just give me time. You needn't promise me anything.

MARY: It wouldn't work.

VICTOR: It can. Just don't make things too obvious locally, that's all? You don't hate me, do you?

MARY: Of course I don't hate you. I suppose I love you in my shabby way.

VICTOR: There's nothing shabby about it. It's different, that's all. When the real teeth fail – I'm sorry. Dentistry again.

MARY: One calls the others 'false' teeth.

VICTOR: If you go away for a holiday now and then, I won't ask you where.

MARY: There's always somebody who finds out.

VICTOR: That's my problem, not yours. They'll sympathize with you.

MARY: Clive would never agree. He told me that he couldn't bear to go on much longer like this. I asked him to go on till after Christmas, but then he wrote that letter.

VICTOR: If he loves you, he can go on. If I can.

MARY: It's a different love. If it is love. I don't care whether it is or not. I love him any way. It's like a sickness, one of those beastly women's diseases. It probably has a Latin name.

[*She is nearly crying and he puts his arms round her.*]

I've tried to cure it. Please believe that.

VICTOR: Don't worry, dear. I'll speak to him.

MARY: If I have to choose . . .

VICTOR: I know. You'll choose him.

MARY: I don't know. I don't want to choose. I don't want to leave you and the children, I don't want to leave him. Victor, dear Victor, why can't we sometimes, just once, have our cake and eat it?

VICTOR: I won't take away your cake, Mary. I'll be what they call a complaisant husband.

MARY: Three people have got to be complaisant. It needs a lot of strength.

VICTOR: I can stand it.

MARY: Yes, but can he?

[*The door opens and* CLIVE *comes in.* MARY *turns abruptly and goes out into the almost dark garden.*]

CLIVE: Well? This interview had to come, hadn't it? Sooner or later.

VICTOR: Yes. Just stay where you are for a moment. Under the light. Now open your mouth. There's just something – I'm afraid you don't have a very good dentist.

CLIVE: What are you talking about?

VICTOR: That filling in the upper canine – it shows too much. Like an old sardine tin. I would say that it's a very old-fashioned amalgam.

CLIVE [*unconsciously feeling with his finger*]: You mean it's a very old stopping?

VICTOR: Better have it done again.

CLIVE: But I can't bear that thing of yours – what d'you call it? The whizzy.

VICTOR: You wouldn't feel a thing. The nerve is probably dead – or I'd use pentothal. Ring up my secretary and make an appointment.

CLIVE: Thanks. Perhaps I will.

VICTOR: We're neither of us young men, Root. The appearance matters. Can I get you another whisky now the party's over?

CLIVE: No thanks. I came back to have a word . . .

VICTOR: With Mary? She'll be back in a moment. I think she's clearing up the mess in the garden. You know how it is after a party. Why not have another Scotch while you wait?

CLIVE [*hesitating*]: It's very kind of you. I haven't been in the mood . . .

[VICTOR *pours out two glasses of whisky.*]

VICTOR: Sit down.

[CLIVE *is about to sit down in the musical chair when* VICTOR *stops him.*]

Not in that chair. Oh, it doesn't matter. The tune's run out. [*He hands* CLIVE *a glass.*] This is good stuff. Black Label. I can only get two bottles a month. I keep it for special friends.

CLIVE: I wouldn't have called myself a special friend.

VICTOR: I think perhaps it would be better if you did. We shall see a great deal of each other from now on, and that is the best explanation, isn't it? Apart from the bookshop. Are dental first editions worth acquiring? Like Zane Greys?

CLIVE: I haven't heard of any.

VICTOR: Speaking as a special friend I wouldn't see too much of Ann. An impulsive child and too young for you.

CLIVE: Is that – quite – your business?

VICTOR: It worries Mary and anything that touches Mary is my business. It was very good of you by the way to give her those ear-rings. She looks beautiful in them.

CLIVE: Yes.

VICTOR: I liked you a lot better when I heard that you'd risked a black-market currency deal to get them for her.

CLIVE: Did she give you any details?

VICTOR: She said something about a currency specialist in Knightsbridge.

CLIVE: She oughtn't to have told you that.

VICTOR: Why? A man and wife don't have many secrets from each other. Except the unimportant ones.

CLIVE: It puts me in your hands.

VICTOR: How?

CLIVE: You could tell the police. I believe I might be put away for two years.

VICTOR: What a strange idea you have of me. It would be a very shabby return for two nice diamonds which I suspect you can't afford. I'm sorry she told the Howards that I had given them to her. She was only trying to protect me. Poor Mary.

CLIVE: Why poor?

VICTOR: You'll know her better in time. Then you'll realize the amount of protection she needs. You and I both have our work. She has no work except the family round. Children, servants, meals – it's not a real vocation. And so to make up she has to have – well, I'd call them illusions.

CLIVE: What illusions?

VICTOR: That she'll love someone for the rest of her life. Physically. In spite of that filling of the upper canine. I'm sorry. That's unfair. I don't suppose my filling would have been any better.

CLIVE: What did you do with the letter?

VICTOR: I tore it up. In time I shall even forget what it said.

CLIVE: I can give you all the evidence for a divorce you want.

VICTOR: I don't want a divorce. The only thing I ask you is to carry on your affair at a distance. You see there are the children to be considered. May I make a suggestion?

CLIVE: Of course.

VICTOR: Mary's mother is dead. Nobody around here knows that. She can be critically ill three or four times a year. If you require it. She lived in Pontefract not in Amsterdam. There's a very good Trust House in Pontefract.

CLIVE: Do you really expect us to live like that, not seeing each other except three or four times a year? In Pontefract?

VICTOR: My dear Clive – I'd better get accustomed to calling you Clive – I hope you'll dine with us almost every week.

CLIVE: No. I'm damned if I will. You can be a complaisant husband if you like, I'm not going to be a complaisant lover.

VICTOR: The two are inseparable.

CLIVE: Then I'm walking out. You won't be bothered with me any more.

VICTOR: If you walk out, I think she'll walk out with you.

CLIVE: But that's the best solution for all of us. Can't you see that?

VICTOR: For you and me perhaps. But we've only one object, you and I, to make it a degree less hard for her. I'll make the effort. Can't you do the same?

CLIVE: What makes you think she'd be happier – with the two of us?

VICTOR: The four of us. There's Robin and Sally. She told me herself she doesn't want to choose.

CLIVE: She wants to have her cake and eat it.

VICTOR: That's exactly what she said. Don't you love her enough to try to give her that kind of cake? A child's cake with silver balls and mauve icing and a layer of marzipan.

CLIVE: Bad for the teeth my nurse used to say.

VICTOR: Not for children's teeth.

CLIVE: You do really love her, don't you?

VICTOR: Yes, I do.

  [*Pause.*]

CLIVE: Me too. Is Pontefract a bracing climate?

[ROBIN's *voice begins to call:* 'Mother, Mother, Mother.']

I suppose you can supply me with the dates of the children's holidays and your dental dinners. I'm sorry. I'm trying to work my sourness off on you. I don't want her to feel it.

[MARY *comes in from the garden.*]

MARY: Robin's shouting from the bathroom. I suppose he's lost his soap.

VICTOR: I'll go and see.

[VICTOR *leaves by the dining-room. Neither speaks till he is gone.*]

MARY: He's talked to you?

CLIVE: Yes.

MARY: What have you decided?

CLIVE: He seems to have done the deciding for me.

MARY: A divorce?

CLIVE: No.

MARY: I suppose that means you are going to leave me.

CLIVE: No. I stay. Under his conditions.

MARY: Thank God.

CLIVE: Are you so pleased?

MARY: Yes.

CLIVE: You certainly must love him.

MARY: I love you too. Clive, can you blame me if I don't want to lose the past or the future? The past is sixteen years of myself and him, the future is even longer of you.

CLIVE: Longer than sixteen years? I doubt that.

MARY [*with complete conviction*]: It's until death, Clive.

[CLIVE *shakes his head.*]

Don't you believe me?

CLIVE: You haven't been to my school. You don't know the lessons I learnt a long time ago.

MARY: What do you know that I don't know?

CLIVE: The future. I'm not being sour, Mary. This is the sad truth, even though I've never loved anyone as much as you. I know that one day I shall get tired of going away at night and leaving you two together. I shall get tired of arranging our holidays to suit his convenience. I shall get tired of all the times when we have to cancel things at the last moment. And I shall get tired of waiting outside the shops in Paris or Brussels while you buy the children's shoes.

[VICTOR *comes back into the dining-room and, hearing their voices, hesitates.*]

MARY: And then you'll leave me?

CLIVE: No. Then, when you see how tired I am, you will leave me. That's what I dread.

MARY [*with fear*]: I don't believe it's true. I won't believe it's true. [*With confidence and returning gaiety.*] It needn't be true.

[VICTOR *comes into the drawing-room and joins them. He stands beside his wife. They are a pair.* CLIVE *is the odd man out.*]

VICTOR: If you'd like to stay for dinner, Clive – there are some cold left-overs.

CLIVE: No thank you. I must get back.

VICTOR [*it isn't easy for him to say it*]: Come on Thursday. No party. Just the three of us.

MARY: Yes, please come. [*In gratitude to her husband she puts her arm around him.*]

VICTOR: We'll open a bottle of good wine.

MARY: I'll buy it myself at the Army and Navy. What shall I get, Victor?

VICTOR: The Cheval Blanc '53 if he'll come. You will come?

[CLIVE *looks at the married pair and sadly accepts his fate.*]

CLIVE: Oh yes, I'll come. [*Pause.*] I expect I'll come.

[*He is turning to go as*

THE CURTAIN FALLS]

Postscript on Censorship

All praise must be given to the Lord Chamberlain who has at last admitted that homosexuality is a theme which may be presented on the English stage. Now we have some reason to hope that in the course of one or two more decades heterosexuality may also be permitted. In the meanwhile readers of this play may have a little fun determining which solitary adjective and which passage of three lines the Lord Chamberlain and his officers have found too indecent for the theatre.

CARVING A STATUE

★

EPITAPH FOR A PLAY

Never before have I known a play like this one so tormenting to write or so fatiguing in production. I am glad to see the end of it, and to that extent I am grateful to the reviewers who may have a little accelerated the end. At the age of sixty there is no reason to work, except to earn a living or to have 'fun'. This play was never fun and I earn my living in another field.

All the same the faults the reviewers find in it are curiously different from the faults I find, which are harder faults to defend, and I may be forgiven perhaps for not pointing them out. I was accused of over-lading the play with symbols, but I have never cared greatly for the symbolic and I can detect no symbols in this play; sometimes there is an association of ideas which perhaps the reviewers mistook for the symbolic – the accurate use of words is difficult, as I know from my own experience as a theatre reviewer, when one writes against time.

I remember that when my film *The Third Man* had its little hour of success a rather learned reviewer expounded its symbolism with even less excuse in a monthly paper. The surname of Harry Lime he connected with a passage about the lime tree in Sir James Frazer's *Golden Bough*. The 'Christian' name of the principal character – Holly – was obviously, he wrote, closely connected with Christmas – paganism and Christianity were thus joined in a symbolic dance. The truth of the matter is, I wanted for my 'villain' a name natural and yet disagreeable, and to me 'Lime' represented the quick-lime in which murderers are said to be buried. An association of ideas, not, as the reviewer claimed, a symbol. As for Holly, my first choice of name had not met with the approval of the American 'star' who considered that the name had (by God knows what association of ideas) a homosexual ring. So I looked through an anthology of bad American verse in search of a prename, and found Holly – Thomas Holly Chivers had some renown in the nineteenth century. So much for symbols.

Other reviewers, because the word God frequently crops up, thought that my play contained that dreaded thing, 'theology'. Theology is the only form of philosophy which I enjoy reading and if one of these reviewers had ever opened a work of theology, he would have quickly realized that there was nothing theological in this play.

What is it about then? I have always believed that farce and tragedy are far more closely allied than comedy and tragedy. This play was to me a game played with the same extremes of mood as *The Complaisant Lover*. The first act is, almost completely, farce: the sculptor was based on Benjamin Robert Haydon, who was obsessed – to the sacrifice of any personal life – by the desire to do great Biblical subjects, already, even in his day, out of fashion. You cannot read the diaries of Haydon without realizing that he had a true daemon and yet he had no talent at all – surely a farcical character, though he came to a tragic end. In my story, as I intended it, the artist lost even his tragic end – no Tom Thumb was capable of shattering permanently his dream and driving him to the saving bullet. He had a greater capacity to recover than poor Haydon.

Graham Greene

CHARACTERS

THE FATHER   THE SECOND GIRL

HIS SON   DR PARKER

THE FIRST GIRL

CAST

Carving A Statue, produced by Peter Wood, with scenery by Desmond Heeley, was first presented at the Haymarket Theatre, London, on 17 September 1964 with the following cast:

THE FATHER	Ralph Richardson
HIS SON	Dennis Waterman
THE FIRST GIRL	Barbara Ferris
THE SECOND GIRL	Jane Birkin
DR PARKER	Roland Culver

SCENES

Act One

A studio in South London.

Act Two

Studio, six weeks later.

Act Three

Studio, a month later.

Act One

An early evening. The scene some suburb south of the Thames on the main road to Brighton. There are moments when we are aware of the heavy traffic outside. When the CURTAIN RISES *the stage is bare of scenery except for various props, which should belong naturally to a sculptor's studio: not a very good sculptor. Perhaps the room was once an old garage. This is not a realistic play, and the characters would seem out of place in a built-up set. A very tall ladder of an exaggerated height is propped up off-centre against a rough stone block surrounded by scaffolding, both ladder and block disappearing out of our view towards an unseen platform (there is an arrangement of pulleys by which the head of the statue can be lowered or raised). The foot of the block has been carved into primitive gigantic feet that stand on a wheeled plinth and reach the height of a stool from the floor. On a table stands a bad plaster copy of Michelangelo's Pietà. On a wall is pinned a reproduction of Holman Hunt's 'Light Of The World' and a big photo of a carving by Henry Moore, one of his recumbent women. Near the footlights stands a magic-lantern. A tarpaulin can be raised across the statue to form a screen. A short staircase right ends on a small landing and a door into the rest of the house. On the left is the door of a tool-shed, and at the back big doors open into a yard. A work-bench on the right.*

There is a sound of chipping from above and small fragments of stone fall on the stage. The figure out of sight coughs, mutters, expectorates and sometimes lets out an oath. The time is evening.

> [*A* BOY *of about 15 or 16 enters carring a tray with two bottles of beer, a loaf of bread and a tin of salmon. He puts the tray on the work-bench and calls up.*]

BOY: Father! [*The chipping goes on.*] Father! I've brought your tea. I could only get brown bread. [*He drops a piece of bread on the floor.*] Oh sakes, we need a woman in the house. [*A long pause while he goes and regards the sandwiches and feels the temperature of the beer. He begins to cut sandwiches.*] Don't you think there's a

chance, just a chance, you might come to marry again? Your
heart's not broken, is it? It's not mother's fault she died the way
she did. Mr Muggeridge has married again. For the third time.
Cancer happens to one in six. I read that in the Christmas
number of the *Literary Digest*. [*A long pause and then defiantly*]
Father, please come down. You've been up there for nine
hours. It's *Spam*, father. I'm going to eat one of the sandwiches.
I'm hungry too. There was nothing but yesterday's kipper for
lunch and half a hard-boiled egg.

> [*This is to attract his father's attention. He is still busy with the
> sandwiches.*]

I'm starting now. I've got my teeth well into it. [*Pause.*] I'm
chewing. I'm chewing hard.

VOICE FROM ABOVE: Don't go and eat more than your fair share.
I'm hungry too.

BOY: I won't eat more than half.

VOICE: Don't you eat more than a quarter. You're only a quarter
my age. If that.

BOY: I'm growing.

VOICE: So am I.

> [*The ladder shakes and slowly the* FATHER *descends into sight,
> holding the ladder with one hand, tools in the other. A heavy figure,
> badly shaved. He is covered, hair, face and all, with the dust of
> stone. He might almost be a statue himself. He pauses about four
> steps from the ground and gazes up.*]

FATHER: You can see the expression of His right eye now, quite
clear. He's coming. He's coming at last.

BOY: It's about time he came. I've known him all my life like that.

FATHER: If you had stayed as you were when your mother got you
I would never have been landed with Him. I needed you badly
as a model then. But you grew too quick. Before I had the folds
of a nappy right, your mother had put you into shorts. A virgin
and child would have been finished long before this.

BOY [*looking up*]: There's a wicked glint in the old fellow's eye.

FATHER: Why wouldn't there be? He made the world.

> [*The* FATHER *takes a sandwich and begins to eat.*] I thought you
> said it was Spam.

BOY: It is.

FATHER: It tastes like tinned salmon.

BOY: I suppose there was some tinned salmon mixed up with it. [*Pause.*] It's a disordered household, father.

FATHER [*looking up*]: There's no disorder here that I can see.

BOY: The place could do with a clean all the same.

FATHER: I'll never suffer a woman fussing around in my studio. [*They both eat.*]

I suffer enough as it is – with Him.

BOY: Did you suffer when mother died?

[*The FATHER pours himself out a glass of beer.*]

FATHER: It was a shocking inconvenience.

BOY: But I suffered?

FATHER: You were too young to suffer. I think I'll turn to Guinness for a week or two. Carving a statue takes a lot out of a man. Remember to buy a case when you do the shopping tomorrow. [*He can't keep his eyes for long off the invisible face. He regards it while he munches a sandwich.*]

BOY: Do you know, sometimes I've wished you were an ordinary man. Then you could have explained things to me here at home. At my school the teachers talked too fast. You don't know any mathematics. Why should you? A blackboard puts the fear of death in you. Blackboard. Black book. Black night. Black deed. What's the act of darkness, father? [*He gets no answer. He moves towards the back of the stage, sandwich in hand.*] I was top in geography. I liked cities with Spanish names and rivers that die out in dotted lines . . .

FATHER [*preoccupied*]: The right eye's not quite as it should be yet. It's not easy working without a living model. You've got to have a very vivid imagination.

BOY [*pointing at the Henry Moore*]: What kind of a model did *he* have?

FATHER: He and I belong to different schools of religious art.

BOY: I wish you had come to my school just once. I used to boast about you, but nobody believed me. I needed evidence.

FATHER: At least I've got real power into the feet. I've done that. And I've got a *bit* of wickedness into His right eye . . .

BOY: The boys with mothers were always a step ahead of the rest of us.

FATHER: The trouble is – He isn't only power. He isn't only wickedness . . . Did He love? Didn't He love? What's love? There's the tricky question.

BOY: We loved you, mother and me.

FATHER: I can't avoid the question like Michelangelo did. [*He indicates the Pietà.*] The Son's dead. It's easy to love the dead – they cause no trouble. But they say He loved the world. They say He even loved his son. It was a queer way He showed it though.

BOY: Did I love mother, father?

FATHER: The feet are right. I defy anyone to question the feet. He's taken a strong purchase like a man with an iron bar in a circus.

BOY: They are comfortable anyway. We've been sitting on them a long time now, and we haven't got piles yet.

FATHER: The knees are an awful problem. He never knelt. His son knelt, and His son's mother knelt, but it's never recorded that He ever knelt. What would He kneel to?

BOY: He sounds rheumatic to me.

FATHER: It's an interesting point of anatomy. A knee is made to bend. If the knee never bends what kind of a knee is it? How do you represent it?

BOY: Perhaps he didn't have any knees.

FATHER: He has to have knees. He made us in His image. Knees and other things. [*Pause.*] What a part He must have had to engender the whole world.

BOY: Heart?

FATHER: I only have to carve what shows. All the same how do you carve a contradiction? He has to be wicked and He has to be loving at the same time and He can't suffer or He wouldn't have sent His son down here to die. He wiped out the whole world except Noah without blinking one stony eyelid. The Egyptians were drowned in the Red Sea like so many Chinamen. Of course I can understand His attitude. I wouldn't exactly suffer if I broke Him up with a crowbar. I would be free of Him as He was free of His son. I suppose I'd feel a bit of waste, that's all. I've been at Him now for fifteen years. Perhaps He felt the same, after all the centuries, when the atom bombs dropped or the plagues came, and the earthquakes . . . A sense of waste, yes. But I wouldn't go so far as to say He suffered.

[*A pause while they both take more sandwiches.*]

BOY: Dr Parker said that mother suffered. I can remember listening outside the door and I heard Dr Parker say to the nurse 'She's gone. It's a good thing she's gone. She suffered terribly.' Where were you, father?

FATHER: Perhaps the knees are not required under the circumstances. Or I could put in embryo knees, like a child in the womb has embryo gills, because if all had gone well with the world, who knows? He might have knelt – in a sort of satisfaction. But it didn't work out that way.

BOY: Is unhappiness the same thing as suffering? Or is suffering something worse? I cried. I didn't scream. Mother screamed. I was unhappy at first when they wouldn't keep me at school. I was failed in Latin. Failed in mathematics. A bad report on conduct. What exactly did they mean by conduct, father?

[*The* FATHER *fills his glass again. He holds it to the light, then drains it.*]

You might answer me. You're too damned preoccupied.

FATHER: It's a terrible thing to have nobody anywhere who has any idea what I'm trying to do.

[*The* BOY *puts his hand out as though he would touch his* FATHER *to show sympathy, but his hand meets a sandwich on the way.*]

Take another sandwich if you are really hungry. But it's a mistake to over-eat at your age. Whatever that may be.

[*The* BOY *takes a sandwich to please his father but doesn't eat it.*]

Sometimes up that ladder I get the vertigo. The floor sways like a sea: I want to plunge, but if I plunged . . .

BOY: You'd drown?

FATHER [*with horror*]: I'd swim. [*A pause.*] Give me another sandwich. [*The sandwich is passed back.*] It *is* tinned salmon. What have you done with all the Spam?

BOY: It went.

FATHER: What do you mean *went*?

BOY: You must have eaten it.

FATHER: I don't eat a tin a day. Who told you to buy tinned salmon anyway? It's boys' food. I have to nurse my strength for work like this. I'm getting old. It was a good thing your mother left me an annuity – enough to keep the two of us.

BOY: In a year or two I could have been earning money for both of us, but it's an awful handicap when you've failed at everything. Even conduct, whatever that may be. I'd like to be a sailor. A first mate on the South American run. I wouldn't have to worry then about what's going to happen to the two of us later. Father, I do worry . . .

FATHER: Worry? [*The* FATHER *is astonished.*] We needn't worry. She left enough to keep us till I die. [*Pause.*] The biggest problem of all is that left eye of His. The right is power and wickedness. But I have to represent a bit of softness in the left. The baby Moses in the bulrushes, while all the plagues of Egypt boil in the other pupil.

[*Pause.*]

BOY: The baby in the bulrushes? The best story in the Bible.

FATHER: He took such care of the child, launching him in that little boat of rushes. The small round belly with the navel like a thumb-mark in clay and the fingers clenched like snails and the tight closed eyes. When the eyes opened they saw a princess of Egypt bending down. He'd arranged it all to the last detail. [*Pause.*] A popular novelist couldn't have done better. [*He stares up the ladder.*] I've got the plagues of Egypt glaring away up there. That's certain. But what infernal chisel stroke do I use for love?

BOY: Did you love mother?

FATHER: Give me another sandwich.

BOY: You've finished them. What did she look like?

FATHER: Who?

BOY: Mother.

FATHER: Like a woman. What do you expect?

BOY [*moving towards the Henry Moore*]: Like her?

FATHER: Your mother wasn't so robust.

BOY: I can't remember anything about her. Not her eyes. Not her hair. Only a smell. My soap smells of her. Why didn't you make a statue of mother?

[*The* FATHER *doesn't answer and the* BOY *continues.*]

I saw a girl at the corner yesterday. She looked pretty. She was fair and her hair was tied in a pony-tail, and she had green eyes.

FATHER: When I've got His head done the body's going to be a big problem. I don't want swirling draperies. That's old Roman hat. He ought to be clothed in the wind and the waves with a touch of fire too. Some people would say I'm a thought too ambitious.

BOY: I went across to the girl.

FATHER: What girl?

BOY: The girl I was telling you about.

FATHER: Michelangelo was never afraid of ambition. Nor Rodin.

BOY: She ran away. I wanted to say Hullo to her. I had some chocolate with me. Fruit and nut. Why did she run away? I don't look like Dracula, do I?

FATHER: There are only three subjects proper for a sculptor. A virgin, a son, and Him. And even Michelangelo never attempted to sculpt Him. It's a terrible thing to be landed with the most difficult of the three by no fault of my own. I meant to work up to Him gradually. Beginning with the virgin.

BOY: I've never got it quite clear about virgins.

FATHER: I was going to use your mother's face. She had a sort of bewildered look as though the Angel Gabriel was at the window making rude signs. I'd examined a lot of other faces, but somehow they weren't right . . . They were on the look-out, knowing too much, or else they were plain stupid.

BOY: Did you start a statue of her?

FATHER: I hadn't even time to buy the stone I needed. We were in here at the time and I was explaining some things to her. Then she put out the light and you began.

BOY: But afterwards?

FATHER: Her face was different afterwards.

BOY: The girl I saw in the street, would she be a virgin, do you suppose?

FATHER: I have a nightmare sometimes, when I've eaten cheese for dinner, that those feet may not be right after all.

[A pause while he stands and regards them.]

They are the feet of a man balancing an iron bar all right. But that fellow up there – He's supposed to be balancing the universe.

BOY: It's a real problem.

FATHER: There are easy ways out if you let the stone dictate to you, but I don't believe in abstract art. I'm a realist. Like Michelangelo. [*He walks to the Holman Hunt.*] Holman Hunt was a realist too. The light of the world. What a subject! But he didn't get it even half correct. That's not the light of the world. That's lamplight on Campden Hill. He lived at Tor Villa and watched the way the light shone above the front door when Burne-Jones came to dinner. I keep it hanging there as an awful warning. I've practised with the iron bar, but I can't practise with the universe. It's a hard thing to be a realist if you have ambition. Michelangelo, Rodin and me. Nobody can deny we try to do big things.

BOY: The milkman says he's much too big – but then the milkman's not a cultivated man.

FATHER: I could have tackled the virgin and son quite easily. I knew what a virgin was. I knew what a son was – more or less. I'd have needed a couple of years perhaps. If your mother had been a bit more patient I'd have had the virgin roughed in before the trouble started, and all she had to do then was keep the baby small for long enough. I wanted to put gin in the milk, but she said gin gave the baby colic.

BOY: What's colic?

FATHER: But what kind of a model can you have for the Father? He's the real difficulty.

BOY: You're a father.

[*It isn't often the* BOY *attracts his* FATHER's *attention. But this time he succeeds.*]

FATHER: Yes. Yes. I suppose I am. I did do a sketch of myself once in the looking-glass. But I couldn't picture Him badly shaved.

BOY: You could have shaved for once.

FATHER: Anyway I thought it might seem a bit conceited to use myself as a model. I produced you, but you aren't exactly the world.

BOY: Mother said I was to her.

FATHER: Women exaggerate. I tried some models for the Father.

For example Mr Muggeridge at 27 Nell Gwyn Avenue, but he couldn't sit still for more than half an hour without a cigar in his mouth. God the Father with a cigar – it wasn't suitable. Then there was Henry Tomlinson from Elm Park Road. I was getting on well with him in charcoal – he had a kind of patient expression. Unlike Muggeridge. But then all the rumours reached me. It was said he wasn't a father at all. His wife had been carrying on for years with Mr Watkins of the Midland Bank. So I thought of trying Watkins instead, but the situation was delicate. It was then I thought of photos. That's been done before by painters. Sickert for example. He was not a man of my ambition, but you can learn from lesser men.

BOY: What exactly is a virgin, father? Of course I know more or less – but then bicycling comes into it.

FATHER: I've got a box of fathers over there. Maybe I'm getting stale and it's time to look at them again. [*He points at the table on which the magic lantern stands. A lot of old cardboard-boxes are on a tray below the table-top.*]

BOY: Can I look at them?

FATHER: There's no interest in them for you. You aren't a sculptor. God knows what you'll ever be.

BOY: A sailor.

FATHER: You can't even tie a knot.

BOY: Oh yes I can. If I had a rope here I'd show you. I know ten different knots.

FATHER: You'd better be a hangman then, while there's still a demand. I tried a murderer for a model once. He's there. In the biggest box. It's marked with an F. F for fathers. That's the one. There's a life-time's collection there. Light the lamp and put on the slides slowly. I want to refresh my memory. [*The* BOY *prepares the lantern.*] I've taken snaps of my friends. I've torn pictures out of the papers. I've found slides in junk shops. Perhaps I should have continued with Henry Tomlinson – but he was only one man, and one man's of little use to me. Michelangelo dissected dozens of corpses before he knew his way around. In that box I've tried to trap the *state* of being a father. In all its aspects. [*He goes and turns out the studio light.*] Put on a slide, boy.

[*An Edwardian photograph appears on the screen of a man with a big black moustache leaning over a frilly child's cot.*]

BOY: What's his name?

FATHER: How would I know? He's one of the junk shop ones. I didn't take to him – his moustache doesn't help. Next.

[*The next slide is difficult to make out since it's upside down.*]

BOY: Sorry.

[*The* BOY *makes an effort to change it, but the* FATHER *stops him.*]

FATHER: Leave it as it is. I meant it that way. The Grand Duke of Lichtenstein. He belongs to my abstract period. You can't have anything much more abstract than royalty upside down. Next.

[*The next photo is one of Landru.*]

Now that's an interesting face. Even the beard had possibilities. Something Assyrian in it. 'When the Assyrian came down like a wolf on the fold.'

BOY: Who was he?

FATHER: He killed a lot of women in France and burnt their bodies in a stove. He's got a wonderfully wicked glint. That gave me an idea for the right eye. But all the same he wasn't entirely satisfactory as a character. He killed a few women, but they were all strangers to him. He lacked the intimate touch. He didn't kill his son. Next slide.

[*The slide shows a man in a straw hat leaning over Brighton Pier.*]

Ah! His name was Davies and I thought I had a real find there. He *had* killed his son. Some question of insurance money and the boy was sick in any case. He was acquitted – the jury found it culpable neglect – and he took a holiday at Brighton. I tracked him down there and quite believed at last I'd found my model. The child had cried out as he lay sick – I read it all in the *News of the World* – 'Father, father, don't leave me alone,' and I thought of Eloi, Eloi, lamma sabacthani. I got him to tell me the story over the third Guinness at Henneky's bar with a piano playing. He wasn't ashamed – and that was godlike of him. He didn't suffer any more than God suffers. (The theologians deny that possibility.) I persuaded him to be photographed on Palace Pier, for here at last, I thought, was a man made in God's image. Don't worry about the straw hat – I'd have discarded it. But leaning there, looking at the to and fro of the waves and the floats bobbing from the anglers' lines and the great sun shining on the Steine, he failed me utterly. He said he was moving house because the neighbours talked. The neighbours. God doesn't move house when a whole nation dies. Put on the next slide.

BOY: But, father . . .

FATHER: They're all fathers. Next slide I said.

[*The next is a slide of a man playing cricket with his children.*]

BOY: Are those his children?

FATHER: I assume so. Junk shop again.

BOY: He's playing with them.

FATHER: A poor type. That fellow up there gave us free will. He threw us into the water, to sink or swim. It's consonant with human dignity. But that man's trying to *teach* his children. He's brain-washing them into cricket. I never made you play cricket, did I?

BOY: No. [*Pause.*] You aren't that much interested, are you?

FATHER: My time is fully occupied.

BOY: If I got sick and died . . .

FATHER: They say He likes us dead. [*The* FATHER *gets up and wipes his mouth. He stretches.*] Time to call it a day.

BOY: Last night I saw a child crying in a room across the street. He must have had a nightmare. Sometimes I have one too. Do you ever have a nightmare, father?

FATHER: He's my only nightmare, and He's there by day.

BOY: I used to be scared when I was alone in the house. When you were out looking for fathers. Sometimes I woke crying like that child. Years ago when I was young, of course.

FATHER: It's a long time since I did any research. I get nothing out of those slides now.

BOY: The door opened and a man came in. He picked the child out of bed and set him on his knee. I think he was telling a story because presently I could see them laughing. It must have been a terribly good story. Do you suppose he was the father?

FATHER: How would I know? Put away the slides. In the right order. I don't want them all mixed up.

[*The* BOY *puts on another slide. A man with a pair of binoculars half lowered, gazing hard.*]

BOY: Here's Dr Parker. Is he a father?

FATHER: There are rumours, but no real evidence. I did consider him once. His victims die often enough, like His.

BOY: Is he at the races?

FATHER: No. He's birdwatching. In every sense of the word.

[*The* BOY *puts away the slides.*]

BOY: Here's a box marked V, father. Was that when you were planning to carve a virgin? Where are you going, father?

FATHER: Out.

BOY: Can I come with you?

FATHER: No. It's my time for reflection.

BOY: Is mother's picture in the box marked V?

[*The* FATHER *finds an ancient bowler hat and puts it on, dusting it first.*]

FATHER [*turning and looking at the statue*]: Tomorrow I'll get to work on that left eye. It's a terrible problem I've set myself. Sometimes I wish I'd been to art-school like the others and learnt their facility. It's an awful thing to work out everything from the beginning for yourself.

BOY: Which is mother's picture?

FATHER: Get to bed in good time, boy. [*Pause.*] But suit yourself. It's up to you. Tomorrow remember to get the Guinness. And don't forget the Spam.

BOY: Please, father, which slide?

FATHER: What a fuss you make about nothing. There are only three slides in that box anyway. She's there, that's all I know – she's one of them.

BOY: Good night, father. I expect I'll be asleep when you get back. [*He goes out.*]

[*The* BOY *hesitates a moment and then opens the box. He takes out the slides: there are only three of them. He tries holding one of them up to the light, but the light is not sufficient. He turns on the lamp of the lantern again and turns out the light of the studio and inserts a slide. What appears is some banal reproduction from a Murillo painting – a lifeless sentimental face of a Virgin and Child. He gives a sigh, a shake of the head, and substitutes a second slide. This is a photograph of a little dead girl spread-eagled in a road – perhaps it is a blitz photograph, perhaps one from the Spanish War, perhaps*] *from the battle of Warsaw. The* BOY *exclaims with horror and approaches the screen. He stares a long time at the picture, then kneels before it and tenderly touches the face.*]

BOY: Who are you? Are you alive? No, you're dead, aren't you? Dead as mutton. Dead as a door-nail. Dead as mother. Or are you asleep? Be asleep and I'll tell you a story, and when you wake up, you'll be happy again. I'll tell you about my father. He's big and strong and gentle too. For nine hours every day he lives up there, thinking of God and every evening he comes down here to me and we talk to each other. About everything in the world. Have you a father? He can be your father too. He's a man as high as a mountain – [*he looks up towards the head of the statue out of sight*] – with a heart as deep as a lake. Nothing bad ever comes where he is, and nothing will ever hurt you again. You'll be safe here. There are no sudden noises to frighten you, and the rushing cars are faint and far away on the road to Reigate. He'll say, 'Stay with us forever', and you'll say 'Forever' and the man as high as a mountain . . .

[*His* FATHER *comes in. He picks up the empty beer bottle.*]

BOY: Who is she, father?

FATHER: One of the junk shop ones. [*He begins to fill the beer crate.*]

FATHER: I may as well take the empties. I'm going that way. I saw Watkins on the road just now with Mrs Tomlinson and Tomlinson a while after looking patient as usual. I wouldn't be surprised if I found Muggeridge in the saloon bar smoking his big cigar. Outside the tube there was Dr Parker watching the typists coming home, carrying their little cases. The place seems to swarm with fathers of a kind today. You'd think I could get a good idea for Him and his left eye with all those fathers around.

BOY: When will you be back, father?

FATHER: I don't know.

BOY: Tonight?

FATHER: How can I tell? I told you I've got to do some research. I need a fresh idea.

BOY: What about the Spam and Guinness?

FATHER: That's your department.

BOY: I'm sorry.

FATHER: I have to be on my own when I think about Him.
　　　　[*He goes out. A pause.*]
BOY [*with his face close to the dead child*]: Oh sakes, sweetheart, I
　　could do with a woman in the house.

CURTAIN

Act Two

The same scene six weeks later. A sunny afternoon. The head of the statue, which is carved from a second block of stone, has been lowered by pulleys and stands in front of the main block. The main block has been pulled round by a winch to make room for it, and we now see it from another angle. Little work has been done. The right eye is out of sight of us. The left eye has been carved roughly out, but it's hardly an eye yet — a blank orb. One side of the head has not been worked on at all and is nearly flat stone. This is uppermost.

> [*The* BOY *enters cautiously through the yard doors and looks around. He has a bottle of sherry under his arm and he carries two half-pint glasses. He puts them down by the statue and calls out towards the wings.*]

BOY: It's all clear.

> [*The* FIRST GIRL *enters.*]

I told you I saw him go out.

> [*The* GIRL's *hair is rumpled and wet after a bathe. She wears blue jeans and a shirt. A towel is slung over her shoulder. Her speech has picked up many Americanisms from the movies. She has an air of toughness, but perhaps she is more vulnerable and inexperienced than she appears.*]

GIRL: I'm not afraid of the old boy. I don't like scenes, that's all. They're crummy. [*Seeing the statue.*] God Almighty, what's this?

BOY: God Almighty.

GIRL: Where does he think he's going to put it up? In Trafalgar Square?

BOY: I never thought to ask him. It's a problem, isn't it? Perhaps there'd be room in Hyde Park. By the Albert Memorial.

> [*The* GIRL *is roaming the studio. She stops at the Henry Moore photograph.*]

GIRL: Boy oh boy, did he make that one too?

BOY: No. That belongs to a different school.

GIRL: Some diaphragm she'd need.

BOY: Diaphragm?

　　[*She stops at the Holman Hunt.*]

GIRL: Mum had that one hanging on the wall when I was a kid. Good King Wenceslas, isn't it? [*She comes to the table where the magic lantern stands and picks up a box.*] Here's fun. What are these? Strip-tease? What does V stand for?

BOY: Virgins.

GIRL: Your Dad's got a proper dirty mind, hasn't he? [*She opens the box.*] He's only got three.

BOY: One of them's my mother.

GIRL: Your mother? What a family! [*She tries to look at a slide, but there's not enough light.*]

BOY [*sharply*]: Not that one.

GIRL: Is it sexy? It looks as if she's lying down.

　　[*The* BOY *snatches the slide.*]

BOY: If you promise not to touch any of them I'll show you my mother.

GIRL: I don't want to see your mother. I hate family photos.

BOY: But I want you to see her. There's something very strange . . . [*He begins to prepare the lantern.*]

GIRL: If you only knew all the photos Dad shows you'd yawn your head off. Mum in Paris. Mum in Ostend. Mum's got width and you can't properly see Ostend. [*The* BOY *chooses one slide, rejecting two.*] Mum on a camel – it was only the zoo at Margate really. And colour films. Mum in Kodachrome. You can't see the sky when Mum's wearing blue.

BOY: Pull down that blind. [*He prepares the lantern.*] Over there. Just above your head. It's something very odd you're going to see now.

GIRL: You are getting me good and scared. If this is what they call an artistic family . . . They aren't vampires, are they? V for vampires. Hold my hand. [*The* BOY *gives her his left hand while he prepares the slide with the other.*] Are you a teenage werewolf – because you're sticky. Gosh, it's not human blood, is it?

BOY: It's only sherry.

GIRL: We ought to have another drink before we see any horror

films. It's always an X certificate for virgins. The Vampire and
the Virgin. The Violated Virgin.

BOY: There's nothing to be scared of.

GIRL: The Violated Virgin Vampire.

BOY: It's my mother. That's all.

GIRL: The Daughter of the Violated Virgin Vampire.

[*The* BOY *puts on the wrong slide and the dead child appears.*]

Mercy! What's this? Did your Dad do her in?

[*The* BOY *quickly removes the slide.*]

BOY: I got the slides mixed up. You confused me.

GIRL: Are all his virgins dead ones?

[*The picture of his mother appears on the screen: a young and pretty
woman with her hair in a knot above her head.*]

BOY: There.

GIRL: Is that all?

BOY: Don't you notice anything?

GIRL: No.

BOY: Look at her face.

GIRL: She's sort of pretty.

BOY: Put your hair up a moment.

GIRL: Why?

BOY: I want you to.

[*She obeys him, screwing it carelessly up.*]

There. You are the living spit of her.

GIRL: Me? You're crazy.

BOY: You can't see yourself. I can. You've got her nose and her
chin. You've got her eyes.

GIRL: Make no mistake, young fellow. I'm not the mother type.

BOY: She wasn't a mother when father took that.

GIRL: Did she want to have you?

BOY: How do I know?

GIRL: Boy, if I got caught . . . Where is she now?

BOY: She died of cancer. In awful agony. In her tender twenties.
Attended by Dr Parker.

GIRL: You talk as if she was someone in a book. Didn't you mind
when she died?

BOY: Father says I was too young to care.

GIRL: And the old man?

BOY: He was too busy to care. You can pull the blind up now.

GIRL: Let's leave the lantern on. It's more romantic that way. With your mother watching over our revels. Come on – we'll have a drink with the old mischief maker.

> [*She goes to the statue and pours out two glasses. They sit down under the head.*]

BOY: We had to lay the head down like this because we needed the ladder for the roof. The rain was dripping through the ceiling. We thought of bringing the beds down here.

GIRL: It's a pity you didn't. [*She hums a little, looking sideways at him.*]

BOY: Father said he couldn't live with him night and day. He's in one of his non-working spells and when that happens he can't bear the thought of him. He keeps away. He hasn't done a stroke of work for six weeks now.

GIRL: What does your Dad do when he stops like that?

BOY: Well – sometimes he looks at the slides – not often, because they are too familiar, and *he* sits there, father says, like a reproach. Sometimes he has a pint of bitter at the Craven Arms. That's so he can reflect a bit, he often likes to reflect. Sometimes he wanders around, looking for models.

GIRL: Girls?

BOY: No, fathers. He's been looking at fathers for nearly sixteen years now. He can't find exactly what he wants. There's always something wrong. A moustache. A cigar. Too many people wear spectacles, he says, and he can't take them off because that wouldn't be realism.

GIRL: Doesn't he ever find a girl?

BOY: God Almighty's not a girl.

GIRL: I mean on a day off.

BOY: He's too much concerned with *him*. He thinks of him even when he's drinking bitter. I wouldn't be surprised if father was a genius. In his own way. Because he doesn't think about ordinary things – except sometimes he gets deadly tired of tinned salmon.

GIRL: It's a hell of a long time sixteen years to chip at a bit of stone.

BOY [*trying hesitantly a new word*]: He's – dedicated.

GIRL: Oh boy what an explosion there'd be if he quit work for a while and started thinking of girls. My sister was crazy about a sailor once – she said after three months at sea he was like fireworks and champagne. I'd have liked to know a sailor too. And all the tricks he learnt in foreign ports.

[*She takes another glass and gives him one. They drink.*]

I wish it was champagne.

BOY: I hadn't the money for champagne.

GIRL: We'll imagine it's champagne. [*She pours two more glasses. They drink.*]

BOY: It's champagne. [*He hiccups.*] You can feel the bubbles if you try.

GIRL: The old man won't come in?

BOY: He hasn't been in here for a month.

GIRL: You can kiss me if you want to.

[*He kisses inexpertly.*]

You've known no foreign ports.

BOY: No.

GIRL: You can touch me if you want. I'm safe in jeans.

[*He kisses her again, one arm round her, his hand on her thigh. She moves it up her thigh while she kisses him and then puts her own hand on his leg.*]

GIRL: You've reached Dover anyway. I bet you'd like to reach Calais.

[*She wriggles closer to him. The dialogue begins to change character – they are both a little drunk – and takes on the tones of a dream. There is no vulgarity in dreams.*]

BOY: I've been at sea a lot of years.

GIRL: How many?

BOY: Three years or more.

GIRL: No ports in all that time?

BOY: No ports.

GIRL: No girl?

BOY: No girl.

GIRL: It's a long time to be at sea, that's certain. Were you unhappy at sea?

BOY: It was all right to start with. There was the Cape of Good Hope and the sun shone on the brass work. They were cheering up in the rigging. I saw a girl with a pony-tail . . .

GIRL: I thought you said you hadn't known a port.

BOY: We didn't tie up there. I waved my hand, that's all, and she ran away in the distance. After that we lived for weeks on Spam and tinned salmon. And then came the Horn. The Horn was terrible. The wind was like a bunch of razors. I thought we'd never get round Point Despair. The waves were mast high and I prayed . . .

GIRL [*slapping the stone*]: To old him?

BOY: No.

GIRL: Who to?

    [*A pause.*]

BOY: I prayed to my mother.

GIRL: What did you pray?

BOY: Oh sakes, I said, we need a woman in the house. [*Pause.*] That's all I could find to pray. [*Pause.*] What's conduct?

GIRL: What we're doing now. [*She kisses him.*] Come closer and tell me more. After the Horn and Cape Despair . . .

BOY: I'm still at sea. But sometimes I long for the land.

GIRL: You can see it now can't you? [*She moves his hand a little.*]

BOY: There's a dark line on the horizon. But it might be a cloud, only a cloud.

GIRL: It's no cloud. Listen – it's the surf. It's a strange land. And I'm waiting on the quay.

BOY: I think I can see the roofs of houses.

GIRL: I can see the top of your sail, I know your ship is coming, and I can't keep still. I've got a jittery tickly feeling. [*She jumps to her feet.*] I'm walking up and down the quay from one bollard to the next.

BOY: What's a bollard?

GIRL: I don't know. Who cares?

BOY: Are there bollards in Elm Park Road?

GIRL: Don't be stupid. This is Valparaiso. I'm not in jeans. I'm in a rose-coloured skirt, with gold shoes, and my skirt swings when I walk. When it swings men can see half way, right up to here. [*She pretends her jeans are a skirt.*] Can't you see me yet, walking on the quay? I tell you I can't stay still. If only there was a juke box somewhere. I want to twist, I want to Madison, I want to do the Hully Gully. I can see the prow of your boat

now. It's pointing like a finger, pointing like something at the
port. There hasn't been a ship in here for weeks, for months,
it seems like years. I want to love the first man who comes
ashore.

BOY: Not me?

GIRL: It will be you if you are quick enough.

BOY: Who are you? Why are you here, all dressed up like that?
    [*Pause.*]

GIRL: I'm the most expensive tart in all Valparaiso. You know
    where Valparaiso is?

BOY: Of course. I was first in geography.

GIRL: I don't care a damn about geography. Come ashore quick.

BOY: How can I? I'm not an officer. I haven't got any money –
    only enough for a glass of rum and water. [*He takes more sherry
    and drinks.*]

GIRL: I slept last night with the governor of Valparaiso and he gave
    me a diamond ring. See it? [*She flashes her cheap ring at him.*] I can
    afford one hour for free. [*She dances in front of him, a twist without
    a partner.*] For free, for a whim, for an hour, for you.

BOY [*after a sullen pause*]: I don't want a tart who's slept with the
    governor for a ring. I want someone to love.

GIRL: Who shall I be?

BOY: The governor's daughter. And I love you for ever and ever.

GIRL: You can keep your virgins. I'm the governor's lady. Every
    night I sleep in a great golden bed with a net around to stop the
    mosquitoes biting my velvet skin. A negro in the morning
    brings us coffee, but he can't see through the net where I lie
    naked. He can't see whether the governor's there or only a
    cabin-boy smelling of tar.

BOY: Where's the governor now?

GIRL: He's killing Indians in the interior. Perhaps he'll never come
    back.

BOY: Do you like the smell of tar?

GIRL: A–hm.

BOY: A–hm yes or a–hm no?

GIRL: A–hm yes.

BOY: Why?

GIRL: It's hot, it's strong, it's summer. I'm sick to death of toilet-water and eau de cologne and after-shave lotion. The governor uses Yardley.

BOY: But there's the smell of a port
            only the local man knows.
       Spume or tar, or even the sort
            of dung that the donkey throws.

GIRL: Where did you read that?

BOY: I made it up. We were told to write an essay on the ports of England, and I wrote that instead. They gave me zero and another bad report for conduct.

GIRL: I suppose it was the donkey did it. Why did you put in the donkey?

BOY: I don't know. He sort of walked in.

[*The dream is over. They are back in reality.*]

GIRL: Oh gosh, I'll have to be on my way. I've got a date.

BOY: Who with?

GIRL: Boy friend.

BOY: In Valparaiso?

GIRL: Stop kidding. The corner of Stanley Terrace. It's a good ten minutes away and I'm late already. [*She takes her comb out of her bag and runs it through her hair.*] Pull up the blind. I can't see to do my face.

   [*The* BOY *goes reluctantly past the screen and the portrait of his mother. He hesitates there a moment looking at her.*]

Oh get a move on, do. My hair's in a tangle and I've got a smut at the end of my nose. Do you never clean the place? Doesn't your Dad notice the dirt?

BOY: He's too busy carving the statue.

   [*He goes and pulls up the blind and the image on the screen fades. He goes reluctantly to the lantern and turns out the light there, withdraws the slide and puts it in the box. The* GIRL *is busy with her face.*]

GIRL: You'd better wipe your face. Your mouth's all smudged with lipstick.

BOY: Who cares?

GIRL: Your old man will notice.

BOY: Will he? I'll bet you a bob . . . Shall I see you tomorrow?

GIRL: A–hm.

BOY: A-hm yes or a-hm no?

GIRL: A-hm no.

BOY: Why not?

GIRL: I've got a date.

BOY: Who's your date?

GIRL: Johnny Salt.

BOY: Do you talk about Valparaiso to him?

GIRL: Hell, no. He's not the dreamy kind. He's wild about sickles.

BOY: What's a sickle?

GIRL: Where were you brought up? A motor-bike of course.

BOY: What do you do?

GIRL: We go riding at a hundred miles an hour.

BOY: Where?

GIRL: It doesn't matter where. Into the country. Down to the sea.

BOY: And when you stop?

GIRL: We don't stop. What's the point of stopping with an Eagle
Rover?

    [*The* BOY *comes up and puts his arm round her from behind.*]

BOY: Do you kiss Johnny Salt?

GIRL: He's not the kissing kind.

BOY: Am I?

GIRL: I'm late.

    [*The* GIRL *breaks away and in the struggle her compact drops.*]

GIRL: Damn you, leave me be. You've broken the glass. It's
unlucky.

BOY: It's lucky. Kiss me again.

GIRL: I'm not in the mood.

BOY: Will you come back soon?

GIRL: How can I tell?

BOY: Wednesday?

GIRL: I've got a date Wednesday.

BOY: Who's your date?

GIRL: Joe Bridges.

    [*The* BOY *tightens his arms around her.*]

BOY: Is he the kissing kind?

    [*She begins to struggle away from him.*]

GIRL: Leave me be. I told you. I don't let anyone take liberties.
Anyone.

[*She kicks back at him with her foot. He falls on the ground. She twists away from him.*]

Take your hand off me.

BOY: I was trying to help you. That's all.

GIRL: You can't take liberties. No one can take liberties.

[*The* FATHER *enters. He has two quart bottles, one under each arm. The* BOY *and the* GIRL *suddenly become still. They sit on the floor silent and entangled as though they hope that he will not notice them and that he will go away.*

He walks around them and deposits the two bottles by the statue. He picks up the sherry bottle, looks at it and puts it back. Then he walks into the tool-shed without a word. A pause. They are both sitting coiled up on the floor.]

GIRL [*whispering*]: Is that your old man?

BOY: Yes.

GIRL: My! He's a big man. Why didn't he speak to you?

BOY: He's thinking of the statue.

[*They neither of them attempt to get up, watching the door where he went out.*]

GIRL: Is he coming back?

BOY: I don't know. Perhaps. Perhaps not.

GIRL: Did he see us?

BOY: You can never tell.

GIRL: He looks sort of rough and hairy. Doesn't he ever shave?

BOY: Perhaps he's been at sea a long time. Like me.

GIRL: At sea? [*She looks at him with surprise. She has forgotten their make-believe.*] He's not a sailor, is he?

BOY: He's about as much a sailor as I am.

GIRL [*with withering contempt*]: You! But my! He's a big man.

BOY: I thought you said you'd got a date.

GIRL: Carving a statue like that – he must need an awful lot of muscle.

BOY: He hasn't got a sickle.

GIRL: Who's talking about sickles? [*She looks sharply at him.*] What's got into you?

BOY: I landed at Valparaiso and there was nobody on the quay.

GIRL: Are you nuts? Where's Valparaiso?

BOY: Like a fool I went into the city looking for a girl.

GIRL [*stroking the stone against which she is leaning*]: How many years did you say he'd been at it, carving this bleeding object?

BOY: They said there was the most expensive tart in the world in Valparaiso, but I only had enough for the rum and water.

GIRL: It's like a convict, isn't it, smashing stones all day? Ten years' penal servitude and then – oh boy, the champagne and the fireworks. My sister was crazy about a convict once.

BOY: I went and looked for the governor's lady.

GIRL: For God's sake stop telling me fairy stories. What's your old man's name?

BOY [*with bitterness*]: I call him father.

[*The* FATHER *enters again and they fall silent watching him. Again he passes them apparently without seeing them. This time he picks up the beer and puts the bottles on the table with the Pietà.*]

FATHER [*paying no attention to the girl but addressing his son*]: I've got to have the head up again. I can't work at Him like this. All the piddling details – they get out of proportion. It was a mistake taking away the ladder. You go and fetch it while I fix Him.

BOY [*rising*]: It's heavy.

FATHER: You don't need to carry it. Just push it down the stairs and through the door.

BOY [*to* GIRL]: You'll stay till I come back?

GIRL: I told you. I've got a date.

BOY: Meet me next Saturday?

GIRL: I can't make a date that far.

[*The* BOY *goes out.*

The FATHER *goes to the arrangement of pulleys and begins to hoist the head up.*]

GIRL: Is it heavy?

FATHER [*mockingly*]: Is it heavy? If I'd left it lying there much longer it would have sunk into the floor like a tombstone sinks in the grass.

[*When the head is dangling out of sight he gives the rope to the girl.*] Here. Hold this rope a moment.

[*While the* GIRL *holds the head in place the* FATHER *turns the winch and revolves the main block into place under the head. While he works the* GIRL *speaks.*]

GIRL: When will it be finished?

FATHER: In a year or two.

GIRL: I bet you'll celebrate that day.

FATHER: Why should I?

GIRL: After all those years.

FATHER: It doesn't bear thinking of. What will I do when that's finished?

GIRL: Start another.

FATHER: I'm too old to start another.

GIRL: Enjoy yourself.

FATHER: How?

GIRL: Your boy brought me here. You don't mind, do you?
[*The* FATHER *takes the rope from the* GIRL *and lowers the invisible head on the block.*]

FATHER [*looking up*]: Now I can see Him properly again with his head in the clouds. Tomorrow I'll get back to work on that left eye. Like it was when He looked at the world and loved what He'd made. At the end of the sixth day. Gentle, mild, satisfied, loving.

GIRL: Your boy wanted to make love to me.

FATHER: They double-crossed Him while He rested on the seventh day. No wonder He took a turn against the world.

GIRL [*with distrust*]: Are you an Adventist? My uncle's an Adventist.

FATHER: It's going to feel good being up there again. On my ladder. Working on the ground gives a man flat feet and a limited outlook. Tomorrow I'll climb . . .

GIRL: Like a sailor up a mast. [*She's getting restless again. She fiddles with a broom.*] A mast. A tall mast. Up a mast.

FATHER: Don't you go cleaning things. I won't have a woman in here cleaning things. Stop fiddling.

GIRL: Your boy wanted to touch me. He kissed me and touched me. Of course I was safe in jeans.

FATHER: You leave that dust alone. Carving and cooking are the same. A clean kitchen spoils the taste of food. Hygiene's like paper. It tastes of nothing.

GIRL: Aren't you angry with him?

FATHER: With who?

GIRL: Your son. He brought me in here – I was buying a packet of envelopes at Smith's, and he took me swimming at the Lido and then he lured me here and tried to make love to me.

FATHER: Where are the envelopes?

GIRL: Gosh, I left them at the Lido. Aren't you angry – I mean he tried . . .

FATHER: He's too young.

GIRL: He gave me a lot of drinks. He got me tipsy.

FATHER: You aren't tipsy. You want a man, that's all.

GIRL: He touched me. It's lucky I'm in jeans.

FATHER: I did those feet before I did anything else. Sometimes I'm afraid they're the best things I've ever done or I'm ever likely to do.

GIRL: I'm telling you. It's not safe for a girl in here alone with your son.

FATHER: My son?

GIRL: He touched me.

FATHER: He wouldn't know how to begin. I thought of using him once – for the Virgin and Child. You don't have to worry about him. Get yourself a man, if you're restless.

GIRL: He says you never think about girls.

FATHER: Why should I? I've got Him.

GIRL: Don't you ever get – sort of disturbed? I mean at night – when you can't work.

FATHER: If I get disturbed I work it off.

GIRL: On him?

FATHER: One way or another. [*But she has a bit of his attention at last.*] Sometimes I get some stuff from Dr Parker.

GIRL: Who's he?

FATHER: A jovial old beast. Jovial. Jove. Jehovah. I nearly used him as a model once, but he's not a father – so far as anyone can prove.

GIRL: Is he married?

FATHER: He never found that necessary. I wrote a rhyme about him once which went the rounds and was much appreciated at the Craven Arms.

[*He circles round the girl, examining her from every angle. She stands still and lets him.*]

Botticelli
Showed the belly
And the little round tail
Through a muslin veil;
But Dr Parker
Prefers 'em starker.

GIRL: You trying to shock me?

FATHER [*with a laugh*]: You're no virgin.

GIRL: I am – sort of. Cross my heart.

FATHER: You mean you need to have the job finished?
  [*He gives her a pat on the seat of her jeans.*]

GIRL: Did you ever love anyone? I mean – swoony. Like your boy
  said about 'I love you for ever'. It's silly, isn't it. But it's nice all
  the same.

FATHER: You want me to show you something?

GIRL: What?

FATHER: Don't complain if it scares you.

GIRL: Something you've carved?

FATHER: Something my father carved for me.

GIRL: Was he a sculptor too?

FATHER: We're all sculptors. Every one of us. He carved in human
  flesh.

GIRL: Oh horrors! X certificate.

FATHER: Come over here and I'll show you. [*He moves towards the
  tool-shed.*]

GIRL: I sort of like horrors. [*She looks into the wings.*] What's in
  there?

FATHER: It's where I keep my tools.
  [*The* GIRL *is scared, but she wants to follow him.*]
  You can bring your bottle if you like and take another drink to
  give you courage.
  [*She picks up the sherry bottle and holds it like a weapon.*]
  Make up your mind. If you don't want to come I'll get back to
  work. Carving Him. It's time I did.

GIRL: My sister loved a monumental mason once.
  [*The* FATHER *goes off with the* GIRL *following him nervously.*]
  Anyway it's safe in jeans.

[*The stage for a moment is empty. From the left wing a nervous laugh. Then from yard at the back the long ladder is pushed slowly in foot by foot, like a snake. The* BOY *enters, holding the other end. He looks around the empty studio and lowers his end of the ladder.*]

BOY: Father! [*Pause.*] Father? [*He assumes that the* GIRL *has gone, but he is happy after his first real adventure.*]

BOY [*addressing statue*]: No answer of course. It's a habit fathers have. *You* would know that. I wish you'd learn to answer. If you are ever stuck up in a cathedral people will always be praying to you. For sun, for rain, for harvest. If there are enough prayers some will be answered. It's the law of averages. I got the jackpot once in a fruit machine. I can hear the music of the tanners now cascading on the floor. Send me another jackpot. Let me see her again next Saturday walking along the quay in Valparaiso. She'll say 'I love you for ever. I won't die or run away. I need you more than Spam or Double Diamond' and I'll say 'I want to give to you. I want to give everything I've got.' [*Pause.*] When I kissed her it was like ice breaking when you tread in the gutter in January. It was like the season changing, a part of you lifts slowly like a branch when the snow begins to slide off it to the ground.

[*The* GIRL *comes in from the left. She looks bemused and tousled. She is without her blue jeans. Her shirt comes down to her knees. She walks by the* BOY, *paying him no attention at all.*

When she reaches the centre of the stage the GIRL *stops. The* BOY *watches her with dismay.*]

GIRL: Where's my jeans?

[*The* FATHER *comes for a moment to the door of the tool-shed and tosses the jeans to her.*]

Where's the bathroom?

FATHER: I told you. On the left at the end of the passage.

[*The* FATHER *goes back into the tool-shed. The* GIRL *goes out, trailing the jeans after her. The* BOY *watches her go then cries to his* FATHER.]

BOY: You think you are strong, don't you? 'My, he's a big man.' You needn't feel so proud. She's only a little tart. I saw through her all the time.

[*The* BOY *collapses in tears with his face pressed against the statue.*
The FATHER *enters dressed for sculpting. He is completely oblivious*
of his son.]

FATHER: Here. Help me with this ladder. I'm ready for a bit of
work now.

BOY: Put up your own bloody ladder.

FATHER: I've got an idea about his left eye. What are you waiting
for? I want to get the ladder up quick. I'm going to start right
away. I'm in the mood. I've been on the ground too long. [*The*
ladder is raised between them and the FATHER *mounts a few steps. He*
is in a state of excitement when for once he is prepared to explain a little
to his son. He turns and addresses him from a few steps up the ladder.]
You wouldn't understand what it feels like when an idea strikes
you. I feel giddy with it. It's like vertigo. Hold the ladder steady
or I'll fall. It's like God Almighty on the first day. When He
divided the light from the dark. You can't rest till you've made
the first start, and anything may follow after that. I bet He
never thought of water when He made the light, and He had no
idea for tigers when He made the first fish. A flat fish, it was,
like a plaice, moving like a mathematical symbol, silent in the
water, and then suddenly the panther, silent, undulating
through the trees. I've been knocking my head against a brick
wall over that left eye. But now I know. I don't have to worry
about love. God doesn't love. He communicates, that's all.
He's an artist. He doesn't love.

BOY: Did He hate his son?

FATHER: He didn't love or hate him. He used him as a subject.
That's what the Son was for.

[*The* FATHER *begins to climb the ladder as the*

CURTAIN FALLS]

Act Three

The same scene about a month later. Afternoon. The BOY *is reading to the* SECOND GIRL *under the statue.*

BOY: This is the world's greatest poet. His name is Joseph Whitaker, and he has been writing poems like this for ninety-six years. You can read him while I'm gone.

[*He sits beside her and taking the book reads aloud while she follows the text with her eyes.*]

'The marriage must be solemnized between the hours of 8 a.m. and 6 p.m. with open doors in the presence of a Superintendent Registrar and a Registrar of the Registration District of that Superintendent Registrar. The parties must make the following declaration. I do solemnly declare that I know not of any lawful impediment why I, AB, may not be joined in matrimony to CD.' I love CD because she is — because she's Calm and Dear.

[*They kiss. The* BOY *indicates another passage.*]

Hell! Here's a piece called Minors. 'Persons under twenty years of age are generally required to obtain the consent of certain persons.' [*A clock strikes.*] I'm late. I must be off.

[*He kisses her again and leaves the studio by the yard doors, waving to her before he goes. She puts her fingers to her lips and reads on.*

Outside there is a crash and an oath. She retreats towards the wall, where she stands in shadow behind the statue. An elderly too-dapper man wearing a dark formal hat and a dark formal suit carrying a dark formal brief-case hops on to the stage from the right — DR PARKER. *He puts his leg gingerly down.*]

DR PARKER: You ought to get that lino repaired. [*He feels his knee-cap.*] There's nothing like hitting the knee-cap to convince a man that he exists. [*He hops down the stairs to the foot of the ladder and stares up.*] You're the lucky one. No knees at all. Perhaps not so lucky. You lack more essential features too. You think me lacking in respect, but you are not in a church yet. Talking

aloud to myself? I'm quite aware of the fact. I do it quite
deliberately. Why should it be thought eccentric to talk to
oneself? It's an enormous relief after talking to less intelligent
people all day. My first appointment was at nine-thirty and
except for lunch-time I have not been alone since then for two
minutes. As for lunch-time I can hardly talk to myself at meals
or I should never finish the meal. So at lunch I listened only, to
my unspoken thoughts. That's no relief at all. I am a listener all
day as it is, God pity me. [*He looks up at the statue.*] If you'll
excuse the expression. [*He sits down on the statue's feet. He pulls
up his trouser-leg and examines his knee with his fingers.*] The patella
is quite undamaged. Apply a little Elliman's Embrocation, the
strong veterinary variety, rubbing it gently in after warming
the bottle. However now that I have you here – at my mercy ha
ha – let's make a more complete examination. After the age of
sixty-five one should be examined regularly. As a precaution
only. No cause for alarm. You are obviously in perfect health.
[*Leaving his trouser-leg still tucked above his knee he opens his
brief-case and pulls out the rubber band used for testing blood pressure.*]
Supposed to be the latest model. Of course the Japs are ahead of
us as always. Ugly little brutes. But inventive. You can't deny
that. Those 'lonely bachelor' boxes they used to sell at Kyoto.
[*He pulls up his sleeve and wraps the band round his arm. Then he
blows it up and checks the pulse beat with his watch.*] 110. Not bad
for a man of my age – a little low, perhaps, but a fault on the
right side. I wouldn't hesitate to let myself know at once if it
were otherwise. What a joy it is to treat a patient without
having to employ a bedside manner. I have the courage to tell
myself the truth. [*He rolls up the apparatus and puts it back in the
brief-case. Absent-mindedly he leaves his left sleeve rolled up as well as
his right trouser-leg.*] A bedside manner is a thing that slowly,
inevitably, destroys a man. A doctor may be clever, charming,
assiduous, he may be loved by his patients, but he belongs to a
world of fantasy. After telling a lot of frightened patients a lot
of reassuring stories I find it hard to believe in my own reality. I
tell little jokes – what is the difference between an elephant and a
flea? – as I feel the cruel tumour under my fingers. [*He pats the
statue.*] My friend, I become like you, a block of stone, indiffer-

ent to human suffering. The thought of you soothes the dying. Just so they wait for my footsteps. Like you I offer false comfort. What other use have you? Can you tell the difference between an elephant and a flea? Can you tell me that? I ask you – and you don't answer. I implore you . . . This comedy has got to end or I shall turn serious.

[*During the last part of this dialogue the* SECOND GIRL *has emerged a little way from the background, staring at the doctor. He looks round and sees her. He is not at all disconcerted.*]

DR PARKER: Good afternoon, my dear. My name is Dr Parker. And who may you be?

[*She makes no reply.*]

I'm just waiting here for our great sculptor. Talking away to myself as is my harmless habit.

[*She stays silent.*]

My clothes are somewhat disarrayed, I know. But for a perfectly good reason. I have been treating myself. [*He pulls down his sleeve, but forgets his trouser-leg.*] There's no other doctor around here that I would trust with a common cold. [*Pause.*] You're rather a silent child, though a very charming one. You might at least bring yourself to say R. [*He raps out a command.*] Say R. [*She says nothing.*] I might be talking to the deaf. [*He shouts at her.*] Are you deaf? [*No reply.*] Are you dumb?

[*The* FATHER *enters.*]

FATHER: She's deaf *and* dumb.

DR PARKER: Who is she?

FATHER: My son found her.

DR PARKER: Where?

FATHER: On the Inner Circle. She was lost, I think.

DR PARKER: Poor child, defeated as we all are by the Metropolitan system. [*He can't keep his eyes off her.*] She's beautiful. Quite beautiful. Turn round, my dear. Oh, I forgot.

[*He crooks his finger and she approaches. He puts his hand on her shoulder and turns her around, examining her figure with an experienced eye.*]

A little Botticelli. I can see her rising from the sea in something silky and diaphanous, through which the pearly skin gleams like an oyster-shell. And what a gift of silence.

FATHER: A gift?

DR PARKER: Oh, perhaps it was odd of your son at his age to pick on someone deaf and dumb, but for me it would have been natural. I long for the restfulness of the uncommunicative. With this child I would be forced to exchange words only at essential moments.

FATHER: And then she wouldn't hear you.

DR PARKER: Oh yes, she would. I know the alphabet.

[*He communicates with his hands. The* GIRL *smiles and turns shyly away.*]

FATHER: What did you say to her?

DR PARKER: I told her that her eyes are very lovely. So they are.

FATHER: Was this an essential moment?

DR PARKER: She pleases me, my dear fellow. So one has to make a beginning with a little compliment. I wonder how your son manages to amuse her?

FATHER: They go out together – I don't know where. It's no business of mine.

[DR PARKER's *eyes follow the* GIRL *who sits on the floor and looks out into the wings, waiting patiently for the* BOY.]

DR PARKER [*wetting his lips*]: Do you suppose the friendship's ripened?

FATHER: Parker, I asked you to look in because I'm frightened.

DR PARKER: Oh well, that's nothing strange. You've reached the age of fear. I'm frightened myself sometimes.

FATHER: What frightens *you*?

DR PARKER: The thought that I shall one day lose my physical attraction for women. [*He stretches out his legs to regard them and remembers that his trouser is turned up. He begins to roll it down.*] That nature will live on in me, hungry and unsatisfied. That I shall be driven in the last resort to unprofessional conduct with the aid of an anaesthetic. [*He makes signs with his hands to the girl.*]

FATHER: Are you telling her your fears?

DR PARKER: Good gracious no! I'm reassuring her, that's all.

FATHER: It's me you've come to see.

DR PARKER: What reassurance do *you* need?

FATHER: When I climb up that ladder now I always get the vertigo.

DR PARKER: You've had it often before.

FATHER: But it's been bad lately, Parker. Now I can hardly stand up to work. My head reels. The floor below crinkles like a moving staircase.

DR PARKER: I warned you a month ago your blood pressure was too high. It's natural at your age. With your temperament.

FATHER: But I've given up beer altogether. I don't go any longer to the Craven Arms. I've not one pleasure left. I work, that's all.

DR PARKER: If I remember rightly your last serious attack was after a little – pleasure.

FATHER: I only had the girl once. She was a slut. I wouldn't let her in the house again.

DR PARKER: You haven't by any chance been playing around with this sweet little Botticelli here?

FATHER: She's my son's girl, not mine.

DR PARKER: So was the other, if I remember right.

FATHER: Doctor, I only need a few more months to finish Him.

DR PARKER: After fifteen years? You'll never finish him.

FATHER: You think I'm slow. Did you never hear of Sir Thomas Lawrence who was painting an earl's wife and baby. The earl wanted the picture back, but Lawrence said he hadn't quite finished. He was nearly satisfied with the countess, but the baby needed another sitting or two. 'You can have my wife,' said the earl, 'but the baby's in the Guards now.'

DR PARKER [*laughing*]: A good story!

FATHER: It's not a laughing matter. Art's stationary. It's a terrifying thing for a conscientious workman like me to watch how quickly his subjects change. Do you think even He kept up with his creation? Before He could turn round beautiful Adam became the unbearable old Israelite Abraham.

DR PARKER: I remember when you began him. Your son was ill. Remember? He wasn't yet three.

FATHER: A childish ailment – I can't remember them all.

DR PARKER: This wasn't one of those. I feared meningitis. You hid yourself down here out of earshot with your block of stone. I believe you slept with it. I call that shocking conduct. What makes you such a selfish old bastard? I've known you for twenty years and you've never faced pain yet.

FATHER: I don't know what you mean. You wait until I've finished Him.

DR PARKER: It won't make a haporth of difference. You'll never get him done.

FATHER: I'll finish Him if I have to work night and day. Then I promise you I'll turn to lighter projects. Perhaps a Virgin and Child.

DR PARKER: You'd better turn to them now, old friend, or one day we'll have you tumbling down and all we'll have to put in the auction catalogue is 'Unfinished Masterpiece'.

FATHER: They won't write Masterpiece. Not in the state He's in now. Do you suppose that girl's a virgin?

DR PARKER: Ask your son.

FATHER: I finished those pills. Give me another bottle to keep me going just for the time.

DR PARKER: We'll have to make a proper examination first. Let's leave this young lady for a while and go upstairs, you and I, take off our shirt, lie down relaxed. [*He watches the girl all the time.*]

FATHER: You did all that last month.

DR PARKER: A month gets more and more important at the age we've reached. Don't you notice how quickly the sand runs out of an eggtimer at the end? In our prime we think of a year as a thirtieth part of the life that's left, but now it's rather more than half perhaps . . . I might have to forbid you to work up there.

FATHER: It wouldn't be any good. It's all I have left – Him.

[*The* GIRL *is wandering out. She looks back and the* DOCTOR *speaks to her with his hands. She smiles and for the first time replies with her fingers before she goes.*]

What were you saying then?

DR PARKER: That she puts a flame in my old body. [*He sighs.*] Time is short. There are things I have to finish too.

FATHER: I'm tired, Parker.

DR PARKER: Couldn't you train your son to do the hard preliminary chiselling for you?

FATHER: If you had a son, would you let him prepare a girl for you?

DR PARKER: You describe things so physically, my dear fellow. I only wanted a little tender unprofessional conversation . . . I should have had a daughter. It's only the young whom I love.

FATHER: Your daughter would be forty by now.

DR PARKER: A shocking thought. In twenty years from now she would be sixty and I no older than Bertrand Russell. What a horror! Kissing her withered cheek morning and night.

FATHER: You haven't got a daughter.

[DR PARKER *has taken up a lantern slide and is holding it to the light.*]

DR PARKER: Who's this? Goodness gracious, it's me! And a very good likeness too. I must say – without false pride – I don't look a day over forty. I wonder what I could have been doing with those binoculars.

FATHER: All I want from you is a bottle of pills, and all *you* do is talk about yourself.

DR PARKER: I'm a doctor, not a chemist. I shall give you no more pills, my friend, until you let me make a proper examination. You can come to my surgery tonight.

FATHER: And sit in a queue for an hour while I might have been working?

DR PARKER: You weren't working when I arrived.

FATHER: A man must sometimes go to the lavatory.

DR PARKER: How are your movements by the way?

FATHER: Oh go to hell.

DR PARKER [*offended at last*]: Not as far as that, my friend. Only as far as my surgery where perhaps we can hold a rational conversation. [DR PARKER *gets up, brushes some dust symbolically off his brief-case and starts to leave. But he pauses and begins to make sign language.*]

FATHER: You're wasting your time. She can't see you up a flight of stairs.

DR PARKER: I was only talking to myself.

[DR PARKER *leaves the studio with cold dignity. A moment's pause and then the* FATHER *turns towards the ladder. He tests it for firmness and then begins to climb with a rope over his shoulder. A few steps up he pauses, clinging to the ladder, like a climber on a rock-face. Another step and again he pauses.*

The BOY *enters. The* BOY *looks around.*]

BOY: Father.

FATHER: Is that you, boy?

BOY: Yes, I've something to tell you.

FATHER: Where've you been? I need you. Hold the ladder.

[*The* BOY *holds the ladder with both hands and his* FATHER *begins to mount again.*]

BOY: I've been to Bentley's garage.

FATHER: You aren't holding the ladder firm.

BOY: It seems firm enough.

FATHER: Don't argue. Keep your hands on it. [*He mounts one step and pauses.*]

BOY: Have you seen my girl?

[*The* FATHER *for once attends to him if only as an excuse for not mounting higher.*]

FATHER: She was in here a moment ago talking to Dr Parker.

BOY [*almost scared*]: Talking?

FATHER: In deaf and dumb language. With the hands.

BOY: I wish I knew that language. What did Dr Parker have to tell her?

FATHER: He was amusing her. At least she smiled at him. You know what Dr Parker is. He can't keep his hands off a girl.

BOY: He touched her?

FATHER: It's too hot to slave up there today. That window's like a burning glass. [*He is seeking an excuse not to climb further.*]

BOY: She smiled? All I can do is take her to the National Film Theatre – silent pictures – Buster Keaton, Charlie Chaplin. She doesn't smile there.

FATHER: Not a bright companion.

BOY: She has a very tender heart. I used to think the movies funny before I went with her. When they threw a custard pie in someone's face or slipped on a banana skin I laughed a lot. She's changed my ideas. She's very profound, father.

FATHER: This heat would make Samson tired. My head will be better in the morning. [*The* FATHER *comes down to the floor.*] Go up and get my tools. I want to give the chisel an edge.

BOY: Father, there's something I had to tell you. About us. It's pretty urgent.

[*The* FATHER *sits moodily down. The* BOY *starts up the steps.*]

FATHER: The days are damned long without one glass of beer.

[*The* BOY *pauses on the ladder and watches his* FATHER *playing with the rope.*]

BOY: I've got an idea for that rope.

FATHER: I want to make a hand-rail round the platform. Something I can hold on to when it sways.

BOY: It won't be long enough for that.

FATHER: It was all I could find.

[*The* BOY *comes down the ladder and takes the rope from his* FATHER.]

BOY: I'll show you what you can do. You can make a loop around your waist – [*he demonstrates*] with a bow-line, and tie the other end to *him*. Under the chin – or whatever he's got instead of a chin. He's quite heavy enough to hold you if you fall. A slip knot like this. I'll do it for you – before I go away. [*He emphasizes the last phrase.*]

FATHER: Tie myself to Him? I'm tied enough already without that.

BOY: I'm going away, father. That's what I've come to tell you.

[*The* FATHER *takes the rope from his son.*]

FATHER: Parker wouldn't even give me my pills.

BOY: What's wrong, father?

FATHER: I'm tired of Him. Tired. Tircd. That means I'm tired of everything. You think I own those blocks of stone? I bought them years ago in Jos. Barrow's Yard at a cheap rate because he was bankrupt. Like the man in the story who bought an old lamp at a sale and when he polished it he thought he owned the djinn who came out of the lamp. This is my djinn. He's taken everything from me, even my evening glass of beer. If I'm not careful, so Dr Parker hints, He'll take my life too. I hate Him and yet He's all I have. If I haven't worked at Him enough during the day I can't sleep, and when I've worked I wake in the morning and know that what I've done is wrong. He owns my sleep, and He poisons it with dreams. He gives me ideas and when I follow them He gives a sneer of stone – I'm wrong again. A woman who lives with a parrot grows a parrot's beak. A man becomes his work. Watch Mr Watkins of the Midland

Bank when he drinks his tea. It's as though he were ladling cash with his brass scoop into a drawer – you almost hear the money chink.

BOY: I'm going away, father.

[*From somewhere outside comes the high squeal of brakes, a confusion of cries.*]

FATHER: What's that?

BOY: Only an accident in Elm Park Road. It's always happening. I'm going away, father.

FATHER: Oh yes? It's time you left. It's time you went into the world. You see I even begin to talk like Him. The world – He sent his Son there to die, didn't he? Go with my blessing and die too among the thieves and publicans.

BOY: I'm only going to work at Bentley's garage. We want to be married. Please give your consent. I love her, father.

FATHER: Emotion suits you, now I come to look at you. You have a good head.

BOY [*bitterly*]: At geography.

FATHER: I mean a head to draw or carve. The Son. After all you are a son. Before the fifteenth century the Sons were always beardless. I could have finished you in a couple of years. You don't change so quickly now. There are no contradictions in you. No mysteries. You're all of a piece. I can imagine you in wood. A bit of suffering would add a flavour – but of course you've never suffered.

BOY: Haven't I?

FATHER: You were too young when your mother . . .

BOY: I'm not talking about my mother.

FATHER: I can imagine you dangling on a cross. Bony and elongated. Stuck up in one of those new cathedrals they are always building nowadays to prove to someone that they still believe. They never show the Father – He's pre-Christian. He worries them. He's incomprehensible. But the Son – He's one of us. A subject for every *petit maître*.

BOY [*whose attention has been wandering*]: It's not like her to go away like that. Where did she go?

FATHER: Who?

BOY: My girl.

FATHER: Perhaps she's exchanging thoughts with Dr Parker's fingers.

BOY: I'll go and find her.

FATHER: Better not. He might be examining her.

BOY: What do you mean? She's not ill.

[*The* BOY *turns to go, but the* FATHER *puts out his hands and holds him. The* BOY *struggles to pull away*.]

BOY: Let go of me. Father!

FATHER: There's nothing like carving a statue to harden the muscles.

BOY: Father!

[*The* FATHER *releases the* BOY.]

BOY: I'd better find her, father.

FATHER: There's plenty of time. I wasn't serious. Parker's safe in his surgery by now. Go and stand on His feet so that I can see you both. After all there's a sort of distant relationship between a father and a son.

[*The* BOY *reluctantly obeys him*.]

There's too much light. I want to get the shadows on your face. [*The* FATHER *draws the blind*.] Too dark.

[*He turns on the magic lantern. The studio is half in darkness now and the boy's face is illuminated*.]

FATHER: Now I've got the shadows right. You can imitate the lines of suffering with shadows. [*The* FATHER *takes a pad and begins to sketch*.]

BOY: They are giving me a room above Bentley's garage and eight pounds a week.

FATHER: I only want to get the bone structure in.

BOY: Bentley wants a girl to help his wife in the house, so we can both earn. I told him she was deaf and dumb. He said, 'All the better. My wife talks enough for two.' We'll be on our own.

FATHER: Of course you aren't a subject of great originality. You've been done too often dead on the cross or dead on your mother's lap like in that Pietà there. It's difficult to think of a fresh way to show you dead.

BOY: I'm pretty alive right now.

FATHER: I might put a bit of you into your Father's face. Struggling to get out. Tenderness buried even in that old Ancient of

Days. Two eyes closed to everything but his own majesty, and the third eye growing, like a window on the world.

BOY: You've had trouble enough with two.

FATHER: One must guard against impatience. Another year's work won't kill me, whatever Parker says.

BOY: I haven't told her yet about the job. In case of accidents. Bentley's only got a single-bed. We'll need a double one. I thought perhaps you might lend us . . . there's a double-bed in the spare room.

FATHER: Damnation. Can't you keep still? [*He tears the sheet off his pad and starts again.*]

BOY: I wanted to be a sailor once. You've seen how good I am at knots. I had dreams of ports like Valparaiso. But all I want now is a borrowed bed and a room over the petrol pumps.

FATHER: It's no good. It won't come. There's nothing in common between you and Him.

BOY: I'll arrange for old Mrs Harris to see after you. And at the weekends we'll look in too. The garage closes Sunday. I'm not deserting you, father.

FATHER: You're stupid-eyed with hope. The world is changing before your eyes. He doesn't hope. He knows. I can only carve a finished thing. No good. No good.

> [*He tears off another leaf and drops it on the floor. The sound of slow footsteps on the right.* DR PARKER *enters. He has a piece of material crushed in his left hand. One can hardly make out his features in the gloom.*]

BOY [*picking up the sketch and looking at it*]: I like it. Can I keep it?

> [DR PARKER *has come to a halt. He says nothing. A pause.*]

FATHER: What's the matter, Parker?

> [*The* BOY *turns and sees his face.*]

DR PARKER: It was nobody's fault. Nobody's. The driver had no chance. She ran out into the street as if she were blind.

BOY: Who?

DR PARKER: It was nobody's fault. I can assure you of that.

BOY: Where's my girl?

DR PARKER: Oh yes, your girl. I forgot. She was your girl. We laid her on the bed in the spare room.

> [*The* BOY *goes past him.* DR PARKER *tries to check him.*]

There's nothing you can do.

[*The* BOY *goes out. Pause.*]

FATHER: What happened, Parker?

DR PARKER: She didn't suffer. If I'd known she was going to tear out of the door like that, I'd have stopped her, but she didn't say a word.

FATHER: She was dumb.

DR PARKER: Yes, I'd forgotten that. The policeman saw it happen. He knows it was no one's fault but hers. The driver put on his brake. He sounded his horn.

FATHER: She was deaf. Why did she run out?

DR PARKER: How would I know?

FATHER: What's that in your hand?

[DR PARKER *looks at his hand as though he doesn't know what it contains: a piece of white material.*]

You'd better not be seen with those. Not by the boy.

DR PARKER: I was only having a game. I meant no harm.

FATHER: She was a virgin, Parker.

DR PARKER: How could I know that? I was being kind to her.

FATHER: You were telling her a lot of pretty things with your fingers?

DR PARKER: How could I talk to her and hold her too? [*He sees he has made a mistake.*] Don't you throw stones, my friend. I know what happened before your last attack.

FATHER: That little slut wanted it. I did no harm.

DR PARKER: Did your boy think that? Shall I ask him? Was she a slut to him?

FATHER: I wouldn't stay to see him again if I were you. We'd better both go out through the yard. Come to the Craven Arms. We could do with a drink.

[*During this dialogue the* BOY *enters. He carries the dead* GIRL *in his arms. He comes slowly towards the centre of the stage. The* FATHER *gives a horrified glance and backs towards the tool-shed door, then plunges through it out of sight.*]

BOY: Father!

DR PARKER: You must excuse me. [DR PARKER *begins to edge out.*] Patients are waiting. I'm sorry. I'm sorry that I could not do more to help.

[DR PARKER *goes. The* BOY *has laid the* GIRL *at the foot of the statue, holding the body in his arms. The sound of a grindstone begins in the tool-shed. The* BOY *is weeping.*]

BOY: Father! She's dead. Come out of there and speak to me, father. I'm alone. I need you. Help me. I'm your son.

FATHER [*from the shed*]: I have to work.

BOY: Work! Do you know what they call you in Elm Park Road?
[*The* FATHER *does not answer.*]

BOY: I'm going away. I'm taking the first train out of here. Express. Non-stop. [*The* BOY *sees the rope and takes it. He climbs a few steps up the ladder.*] You wanted a new way to see me dead. I'll hang from God the Father's neck. Ask me not to go, father.
[*The* FATHER *comes out of the tool-shed. The* BOY *stops.*]

BOY: You are a father, aren't you? Indifference in the right eye and a bit of tenderness in the left. But you could never get round to finishing the left eye, could you?

FATHER: Why are you blaming me? I did nothing.

BOY: Nothing for me and nothing for mother. You know all about indifference, don't you, and nothing about love.

FATHER: There wasn't time for two lives with all I had to finish.

BOY: I'll finish quicker than you. [*He runs up the ladder to the catwalk.*]

FATHER: Come down from there, son.

BOY: Give me one good reason. Would you suffer or would it be a 'shocking inconvenience'?

FATHER: You've been burnt yourself. Can you blame a man who's afraid of fire? Oh yes, you can. You've the courage of ordinary folk. I haven't. It wasn't courage which made Him. You don't have to tell me how bad He is. He'll never stand in any cathedral. I haven't even the excuse of excellence.

BOY: I asked you for one word, father, but you are still talking about a bit of stone.

FATHER: This studio is a cave where I hide. With my great mudpie standing there, and my lantern slides. I'm laughable. But then I remember how they laughed at Gauguin his first week in Pont Aven. It's been a long week of laughter in Elm Park Road. [*The* FATHER *begins to break the slides.*] There go your fathers, Father Landru, Father Grand Duke and Father Davies at Brighton who killed his son with phenobarbital. And now for the Eternal Father – you'll see – I'll smash Him too.

BOY: Put the bar down. You'll only hurt yourself. Stop playing and answer me.

[*The* FATHER *drops the bar.*]

FATHER: Help me. You're my son. You're young. I'm old. I'm ashamed. I know how my conduct seems to you.

BOY: What's conduct, father?

FATHER: It wasn't all my fault. He was like the djinn of the lamp. He held me in his hands.

BOY: How could he? You never got as far as the hands.

FATHER: Please come down. Come down a little nearer. I can't even see you where you've gone.

BOY: I was proud of you. I thought you were strong. I admired you. I thought you were dedicated. I thought you'd sacrificed your life for your art. Father, who was sacrificed?

FATHER: You know a lot about me now. Pain teaches quickly. I'm frightened of pain.

BOY: I'm not. It's the only thing I have left that belongs to her.

FATHER: Come down. It's not too late for you and me . . .

BOY: Give me one true answer and I'll come. Where were you when mother died?

[*A long pause. Will it be an excuse or the truth?*]

FATHER: When your mother died I ran out of the room before the breathing stopped. I began to work. It was all I could do. [*He calls up to his son a last justification.*] I can't take life except at second-hand, but I work. I work. In dryness I work. In despair I work. As long as I work I can hold the pain of the world away from me. That's the only subject I've got – my indifference and the world's pain.

[*A long pause. The* BOY *flings down the rope.*]

BOY: Poor father.

FATHER [*inaudibly*]: No good.

BOY: What did you say, father? I can't hear you. What did you say?

FATHER: It was so beautiful standing there that first day. Waiting untouched. For the first chisel stroke. Like the world was before Adam came. But now . . . now . . . Look at it now. I've ruined a fine piece of stone.

[*The* BOY *is coming down the ladder.*]

FATHER: Forgive me. I've made mistakes. I'm not a clever man. And yet when I look up there . . . there's something. Even if the eyes are wrong.

[*The* BOY *pauses on the last steps of the ladder and watches him.*] It's not God the Father. I know that now. No love or tenderness there. Only pride. Like Lucifer's. Lucifer had reason to be proud. The brightest of the angels. Now he's dropped like a parachutist through the skies. Look – his feet touch the earth and he stands there, the conqueror of the world. [*He makes for the ladder.*]

BOY [*watching the obsession return with horror*]: Father!

FATHER: All I've done is not wasted. I can start again. I've got to climb up there and see him close. The ladder's firm. It wasn't vertigo. All I needed was a new idea.

CURTAIN

THE RETURN
OF A. J. RAFFLES

★

An Edwardian Comedy
in Three Acts
Based Somewhat Loosely
on E. W. Hornung's
Characters in
The Amateur Cracksman

AUTHOR'S NOTE

This story cannot of course be accepted as strictly true to history. I have in one respect seriously deviated from the truth – the Marquess of Queensberry met his end in January 1900 and I have extended his life into the late summer of that year. It is very questionable too whether the Prince of Wales would have been on terms of friendship with the Marquess, and I have no evidence that the Marquess had a country house in Hertfordshire.

On the other hand the gold box presented by the theatrical profession to the Prince of Wales is in no way fictitious, nor the difficulties the Prince had with foreign uniforms. And I am prepared to defend the truth of Raffles' return from South Africa alive. His chronicler, and his close companion, Bunny, wrote a moving account of Raffles' death and claimed to have been beside him when he was 'killed', but Bunny had every reason for falsifying history, to disguise the fact that, far from being in South Africa, he was, at the date of Spion Kop, incarcerated in Reading Gaol, where he had the good fortune to meet Oscar Wilde.

Graham Greene

CHARACTERS

(not in order of appearance)

A. J. RAFFLES

BUNNY

LORD ALFRED DOUGLAS

'MR PORTLAND'

INSPECTOR MACKENZIE

THE MARQUESS OF QUEENSBERRY

A LADY CALLED ALICE

A LADY'S MAID CALLED MARY

MR SMITH, HEAD PORTER OF
   ALBANY

CAPTAIN VON BLIXEN

SCENES

Act One

Raffles' old chambers in Albany, Piccadilly, late summer of 1900.

Act Two

The Marquess of Queensberry's bedroom in his country house in Hertfordshire a few nights later.

Act Three

Raffles' chambers in Albany early the next morning.

Act One

The date is the late summer of 1900, a few months before the death of the old Queen. The scene a set of chambers in Albany, which was once described by Conan Doyle as an 'aristocratic rookery'. Even if we did not know it was Albany, where at that date no woman, cat or dog was allowed to reside, we would recognize a bachelor's apartment – the rather heavy furniture, the comfortable leather armchairs, the photograph on the desk of an elderly woman – a rather obvious mother – on the back wall the photograph of a cricket team and hanging on either side of it a cricket bat on which the signatures of a team have been inscribed and a red leather cricket ball dangling in a net from a nail. Below them a large chest with a flat top like a cabin trunk. Hornung has described the room when Raffles occupied it: 'That dear den of disorder in good taste, with a carved bookcase, the dresser and chests of still older oak, and the Watts and Rossettis hung anyhow on the walls.' A man in his early thirties in full evening dress is moving restlessly round the room, sometimes consulting his watch. He is good-looking in a rather weak way with depraved aristocratic features. On the right a door into the hall stands open, curtains are drawn over the windows on the left, and in the back wall a door leads to a bedroom. The young man knocks impatiently at this door.

LORD ALFRED: Bunny! Bunny! For God's sake hurry up. The curtain at Covent Garden won't stay down for us. I asked Stephen to meet us first at the Criterion. Drinking brandy and selzer too fast always gives me the hiccups. One mustn't have hiccups at *Carmen* – too middle-class.

[*He tries the handle of the door, but the door is locked.*]

Let me in, Bunny. Why lock the door? You needn't be so careful of your precious virtue. I like a bit of flesh and prison benches make for hard bottoms.

[*Lord Alfred goes to the wall and unhooks the cricket bat, then he takes the ball out of the net, arranges it carefully like a golf ball and strikes it at the door.*]

LORD ALFRED: A goal! A goal! If that's the right term.

[*The door is quickly opened and Bunny, a small thin young man in his early thirties, comes furiously into the room. He is in his evening shirt sleeves, with his white tie dangling unfastened. His hair is cut very short.*]

BUNNY: How dare you, Bosie. Put the bat back.

LORD ALFRED [*obeying*]: A sacred relic. Do people always write on these things?

BUNNY: Of course not. That was Raffles' bat in the last Test he played in. He made 105 not out against Australia and won us the Ashes.

LORD ALFRED: Ashes? How very morbid. But, Bunny, we *must* be off. Poor Stephen will think we've gone without him.

BUNNY: I can't tie this wretched tie.

LORD ALFRED: Turn round. I'll tie it for you.

BUNNY: I was never very good at it. Raffles always had to help me. And one forgets things after two years picking oakum in prison.

LORD ALFRED: Chokie Oscar always calls it. He's forgotten nothing – except his friends. Now that's a very fine bow, Bunny. Raffles couldn't have done better. [*With a caress of his fingers*] I must admit the back of your neck has a certain epicene charm, but I wish your hair would grow faster. It has a distinctly penal look. All right for the gallery, of course, but unusual in a box. And very noticeable I would say at the Criterion.

BUNNY: I've no intention of going to the Criterion. I don't like Stephen. He was very offensive to me last week. He said his valet had known me at Reading. I hadn't even exchanged whispers with him in the exercise yard. I shall go direct from here, Bosie, to your box.

LORD ALFRED: Stephen is rather highly-coloured, but I thought he might cheer you up after all the greyness of gaol.

[*He tosses up the cricket ball and fails to catch it.*]

Butterfingers! Unlike your Raffles I was never any good at outdoor games. So much depends on the boring weather the English like to talk about. But in a bedroom . . . rain or snow, sun or showers . . . who cares? Are you always faithful to your Raffles?

BUNNY: Always. He was a great man, Bosie, and he died a hero's death at Spion Kop. I'll be ready in a moment.

[*Bunny goes to fetch his tails while Lord Alfred prowls around the room. He pauses by the photograph of the cricket team and calls out to Bunny in the bedroom.*]

LORD ALFRED: And this photograph? Which of the flannelled fools is Raffles?

BUNNY [*returning and putting on his tails*]: You wouldn't have called him a fool if you'd faced him as he came up to bowl. He's there on the left of the captain. It's the Gentlemen's team against the Players in '94. They hadn't yet learned that he could bat just as well as he could bowl.

LORD ALFRED: And the gentleman with the enormous beard on the captain's right?

BUNNY: Don't pretend you don't know that fellow W. G. Grace?

LORD ALFRED: So Raffles could bowl as well as he could bat? Was he bisexual too, Bunny?

BUNNY: Of course not. He never looked twice at a woman. If you want to meet Stephen you'd better be off. I'll meet you in the box.

LORD ALFRED: Bunny, whatever have you got around your sleeve?

[*Bunny is wearing a black armlet.*]

BUNNY: It's only six months since the Boers killed him, Bosie.

LORD ALFRED: You can't possibly go to Covent Garden wearing that. Take it off at once. They'll think the Queen has died. It would be a bit exaggerated even then.

BUNNY: Can't I mourn him for six months? You don't know all the things he did for me.

LORD ALFRED: I know what you told Oscar in Reading Gaol – that Raffles escaped to the war and left you to carry the blame.

BUNNY: I know I told Wilde that. I was bitter at first, but it was all my own fault I was caught. Raffles was right to escape. He wouldn't have got off with a two-year sentence. That old monster Mackenzie of Scotland Yard had been on his trail for years. I was only small game. Why, Mackenzie even spoke up for me at the trial. I can see him now, the old greybeard, in his heavy musty tweeds. His nose was always running. He said I had a weak character and I had been seduced by an arch-criminal. He said it in a self-righteous Scotch accent which made it worse.

LORD ALFRED: Seduced, Bunny?

BUNNY: He only meant mentally. Why aren't you off to your highly-coloured friend Stephen, Bosie?

LORD ALFRED: I can't go with you to Covent Garden if you are wearing that thing. But for you I'll give up the Criterion. Stephen is beginning to bore me. He has developed a hideous taste for pink champagne. It makes me think he has secret connections with women. I begin to love you, Bunny. No, no, don't moue at me. Like a brother of course. Ever since Oscar went to chokie I've discovered a strong interest in the criminal classes. Wouldn't you sometimes like to return to a life of crime?

BUNNY: There'd be no fun in it without Raffles. And no future. In a tight spot I always knew he was there. Do you know, I really believe he chose to die at Spion Kop to help me in the only way he could? He couldn't spring me from prison, but he made his will the night before he was killed. They found it on his body stained with blood. He left me everything. These chambers and everything in them.

LORD ALFRED: Including the bat and ball. What do you keep in this old chest? The Crown Jewels?

BUNNY: The last thing Raffles stole.

LORD ALFRED: Show me.

[Bunny opens the chest and Lord Alfred peers inside.]

LORD ALFRED: It's empty.

[Bunny releases a catch and a false top falls from the lid, making a tray which he lifts out and places on top of the chest.]

LORD ALFRED: A lot of old junk.

BUNNY: They are the Raffles Relics from the Black Museum at Scotland Yard.

LORD ALFRED: How did he get them?

BUNNY: You'll never get to Covent Garden if I begin to tell you that. They were labelled Relics of an Amateur Cracksman.

They could never pin anything on him. He got them from under the nose of Inspector Mackenzie himself.

[*Bunny lifts out the relics one by one for inspection.*]

BUNNY: His revolver. He never fired it. He only used it to frighten. Here's a life preserver. There's blood on that. Raffles was ashamed of that blow, but it saved me from prison. He never carried it again. Here's an evening waistcoat, white on this side, black on the other. In a moment he could turn from a guest to a waiter. Here's a brace-and-bit, bottle of rock-oil, gimlet, wedges – just slivers of wood, but how useful they can be – safe-keys. Quite a collection of those. His special opera hat.

[*Lord Alfred takes the hat and turns it over.*]

LORD ALFRED: What's special about it?

BUNNY: Open it and you'll see. It was his idea to make a dark lantern out of an opera hat. You can't carry a dark lantern with evening dress, and Raffles nearly always worked in evening dress. He said it gave him a sense of moral superiority to any constable who ventured to stop him. Look inside. See the metal socket attached to the crown. He always carried a candle in his pocket and all he had to do was fix it – so.

LORD ALFRED: I would have liked to meet your Raffles on a dark night.

BUNNY: And look here. This is a very special walking stick. What do you think of that – ?

LORD ALFRED: I imagined a burglar did more climbing than walking.

BUNNY: And how right you are. This helps you to climb.

[*Bunny unscrews the ferrule and shakes out of the cane a diminishing series of smaller canes, like a fishing-rod, which he joins together. He takes off the tray a double hook of steel and attaches it to the tip of the top joint. Then he attaches the hook to the top of the open door.*]

BUNNY: Imagine that's a balcony. And now for the finest of Manilla ropes. [*He takes a coil of rope from the tray*] Fine enough to tie up a parcel and strong enough to risk your life on. See the foot loops. He could wear this round his waist and nobody could tell. I've seen him waltz in it.

LORD ALFRED: You fascinate me, Bunny. I have the glimmerings

of an idea. A glorious idea. An idea that would have appealed to
Raffles.

[*There is a double knock on the outer door. Bunny seizes the
tablecloth and throws it over the chest. The opera hat lies forgotten
on a chair. A second knock, louder this time. The cane remains
hanging from the door.*]

BUNNY: Come in.

[*The head porter of Albany, Smith, in top-hat and tail-coat enters
from the hall: a very sturdy man with a sergeant-major's air of
authority and a sergeant-major's moustache.*]

BUNNY: What is it, Smith?

SMITH: Well, sir, being new in this situation I want to do what's
right.

BUNNY: I'm sure you do.

SMITH: And Betteridge before he went off to the war told me as
how Mr Raffles always wanted him to report anything what
struck him as unusual, Betteridge being a very sensitive sort of
man with a nose for such.

BUNNY: You've seen something unusual?

SMITH: I said to myself, sir, Betteridge might think it unusual.
You see there's an elderly man lingering around. He asked for
you, sir, and me knowing you were with his lordship here, I
told him you was out, but he hasn't gone away, sir. He walks
up and down the Ropewalk from the back door to the front.
You could almost say, sir, that he prowls.

LORD ALFRED: A fine choice of words. I can see you are as
sensitive as Betteridge.

SMITH: Thank you, sir.

BUNNY: What does he look like?

SMITH: Not a gentleman, sir.

BUNNY: Couldn't you be a little more precise? Fat or lean? Tall or
short?

SMITH: I wouldn't say he was either fat or lean – somewhere
between the two.

BUNNY: His height then?

SMITH: If you said about the middle height, sir, you wouldn't be
far wrong, give an inch or two either way. There was one thing
I noticed – he has a grey beard much like His Royal Highness's.

LORD ALFRED: Perhaps it is the Prince. My friend has ties in the highest society.

SMITH: Oh no, sir. His Royal Highness would never wear such tweeds as this man wears. I've never seen the like before in Albany.

BUNNY: By God, Bosie, I believe it's Inspector Mackenzie. Has he a Scotch accent?

SMITH: He has some sort of accent, sir. I wouldn't like to define it.

BUNNY: Tell him – tell him you've received a telegram that I've gone for a week to Boulogne. No. Better say to Monte Carlo – otherwise he'll be slipping across on a cheap excursion.

[*A footstep in the hall and Smith turns. An elderly bearded figure in atrocious tweeds appears in the doorway.*]

BUNNY [*with a touch of dismay in his voice*]: It *is* Inspector Mackenzie.

SMITH: What are you up to, my man, coming in without so much as a knock?

DETECTIVE: The law doesna knock, porter. The law enters.

BUNNY: What do you want, Inspector?

DETECTIVE: Oh, just a wee word or two, but I mickle doubt if you'd want them spoken in public.

BUNNY: You can go, Smith. But when this gentleman leaves see that he really leaves.

SMITH: That I will, sir, but if you want him thrown out . . .

BUNNY: No, no, one doesn't throw a policeman out.

SMITH: There's many a gentleman in Albany would be glad to lend a hand. Mr Digby on Staircase C spent a night in the cells last Boat Race Night.

BUNNY: Mr Digby mustn't be disturbed on my account.

SMITH: Well, if you say so, sir. [*He looks with scorn at the detective.*] The tweeds alone deserve it.

[*Smith goes out through the hall and we hear the closing of the front door.*]

DETECTIVE: He'll come to no good end if he hasna maer respect for the law. And now perhaps this gentleman too will be guid enough . . .

BUNNY: This gentleman, Inspector, is my friend Lord Alfred Douglas, son of the Marquess of Queensberry. You'll have heard of the Marquess. He's put up many a boxing match for the aid of police charities.

DETECTIVE: All the same, sir, I wouldna think you'd lak a lord to hear what I hae got to ask you.

BUNNY: You can't blackmail me, Inspector. Lord Alfred knows all about my past.

DETECTIVE [*He takes stock of the room while he speaks*]: That's mair than I can say, sir. You askit for four counts to be takken into consideration at your trial, but I'm thinkin' you left out ane or twa that you workit wi' Mr Raffles.

BUNNY: You never proved anything against Mr Raffles. You ought to have the decency to let the dead sleep in peace. Mr Raffles died like a hero.

DETECTIVE: Oh, we ken weel how the dead are all heroes, sir. There'll be thousands of heroes before this war is over, and the wounded, why they be just pensioners in Chelsea – a mickle somethin' for a lost leg and a mickle somethin' for a lost arm an' maybe an extra saxpence a week for baccy. Weel, there be still questions I'd have askit your great hero, Mr Raffles, if he were here now.

[*The detective moves around the room as he speaks. He sees the opera hat on the chair and picks it up, but Lord Alfred holds out his hand.*]

LORD ALFRED: My hat, Inspector. [*The detective surrenders it.*]

DETECTIVE: An' what was the name you gave, sir? Lord . . . ?

LORD ALFRED: I gave no name. My friend presented you to me. I am Lord Alfred Douglas.

DETECTIVE: Ah, I thocht that was the monicar.

[*The detective looks at the tablecloth covering the chest. He twitches a corner of it with his eyes on the two men. It is as if he were sniffing for the smell of fear. Still holding a corner of the cloth he looks up at the photograph of the cricket team.*]

DETECTIVE: A pity he didna stick to cricket – though it's not the equal to ma mind of the true sport o' kings. I'd have takken him on at golf mysel' an' thrashed him. [*He turns, still holding the cloth.*] Your name's weel known to me, my lord. The Oscar Wilde case. You seem to make a strange choice of friends.

LORD ALFRED: You are being impertinent, Inspector.

DETECTIVE: Ah weel, Lord Alfred, I hae a likin' for straight-forward crime. It's cleaner than muckin' aboot wi' boys.

LORD ALFRED [*amused*]: That too has been the sport of kings.

DETECTIVE: Your English kings. Oh, I ken ma history books.

LORD ALFRED: James the First was Scottish.

DETECTIVE: Aye, but his mither was reared in France. [*He picks up the corner of the cloth again.*] Ah weel, you an' I, we'll argue aboot history anither time. [*He whips the cloth off the chest.*] The Raffles Relics, eh. This would put your grand hero into prison if he wasna deid. A braw pity it was the Boers got at him before me.

BUNNY: How would you have charged him, Inspector? If they are Raffles Relics they belong to Raffles. You can't accuse a man of stealing his own belongings.

DETECTIVE: Housebreaking implements. It's an offence to hae them on the premises. [*In his turn he begins to name them.*] Brace-and-bit, gimlet . . .

BUNNY: He was fond of carpentry. All the pictures you see here – he made the frames himself.

DETECTIVE: Rock-oil. Ye ken what that's for.

BUNNY: Indeed I do. That was for oiling his bat. I'm afraid you know little about cricket, Inspector.

DETECTIVE: A life preserver. Now how will ye explain that?

BUNNY: Mr Raffles liked his steaks tender. He used to beat them with it. You can see the stains of gravy.

DETECTIVE: Gravy stains, eh? And this rod hangin' on the door. Maybe ye'd lak me to show ye the way it works?

BUNNY: No need. I've been showing it already to Lord Alfred. Mr Raffles was always afraid of fire in Albany. The safety pre-cautions are hopelessly out of date, so he made his own. With this he could always get out on to the roof of Burlington Arcade and so into Bond Street. Of course there's a bit of Royal Academy roof to pass, but Raffles always said that the Academy would put out any fire.

DETECTIVE: An' I dessay ye've tried it yoursel'.

BUNNY: Oh, we used to have an occasional fire practice.

DETECTIVE: An' this revolver?

BUNNY: Any gunsmith will tell you it's never been fired. Perhaps a technical breach of the regulations, but Mr Raffles was always

fond of amateur theatricals. I remember once he played the part
of you at Lady Melrose's. Do you carry a revolver, Inspector?

DETECTIVE: No, but I hae a pretty brace of handcuffs which I find
unco' useful. Ye ken Lady Axminster? She's muckle worried
about her pearls.

BUNNY: You should know me better, Inspector. Even in my
misguided youth before Mr Raffles reformed me I would never
have touched pearls. You can't recut or melt down pearls and
they have to be worn to keep their lustre. Can you see me
wearing Lady Axminster's pearls? I've never been a transvestite, Inspector.

DETECTIVE: I thocht maybe ye might have larned about such
goings on with Mr Wilde in Reading Gaol. Or from his
lordship here.

LORD ALFRED: You seem to have a poor opinion of me, Inspector
Mackenzie.

DETECTIVE: Ah keep ma thochts to masel'. [*To Bunny*] Ye wouldna mind, sir, you being as innocent as a new-born bairn, if I
took a wee peek aroun' your apartment?

BUNNY: Known as chambers, Inspector, in Albany. Have you a
search warrant?

DETECTIVE: I've not. I thocht ye being such a braw innocent chiel
wouldna cause me all that trouble. I can easy telephone a
magistrate.

BUNNY: No, go ahead, Inspector. My bedroom is through there.
My bathroom opens out of it, but I suspect you know your
geography. The kitchen is up the stairs outside, but you'll want
to leave that to the last in case I sport my oak on you.

[*The detective moves towards the bedroom door.*]

LORD ALFRED: May I come with you? My favourite game as a
child was Hunt the Slipper.

[*The detective disdains to reply and shuts the bedroom door behind
him.*]

LORD ALFRED: You were superb, Bunny. You must be very
used to the police. Have you really got Lady Axminster's
pearls?

BUNNY: Of course not.

LORD ALFRED: Just before your porter arrived I had a wonderful idea. Ever since poor Oscar's trial I've been puzzling how to revenge him on my odious father. Now here I am with a cracksman as a friend. I want you to burgle my father's house. He's mean as hell, but he always has a lot of ready cash in his safe for baccarat. He won't accept an IOU from his best friend, so of course he has to be prepared to pay up himself – though I've never known him lose.

BUNNY: I was never any good as a cracksman without Raffles.

LORD ALFRED: But you can't imagine the depth of my beastly father's stupidity. You remember he couldn't even spell Sodomite on the card he left at Oscar's club. I'll help you. It will be as easy as robbing a blind man.

BUNNY: No, Bosie, I've lost my nerve for the game – half my nerve was knowing that Raffles was with me. I've never told you about the only time he left me to case a joint alone.

LORD ALFRED: I love your professional phrases. Case a joint. So picturesque.

BUNNY: The house was in Surrey. One of those sham Tudor stockbrokers' houses. Raffles was playing for the Gentlemen in Manchester. I got into the hell of a jam, practically taken with my fingers on the safe, and then suddenly there was Raffles. Rain had stopped play and he'd caught an express to London. You don't understand, do you, all he risked for me?

LORD ALFRED: Quite a few years, I suppose.

BUNNY: He would never have thought of that. But suppose the rain had stopped he would have ceased to be a Gentleman.

LORD ALFRED: Why? I don't . . .

BUNNY: He would have lost his place on the team.

LORD ALFRED: So he would in prison surely?

BUNNY: But without the disgrace. The Gentlemen would have understood a thing like that. Prison is like an act of God. It can happen to any man.

LORD ALFRED: How interesting. Morality is one of those things I've never been able to keep up with. It changes more quickly than the shape of one's lapels. But, Bunny, can we talk of serious things? Next week my abominable father . . . he's always cropping up and the only thing I can do is to change the adjective . . . my moronic father has a house party. Men only.

For baccarat. Of course there may be one or two female appendages. Some men seem unable to go away for a weekend without carrying a woman with them. So thoughtless and egotistical. We have to be polite to them.

VOICE: Would it be his country house or his town house you plan to rob, Lord Alfred?

[*A. J. Raffles enters from the bedroom. He is wearing the hideous tweeds, but the beard has gone except for one patch. The two others stare at him in astonishment.*]

BUNNY: A.J.?

[*Bunny runs to Raffles and puts his hands on his shoulders.*]

BUNNY: But you are alive?

RAFFLES: Very much alive, Bunny, and in great need of a Sullivan.

[*Bunny rushes to the desk and fetches a box of cigarettes.*]

RAFFLES: The first I've had in eighteen months. You've always been inclined to dispose of me prematurely, Bunny. You remember when I drowned in the Mediterranean under the eyes of old Mackenzie? By the way, these tweeds are quite his style, aren't they? I spotted them in a second-hand clothes shop in Harwich when I landed this morning. So this is Lord Alfred Douglas [*offering his hand*]. I've read a lot about you, sir, in the *Cape Times*.

BUNNY: But Raffles . . . Spion Kop . . . that will stained with your blood . . .

RAFFLES: Not my blood, Bunny. The poor devil beside me had his face blown off, so I took the opportunity to exchange papers before the Boers got to me. Some of the blood was his, though just in case I had used a lot of tomato sauce on the paper the night before. I didn't think that they'd check the genuineness of blood on a battlefield.

LORD ALFRED: And the Boers got you, Mr Raffles?

RAFFLES: The Boers got me, Lord Alfred, but they were no cleverer than poor old Mackenzie. In fact I took a souvenir away with me. [*Raffles takes a gold watch from his waistcoat pocket.*] General Botha's, inscribed by President Kruger himself. I had to leave the chain behind.

BUNNY: Oh A.J., A.J., I feel alive again. But why, why did you dress up as Mackenzie?

RAFFLES: It was the sight of these hideous tweeds that did it. Besides it's better for Raffles to stay legally dead.

BUNNY: One thing worried me. Old Mackenzie's sniffle. You forgot his sniffle.

RAFFLES: Bravo, Bunny. My accent was a bit uncertain too. I can manage real Devonshire, very fair Norfolk and three Yorkshire dialects, but Scots — I don't know the difference between Highlands and Lowlands. I tried to remember some Burns, but all that came to mind was 'Scots wa hae wi Wallace bled, Welcome to your gory bed,' and I've had enough of gory beds. And now, Lord Alfred, what is all this about avenging Mr Wilde?

LORD ALFRED: How did you hear that?

RAFFLES: This little gadget here. [*He goes to the wall and indicates the mouth of a blower*] What do you suppose this is?

LORD ALFRED: A blower to the kitchen, I suppose.

RAFFLES: It served that purpose once, but I thought of diverting it to the bedroom with a little electrical device for increasing the sound. It pays sometimes to be an eaves-dropper.

BUNNY: You never showed me that.

RAFFLES: My dear Bunny, there have been times when I have felt a little jealous, and this was one of those occasions. Finding you with Lord Alfred . . .

BUNNY: How could you suppose, A.J. . . . ?

RAFFLES: Your friend dead and Lord Alfred's friend in exile . . . I felt a little insecure, Bunny, in spite of that black band. But you should never wear a thing like that with evening dress. I'm not conventional but it shocks me. One must choose carefully what conventions to defy.

BUNNY [*pulling the band off*]: It's gone. Never to return.

RAFFLES: Oh, I don't expect to rise from the dead again. That would shock the Archbishop.

LORD ALFRED: You asked me, sir, about my detestable father's house. The baccarat will be at his country house. I hope now that he has you to help him, Bunny will agree to a little burgling.

RAFFLES: Ah, but will I help him, Lord Alfred? I've had time for reflection as well as Bunny. I was in a kind of prison too. Stone rocks instead of stone walls. And open to the sky. 'That little tent of blue that prisoners call the sky.' That's a remarkable poem of Wilde's you have beside your bed, Bunny. It was another sort of sky for me – a merciless glaring sky above the dried veld. I've had two passions in my life, Lord Alfred. Cricket and burglary. I have been pretty good at both, but I've begun to wonder whether it's really possible to keep practising them together. [*Pause*] I believe your father's house is in Hertfordshire, a county singularly without character.

LORD ALFRED: It is.

RAFFLES: I once spent a very sad weekend at Hemel Hempstead.

[*Raffles goes and looks at the photo on the wall. He touches his bat with tenderness.*]

Lying out there on Spion Kop I had a dream, Bunny. The old Raffles would be dead and someone, perhaps with the insignificant name of Jones, would land at Harwich. He knows a little about cricket – in Cape Town he had shown some promise. Perhaps he could find his way into a minor county eleven. Perhaps he might even turn professional – I imagine we are pretty short of ready cash, Bunny? Who knows? After a time Jones's talents might be spotted. A good slow bowler and no mean batsman. He might at last find himself a place with the Players and bowl that pseudo-Gentleman Grace for a duck first ball. That would make him forget the 400 not out you are too young to remember. Do you know – lying flat with my nose on the burnt grass of Spion Kop, I imagined I was smelling the turf at Lord's on a hot summer's day.

BUNNY: They'd recognize you at once, A.J.

RAFFLES: You didn't recognize me in Mackenzie's beard. That fraud W. G. Grace – would you recognize him *without* his beard? [*Pause*] Where does your father keep his cash, Lord Alfred?

LORD ALFRED: A safe in his bedroom. A very old-fashioned one. Behind the painting of a dog in a basket by Landseer. That's all he cares for – dogs and pugilists. Will you do it, sir?

RAFFLES: And what will you get out of it, Lord Alfred?

LORD ALFRED: A story to make Oscar laugh.

RAFFLES: I prefer to work with men who want money. They are more reliable.

LORD ALFRED: Give me any share you like. I'll send it to Oscar. He's in Paris, miserably poor.

RAFFLES: I much admire your friend. He was reckless in the pursuit of one passion. It's even more reckless to be divided between two, but how is one to decide? There is such poetry and drama in them both, though the poets I think have only celebrated cricket. Do you remember Francis Thompson:

'For the field is full of shades as I near the shadowy coast −'

I was near enough on Spion Kop −

> 'And a ghostly batsman plays to the bowling of a ghost,
> And I look through my tears on a soundless clapping host
>   As the runstealers flicker to and fro,
>   To and fro,
> O my Hornby and my Barlow long ago.'

Thank God he didn't add Grace, but he should have seen *me* at my best, Bunny. And then there's Newbolt, a fine poet underrated by writers of your school, Lord Alfred.

> 'There's a breathless hush in the Close tonight −
>   Ten to make and the match to win −
> A bumping pitch and a blinding light,
>   An hour to play and the last man in.
> And it's not for the sake of a ribboned coat,
>   Or the selfish hope of a season's fame,
> But his Captain's hand on his shoulder smote . . .'

I don't much like that last line. It smacks too much of Inspector Mackenzie. [*Pause*] I think I could be happy enough with cricket and to hell with burglary, Bunny, but what would you do all the long summer?

BUNNY: I'd be in the crowd cheering your hat trick or your century.

RAFFLES: You see, Lord Alfred, Bunny votes for cricket.

LORD ALFRED: There's not only my disreputable father's cash in the house, Mr Raffles. There are always a few doxies around with their diamonds and their gold bracelets. Think what a fool he'd look if you *looted* the place.

RAFFLES: It's a good thing the summer's nearly over. I'll have a lot of work to do at the nets, Bunny, before I try my luck again. I've still got a bit of shrapnel in the left shoulder, but a spot of surgery will soon put that right.

BUNNY: Thanks to you I think I've got enough to see us through the winter.

RAFFLES: Ah, those winters, Lord Alfred. The winters Bunny and I have had together, here in old Albany. No women to trouble our peace like Byron had. A wood fire. A Wisden to set our memories working over a glass of old Madeira. Then a leisurely dinner at the Café Royal round the corner, making our last plans over a Château Lafite. And then a hansom to the dangerous suburbs. You as a poet, Lord Alfred, will appreciate that burglary has poetry as much as cricket. An unknown house – all houses after midnight are unknown, however much you've examined them in sunlight. Will there be a watch-dog in the garden? No, not in suburbia. Here's a grass border. [*He acts the whole affair*] Walk it as you'd walk a plank. Gravel makes a noise and flowerbeds tell a tale. Never use the heel. [*He arrives at the door and the dangling cane*] Up there, look, there's a balcony. This cane will prove useful. Or perhaps the front door is an easy one to open with the right tool. Think of the broad staircase that faces you, leading up from the dark hall. No voices from the servants' quarters, a murmur from the dining-room. Here they sit late and sleepy over the wine. Give me my opera hat, Bunny. I must light a candle. These shoes were specially made by Lobb's. They never give a tell-tale squeak. I am on the first landing now. The room on the left looks out on to the garden, but who sleeps in it? No daylight inspection could tell that.

BUNNY: Where am I, A.J.?

RAFFLES: Where you ought to be, of course. Up on the balcony with the rope fixed to the rail. There must always be two ways of escape.

LORD ALFRED: Every guest will have brought cash to pay his losses. No IOUs. There will be thousands of pounds in the house that night.

RAFFLES: The cracksman is worthy of a poet, Lord Alfred. The French have Villon, but there's a sad gap in our literature, though I've sometimes thought that Francis Thompson had Inspector Mackenzie and me in mind when he wrote *The Hound of Heaven*.

> 'I fled him down the nights and down the days,
> I fled him down the arches of the years.'

I'm not convinced of the existence of God, but I'm quite sure of Inspector Mackenzie.

> 'Still with unhurrying chase
> And unperturbed pace'

– a fine description of a Scotland Yard flatfoot.

LORD ALFRED: The house party arrives on Friday.

RAFFLES [*taking the ball out of the net and twisting it in his hands*]: Burglary or cricket. What a choice! It's the same game, really. One man's skill against another's, and luck always taking a hand. 'Ten to make and the match to win.' Surely this is going to be the tired ball I've been waiting for. The moment's come to step out of the crease and smash it to the boundary – or is it not so simple as it looks? Is there a trap there? All the field's alert, but what's the good of a drawn match? I hate stone-walling. The risk makes the game. The risk, Lord Alfred. [*Pause*] I'll need a list of all the house guests and the rooms they occupy.

LORD ALFRED: I can get it from the housekeeper tomorrow.

RAFFLES: And a plan of the house floor by floor.

LORD ALFRED: I'll draw you one now if you'll give me a sheet of paper.

[*Lord Alfred sits down at the table. Bunny gives him a sheet of paper. Lord Alfred begins to draw.*]

RAFFLES: Are our bicycles in trim for a country ride, Bunny? It's not the job for a hansom.

BUNNY: They are.

RAFFLES: My Beeston Humber and your Royal Sunbeam, and the good Dunlop tyres. They leave tracks like a rattlesnake, Lord Alfred, but they are the most popular brand – nothing to distinguish our snake from all the other snakes on a wet road.

[*Thoughtfully*] What a devilishly clever tempter you have always been. You tempted your friend Wilde to defy your father – the Scarlet Marquess they call him, don't they? – and Wilde ended in Reading Gaol.

LORD ALFRED: Are you afraid?

RAFFLES: Of course I'm afraid. Very much afraid. What poetry would be left in life if one couldn't feel fear?

LORD ALFRED [*pointing at his plan*]: This is my father's bedroom. Here's the Landseer painting I told you about. Behind is the safe. Very old. Easy to open.

SLOW CURTAIN

Act Two

A bedroom in the Marquess of Queensberry's country house. A little light is coming through an open door in the right wall leading to a dressing-room and bathroom. Standing out from the back wall is a double bed. On the wall to the left of it hangs a Landseer painting, and to the right of the bed a door leads to the passage outside. A dressing-table stands beside the dressing-room door, and on the left of the room double curtains hide double windows and a balcony. The room is in darkness, except for the light from the dressing-room, and it is empty when the curtain rises. After a moment furtive sounds — scratches and rubbings and the clink of metal — come from behind the curtains.

They cease abruptly when there is a knock on the door. The door to the passage opens and a waiter, a young fair-haired man with a moustache, enters. He carries a bottle of champagne in an ice-bucket shoulder high. He turns on a centre light by the door, goes and looks through the door of the dressing-room and then puts the tray down on the dressing-table. A gold box on the dressing-table catches his eye. He lifts the lid and looks inside. At that moment a sneeze sounds behind the curtains. He hastily puts the box down and leaves, turning out the light. A short period of silence, and then the furtive noises begin again. The curtains sway, a voice says, 'Damn!'

Bunny emerges in evening dress with a cloak. He has the end of a cord in one hand and an opera hat reversed in the other — the Raffles Relic — with a candle burning inside it. He blows out the candle, drops the end of the rope and kicks it out of sight behind the curtain. Then he inspects the room, as the waiter did, peering first into the dressing-room. Next he identifies the picture on the back wall and is about to lift it down when he is disturbed by a knock on the door. He hastily retreats behind the curtain. The door to the passage opens, and this time it is Raffles in evening dress who enters and turns on the light. He too carries a tray with a bottle of champagne on ice. Unlike the waiter he carries it unprofessionally in both hands. He pauses at the dressing-table and is a little disconcerted at the sight of the other bottle. He hesitates and then puts down his ice-bucket *beside the other. He sees the gold box. He lifts it in his hands and mentally weighs it.*

BUNNY [*entering from behind the curtains*]: A.J.!

RAFFLES: Admirably on time, Bunny.

BUNNY: You've forgotten to turn your waistcoat and where's your black tie?

RAFFLES: I saw myself in the glass and couldn't bear it. A hero of Spion Kop can become a Chelsea pensioner, but never a waiter. Anyway, I intend to mingle with the guests, Bunny.

BUNNY: Carrying a bottle of champagne on a tray?

RAFFLES: I admit I took that in a misguided moment. And now there seems to be one bottle too many.

BUNNY: And one waiter too many. I thought it was you for a moment.

RAFFLES: I'm sorry. One should never improvise. I followed a fellow to the cellar and I couldn't resist snatching a bottle myself – there was a tray handy. I quite forgot I was a guest and not a waiter, but no harm's done. Now sketch me the battle-field, Bunny. The rope safely attached to the balcony?

BUNNY: Of course. There's a dressing-room through there and a bathroom beyond. And look, A.J., there's the Landseer.

RAFFLES: And here's a very handsome gold box. Not in the best of taste, but melted down . . . I bet you it weighs around a hundred ounces. And some diamonds of the first water in the lid. A plume and feathers. Obviously a present from the Prince of Wales. It sounds unpatriotic, but I long to pry them off, Bunny.

BUNNY: Are they large enough to recut?

RAFFLES: The best ones are. There's a smut on your nose, Bunny. That doesn't go with evening dress.

BUNNY: It was an infernal scramble to get on to the balcony. What first, A.J.? We'd better move fast.

RAFFLES: Bunny, Bunny, you've forgotten all my lessons. One must never burgle in a hurry. Bad for the nerves, like putting on your pads too soon. The men are all sitting down happily to their baccarat. The Scarlet Marquess never goes to bed before one.

BUNNY: But look at the dressing-table. Scent. Powder. All sorts of frippery.

RAFFLES: Either the Scarlet Marquess takes after his son or he's got a woman with him. That's awkward. You can never depend on a woman's bedtime. A sick headache, a quarrel with her lover. Life would really be so much easier without them.

[*While Raffles talks he has moved across the room and taken down the Landseer, disclosing a small safe. He leans the Landseer against the head of the bed.*]

RAFFLES: A nice old-fashioned model. My safe-keys, Bunny. Burroughs of Birmingham. Went out of business in the fifties. Those dear old trustful times.

[*Raffles tries a few keys before finding the right one. He opens the door of the safe and gazes in with satisfaction.*]

RAFFLES: How satisfying the sight of gold is. To think there are economists who want a paper currency. Bunny, that gold box on the dressing-table. Bring it here. Gold cries for gold.

BUNNY: It's full of letters.

RAFFLES: Get rid of them then. No, no, Bunny, not on the floor. In your pockets.

[*Raffles begins to fill the box with sovereigns.*]

BUNNY: Let's be off, A.J. The box alone . . .

RAFFLES [*handing him the box*]: There. Put that under your cloak.

[*Raffles begins to fill his pockets with coins. Bunny opens the door of a large wardrobe full of women's dresses.*]

BUNNY: A.J. For God's sake, look. This is a *woman's* room.

RAFFLES: I can hear a woman talking in the passage. That damned friend of yours! Quick, Bunny, on to the balcony.

[*Raffles closes the safe and turns out the centre light. He follows Bunny. The Landseer remains leaning against the head of the bed. The door opens and a lady in a long sweeping evening gown stands silhouetted against the light of the passage. She is around thirty years old with great beauty and poise. She crosses to the dressing-table and looks at herself in the glass. An invisible spot demands attention: some cotton wool from a drawer, a squeeze with the fingers, a touch of alcohol from a bottle, another examination, a dab of powder. She sits down at the dressing-table and undoes her elaborate coiffure. She puts a jewelled ornament she has worn in her*]

hair into a drawer. Her hair hangs down to her waist. There is a tap
on the door.]

LADY: Come in.

[*A young lady's maid enters. We can soon tell from her manner that*
she is devoted to her mistress.]

MAID: You never rang, ma'am.

LADY: I don't really need you tonight, Mary. You were up very
late yesterday.

MAID: I'm not a bit tired, ma'am. You'll never manage . . .

LADY: I undressed myself easily enough before I married. I don't
suppose I've forgotten how.

MAID: You'll get yourself all tangled up. I'm sure you will.

LADY: Well, go and turn on my bath and we'll see.

[*The maid goes through the dressing-room door and we hear a*
distant tap running. The lady gets out of her dress easily enough.
She goes and lays it on the bed. She has an air of happiness and
relaxation. She sings to herself as she sits again at the dressing-table,
undoes her flowered garters which she leaves under the looking-
glass. The song is a sentimental drawing-room ballad which will be
made famous later by Yvette Guilbert.]

LADY [*singing*]:

    I will give you the keys of heaven,
    I will give you the keys of heaven,
    Madam, will you walk? Madam, will you talk?
    Madam, will you walk and talk with me?

[*She pulls off her long stockings and plays with them thoughtfully,*
swinging them in time with her song.]

    Though you give me the keys of heaven,
    Though you give me the keys of heaven,
    Yet I will not walk; no, I will not talk;
    No, I will not walk or talk with thee.

[*The lady drapes her stockings over the chair, but now she has a little*
difficulty with her stays. She gets up and looks for aid in a long pier
glass, but after a short struggle she loses interest for a moment in the
stays as she regards her own image and sings to it. The tap is turned
off.]

    I will give you a coach and six,
    Six black horses as black as pitch.

[*The maid comes to the door carrying a dressing-gown of rose-coloured silk. She watches her mistress with amusement.*]

    Madam, will you walk? Madam, will you talk?

    Madam, will you walk and talk with me?

MAID [*singing*]:

    Though you give me a coach and six,

    Six black horses as black as pitch;

    Yet I will not walk; no, I will not talk;

    No, I will not walk or talk with thee.

LADY: Why, what a pretty voice you have, Mary.

MAID [*helping with the stays*]: You see, ma'am, it's not so easy to undress yourself as you thought.

    [*The curtain moves as Raffles makes a crack to see through. The maid as she folds up the stays notices the curtains move and goes towards the window.*]

MAID: Oh, ma'am, there's quite a cold draught from the window. I'd better close it.

LADY [*as she gets out of her big drawers*]: No, let it be, Mary. He likes the room fresh. He says it makes the bed warmer. Besides he likes to smoke his last cigar.

MAID [*a little shocked*]: A cigar? In the bedroom, ma'am? But do you like that?

LADY [*a little sadly*]: I like what he likes, Mary.

MAID: That's love, isn't it? Real love.

LADY: Yes, I suppose it is.

    [*She is quite naked now. The maid approaches her, carrying the dressing-gown, but stops a moment before draping it over her to look at her mistress with admiration.*]

LADY: What is it, Mary?

MAID [*singing softly*]:

    I will give you the keys of my heart,

    And we will be married till death us do part;

    Madam, will you walk? Madam, will you talk?

    Madam . . .

    [*Something in the song now has touched her mistress on the raw. She snatches the dressing-gown from the maid and speaks abruptly.*]

LADY: That's enough, Mary. Go to bed.

[*She moves to the dressing-room door but relents before she leaves and speaks kindly.*]

LADY: Good night. Sleep well.

MAID [*a little dashed, the brief intimacy over*]: Good night, ma'am.

[*She leaves the room. A few moments pass.*]

[*Raffles comes from behind the curtains followed by Bunny. They speak in low voices.*]

RAFFLES: You clear off by the balcony, Bunny. Where are the bicycles?

BUNNY: Hidden in the shrubbery to the left of the door as you come out. I'll be waiting for you there.

RAFFLES: No. You'll leave at once with that box.

BUNNY: I don't leave unless you come with me.

RAFFLES: Don't be an ass. How can I leave with all that lovely money lying around the baccarat table?

BUNNY: Somebody's sure to spot you, A.J. These are the sort of fellows who go to Lord's.

RAFFLES: Only bishops go to Lord's. Besides, I'm dead, Bunny, don't you realize that, I'm dead.

BUNNY: You've always said there must be two ways of escape. I'll guard the balcony until you are clear.

RAFFLES: It's not the young woman, is it, Bunny? Tell me the truth. I grant you she has the slender flanks of a young fawn.

BUNNY: What a fool you are, A.J.! Have I ever looked twice at a woman?

RAFFLES: Well, I thought that you looked rather more than twice from behind the curtain.

BUNNY: First you were jealous of Bosie, and now – this female object.

RAFFLES: I've been occasionally attracted by a female object myself. In the absence of a good chef, Bunny, they serve to warm the soup. [*Voice singing again*] She would have made a nice choirboy if she had cut off all that redundant hair.

[*A soft knock on the door to the passage.*]

RAFFLES: Back, Bunny. [*Bunny hesitates*] Go on, you ass. No argument. I can manage this. [*A second knock*] Take the box and get back to Albany.

[*Bunny disappears behind the curtains. A rattle as he retrieves the rope. A third knock, louder this time.*]

VOICE: Alice, it's Bertie.

[*The door opens and a bearded figure, familiar to all the world, stands in the doorway.*]

RAFFLES [*with an astonishment he can't conceal*]: Your Royal Highness.

[*The somewhat stout figure of the Prince of Wales advances with ponderous authority into the room.*]

PRINCE: Who the hell are you?

[*The Prince speaks with a heavy Teutonic accent.*]

RAFFLES: Jones.

PRINCE: Jones? What Jones?

RAFFLES: I know it's a somewhat *usual* name, Your Royal Highness.

PRINCE: My name is Portland, Mr Portland.

RAFFLES: I thought . . .

PRINCE: I advise you not to think along those lines, Mr Jones. I am Mr Portland.

RAFFLES [*obediently*]: Mr Portland.

PRINCE: And now what the hell are you doing in this room?

RAFFLES: I understood it was Lord Queensberry's room, sir. He asked for champagne.

PRINCE: It is Lord Queensberry's room. But he has been kind enough to lend his room to a friend of mine. [*He goes to the dressing-table and looks at the two bottles of champagne*] Did Lord Queensberry order two bottles? That's most unlike him. [*The Prince examines one bottle*] Pommery. A very common Pommery.

RAFFLES: I felt sure there had been a mistake, Mr Portland, so I brought another bottle. Mumm '84.

PRINCE: By God, you are an intelligent fellow, Jones.

[*The Prince goes to the dressing-room door and knocks. There's no reply – only the sound of splashing. The Prince knocks again.*]

PRINCE: Alice, how much longer are you going to be?

LADY'S VOICE: Only two minutes, Bertie.

PRINCE: Only two minutes! Multiply that by ten, Jones, and you'll be near the truth.

[*The Prince sits down by the dressing-table.*]

PRINCE: By the way, how is it that you are wearing a white tie?
And a white waistcoat?

RAFFLES: I haven't got black ones, sir.

PRINCE: What sort of a waiter are you?

RAFFLES: An amateur one, sir. I'm sure you know what it is to be
temporarily short of funds. I put my name down at an agency.
Extra assistance was required here in a hurry, and I quite forgot
about the tie – and the waistcoat.

PRINCE: You mean that's your own suit? You've got a good tailor,
Jones.

RAFFLES: I'm afraid, sir, it smells of mothballs. I have been away in
South Africa.

PRINCE: Looking for diamonds?

RAFFLES: Wounded and taken prisoner at Spion Kop, sir.

PRINCE: You were there? Why, sit down, my man, and tell me
more. A soldier mustn't stand in front of a non–combatant.

RAFFLES: I would rather stand, sir, in your case.

PRINCE: Sit down, I said.

RAFFLES: If it's a command . . .

PRINCE: It is.

[*Raffles sits.*]

PRINCE: Your name is Jones, eh?

RAFFLES: As certainly, sir, as yours is Mr Portland.

PRINCE: Ach! What regiment?

RAFFLES: Mounted Light Infantry, sir.

PRINCE: An amateur soldier as well as an amateur waiter. Your
commander?

RAFFLES: Colonel Thorneycroft, sir. Under General Woodgate.

PRINCE: You were in the first assault then?

RAFFLES: Yes, sir. With some Lancashire companies and the Royal
Engineers.

PRINCE: So you really were there, Jones. You mustn't mind
my questions. I've met a good few beggars in Piccadilly
who claim to have been at Spion Kop. Are you South
African?

RAFFLES: No, sir. But I enlisted at Cape Town.

PRINCE: What were you doing there?

RAFFLES: To you, Mr Portland, I would like to tell the truth. I was travelling abroad for my country's good.

PRINCE: Ach! I've done a bit of that myself. We seem to have more than one thing in common, Jones. [*The Prince takes out a cigar case*] Have a cigar. Alice is a good girl. She lets me smoke.

RAFFLES: If you don't mind, Mr Portland, I'd rather have a Sullivan.

[*Raffles too takes out a case and the two men light up.*]

PRINCE: I think you and I might try the champagne.

RAFFLES: You honour me too much, sir.

PRINCE: I wish I could honour every man who fought at Spion Kop. I think for us, Jones, the Mumm. Pommery is good enough for the ladies.

[*Raffles opens the bottle and serves the wine.*]

PRINCE: How did you escape?

RAFFLES: It's not so hard, sir, from a Boer prison. I've been in tighter spots at home. I even brought away a souvenir. [*He takes out his watch and hands it to the Prince*] I had the honour of being interrogated by General Botha himself.

PRINCE [*examining watch*]: Louis Botha . . . President Kruger . . . By God, Jones, you're a man after my own heart. I only wish I could show this to my mother. It would make the old lady's eyes sparkle.

RAFFLES: Give it to her, Mr Portland.

PRINCE: No, no . . .

RAFFLES: I would be proud to feel that I had given her a moment's pleasure.

PRINCE: Impossible. You earned this at Spion Kop.

RAFFLES: She has earned it, Mr Portland, more than any of us.

PRINCE: You make me ashamed, Jones. If you ever need a reference . . .

RAFFLES: I'll write to Mr Portland.

PRINCE: What address?

RAFFLES: London W. I think would be sufficient, sir.

PRINCE: Must I call it a present from Private Jones?

RAFFLES: Corporal Jones, sir. Say one of the *English* Joneses.

PRINCE: Do you know, if it wasn't for my mother, you and I wouldn't be talking together here. You see, I made her a rash promise a few years back to play no more baccarat. Presumably, Jones, you have been blessed with a mother?

RAFFLES: She died too early, sir, for me to have encountered her socially.

PRINCE: Ach! She talked to me very severely about gambling. I tried in vain to persuade her that a game of baccarat played by rich men for stakes they can afford is no more gambling than a bottle of champagne at dinner is alcoholism. Oh well, I've kept my promise. We've been playing bridge all the afternoon. Naturally the boys down there wanted to change to something stronger, so up I came to talk to Alice.

RAFFLES: I'm hardly such good company.

PRINCE: Well, one doesn't want to talk to a lady about Spion Kop. [*The Prince picks up the garters from the dressing-table, and lays them down again*] What an awful muddle, Jones, that was. Poor General Woodgate. I knew him slightly. He was lucky to die.

RAFFLES: I was lying close by when they came to carry him away, shot through the eye. I heard him sobbing, 'Let me alone. Let me alone.'

[*A long pause.*]

PRINCE: I have a German nephew, Jones. An intolerable ass. He fancies himself as a soldier and laughs at me as a useless non-combatant. This tummy of mine would have made a good mark, wouldn't it, on Spion Kop? The papers jeer at General Buller for his incompetence, but I doubt if Mr Portland would have done any better – nor my nephew Willy either.

RAFFLES: I think I have seen photographs of your nephew, sir. A rather brazen moustache.

PRINCE: And probably sitting on a white horse. He had the effrontery once to write to my mother . . . why does one tell family secrets to Mr Jones?

RAFFLES: Perhaps because I am like a stranger in the train. Once in everyone's life a man feels the need of a stranger in the train.

PRINCE: My strangers have generally been women. They are wonderful listeners. Do you know, my nephew had the effrontery to write to my mother that an honorary colonel of the Prussian Hussars had no right to be embroiled in a gambling case?

RAFFLES: Should I have been addressing you, sir, as *Colonel* Portland?

PRINCE: Ach! You know, Jones, these foreign uniforms they send me, they never fit. They call me Tum-Tum behind my back, but they never allow for it in their measurements.

[*He gets up and goes to the dressing-room door. He knocks again.*]

PRINCE: Alice! You've kept me long enough. [*Pause. He puts his ear to the door*] Two minutes still. She's got that boat in the bath with her. She calls it the *Britannia*. She likes sailing it up and down between her legs. Scylla and Charybdis she calls them. I've been wrecked there sometimes myself. [*He comes back and sits down*] Another ten minutes at least. Good women have such a passion to be clean. If they only knew what really takes our fancy. [*Again unconsciously he picks up the garters*] Do you know Paris well?

RAFFLES: I've spent a little time there.

PRINCE: Do you know La Goulue at the Moulin Rouge?

RAFFLES: I haven't had that chance, sir.

PRINCE: A fine, fine woman. I can talk to her as I can talk to you – as if I were real.

RAFFLES: Aren't we all real, sir?

PRINCE: I will tell you a parable, Jones. Once I took a walk with friends in the East End of London. I saw the very poor and how they lived. When I tried to give them money my friends hustled me into a cab. I was wrong, of course. You don't, if you think, give a starving cat milk, and you can't solve the problem of poverty with a handful of guineas. But what hurt me was that I had come there to talk to them, and my friends had carried me around like a wooden doll. I wasn't real any more than a plaster image in a Roman church. To be real for a little while we have to pretend . . . that you are Jones and I am Mr Portland. I like women – because they let one pretend. It's only with a chance encounter like ours one can speak of Spion Kop and La Goulue in the same breath. The dying of poor Woodgate and the dancing of La Goulue. A dancer's honour and a soldier's honour. My father wouldn't have understood the connection, and I'm quite sure my son doesn't. You and I, Jones, belong to a very special moment of time. *La Fin de Siècle* the papers call it, don't they? But it's more than just the end of any century. I have an awful fear that my nephew Willy, with his talk of Huns and Attila and inspiring fear, represents the future. I prefer my old mother . . . and senseless honourable Spion Kop. And La Goulue, of course. [*Pause*] You'd better go back to your job, Jones. I don't want you to lose it by keeping a lonely man company for . . .

[*A rush of feet along the passage outside and a furious beating on the door.*]

MAN'S VOICE: Sir, let me in. Let me in, sir.

PRINCE: The Scarlet Marquess. [*In a louder voice as the knocking is repeated*] The door is not locked, Queensberry.

[*The man who enters, the Marquess of Queensberry, is a small man with curly red hair, heavy eyebrows and long whiskers, and a heavy ugly lower lip. He is in a state of great excitement.*]

MARQUESS: Sir, there's an inspector from Scotland Yard downstairs.

PRINCE: Of course there is. I carry policemen about with me like an umbrella.

MARQUESS: This is not one of your troop, sir. There's a Special Branch man with him.

PRINCE: Just anarchists again, I suppose. Is it me or you they want to blow up?

MARQUESS: The inspector says there's a plot to rob your friend.

PRINCE: Alice, poor girl? I doubt if all her jewellery is worth a hundred pounds.

[*Throughout the conversation Raffles remains seated with his back to the Marquess and the door. The Marquess sees the Landseer propped up on the bed. He gives an anguished cry.*]

MARQUESS: My Landseer!

PRINCE: Your what?

MARQUESS: Who put it on the bed?

[*The Marquess runs to the safe taking a key from his pocket, opens it.*]

MARQUESS: I've been robbed.

PRINCE: So it was you not Alice they were after. I'm glad.

MARQUESS: But I've been robbed, sir.

PRINCE: So you have mentioned.

MARQUESS: Five hundred pounds gone.

PRINCE: Only bank cashiers calculate exact amounts of money without vulgarity. Just leave it that you've been robbed. Now have a glass of your excellent champagne.

MARQUESS: You sit there swilling my champagne as though nothing important had happened. Don't you understand, sir, what five hundred pounds means?

PRINCE: I begin to understand what it means to you.

[*The Marquess rushes into the passage and can be heard calling 'Inspector, Inspector.'*]

PRINCE: One must forgive him, Jones. The Marquess consorts too much with pugilists for his manners.

[*The real Inspector Mackenzie appears in the doorway with the Marquess behind him. The imitation by Raffles was not a bad one. His tweeds are as bad, but his accent is a lot less pronounced and is of course genuine Scots. He is much given to loud nose-blowing with a large bandanna handkerchief.*]

INSPECTOR: Inspector Mackenzie, Your Royal Highness.

PRINCE [*not rising*]: I am Mr Portland in this house, Inspector. Please remember that.

MARQUESS: Look there, Inspector. My safe broken open. Five hundred pounds gone.

[*The Inspector approaches the safe in a heavy leisurely way. He blows his nose and looks inside.*]

INSPECTOR: Not *broken* open, my lord. There are a few sovereigns left. Five, six, a round dozen maybe. The thief seems to hae been disturbed.

MARQUESS: Aren't you going to take finger-prints?

INSPECTOR: Oh, every thief kens all aboot finger-prints, sir. That Monsieur Bertillon taught 'em to wear gloves. I niver fash mysel' to carry pouder around with me.

[*Raffles remains seated near the Prince with his legs crossed and his back turned to the Inspector.*]

INSPECTOR: How long would you hae bin here, Your . . . sir?

PRINCE: Ten minutes. Perhaps a quarter of an hour.

[*The Inspector goes and draws back the curtains. Raffles watches him over his shoulder. The windows are open.*]

INSPECTOR: We are on the first floor. It's not a long leap from the balcony. [*He moves forward through the window on to the balcony and a moment later returns trailing a rope with him.*] He didna' need to leap. This is the way he came an' went. He's left his rope behind. A verra fine Manilla rope – it puts me in mind of a cracksman called Raffles who led me many a dance, but he's deid, God rest his soul, though I'd like to have takken him mysel' before God did.

PRINCE: You spoke of a plot, Inspector?

INSPECTOR: Yes, sir, I talked in London with a gentleman from the Special Branch. They deal with plots. I only deal with crime.

PRINCE: What sort of a plot?

INSPECTOR: Weel, it seems, sir, they hae an agent in the German Embassy. What we call an informer, an' he's told 'em that they are out to get certain letters.

PRINCE: Have you been indiscreet again, Queensberry?

MARQUESS: Indiscreet? When have I ever been indiscreet? God damn it, Inspector, five hundred pounds gone and you babble about letters.

INSPECTOR: It's not exactly your lordship who's concerned . . .

PRINCE: Well, who is? Come to the point, man.

MARQUESS: What's it all got to do with my safe? I didn't keep any letters there.

INSPECTOR: No, your lordship. These letters, well, it's like this, if the information is correct an' I'm not saying it is . . .

PRINCE [*impatiently*]: Inspector!

INSPECTOR: These letters were addressed to a lady staying here. A lady his lordship lent his room to.

PRINCE: What in heaven's name would the Germans want Alice's letters for?

INSPECTOR: To publish them in the German Press, sir. Mind you, that's what the Special Branch say.

PRINCE [*with a loud laugh*]: By God, it's possible. A typical idea of Willy's. I suppose I *would* look a bit foolish. One shouldn't write letters like that in prose, but we are not all poets like your son, Queensberry. All the same it hardly seems worth a plot. Poor mother, it's a pity she reads the German Press. My wife will only laugh. You know, Jones, or perhaps you don't, the laughter of someone you love can be a lot more painful than anger.

MARQUESS: I don't know what you are all talking about. He's stolen *five hundred pounds*.

PRINCE: If you must talk like a bank cashier, Queensberry, be accurate. Five hundred minus twelve.

INSPECTOR: Where were the letters kept, sir, if not in the safe?

PRINCE: The lady kept them, I believe, in a gold cigar box I had given her. It was a present to me from some friends in the theatre. It was decorated with my arms in diamonds, but as no doubt you know, Inspector, sandalwood is a much better receptacle for cigars than gold and diamonds. It was her whim to put my letters in the box instead of throwing them into the waste-paper basket as I advised her to do. They were really not worthy of so important a setting.

INSPECTOR: They were dangerous, sir?

PRINCE: They were worse, Inspector. They were badly written.

INSPECTOR: And this gold box, sir? She didn't keep it in that safe there?

PRINCE: No, no, the safe belongs to Lord Queensberry. We are only weekend guests.

INSPECTOR: Then where would she keep it, sir?

PRINCE: Well, the last time I saw the box – it was earlier this evening before dinner – I had come to take her down – I teased her a little about it.

INSPECTOR: Where was it, sir?

PRINCE: Here on the dressing-table.

INSPECTOR: And it's not there now.

PRINCE: No – now you mention it – it isn't.

INSPECTOR: Where is the lady, sir? With your permission I would like to ask her a few questions.

PRINCE: It would be a little inconvenient, Inspector. She is in her bath, or rather Lord Queensberry's bath – the only one in the house. If you don't mind waiting, I don't think she will be more than half an hour. She told me she would be two minutes a quarter of an hour ago.

INSPECTOR [*looking at his notebook*]: I think, sir, you said that you and this gentleman came up about that time.

PRINCE: Oh no. Mr Jones was here when I arrived . . .

INSPECTOR: Here?

[*Raffles uncrosses his legs. He looks as if he might be preparing to rise.*]

PRINCE: He had brought me a rather better champagne than Lord Queensberry's first waiter had sent up. A very good Mumm '84.

MARQUESS: A Mumm '84! I've only two dozen bottles left. I provided no champagne. Neither you nor the lady asked for it.

PRINCE: Yet here are the two bottles. Perhaps your butler was more thoughtful than you.

MARQUESS: My butler does nothing without my orders. Who is this Mr Jones?

[*Raffles makes to rise, but the Prince signals him to remain seated.*]

PRINCE: A gentleman I'm proud to have met who fought at Spion Kop.

MARQUESS: Where's Spion Kop?

PRINCE: I forgot, Queensberry, that while England has been fighting the Boers, you have been fully engaged fighting Mr Oscar Wilde.

MARQUESS: I insist on knowing who this man is. This is my house.

RAFFLES [*speaking over his shoulder without rising*]: I am the second waiter with the Mumm '84, Lord Queensberry.

MARQUESS: How dare you sit there in my room like a gentleman?

RAFFLES: Mr Portland ordered me to sit. Mr Portland unlike you has a natural authority. So I sat and he hasn't asked me to rise.

MARQUESS: Who the hell are you? You aren't one of my men.

RAFFLES: Thank God, no.

[*The Inspector begins to approach.*]

RAFFLES: Forgive me, Mr Portland, if I get up.

[*Raffles jumps to his feet and makes a dash for the window, but the Inspector is too quick for him. He takes him by the left shoulder and spins him round.*]

INSPECTOR: A. J. Raffles! Come back from the deid. It's lak an answer to prayer. Many a time I've prayed to the guid God to let me put my hands on you.

RAFFLES: Be careful of my shoulder, Mackenzie. There's still a bit of Boer shrapnel lodged there.

PRINCE: *Raffles*, Mr Jones?

RAFFLES: I did hint to you, sir, that I was incognito like yourself.

PRINCE: *The* Raffles?

[*The Inspector as the Prince speaks has clapped on a pair of handcuffs.*]

RAFFLES [*looking glumly at the handcuffs*]: I haven't met another. I was an only child, but distant cousins of course are always apt to pop up.

PRINCE: I saw you in '96. At Lord's. 105 not out against Australia. You won us the Ashes.

RAFFLES: Well, I regret to say, sir, W. G. Grace also played a small but grandiloquent part.

MARQUESS: You infernal scoundrel, where is my money?

RAFFLES: I gather there are some twelve pounds still in the safe. As for the rest you can find some of them if you search me, but I would prefer the cleaner hands of Inspector Mackenzie.

[*The Marquess raises his hand to strike him.*]

PRINCE [*sharply*]: Marquess! Remember the Queensberry rules. You were really at Spion Kop, Raffles?

RAFFLES: Yes, sir, to you I have told no lies.

PRINCE: Take off the handcuffs, Inspector. This man has fought for his country, which is more than you or I have done.

MARQUESS: He's a common thief.

PRINCE: An uncommon one, I should say.

MARQUESS: He's robbed me and he's robbed you.

PRINCE: On the contrary he has given me a present of inestimable value. He will go quietly to Scotland Yard. I make myself responsible.

INSPECTOR: I'm afraid I can't obey you, sir.

PRINCE: You can't obey me?

INSPECTOR: I can't obey Mr Portland, sir.

PRINCE: I shall not always be Mr Portland.

INSPECTOR: I ken that weel, sir.

MARQUESS: Bravo, Inspector, no man is above the law, eh?

INSPECTOR: Verra true, my lord, but it doesna need all that emphasis.

RAFFLES: You know, I'm quite happy with these bracelets. A better lock than you had on your safe, Marquess. [*To the Prince*]

I am sorry, sir, for disorganizing your evening. It wasn't my intention. And if I had known that the gold box belonged to a friend of Mr Portland . . .

MARQUESS: I hope you'll lock him up in your coldest cell for the night, Inspector.

INSPECTOR: We have our Queensberry rules too, your lordship. We charge him, he telephones – if that's what he wants – to his lawyer, an' then we give him a nice cup o' tea – and a sandwich if he feels so inclined.

RAFFLES: Oh, that won't be necessary, Inspector. I dined well at the Café Royal before I came. Your sandwiches, I fear, would be of the railway station variety.

MARQUESS: I'll get my coachman out of bed and drive you to London myself. I intend to see justice done on this scoundrel.

RAFFLES [to the Prince]: I think, sir, you are more interested in the letters than in the gold box?

PRINCE: One can buy a new box at Asprey's. I would hate to rewrite my letters.

RAFFLES: I think I might be able to recover the letters, sir.

MARQUESS: And my gold?

RAFFLES: Ah, that is a separate matter. Mr Portland's interests must come first. There seems to be a basis for a bargain.

INSPECTOR: Ye canna bargain with the law, man.

RAFFLES: I'm told the Special Branch are sometimes more amenable. If I helped you to lay your hands on the mystery man . . .

INSPECTOR: The man with the rope?

RAFFLES: No, no, the waiter with the Pommery, of course.

[A key turns in the dressing-room door and the lady enters singing softly with a towel wrapped round her waist. The song dies on her lips as she looks at the four men in the room.]

LADY: Bertie, what on earth are all these people doing in *our* room?

CURTAIN

Act Three

The chambers in Albany early next morning. Half dark. A light burning on the table. Lord Alfred Douglas asleep in an armchair. A key grates in the hall lock. Bunny enters, his evening dress in a very tousled condition.

BUNNY: Bosie!
   [*Lord Alfred wakes with a start.*]
LORD ALFRED: My dear Bunny! You gave me quite a start, slinking in like a thief.
BUNNY [*bitterly*]: I am a thief.
LORD ALFRED: Oh yes, I had forgotten. It would have been more tactful to say 'calling early like the milkman'.
BUNNY: Raffles is caught.
LORD ALFRED: That's unfortunate.
BUNNY: It won't be long before the police are here. They know we always worked together.
   [*Bunny opens the chest and returns the opera hat to the secret drawer.*]
BUNNY: I left the rope behind. I hoped Raffles would use it. I hid in the shrubbery with the bicycles, until I saw him driven away in handcuffs with Inspector Mackenzie and another man.
LORD ALFRED: The burglary failed?
BUNNY: Oh, we did what you wanted. While I was hiding I could hear your father baying like a pack of foxhounds for his money. Here it is. [*He takes the gold box from under his evening cloak*] Or part of it. By this time Inspector Mackenzie has the rest.
LORD ALFRED: Whose box is it?
BUNNY: Your father's, I suppose. A present from the Prince of Wales.
LORD ALFRED: Impossible. My father would have pawned it long ago.
BUNNY: Open it. You'll find about half the money he had in the safe.

LORD ALFRED [*opening the box*]: He'll be fighting mad.

BUNNY: Take your share and get out before the police come.

LORD ALFRED: No, I owe you an alibi. Put on your pyjamas and lend me a pair. We both spent the night here.

BUNNY: And go to prison like Wilde? I prefer felony. They treat felony better. I suppose everyone, even a judge, has stolen something in his time, if only a woman, but sodomy is beyond his imagination.

LORD ALFRED: The boat train from Victoria leaves at nine. Come with me, Bunny. Oscar's in Paris at the Hôtel d'Alsace. He'll be glad to see us. Poor devil, he badly needs the money.

BUNNY: Take it all and clear out. I won't need it in jail, and at least they won't have *that* evidence. You've done enough harm, Bosie. Your errors of judgement always lead others to prison.

LORD ALFRED: What do you mean, Bunny?

BUNNY: There was a woman sleeping in your father's room.

LORD ALFRED: I suppose he keeps a whore. He's never been able to keep a wife.

BUNNY: This was no whore.

LORD ALFRED: How very odd. If you'd found a boxer, I could have understood it. My father has a passion for boxers – not in the interesting sense of the word. Revolting types with muscles like a coil of snakes and breasts like fat women at fairs. A broken nose or a cauliflower ear are marks of beauty to my disgusting parent.

BUNNY: There wasn't one woman on the guest list you gave us.

LORD ALFRED: Strange. A woman incognito. It wasn't our dear old Queen by any chance, was it?

BUNNY: It wasn't. I saw her undress.

LORD ALFRED: You seem to have had a *mouvementé* evening.

BUNNY: You find it amusing, don't you? Poor Raffles. He told me to take this box and go. He was so sure he could manage things. He always did manage somehow in the old days.

LORD ALFRED: I suppose even a burglar gets out of practice.

BUNNY: Be off, Bosie. It's not going to be so funny when the police arrive.

LORD ALFRED: But I've done nothing, Bunny. I've been innocently asleep. I had a dream of an enormous pineapple.

BUNNY: They'll make you out an accomplice before the fact or after the fact or both.

LORD ALFRED: My avaricious father stopped my allowance when I refused to leave Oscar. So you might say that this is part of his debt to me. I know man doesn't live by bread alone, but I've even had to give up caviare. Really, they can't charge me with drawing my own allowance. Anyway I don't much fancy Paris in a cheap hotel all alone with poor Oscar. Not necessarily alone either, though I shudder to think of what he can buy on two pounds ten a week. That's what his wife allows him.

BUNNY: All the more reason to take this and go.

LORD ALFRED: But what about Raffles' share?

BUNNY: The box will be our share, if I can hide it. It's worth more than the cash, but you wouldn't know the right market.

LORD ALFRED: I suppose it would save a bit of argument with the police if neither I nor the gold were here. I hate arguing with inferiors. They are so apt to raise their voices.

[*He begins to gather the money into his pockets.*]

BUNNY: Have a good time in Paris.

LORD ALFRED: I doubt if I shall. Oscar writes that the place is full of Americans and Germans. Do change your mind, Bunny, and come too.

BUNNY: I was alone for two years in prison without Raffles. I'm not going to let him suffer the same way.

[*Sound of the hall door closing. Footsteps in the hall. Bunny turns.*]

BUNNY: Too late, Bosie. Here they come.

[*The door opens, but it is not the police but the first waiter with the blond moustache who enters, still in his waiter's tails, wearing a black overcoat. When he speaks it is with a slight foreign accent.*]

WAITER: Excuse me. The door was open.

BUNNY: What are you doing here?

WAITER: I will explain, sir. You and I belong to similar services. I was hiding in the same bushes. There were two bicycles. You took one, I took the other.

BUNNY: You took Raffles' bicycle – his Beeston Humber? You're a damned thief.

WAITER: Those are not terms we employ in my service or yours.

BUNNY: What the hell are you talking about?

LORD ALFRED: I think I've met you somewhere before.

WAITER: Yes, my lord, that is true. At the Narcissus Club in Archer Street.

LORD ALFRED: Are you a waiter there?

WAITER: *Nein, nein.* I am a member like you, Lord Alfred. On a secret mission one suffers loneliness. No one to speak to. That is bad for the health. It is a security risk. So I go to the Narcissus Club, Archer Street. That was the address recommended by my service for agreeable uninquisitive company.

BUNNY: Would it be against security to tell me who you are?

WAITER: Between our services there is no question of security. [*He clicks his heels together*] Captain von Blixen of the Prussian Hussars. Seconded for a secret mission in England because of my knowledge of English. You, I believe, are Captain Yevgeny Petrovitch.

BUNNY: No.

VON BLIXEN: *Nein?*

BUNNY: *Nein.*

VON BLIXEN: In Berlin we are taught not to have secrets from fellow officers engaged on similar missions. Let the best man win as in chess.

BUNNY: It was you I saw between the curtains bringing the bottle of champagne.

VON BLIXEN: Yes, I did it well? Tray on the level of the right shoulder. I received special instruction at the Hotel Adlon. High commendation from the head waiter.

BUNNY: What on earth do you want? I warn you the police will be here any moment.

VON BLIXEN: Do not worry, Captain Petrovitch. We have much time to arrange our affair. I have studied very hard the methods of the English police. I took that course under a most distinguished professor, Dr Heinrich Engelbeim, author of the classic work, *English Methods of Law Enforcement from Ethelred the Unready to Sir Robert Peel.* I was head of my class as at the Adlon Hotel. I have the impression, Captain Petrovitch, that they do not train so well at St Petersburg. Your colleague was wearing a white tie, and he carried the champagne with both hands. And you – you sneezed behind the curtain. They did not teach you not to sneeze at St Petersburg? *Nein?*

BUNNY: *Nein.*

VON BLIXEN: You disturbed me when you sneezed, Captain. Ah, I said at once to myself, that is Captain Yevgeny Petrovitch. Now we in Berlin are trained not to sneeze.

BUNNY: Bosie, is this fellow mad or am I mad?

LORD ALFRED: Tell me, Captain von Blixen, how do they train you not to sneeze? A finger on the upper lip?

VON BLIXEN: That is not to be relied on. It is not scientific. If you feel a sneeze about to arrive, you take a pin prepared by our great pharmaceutical firm of Bayer and you prick the nose. Close to the nostril. You see, [*He turns up his lapel*] here I carry pins. Three pins. It is the allowance for one mission.

LORD ALFRED: Suppose a fourth sneeze arrives?

VON BLIXEN: That would mean a real cold. We have a very strict examination before a mission and many injections.

LORD ALFRED: One catches cold very easily in England, Captain, even in summer.

VON BLIXEN: If I catch a cold, then I retire. Another takes my place.

LORD ALFRED: Trained at the Adlon?

VON BLIXEN: *Ja, ja.* Naturally.

LORD ALFRED: I once passed a happy weekend at the Adlon with Oscar. We little knew that the waiter who brought us our morning coffee might be training as an agent. It's true he proved very well trained in other ways. Please tell me, Captain von Blixen, what exactly are you after?

VON BLIXEN: That gold box on the table, Lord Alfred.

LORD ALFRED: And I suppose you think I am in competition with you? As a graduate of the St Petersburg school.

VON BLIXEN: Not you, Lord Alfred. We know your interests very well. In Germany we are not hypocrites. We have much sympathy for you and much admiration for your great poet, Mr Oscar Wilde. But this gentleman . . . that is a different affair. I can recognize the kind of inferior training he has received.

LORD ALFRED: At St Petersburg?

VON BLIXEN: *Ja.* St Petersburg.

BUNNY: Bosie, the man's mad.

VON BLIXEN: You and I, Captain Petrovitch, know that to pretend madness is part of the training of any agent. We understand each other – but the stupid police, they will think we are both mad. So we save the secret of our services. That I learnt in the psychology course under Professor Himmelstuber. I make myself clear? *Nein?*

BUNNY: *Nein.*

VON BLIXEN: And now the police will have finished their interrogation of your comrade. They will have broken him, or he will have taken his pill of cyanide. It is time for me and you to leave. So the gold box, please. [*He picks it off the table and opens it*] *Gott in Himmel*, it is empty!

LORD ALFRED: The money has been transferred to my pocket, Captain.

VON BLIXEN: Money? What money? I am not sent to steal money. Where are the letters?

LORD ALFRED: What letters?

VON BLIXEN: The letters were in the box, I saw them.

[*He draws a revolver from his pocket and points it at Bunny.*]

LORD ALFRED: Have you any letters, Bunny?

BUNNY: Why, yes, I suppose I have. [*He feels in his pockets*] Unless they've fallen out on the road. I remember a bump in Boxmoor High Street.

VON BLIXEN: You've dropped the letters? Then you are a disgrace even to St Petersburg.

BUNNY: It comes of riding a bicycle in tails. They kept on getting caught in the brakes. There seem to be a few left.

VON BLIXEN: Give them to me.

BUNNY: Why should I?

VON BLIXEN [*waving the revolver*]: This is your excuse, Captain Petrovitch. An agent must never kill another agent, but I am permitted to shoot you in both legs.

BUNNY: You really do want the letters. Why? Who wrote them?

VON BLIXEN: Why pretend ignorance with me? That is not football.

BUNNY: Cricket.

[*Bunny begins to remove letters from his various pockets. Von Blixen snatches two of them and begins to read.*]

VON BLIXEN: 'My dear Alice. It was a bitter disappointment to me not to find you at Lady Melrose's party . . .' 'Dearest of all Alices' – that is better – 'Alas! I have an appointment with my tailor at three. That ass Willy has sent me another of his damned foreign uniforms . . .' [*Von Blixen's voice falls away with disappointment and embarrassment.*]

LORD ALFRED: Hardly worth a hold-up surely? Wouldn't you rather take the gold box?

VON BLIXEN: Do you think a captain of the Prussian Hussars can be bought with gold?

[*The Prince of Wales enters from the hall.*]

PRINCE: Put down that gun, Captain.

[*Von Blixen turns so that his gun points at the Prince.*]

VON BLIXEN: Your Royal Highness.

PRINCE: Your colonel, Captain. If only an honorary one. Please point your revolver in another direction. The ceiling is more suitable. Or the floor. [*Von Blixen drops his revolver on the table*] Thank you. I don't think the Emperor would have been pleased if you had shot his uncle. It would have been difficult to hush up – even in Albany. Lord Alfred, what is your part in all this?

LORD ALFRED: It's all my obnoxious father's fault, sir. I'm running out of adjectives. It's like rhymes for love.

PRINCE: What's your father got to do with it?

LORD ALFRED: He stopped my allowance, sir. So Mr Raffles and my friend Bunny here – whom this gentleman insists on calling Captain Yevgeny Petrovitch – were good enough to offer their services and extract it for me.

PRINCE: And the letters?

BUNNY: We had nothing to do with the letters, sir. Only Captain von Blixen was interested in the letters.

PRINCE: They don't read aloud well, Captain. I'm glad you didn't reach the more passionate parts. I don't fancy seeing them published in the *Frankfurter Zeitung*.

VON BLIXEN: I have failed my Emperor. I shall resign my commission. I shall go to Africa.

PRINCE: If you are looking for lions, my dear fellow, you have only to go as far as Trafalgar Square.

VON BLIXEN: Mock me if you must, Your Royal Highness, but beware that man [*pointing at Bunny*]. Whatever he says, he is an agent of the Emperor Nicholas and his pockets are stuffed with your letters.

BUNNY: I'm sorry. I don't think I have any more. Most of them fell out in Boxmoor High Street.

LORD ALFRED: What has happened to Raffles, sir?

PRINCE: As far as I know he is on the roof with your father and Inspector Mackenzie.

LORD ALFRED: Why the roof, sir?

[*An enormous crash of broken glass.*]

PRINCE: Ach! I hope they are not fighting among themselves. Raffles was convinced we should find this fellow here looking for my letters. He persuaded the Inspector to release him on parole and help block the escape route.

BUNNY: Over the roof of the Burlington Arcade. A rather private way in an emergency. I doubt if the Captain knows of it.

PRINCE [*to Lord Alfred*]: It was not the Captain your father was concerned about. He was afraid your friend would escape with the box and the money. He insisted on accompanying Mr Raffles and the Inspector. I came the conventional way helped by your friendly porter whom I found sleeping with an empty bottle of Spanish wine. I had to persuade him that I was not Inspector Mackenzie. He seemed to find a resemblance. Surely it can only be the beard? I haven't picked up a Scotch accent at Balmoral? No, no, Captain, please do not move. I want you to tell me why my nephew Nicholas would want my letters. Willy I can understand, but not Nicky.

VON BLIXEN: Everything my Emperor wants, Your Royal Highness, Russia always tries to snatch. One day it will be a war of armies – now it is a war of agents. This man has all the faults of the St Petersburg school.

LORD ALFRED: The Berlin school has hardly done better . . .

[*Raffles enters through the bedroom door.*]

LORD ALFRED: What's happened, Raffles?

RAFFLES: Your father has fallen through the roof into the Burlington Arcade.

LORD ALFRED [*hopefully*]: Is he dead?

RAFFLES: I think so. I can't be sure. I thought I saw his leg twitch. Inspector Mackenzie is climbing down to see.

LORD ALFRED: Perhaps if I went to help I might be able to give him the *coup de grâce*.

RAFFLES: Unwise in the presence of the Inspector. So, as I told you, sir, you've found the waiter with the inferior Pommery. Have you recovered the letters?

PRINCE: Your friend seems to have dropped most of them in a place called Boxmoor.

RAFFLES: That's unfortunate. The waiter might return and recover them. That has to be prevented. Is that your revolver, waiter?

VON BLIXEN: I am not a waiter. I am Captain von Blixen of the Prussian Hussars seconded for special services.

RAFFLES: Allow me to borrow your revolver, Captain. [*He helps himself*] And now it will be my painful duty to ensure that you don't return to Boxmoor.

VON BLIXEN: It is no good to threaten me. Even death would be less hard than the thought that I have failed my Emperor.

RAFFLES: An admirable sentiment. I can hear Irving pronouncing it at the Lyceum. One thing, though, troubles me. Killing you is child's play, but how . . . how . . . do we dispose of your corpse?

LORD ALFRED: You could incinerate him.

RAFFLES: But I have no incinerator.

PRINCE: I have read that a bath of acid has sometimes been used, Mr Raffles.

RAFFLES: In Albany? We shan't even have constant hot water for another twenty years.

BUNNY: I suppose we might dismember him. A head, two arms, two legs and a torso – they would fit into that chest.

RAFFLES: If only one of us were a surgeon. A job like that has to be done neatly. Otherwise all sorts of undesirable bits and pieces fall out.

[*Captain von Blixen is more and more uneasy.*]

LORD ALFRED: Surely, Captain Petrovitch, they taught you to carve at the St Petersburg school?

RAFFLES: Petrovitch?

LORD ALFRED: It seems that this is Captain Yevgeny Petrovitch of the Russian Secret Police.

BUNNY: At St Petersburg we only had bears to practise on. Perhaps I could manage if Captain von Blixen would look a little more like a bear. Another thing – we had proper surgical knives. Here I've only got a blunt bread knife. And a serrated edge may prove messy.

VON BLIXEN: I insist on being shot as an officer and a gentleman.

RAFFLES: Of course, of course, we are not barbarians. We will shoot you first, Captain. I wouldn't dream of letting him carve you up alive. But I'm troubled about the bloodstains you'll leave on the carpet.

PRINCE: Surely your friend could spread some newspapers on the floor. *The Times* is better for that than the *Telegraph*.

LORD ALFRED: I'm sorry, sir, the sight of blood always makes me feel ill. Besides, the Captain and I belong to the same club. With your permission, I will go and see if my infernal father is still alive. I might seize an opportunity of strangling him if the Inspector turns his back.

BUNNY: Better leave by the door, Bosie. You have no head for heights.

LORD ALFRED: If you will excuse me, sir. [*He leaves.*]

PRINCE: Strangling. Ach! That is quite an idea. It would avoid blood.

VON BLIXEN: I appeal to you, Your Royal Highness. As my honorary colonel. Grant me a clean death like a soldier.

RAFFLES: A *cliché*, Captain. A soldier's death is very seldom clean. By the way, is that your own suit? It doesn't fit you very well.

VON BLIXEN: It is a hired suit from the Brothers Moss in Covent Garden. If I have to die, please see that the suit is returned. They trusted me without a deposit.

RAFFLES: I don't like the idea of strangling, sir. All very well for Lord Queensbury – not for a man who dies in the service of your nephew.

PRINCE: I was merely making a suggestion. I don't insist, Mr Raffles.

RAFFLES: I would feel like a hangman. Don't you agree, Captain Petrovitch?

BUNNY: Oh, in Russia a hangman's is an honourable profession.

RAFFLES: All the same, as between one agent and another, wouldn't it be possible to accept his word of honour – as a captain of the Prussian Hussars – that he will not bicycle back to Boxmoor?

VON BLIXEN: I will never give it. I would rather be cut up.

RAFFLES: Yevgeny Petrovitch.

[*Bunny comes to Raffles' side and Raffles whispers in his ear. Bunny goes to the bedroom and a little later comes back with several copies of* The Times.]

RAFFLES: Your request is granted, Captain von Blixen. You will die a soldier's death and your clothes will be returned untarnished to Moss Bros. Take off your coat and your jacket. [*Von Blixen obeys.*] Now would you remove what our great writer Mr Henry James has called 'the nether integuments of a gentleman'?

VON BLIXEN: I do not understand.

RAFFLES: Your trousers.

VON BLIXEN: *Nein, nein*. I refuse. If you shoot me through the heart the trousers will not be damaged.

RAFFLES: Blood has a tendency to splash, Captain. Anyway I am not a good marksman. Off with your trousers, please.

[*Von Blixen miserably obeys. He is wearing long combinations.*]

RAFFLES: Were your combinations hired too at Moss Bros?

VON BLIXEN [*gloomily*]: They are my own.

RAFFLES: When you've spread the papers, Captain Petrovitch – a double thickness, please, blood soaks so – take the Captain's clothes and lay them safely in the bedroom. There's a little mud on the trousers, but we will have them cleaned before we return them to Moss Bros.

[*Bunny busies himself.*]

RAFFLES: You won't reconsider giving your word, Captain?

VON BLIXEN: *Nein*.

PRINCE: A brave man, Mr Raffles, even if absurd.

RAFFLES: We all look absurd, sir, when we are reduced to combinations.

VON BLIXEN: I will protest with my dying breath that in civilized countries one agent does not kill another agent. An agent is always exchanged.

RAFFLES [*to the Prince*]: Perhaps after all, sir, killing is not strictly necessary. An officer of the Prussian Hussars can hardly bicycle to Boxmoor in his combinations.

[*A loud knock on the outer door.*]

BUNNY: Come in, whoever you are.

[*Smith, the Albany porter, enters, eloquently the worse for Spanish wine, though for a long moment he is flabbergasted and silent at the sight of von Blixen in his combinations.*]

BUNNY: Well, Smith, what is it?

SMITH: I don't know, sir, what Betteridge would have done in my place. Anything unusual, he said, you report it. First I have someone who looks like His Royal Highness asking to be let in . . .

PRINCE: Yes, porter, I'm sorry I had to shake you awake.

SMITH: It's nearly six in the morning. A man's not himself at six in the morning . . . A man can't think clearly at six in the morning. I only want to do the right thing, but there's things afoot I can't understand. I dunno what Betteridge would have done at six in the morning.

PRINCE: Perhaps Betteridge did not indulge in Spanish wine.

SMITH: It's not the Spanish wine, sir. It's them at the door with a stretcher and a corpse demanding to be let in. It's not what we are accustomed to at Albany. No dogs, no cats, no women – that's the rule. But what about a corpse, sir, I ask you?

RAFFLES: Is it a woman's corpse?

SMITH: No, sir, a man's as far as I can make out from the boots – which is all I can see, for the face is covered with a handkerchief.

RAFFLES: There are no rules against admitting a *man*'s corpse, are there, Bunny?

BUNNY: Don't ask me. I give up. I give up.

SMITH: Do I understand I'm to let them in, sir?

BUNNY: Let them all come.

[*Smith goes out to open the front door.*]

VON BLIXEN: Please. I give in. I will promise anything. Only let me put on my trousers.

RAFFLES: Your promise comes too late, Captain. And a corpse won't care about your combinations.

[*All stare in suspense at the door. Inspector Mackenzie enters first backwards at one end of a ladder which is serving as a stretcher. On it, the body covered with an overcoat and the face with a handkerchief, lies the body of the Marquess of Queensberry. Guiding the other end is Lord Alfred Douglas. Raffles removes the handkerchief. The Prince and Bunny come and look down at the Marquess.*]

RAFFLES: Nothing in his life became him like the leaving of it. [*He puts back the handkerchief.*]

PRINCE: Is he dead?

INSPECTOR: He hasna moved since he fell, sir, but for one wee twitch i' the right leg.

PRINCE: He will be mourned by the boxing profession. I don't know who else.

BUNNY: I suppose we ought to get an ambulance.

LORD ALFRED: No hurry, Bunny. If he's dead it's too late, and if he's dying we don't want to *encourage* life, do we?

> 'O let him pass; he hates him
> That would upon the rack of this tough world
> Stretch him out longer.'

PRINCE: All the same, Lord Alfred . . . Porter, which is the nearest hospital?

SMITH: I'd say, Your Royal Highness, it would be the St James's Hospital for Diseases of the Skin round the corner in Soho.

PRINCE: I suppose they'd have an ambulance?

SMITH: I couldn't be sure, sir, they deal more with walking cases.

RAFFLES: Try them anyway on your telephone.

[*Smith leaves.*]

RAFFLES: Bunny and I don't want to spend what's left of the night with a dead marquess. It would spoil our breakfast.

INSPECTOR: Neither of you will take your breakfast here, sir. We'll serve you that at the Yard.

RAFFLES: No, no. I must refuse your invitation, Inspector. The Yard as a restaurant doesn't attract me. Bunny and I are going to have a little race down the Ropewalk, and you are blocking our way.

[*Raffles raises the revolver.*]

INSPECTOR: You are only bluffing, Raffles. The safety catch is on.

RAFFLES [*clicking it off*]: Thank you for reminding me.

INSPECTOR: You are still bluffing. I ken my man, Raffles. I've been at your heels a long time like a faithful dog. You are not the killing type.

RAFFLES: Oh, but I've changed, Inspector. In South Africa they taught me to kill. Even dogs when food was short.

INSPECTOR: Be a sensible laddie. Give me that gun, and I promise to speak up for you at the trial like I spoke up for your friend.

RAFFLES: No, Mackenzie. I've always said I prefer a rope and a quick drop to a long dull old age. Get away from the door. There are many men I'd much rather shoot than you.

INSPECTOR: I tell you – give me that gun.

[*Raffles raises it and Mackenzie doesn't move. Raffles hesitates and then tosses the gun to the floor at Mackenzie's feet.*]

RAFFLES: You win, Mackenzie. Bring out your bracelets. If only you'd been in uniform – but I can't bear spoiling those bloody tweeds of yours.

PRINCE: Excuse me interrupting a rather personal scene. My knowledge of the law is limited. But on what charge are you arresting him?

INSPECTOR: Why, for one, sir, stealing that gold box there.

PRINCE: My box. And I make no charge.

INSPECTOR: There remains, sir, a matter of five hundred sovereigns.

RAFFLES: Minus twelve, and all you recovered from my pockets.

LORD ALFRED: Mr Raffles at my request was recovering a debt. They were the allowance that dead monster owed me.

INSPECTOR: Ye should learn, ma lord, to spik wi' more respect of the departed. When he slipped on the roof up there and crashed through the glass, he offered up a prayer to the Almighty. Whatever his sins it will not ha' gone unheard.

LORD ALFRED: What did he say?

INSPECTOR: He said 'My God', my lord. [*The Inspector blows his nose loudly.*]

PRINCE: Well, Inspector, there seems little we can do against Mr Raffles.

INSPECTOR: There are still the letters, sir.

PRINCE: They were not stolen by these gentlemen. On the contrary they saved them from the hands of a foreign agent sent by my nephew, the Emperor of Germany. That fellow there in combinations.

INSPECTOR [*with mounting irritation*]: At least you'll let me arrest *him*, sir?

PRINCE: I think you would find difficulty in proving anything. There are no letters on him, and you have no warrant. Better consult your friend in the Special Branch. I think he will want to exchange him — or to turn him. Isn't that the correct expression, Captain?

VON BLIXEN: I am not one who can be turned, Your Royal Highness.

PRINCE: Bravo.

INSPECTOR: Are all the letters recovered, sir?

PRINCE: Not all. Quite a number must be blowing about the High Street of Boxmoor. Don't worry. Alice is a common name — and so, I'm afraid, is Bertie. Let us hope they don't lead to any misunderstandings among the inhabitants of Boxmoor.

VON BLIXEN: Your Royal Highness, would you allow me to put on my trousers? I feel a cold coming on. [*He sneezes.*]

PRINCE: Probably caught from Inspector Mackenzie.

BUNNY: Go and take a pin, Captain.

[*Von Blixen goes towards the bedroom. He pauses in the doorway.*]

VON BLIXEN: Herr Raffles, I will admit to you now what I could not admit under the threat of death. I would not be able to return to Boxmoor. Your bicycle has a puncture in both tyres. English tyres, of course.

[*He goes.*]

PRINCE: We seem at last to be reaching what I have always desired in politics, a peaceful understanding.

RAFFLES: We owe it to you, sir.

PRINCE: Don't feel downhearted, Inspector. We owe it also to your tact and diplomatic sense. I think I have never enjoyed a long night more. Now I look forward to a little breakfast at

Marlborough House – some kidneys and bacon, a well-done steak, and a pint of claret. Then I can face the humdrum world again. I would invite you, gentlemen, to join me, but you have a corpse to guard, and you, Inspector, will no doubt wish to return to Scotland Yard. You will have a rather complicated report to write, but I'm sure you will do it with all the finesse for which your countrymen are famous.

INSPECTOR: But, sir, what about the foreign agent?

PRINCE: Oh, leave him to the Special Branch. I have little doubt he can claim diplomatic immunity.

INSPECTOR: He may flee the country, sir.

PRINCE: Then look for him in Africa. Most of the lions are in British territory.

INSPECTOR: And the deceased?

RAFFLES: We will see it safely delivered to the hospital.

PRINCE: Your report will not wait, Inspector.

INSPECTOR [*unwillingly*]: Then I must wish you good night, sir?

PRINCE: No, good morning, Inspector. The sun has risen.

RAFFLES: No hard feelings, Inspector?

INSPECTOR: I'll not be saying good-bye to you, Raffles.

   [*The Inspector leaves.*]

LORD ALFRED: With your permission, sir, I will leave for Victoria Station and Paris. My elder brother will bury the corpse in an adequate way. I see no reason to attend the funeral.

PRINCE: No doubt you are off to your friend, Mr Wilde?

LORD ALFRED: We may happen to run into each other, sir.

PRINCE: I don't like his tastes, but I like his plays. I will never forget that he was a good friend to an old friend of mine, Mrs Langtry.

LORD ALFRED: Your message will hearten him, sir.

PRINCE: Just let him stay out of England. They manage these things better in France. Good-bye, Lord Alfred.

LORD ALFRED: Good-bye, sir.

PRINCE: Be careful, my boy.

   [*Lord Alfred leaves.*]

PRINCE: And now, Mr Raffles – I would have preferred to speak to Mr Jones who fought at Spion Kop – I have a request to make.

RAFFLES: You have been very generous, sir. You have only to command.

PRINCE: It has been an unprofitable night for you. You have risen from the dead – unlike Lord Queensberry. Inspector Mackenzie will not forgive that. Promise me that in future England will know only Raffles, the cricketer, and not Raffles, the amateur cracksman.

RAFFLES [*after hesitation*]: Very well, I promise, sir.

PRINCE: Then good morning to you both. Look after your shoulder, Mr Raffles. I expect to see you take the field next summer. [*He walks towards the door and turns*] Wearing a white tie, Mr Raffles, was a bad mistake. It was time for you to retire.

RAFFLES: Sir, you have forgotten the box.

PRINCE: A present to Mr Jones from Mr Portland – of less value than the one he gave me.

[*He leaves.*]

RAFFLES: A great gentleman, Bunny. He'll make a great king – if the gods allow him time.

[*A pause. Bunny moves round the room turning out lights. The morning sun comes in.*]

RAFFLES: Well, Bunny, you voted for cricket and cricket it will have to be.

BUNNY: Do you regret it very much, A.J.?

RAFFLES: There's a long penurious winter ahead.

BUNNY: At least there's the box to melt down – and the diamonds are fine ones.

RAFFLES: One doesn't sell a present like that. I shall keep my Sullivans in it – cigarettes unlike cigars don't need sandalwood.

BUNNY: Then how shall we manage, A.J.?

RAFFLES: I think a winter on the Continent is indicated, Bunny. I made no promise about the Continent. Versailles perhaps is too large for us – and a little too vulgar. We should be treading in the footsteps of so many trippers. Perhaps we might case one of the smaller châteaux of the Loire, Bunny?

BUNNY: You were never much good at French, A.J.

RAFFLES: True, but I rather fancy my American accent. American visitors are very welcome on the Loire. There's always a needy château in search of a rich marriage. I could be one of the obscurer Rockefellers.

[*Von Blixen enters dressed again as a waiter.*]

RAFFLES: Ah, Captain, I hope you bear us no ill will for our little comedy.

VON BLIXEN: I am ashamed. To have been beaten by St Petersburg.

RAFFLES: Not by St Petersburg, Captain. By Rugby. The school not the railway junction. We are two amateurs.

VON BLIXEN: That is worse.

RAFFLES: No, no. Here in England the Gentlemen quite often beat the Players.

[*Smith enters with a tarpaulin over his arm.*]

SMITH: Sir, they've sent an ambulance. It's down in the forecourt, but the men are all dressed up in white coats an' I'm afraid to disturb some of the old ones here like Mr Grosvenor on Staircase B. It's not pleasant if you are ninety to look out of the window an' see a corpse carried down the Ropewalk.

BUNNY: Very thoughtful of you, Smith. What do you suggest?

SMITH: Well, sir, a ladder's different to a stretcher an' if we cover the corpse with a tarpaulin it might well be some pots of paint the workmen have left behind.

RAFFLES: You are a worthy successor of Betteridge. This gentleman is leaving and I'm sure he'll lend you a hand. Please, Captain. I would not ask it if you were in the uniform of the Prussian Hussars.

VON BLIXEN: I am your prisoner. I must obey.

RAFFLES: To carry a stretcher – if it is not a military one – is not forbidden by the Geneva Convention.

[*Smith spreads the tarpaulin in place of the coat. Von Blixen unwillingly takes up the end of the ladder and they begin to carry the body towards the door. Suddenly the tarpaulin is thrown aside and the Marquess sits up with a wild expression.*]

MARQUESS [*looking from von Blixen to Smith*]: Where am I? Who the devil are you?

RAFFLES: Please lie down and be quiet, Lord Queensberry. There is nothing to be alarmed about.

MARQUESS: Where are they taking me?

RAFFLES: To St James's Hospital, my lord, for Diseases of the Skin and Venereal Infections. Carry on, Smith.

CURTAIN

THE GREAT JOWETT

★

CHARACTERS

(in order of speaking)

COMMENTATOR
MR GRIGGS, *an Oxford guide*
MR FOSTER, *head porter of Balliol*
BENJAMIN JOWETT
MATTHEW KNIGHT, *his servant*
ARTHUR STANLEY
GREEN ⎫
PEEL   ⎪ *Fellows*
ROSS   ⎬ *of Balliol*
SMITH ⎭
THE VICE-CHANCELLOR
PAINE ⎫ *Undergraduates*
PLUMER ⎭
ALGERNON SWINBURNE
DR SCOTT, *Master of Balliol*
MRS SPARKS, *a landlady*
ARCHBISHOP OF CANTERBURY
MATTHEW ARNOLD
MISS KNIGHT, *Jowett's housekeeper*

The Great Jowett was first written as a radio play for the BBC, and was broadcast on Saturday, 6 May 1939. It was produced and narrated by Stephen Potter.

COMMENTATOR: Tonight I am going to try to present to you in dramatic form an undramatic life. The scene of the play is Oxford, our chief character a don – Benjamin Jowett, who was born in 1817 and died in 1893. So it is not quite the Oxford you may know today. There are no motorworks at Cowley; indeed there are no motors anywhere – smart undergraduates go spanking along the Iffley road in dog-carts. Take a walk with me down Cornmarket, stepping carefully over the metal lines of the horse trams. In Broad Street, Balliol, the main scene of our play, has only just got its new front: a new chapel, a new Hall. Victorian masonry glares at you – shinily.

But the rooks are there in the Balliol elms, and at nine o'clock Big Tom can be heard striking a hundred and one times all across Oxford from St Ald's. If you were able to turn the ring on your finger and wish yourself back to those days, you would feel yourself quite at home, for the men don't change much more than the old grey flaking stone – scholarship is there hiding behind a closed oak, snobbery off to a wine in Magdalen. There are the same intrigues in Convocation and Senior Common Room, young earnest conversations as if all time lay ahead – about Newman instead of about Eliot – and the same hollow, careful, unbearable voices.

I have told you this is not a dramatic life. It is a life mainly concerned with the struggle to be Master of a college, with translating Plato, with old dead theological disputes. During Jowett's Oxford career England found herself at war in the Crimea, the Light Brigade charged at Balaclava, Sebastopol fell: Gordon died in Khartoum: it was the heroic age of Lawrence of Lucknow: Gladstone and Disraeli fought for power, there were Home Rule Bills, great political crises, crimes of passion and interest. But life in Oxford, at Balliol, must have seemed to Jowett just as dramatic. It contained failure (when another man was elected Master in his stead), disgrace (when the Vice-Chancellor summoned him, like any young curate, to sign the Thirty-Nine Articles or lose his Fellowship), and it contained triumph – when he became, in spite of his enemies, Master of Balliol, when his Plato was published, and when Balliol Hall was built – his thumbmark fossilized in stone upon his college for ever.

And the man – you cannot see him on this invisible stage of ours, but I want somehow, through the ether, to convey an image to you – of a rather small clerical gentleman with scanty whiskers and twitching eyelids and an aureole of whitening hair. He has sloping shoulders and a tiny chin. His voice is piping and he wears a white neckerchief loosely tied about an upright collar. He hums as he walks and if he is cold he just breaks into a run. The scene is set, September 1893 – the end of the long vac when strange faces and accents are heard all over Oxford and the guides linger in the High, pulling on gloves with battered gentility, carrying folded umbrellas.

MR GRIGGS: An' now, ladies and gentlemen, we'll just turn down Broad Street – known to university men all the world over as the Broad.

WOMAN: Why?

MR GRIGGS: Because of its width, ma'am. What you're now looking at – no, look this way, please, ma'am, what you're *now* looking at is Balliol College – disrespectfully known to some as Belial, founded by a lady with the name of Devorguilla in Anno Domini 1265. The front you're looking at needless to say doesn't go back to those barbaric days. It's only been up a few years, thanks to the Master. Good evening, Mr Foster. Any objection to my showing these ladies and gentlemen through the college?

MR FOSTER: Go ahead, Mr Griggs. But no scandal, mind.

WOMAN: Who's he?

MR GRIGGS: The head porter. A good friend of mine, and a very responsible position. When Big Tom stops striking nine, he shuts that gate – and no gentleman can get in without a fine. You should see them running along the street: they say as they can leave Wadham on the first stroke and get here before Mr Foster gets the bolt in.

AMERICAN: Who gets the cash?

MR GRIGGS: Ah, that's what *they'd* like to know. Now, ma'am, *if* you'd look over this way, you'll see the new 'all. The greatest architectural achievement in Oxford since the Middle Ages. Them as have a right to speak say it's finer than Keble College.

AMERICAN WOMAN [*reverently*]: I guess I'd find it easy to pray there.

MR GRIGGS: You don't pray there, ma'am, you eats. Let me tell you this – the Master's particular about the food. They didn't always eat well in Balliol, but when the old cook got taken –

VISITOR: Who took him?

MR GRIGGS [*ghoulishly*]: One, ma'am, as needs no reference. An' when the Master heard of it, all he said was, 'Now we'll show them Balliol can give as good a dinner as Trinity.'

VISITOR: What's the Master's name?

MR GRIGGS: Benjamin Jowett. Known to his intimates as Jowler.

WOMAN: I suppose he's very old and very good?

MR GRIGGS: Old, yes, ma'am. [*He drops his voice*] Good, that's as may be. They say 'e loves a lord. An' for why? Because 'e's the son of a London furrier. 'E was so poor when 'e was an undergraduate, they say people wouldn't take tea with him – for fear of ruining him. An' sharp? You should 'ear the tradespeople. Learnt it from his father, I daresay. Why, 'e's not even a Christian like you an' me. Messin' about with Greek prophets. Pluto. You know who *he* was. Lord of Hades. Oh, 'e's a great man in Oxford now is Professor Benjamin Jowett – but it wasn't always that way. He's 'ad 'is enemies. He wasn't always Master of Balliol.

[*Fade out into sound effects and through them into a clock striking eight in Jowett's room. A knock.*]

JOWETT: What is it, Matthew?

KNIGHT: Mr Stanley, sir.

JOWETT: Come in, Arthur, come in. You find me keeping vigil. I should be praying over my armour in the chapel – but this new chapel the Master put up . . .

STANLEY: *De mortuis*, Benjamin. So they are holding the election at this moment, are they?

JOWETT: I can't imagine what's keeping them so long.

STANLEY: It's a serious matter, I suppose, electing a Master of Balliol.

JOWETT: They have no choice, Arthur. There's only me.

STANLEY: There's Scott.

JOWETT: Oh, I don't think so. [*As if that settles it*] A country parson, they couldn't elect him. [*He hums a tune*] Do you know, Arthur, I shall be the only Master in Oxford under forty?

STANLEY: And I suppose you have everything planned.

JOWETT: Of course. Now I've finished St Paul I shall read a little Aristophanes.

STANLEY: And then Plato.

JOWETT: Always Plato . . . and we must have a new cook . . . and I have a plan for free students . . . and a new Hall.

STANLEY: They'll never agree.

JOWETT: A Master must know how to put pressure on everybody. And, Arthur – there's talk of a professorship. Moral Theology.

STANLEY: There's other talk too. Your book on St Paul . . . have you shown the proofs to anyone?

JOWETT: Oh, Ross has seen them. You remember when we first talked about it. In that stone quarry out past Headington?

STANLEY: It was raining.

JOWETT: We began about the college port and went on to St Paul.

STANLEY: And there was thunder . . .

[*Fade out and in to the election.*]

A FELLOW: I suggest we now put the names to the vote. Will you pass your slips to me? I have seven in favour of Dr Jowett . . . and in favour of Dr Scott . . . four, five, six, seven also. Well, somebody will have to give way, I suppose. On one side or the other.

GREEN: I'm surprised Dr Scott's had so many votes. Of course he and Liddell did a fine job . . . the lexicon, but Jowett . . . Jowett's one of the most brilliant scholars we have. What's more he gets on well with the young.

PEEL: If they are of good birth, Green.

GREEN: That's not fair. What you dislike, Peel, is his opposition to the new chapel. Well, it *is* hideous. And he wouldn't support that motion of yours about the SCR port. Is a man to be turned down because he quarrels with you about a vintage?

PEEL: Are we going to have a Master of Balliol like Melchizedek, a man without father, without mother, without descent? Any *gentleman* knows he was wrong about the port.

ROSS [*a mellow parson's voice*]: He reads Plato on Sundays.

GREEN: Oh, this is farcical.

SMITH: Not so farcical, Green. I voted for Jowett myself, but that's no reason why we shouldn't listen to what Dr Ross has to say.

ROSS: What I am suggesting is this: it wouldn't be good for the college to elect a Master who may be condemned for his religious opinions. We all know about Ward and Newman: we don't want Balliol mixed up in un-Christian controversy.

GREEN [*mockingly*]: This is terrible, Ross. What's Jowett done?

ROSS: You may laugh, Green, but in my opinion he reads too much Plato – and too much Hegel.

SMITH [*shocked*]: He reads German criticism?

ROSS: He does. And let me tell you this – his work on St Paul will raise a storm – and rightly. I shall raise it myself if no one else does.

SMITH: Have you read it, Ross?

ROSS: He lent me the proofs. Let me read you *one* passage.

GREEN: I protest. This has nothing to do with the Mastership of Balliol.

SMITH: I don't agree with you, Green.

ROSS: Dr Jowett we all know hopes to become Professor of Moral Theology. Well, this is how he writes on the Atonement. 'One cannot but fear whether it be still possible so to teach Christ as not to cast a shadow on the holiness and truth of God.' If that is not blasphemy, Green . . .

[*A long silence and then fade in to Jowett's study.*]

JOWETT: Oh, dear me, Arthur, nobody here in Oxford, in Balliol, could object to a word of it. Religious minds couldn't be offended.

STANLEY: You aren't dealing with religious minds. You are
dealing with parsons' minds.

JOWETT [*laughing*]: You remind me of Buller's remark. 'Destroy
the Church of England? You must be mad, sir. It is the only
thing which stands between us and real religion.'

STANLEY: I'm not joking.

JOWETT: No, no, Arthur, these are nightmares. There's nobody
else they can elect. Do you know the first time I ever met a
Master of Balliol? I was a schoolboy, up from St Paul's for a
scholarship. (They used to call me Miss Jowett there.) I came
into the Master's dining-room. I was so nervous I left my cap
on. Jenkyns came in. 'Do my eyes deceive me,' he said, 'or do I
see a gentleman in my dining-room with his cap on?' You
know, Arthur, it took me years to forgive him that rebuff. It
taught me to be careful. Young men are so sensitive. You will
find one burning with indignation for some neglect of which
you were profoundly unconscious. No. It never does to speak
roughly to them. When I am Master . . .

[*A knock at the door.*]

KNIGHT: Mr Green, sir.

JOWETT [*with sudden anxiety*]: Come in, Green. [*He won't ask a
question*] Sit down. Will you have a glass of port? My port – not
Peel's.

GREEN: No, Jowett, no, thank you. How are you, Stanley?

JOWETT: Arthur and I were just talking . . . about St Paul's . . .
Jenkyns . . .

STANLEY: How has the election gone?

GREEN: I'm afraid . . . badly.

[*No word from Jowett.*]

STANLEY: Badly?

GREEN: They have elected . . . Scott.

STANLEY: I was afraid . . .

JOWETT: You have not elected a man, Green. You have elected
half a lexicon.

STANLEY: Your time will come.

JOWETT: Masters live long. Thank you for coming, Green. There
are always plenty who come when one wins, but you are a
losing friend.

GREEN: The voting was very close, Jowett.

JOWETT: So I nearly beat the lexicon. Thank you, Green. Well, I must say goodnight to you both. You see, I am bursar of this college still, and I have to go through a good many accounts. Somebody has been exceeding on battels and we spend too much – on candles.

STANLEY [*undertone*]: We'd better go. Goodnight, Benjamin.

GREEN: Goodnight, Jowett.

JOWETT: Goodnight. Goodnight.

[*A door shuts. Footsteps on stairs and then gravel.*]

GREEN: He's bitter.

STANLEY: It's hard for him to have got so far and not got further.

[*Footsteps.*]

PEEL [*maliciously*]: Ah, Stanley, been with your friend, the philosopher? You hear we've got him on the run now?

STANLEY: He'll give you a long run then.

PEEL: Out of Oxford altogether, perhaps.

[*Fade out into clatter of newspaper presses.*]

VOICE [*mechanically*]: Books received for review: *A Commentary on St Paul's Epistles*, by Dr Benjamin Jowett.

VOICE [*mechanically*]: We would question the propriety of an Oxford Fellow writing in these terms on the Atonement.

VOICE: Mr Ward and Dr Newman have accustomed us to assaults from Oxford on the Established Church, but we are not prepared for so blunt an attack on all revealed religion . . .

VOICE: Dr Jowett knows German . . . reads German . . . studies German . . .

VOICE: Contrary to expectation, Dr Jowett has not been elected Professor of Moral Theology.

PEEL: We have Dr Jowett on the run now.

[*Clatter of teacups.*]

WOMAN'S VOICE: My husband heard yesterday from the Master. In confidence. He says Dr Jowett will be *condemned*. Another cup of tea, Mrs Bullen?

ROSS: I'm afraid it's the end of poor Jowett.

VOICE [*mechanically*]: A book unwise from any pen, but more than unwise from a Fellow of Balliol who by university statute, if he is to hold his Fellowship, must subscribe to all the Articles . . .

PEEL: The next move is with the Vice-Chancellor.

ROSS: Much as I feel for poor Jowett, I felt it my duty to appeal to two members of Convocation, McBride and Dr Golightly, to see the Vice-Chancellor.

VOICE: Mr Vice-Chancellor, we have come to you to denounce Dr Jowett for having denied the catholic faith and to demand that you summon him before you and ask him to subscribe to the Thirty-Nine Articles. Otherwise proceedings must be started to deprive him of his Fellowship.

[*A door slams.*]

KNIGHT: Good morning, sir, I've put the tea on the hob and the kidneys on the fender.

JOWETT: Thank you, Matthew. How goes the Latin grammar? We'll have you reading Virgil soon. And then Greek . . . and Plato.

KNIGHT: There's a note for you, sir.

JOWETT: Thank you, Matthew.

KNIGHT: It came by hand. They said it was urgent.

JOWETT: It looks very official.

KNIGHT: Won't you read it, sir?

JOWETT: I like letters from my friends. Others can wait. Can you read my writing, Matthew? I want somebody to help me. To make fair copies of this manuscript.

KNIGHT: What is it, sir?

JOWETT: Plato – the greatest writer who ever lived.

KNIGHT: The kettle's boiling, sir.

JOWETT: Never mind. I'll see to that. See if you can read my writing.

KNIGHT [*uncertainly reading*]: 'And if there is no war, they stay at home, and do many little pieces of mischief in the city.'

JOWETT: It's Socrates who's speaking. And Adeimantus says . . .

KNIGHT: 'What sort of mischief?'

JOWETT: 'For example, they are the thieves, burglars, cut-purses, foot-pads, robbers of temples, man-stealers of the community. Or if they are able to speak they turn informers, and bear false witness . . .' and go to the Vice-Chancellor.

KNIGHT: You shouldn't have read your letter, sir. The kidneys will be cold.

JOWETT: Take them away, Matthew. I have to be off. Never put off unpleasant duties.

KNIGHT: Is anything wrong, sir?

JOWETT: Oh, dear me, no. I am being teased, that's all. By a little monkey of an old gentleman, who dresses himself in black and has three pokers walk before him . . .

KNIGHT: Will you be dining in Hall tonight, sir?

JOWETT: No, I shall not be dining there again – for a long time.

[*The door shuts. Street noises.*]

VOICE: There goes Jowett.

VOICE: Black as thunder.

VOICE: His first lecture this morning on Plato.

VOICE: There won't be any lecture. He's been summoned.

VOICE: The Vice-Chancellor? Will he sign?

[*Street noises. Silence. A door opens.*]

SERVANT: Dr Jowett, sir.

VICE-CHANCELLOR [*pompously*]: Come in, Dr Jowett. You know why I have sent for you. It is a painful situation for me and a dreadful one for you – I realize that. I have never before had to call on a man in your position. . .

JOWETT [*interrupting*]: Mr Vice-Chancellor, I am here to sign the Articles. Where are they?

VICE-CHANCELLOR: They are on my desk, Dr Jowett. Of course I am relieved to hear of your consent, but I hope you will bear in mind as you sign them the sacred obligations . . .

JOWETT: This pen scratches. May I take a new one?

VICE-CHANCELLOR: Yes, yes. But what I am saying is – this is not mere legal form; it represents . . .

JOWETT: Good morning, Mr Vice-Chancellor.

[*Door slams. Outside noises.*]

VOICE: There comes Jowett.

VOICE: Black as thunder.

VOICE: Today's his first lecture.

VOICE: There won't be a lecture. He's been summoned.

VOICE: Did he sign?

VOICE: Has he lost his Fellowship?

VOICE: You saw his face. He's lost something.

[*Street noises. Silence. A door slams.*]

GREEN: Your servant told me. I waited to see you. What happened?

JOWETT: They have done me harm, Green. But I shall live it down.

GREEN: All the younger fellows are for you. Peel and Ross will not live for ever.

JOWETT: It was a schoolboy degradation they put me to.

GREEN: It will be forgotten in no time at all. You mustn't think of Oxford as the world: it's a small town in a small island in one of the smaller continents.

JOWETT: Nobody lives in what *you* call the world – everyone has his own world. Oxford's mine.

GREEN: And Greece. You'll be late for your lecture, Jowett. The hall's crowded.

JOWETT: Oh yes, they want to see how I take it, I suppose. I have no pleasure in looking forward to my lectures now.

GREEN: I'll walk across with you.

[*A door closes. Footsteps on gravel.*]

JOWETT: You know, Green, after the first sting, the power of feeling is almost lost. Perhaps it's worth while to be attacked for the sake of being free from attacks for the rest of your life.

[*Fade out. Voices increasing in volume.*]

VOICE: He wouldn't sign. Cavendish told me.

VOICE: He threw the pen on the floor.

VOICE: Barker knows the Vice-Chancellor's niece. She said her uncle was quite *pale*.

VOICE: It's the end of poor Jowler.

[*Sudden silence. Steps on wood. Jowett clears his throat.*]

JOWETT: Now, blowing the dust off the outside of this venerable volume, let us proceed to examine what I may call the *greatest uninspired writing*. Plato's *Republic*.

[*Fade out.*]

COMMENTATOR: Jowett retired like Achilles to his tent: he no longer appeared in Hall or Common Room. His election to the Professorship of Greek made no difference to his attitude. He had given up the Fellows for the undergraduates; it was at his tutorials that he tried to find his friends. The opening of a winter term.

PAINE: Jowler's so obscure. Do you know what he said to me at the end of last term when I handed in an essay on Plato? He said, 'Have you any taste for mathematics?' What did he want you for last night, Plumer?

PLUMER: He asked me if I would have a glass of wine, so I poured out a glass and drank it. Then he asked me if I would eat an apple, so I ate an apple. But he said nothing and I said nothing. I'm told he asks you to wine so that he can find out what sort of a fellow you are, but I wasn't going to let him see what sort of a fellow *I* am.

PAINE: Here he comes.

[*A faint humming is heard.*]

JOWETT: Ah, yes . . . exactly . . . who have we here? . . . yes . . . let me see . . . Paine, my dear boy. I hope you had a good vacation. How is Lady Mary?

PAINE: Blooming.

JOWETT: And Plumer . . . I hope Sir Ronald is very fit. Great rumours came down from Scotland through Lady Abercon-way. And let me see. Our dumb friend here . . . your name is . . .

SWINBURNE [*in a high voice like Jowett's own*]: I am Algernon Swinburne.

[*An awful silence.*]

JOWETT: I see we have much in common, Mr Swinburne. Do they breed voices like yours in Northumberland as well as in Balliol? Now, gentlemen – as to lectures for the term. I wish you to go to Professor Davis on Aristotle's *Poetics*, Dr Carmichael on Hegel and to myself on the *Republic*. You will bring your English essays to me. And as for your first essay . . . let me see, we will make it 'Why was Plato the enemy of poets?' I trust we have no poets among us. You, Plumer?

PLUMER: Never written a line, sir.

SWINBURNE: I am a poet.

JOWETT: Oh, dear me, Mr Swinburne, I trust you are of the severe type Plato trusted. Otherwise – you know what he said. 'We must inform him that in our state such as he are not permitted to exist; the law will not allow them. And so when we have anointed him with myrrh, and set a garland of wool upon his head, we shall send him away to another city' – to Cambridge perhaps.

SWINBURNE: Plato also said, sir, 'We will fall down and worship him as a sweet and holy and wonderful being.'

JOWETT: Excellent, dear boy, excellent. I shall look forward to your holiness. In the meanwhile bring your essays to me today week at eleven. Good morning, gentlemen.

VOICES: Good morning, sir.

JOWETT: One moment, Mr Swinburne.

[*A door closes.*]

How is the admiral?

SWINBURNE: Well, thank you, sir.

JOWETT: And your mother?

SWINBURNE: Well, too.

JOWETT: So you are not following the sea, Mr Swinburne?

SWINBURNE: The sea, sir, is something to be loved not used – a mistress not a wife.

JOWETT: Oh, dear me, your images are a bit bold for an old bachelor. I begin to be doubtful if Balliol will be able to hold a poet. Don't think me unsympathetic, Mr Swinburne. I have some acquaintance with poets. Mr Tennyson trusts a good deal to my criticism. And I know Mr Browning too. Not a great poet like Mr Tennyson. *Porphyria's Lover* – poor sad stuff, but he deserves a *shady* first. Have you thought of entering for the Newdigate? One man, you know, is as good as another until he has written a book.

SWINBURNE: Oh, I expect I shall enter.

JOWETT: You have great confidence, Mr Swinburne. But take my advice. Poetry is a way of writing, not a way of living. Poetry feeds and waters the passions – Plato said that. You smile at me, but you will find everything in Plato.

[*Distant shouts have been heard increasing in volume.*]

Burns's genius wasn't in his glass. You hear that?

[*Window opened and sounds come distinctly in. A gang of hearties is singing* 'Gordoulie' *by Trinity wall.*]

Drunk, but those people take it out in sweat. Galley-slaves, Mr Swinburne, tied to an oar. But you and I who are poets . . .

SWINBURNE: You a poet, sir?

JOWETT: I translate Plato. If Plato found no room in his republic for poets and *their* madness, I wonder what he'd have done with that kind of insanity.

[*He closes window. Fade out.*]

COMMENTATOR: As the years pass Jowett remains in retirement, but the balance of power is shifting. His own pupils are Fellows of the college now. His enemies are still as bitter, but they are outnumbered. When he appears at a college meeting, it is they these days who are on the run. They can only strike at him through his friends. A meeting of Fellows.

JOWETT: The point I wish to make is this. Not the tenth part of the ability of the country comes to Oxford. The scheme I want you to adopt for Balliol will allow a poor man to get cheap lodgings and free lectures.

PEEL: Professor Jowett is playing a new role. He has already got us to waste money building a new front to the college. But this is a new front to Dr Jowett. The friend of the poor.

JOWETT: I know that Dr Peel and I once disagreed over port. But this isn't a personal matter.

PEEL: What do you say, Master?

SCOTT: I don't see the value to the University of bringing in a great many illiterate men.

JOWETT: Have we got to judge their value to us or our value to them?

GREEN: I agree with Jowett. If we don't reform ourselves the State will do it for us.

PEEL: I don't wish to be personal – but after all this is not a public meeting. We all know each other, and I for one see in this attempt nothing but Dr Jowett's inability to control men of birth. But will a miner prove any less of a drunkard under his care than young Swinburne?

JOWETT: We are not discussing Swinburne.

PEEL: Not today perhaps.

JOWETT: Then may we put *my* proposal to the vote, Master?

SCOTT: Those in favour . . . My vote can't stop you winning, Jowett.

PEEL: Now that Dr Jowett's settled that to his satisfaction, may we hear if he has any other plans up his sleeve?

JOWETT: I want soon to bring forward plans for a new Hall.

SCOTT: Really, Jowett, the college funds aren't bottomless.

JOWETT: We can appeal to old Balliol men.

SCOTT: Nonsense, you'd never raise enough money. Well, gentlemen, the meeting's closed. Shall we have in the sherry?

JOWETT: Not for me. I have work to do.

　　[*Door closes. Footsteps on gravel.*]

VOICE: Good evening, Jowett.

JOWETT: Good evening. How's *your* Master, Elton? He's an astute man who works by winning confidence. Here we have a bare struggle for power. Goodnight.

　　[*Opening and closing door.*]

KNIGHT: There's a lady to see you, sir.

JOWETT: A lady, Matthew? For me?

KNIGHT: What about your dinner, sir? This Plato will be the death of you.

JOWETT: I have a gentleman coming in later with some work. I must get through my own first.

　　[*Feet on stairs. Opening door.*]

And to what, dear lady, do I owe the pleasure?

MRS SPARKS: No pleasure. My name's Sparks. Mrs.

JOWETT: Sit down, Mrs Sparks, sit down.

MRS SPARKS: I can say what I've got to say standing.

　　[*A pause. Jowett starts to hum.*]

Well?

JOWETT: My dear lady, I don't know who you are.

MRS SPARKS: I've come to tell you I've had me fill of Balliol gentlemen.

JOWETT: I feel like that too sometimes.

MRS SPARKS: You can't talk round me. My mind's made up.

JOWETT: Yes. But about what exactly?

MRS SPARKS: Carried in 'ead first, night after night. Put to bed at all hours by strange gentlemen – from other colleges.

JOWETT: Yes, but who? If I may inquire.

MRS SPARKS: It's Mr Swinburne I'm referring to.

JOWETT: Oh, dear me, I was afraid of that.

MRS SPARKS: 'E may be drunk as a lord, but 'e's not a lord, an' that makes a difference.

JOWETT: I'll speak to him, Mrs Sparks.

MRS SPARKS: I don't have 'im in the 'ouse any more. An' he's got to pay for six pairs of spoilt sheets.

JOWETT: He shall pay.

MRS SPARKS: I'll see to that. I've wrote to the Master as much.

JOWETT [*sadly*]: Then certainly you won't be troubled again by Mr Swinburne. Goodnight, Mrs Sparks. I see you agree with Plato about poets.

[*Door closes. A knock.*]

KNIGHT: Are you ready, sir?

JOWETT: No work tonight, Matthew. I must see the Master.

[*Fade out and in.*]

May I have a word with you, Master? Oh dear, I see you've read Mrs Sparks's note already.

SCOTT: The poor woman has been much abused. Of course, he must go.

JOWETT: I was afraid you'd say that. But don't be hasty. We don't want Balliol to make itself as ridiculous as University made itself over Shelley.

SCOTT: I have as much feeling for Balliol as you, Jowett. Why bring in Shelley? Swinburne has no mark of a poet but drink. Twice he's failed to win the Newdigate! What sort of poet does that make him?

JOWETT: What sort of judges does that make them?

SCOTT: I did not know you were a judge of modern poetry, Dr Jowett.

JOWETT: I'm the friend of many poets, Master, and I do implore you to think very carefully . . .

[*Fade out and in.*]

KNIGHT: What about your dinner, sir? Can't you take a bite now?

JOWETT: No time, Matthew. Fetch Mr Swinburne. He may be in Hall or the JCR.

[*Silence. He hums to himself.*]

SWINBURNE: Well, Jowler, you wanted me.

JOWETT: Yes, Algernon. I've got bad news for you. Your land-lady's complained.

SWINBURNE: She only wants money. That's all Oxford landladies ever want.

JOWETT: She's complained to the Master.

SWINBURNE: Oh!

JOWETT: I've done my best for you.

SWINBURNE [*hysterically*]: They are going to send me down, is that it?

JOWETT: The Master *wanted* to send you down.

SWINBURNE: Then I stay?

JOWETT: No, Algernon, you don't stay. You leave of your own accord. Your name remains on the college books.

SWINBURNE: Do you think my father will understand the difference? They don't learn subtleties in the Navy. [*Hysterically and melodramatically*] I can't face it. I shall shoot myself.

JOWETT: Not on this carpet, Algernon.

SWINBURNE [*toned down a little*]: I shall be leaving Oxford a total and scandalous failure.

JOWETT: Oh, dear me, no. You'll come back and stay with me as often as you please. My dear boy, you'll be welcome. You know there's no one else who can help me with my Plato.

SWINBURNE: Oh, they'll repent of this one day.

JOWETT: Of course they will. When we have your portrait hanging in Hall. But you know, Algernon, you've made things rather difficult for us.

[*A knock.*]

KNIGHT: I thought I'd tell you, sir. Mr Plumer's coming across the quad.

SWINBURNE: I don't want to see anyone, anyone at all. Leave alone that dummy Plumer.

JOWETT: Thank you, Matthew. Plumer won't keep me long, Algernon. Slip into my bedroom. Take my manuscript with you, the printers are pressing for copy. Just take a look through the tenth chapter of the *Republic*, there's a dear boy.

SWINBURNE: Oh, I'll look at it, but I shan't *see* it. I shall just see disgrace . . . failure . . .

[*A knock.*]

Barrenness . . . old age . . .

JOWETT: Good evening, Plumer.

[*A door slams.*]

PLUMER: Good evening, sir.

JOWETT: A glass of wine?

PLUMER: Thank you, sir.

[*Pause.*]

JOWETT: An apple perhaps?

PLUMER: Thank you, sir.

[*Pause.*]

JOWETT: Your copy?

PLUMER: Here, sir.

[*A pause. Jowett hums.*]

JOWETT: Well . . . well . . . this is not quite so *Greek* as the last you did for me, Plumer.

[*A pause. Jowett hums.*]

Yes . . . yes . . . have you perhaps a taste for mathematics, Plumer?

SWINBURNE [*from bedroom*]: Jowler. Jowler.

JOWETT: Yes, Algernon?

SWINBURNE: A howler, Jowler, an awful howler.

[*Pause.*]

JOWETT [*meekly*]: Yes, Algernon.

[*Fade out.*]

COMMENTATOR: The time for which Jowett has waited so long comes at last. In June 1870 the Master of Balliol was appointed Dean of Rochester, sixteen years after that first disappointment. There was no question now of a rival. The same month as Jowett's election was announced, the first volume of his Plato was published. It was his happy time. He moved into the Master's Lodge, taking his servant Matthew Knight with him. Now that he was Master, what would he have to show for all those years of waiting, what ideas?

JOWETT: We must be hospitable, Matthew, we must be hospitable.

COMMENTATOR: There is the story of a guest who arriving late at the Master's Lodge noticed some concern on Knight's face and asked him, 'I hope you have no cause for anxiety at home.'

KNIGHT: No, sir, it's nothing. Only the Master invited twelve to dine this evening, sir, and you are the eighteenth who has come.

COMMENTATOR: Yes, the furrier's son is remembered now mainly for his snobbery and his hospitality to the great. But it wasn't
snobbery which dictated the new reforms, small rules like that
which restricted each man to one guest at dinner a week. Jowett
remembered his own undergraduate days of poverty, when
hospitality was such a burden that men refused his invitations
to tea. (Perhaps he remembered those days, too, when the
archbishops and the peeresses and the poets sat down to his
table in the Master's dining-room.)

Balliol was to be a college where a poor man could be happy
. . . and so it has remained. Even the laundresses had to revise
their charges. They went in deputation to the Master.

JOWETT: Will you work for Balliol at this price?

VOICES: No. Slavery I call it. We won't. Call yourself a gentleman.

JOWETT: Then, Knight, show these ladies downstairs.

COMMENTATOR: If Jowett loved a lord, he was at any rate
determined that other poor men too should have their chance to
love one. At one of the first college meetings he held as Master,
he proposed a scheme for extending the benefit of university
teaching to other cities. If the University wouldn't do it, then
Balliol would do it alone. The result was the foundation of
University College, Bristol, with the help of Balliol and New
College.

At about the same time the Liberal Government appointed a
commission to investigate the way in which Oxford and
Cambridge spent their huge incomes. Jowett at that inquiry
fought beside the reformers – for cheaper teaching, for better
conditions for the non-collegiate students (he had already
obtained them free teaching and cheap lodging). The man who
had once been so unpopular in his own college was now
unpopular in the University. Eighty years before Balliol had
been in a state of decay: now it was playing too big a part. But
they could not prevent him becoming Vice-Chancellor: that
office goes by rotation.

Now he had himself become the little monkey of a gentleman who dresses in black and has three pokers walk before
him. His ideas were lavish.

JOWETT: We have all this money to spend. Don't let's spend it in a commonplace way.

COMMENTATOR: He had noted down the previous vacation seventeen things he wanted to do – from putting stained glass into St Mary's to founding an Indian Institute. The Institute was founded with immense glitter: the Prince of Wales was there, Indians in cloth of gold and jewels. Corn was strewn and oil poured on the foundation stone. It was all very Oriental. For it was in Jowett's day that Trinity's famous taunt began:

VOICES: Balliol, Balliol, bring out your bloody blacks.

JOWETT: I see no reason why an English blackguard should not be sentenced by a respectable native.

COMMENTATOR: But perhaps what undergraduates have most to thank him for was the founding of the OUDS – though the outside world may think it a mixed blessing. For all those adolescent Hamlets with Oxford accents, and awkward extras sloping spears in tow-coloured wigs, Jowett is responsible.

Sneers about his snobbery grew – he was the friend of Lord This and Lady That: he liked the company of the famous, of Tennyson and Browning – he even brought them into his sermons. His sermons in Balliol Chapel were an easy mark – full of worldly wisdom about taking credit and writing books. That high, pedantic voice was the enemy of all enthusiasm. He deprecated too much theology in one sermon, in another he told the undergraduates:

JOWETT: The mere reading for Honours is certainly rather degrading.

COMMENTATOR: He advised them against fine writing from the pulpit and discussed the art of conversation and warned them to be temperate even about temperance.

JOWETT: Do not become intoxicated with water.

COMMENTATOR: You wouldn't have called a man like that a leader – and yet, somehow, between the dinner parties to the great and the translations from the Greek – he created an atmosphere in which leaders were born – Arnold Toynbee, the philanthropist, statesmen like Milner and Asquith and Curzon, writers like Mallock, who in the *New Republic* gently caricatured his Master. Not the greatest men, perhaps, who emerge from stormier worlds than Balliol . . . but men with a sense of philosophy and common sense, who didn't, any more than Jowett, expect too much of the world. To Jowett perhaps the great moment was when the new Balliol Hall was at last opened, and a great dinner was held. Among the speakers were the Archbishop of Canterbury, Mr Matthew Arnold, the poet, and Jowett's old friend, Dean Stanley.

[*Dinner noises fading.*]

JOWETT: Thank you for wishing me a long life. I think I do desire that, sans teeth, sans eyes, sans ears, sans everything except mind. It seems to me I have made so many mistakes.

['*No! No!*' *Laughter.*]

Yes, so many. About port and St Paul some would say.

VOICE: Not about Plato.

JOWETT: You have been good enough to compliment me on my Plato. Plato has been a great labour certainly. Yet I like being in such good company. There's nothing better in style and manners – not even in 'the first circles'.

VOICE [*in a whisper*]: There speaks Jowler.

JOWETT: But I haven't finished with him. Now I must begin to revise.

[*Laughter.*]

You have got me talking about myself. It is because I am among friends. There are many opposite opinions among us, I have no doubt, but there is one common sentiment – we were all educated at Balliol.

[*Applause.*]

TOASTMASTER: Silence for his Grace, the Archbishop of Canterbury.

ARCHBISHOP: *Si monumentum requiris, circumspice.* Her Majesty once asked me if I knew Dr Jowett and to describe him to her. I confess I found it difficult. But I realize now that Dr Jowett is simply – Balliol. I should describe to her Balliol Hall, its comfort and its dignity: I should describe this Balliol gathering – for we all owe something of ourselves to Dr Jowett – the statesman, the poet, the churchman . . .

[*Laughter and cheers. Fade.*]

TOASTMASTER: . . . for Mr Matthew Arnold.

ARNOLD: I sit here among the shadows of my past life. I see the members of the old Balliol boat, the shades of ancient tutorials. Chateaubriand, on revisiting Venice, found a charm gone; but from school and college the charms never quite pass away. Here we can dream once again that we are young . . .

[*Fade out into Big Tom striking two.*]

KNIGHT: Tired, sir? We're not as young as we were. I've put a hot brick in your bed.

JOWETT: Thank you, Matthew.

KNIGHT: It's been a great occasion, sir.

JOWETT: I wanted to show them Balliol could cook a good dinner . . . You know, Matthew, no day passes when I don't feel the defects of early education. I was never taught how to play at cards, or even at billiards, and it seems too late now. Do you think I could learn to waltz?

KNIGHT: *Waltz*, sir?

JOWETT: I'm going to have a ball. In the new Hall. We old men have finished celebrating. It's the turn of the young men now . . .

[*Fade out and in to waltz music.*]

PEEL: Green, Green – I've seen what I should have thought impossible – ladies coming in to the Common Room. A ball – attachments – matchmaking – matchmaking in college – most inappropriate.

GREEN: Well, here's Jowett. Complain to him.

JOWETT: What, Peel. Going home! At three o'clock?

[*A strangled note of rage. Sound of feet going off.*]

Poor Peel.

GREEN: He's an old man, Jowler.

JOWETT: Aye, it's hard to be beaten by old age. Did you ever hear the story of the man who asked his doctor if he was not dangerously ill. 'No, sir,' the doctor said, 'but you are dangerously old.' Well, I've come to the creaky places of life myself.

[*Sound of feet.*]

KNIGHT: Shall I give your compliments to the band, sir, and say you would like to hear them play *God Save the Queen*?

JOWETT: Do you think they've had long enough? Oh well, if *you* think so, Matthew.

[*Sound of feet.*]

Sometimes I look suddenly up at Matthew and see a middle-aged stranger. Not the boy I taught Greek while he served my dinner. He was cross with me this morning for taking all my medicines at once before breakfast.

GREEN: At once!

JOWETT: I thought it would save time. You know, Green, no one has written on old age.

GREEN: Not even Cicero?

JOWETT: Oh, I'm not forgetting that lovable book. But I mean no one has written on the management of old age. No one has given practical advice to old men. We all have to work it out for ourselves.

[*The band plays* God Save the Queen, *voices stop, music fades, silence.*]

MR GRIGGS: So that, ladies an' gentlemen, is Balliol College. Founded by a lady called Devorguilla in Anno . . .

WOMAN: You told us all that. What I want to see's Dr Jowett. Is he here?

MR GRIGGS: Him here? Oh, you may be sure he's in one of the great houses. Lord This or Lord That. If he loves anything it's a lord. That's where he really belongs. Now, if you'll just follow me back into Broad Street, we'll take a look at Trinity College.

WOMAN: Oh, dear. More colleges?

MR GRIGGS: We haven't seen the half yet, ma'am.

WOMAN: An' all as like as two pins.

PORTER: Now, Mr Griggs, no scandal, I hope.

MR GRIGGS: I sticks strictly, Mr Foster, to history. And how, if I *may* ask, is old Jowler?

PORTER [*sternly*]: The *Master*, Mr Griggs, is a very sick man.

MR GRIGGS: Well, we'll see him here, I suppose, when term starts.

PORTER: If he can, Mr Griggs, he'll be here.

COMMENTATOR: But the Master was a dying man. He did not live to see another term. It may have been some consolation to him that he was dying in the best circles. The Tennysons came to see him in London, and almost at the last his Oxford housekeeper, Miss Knight, arrived, sister of his old servant and pupil.

MISS KNIGHT: 'Master,' I said, 'you know me?'

JOWETT: Yes, my dear child, but I did not know you were here.

MISS KNIGHT: After pausing a moment or two he said . . .

JOWETT: You know I am dying?

MISS KNIGHT: I said, 'Yes. Won't you give me a message for my brother?' He unclosed his eyes and said with a smile . . .

JOWETT: Oh, yes. Give Matthew my love. Tell him he must be sure to bring out that little book he is doing for himself. Selections from Plato, I mean.

[*Fade out into Oxford sounds. Traffic noises.*
Last Big Tom.]

YES AND NO

★

CAST LIST

Yes and No was first performed at The Haymarket Studio Theatre, Leicester, on 20 March 1980, with the following cast:

DIRECTOR   *Derek Smith*
ACTOR   *William Hope*

Scene: The stage of an empty theatre, cluttered densely with the furniture of the current play. If this is easier there could be a backcloth with a design made of various articles of furniture making up the set of the play. In that case two chairs are set before the backcloth. The Actor, a young and nervous man, paces up and down, looks at his watch, examines the backcloth or the furniture of the set. He carries a script. The Director enters, also carrying a script, a middle-aged man, with an ebullient manner, who likes the sound of his own voice.

DIRECTOR: Ah, punctual, I see. A great virtue in a young actor. Have you been here long?

ACTOR: Yes.

DIRECTOR: I'm sorry. I was held up by the *traffic*. Never mind. You've had an opportunity to learn your lines properly, I hope. You were not exactly word perfect at yesterday's rehearsal.

ACTOR: No.

DIRECTOR: *Well*, it *is* rather an ordeal for a young actor like you to rehearse for the first time with Sir Ralph and Sir John. Two great men of the theatre. That's why I asked you to come this morning because I had the impression yesterday that you didn't really understand the play as a whole. I know you only come on in the first act, but I suppose you have read the play – as a whole?

ACTOR: No.

DIRECTOR: No? A bad fault, young man. A play, thank God, is not one of your wretched movies. In the theatre we respect the word and the writer of the word and the actor who interprets the word. I help to the best of my ability, but the actor is not a puppet as he is in the movies. You can't interpret the part without knowing the whole play. By the way, the play they're doing in this theatre is by the same author as ours, Frederick Privett, and it's been running now for six months. I only hope our Privett does as well. An interesting cluttered set by the way. He didn't want the actors to move about too much between his lines. The play here is in Privett's *staccato* style. You understand me?

ACTOR: No.

DIRECTOR: In this play he uses the very shortest sentences. Sometimes they are only one word long. In our play it is not the sentence but the pauses which count. I oughtn't to say this, but he has learnt a lot from Pinter. Though he's not an imitator, mind you. His pauses are quite different from Pinter's. They are Privett pauses. You must study the pauses very carefully. Even in a small part like yours. You do understand me, I hope?

ACTOR: Yes.

DIRECTOR: Good, now let's begin your scene. Don't look at your script. I'll prompt you if it's necessary.

ACTOR: Yes.

[*A long pause.*]

DIRECTOR: Go on. Begin. This is not the moment for a pause.

ACTOR: Yes.

DIRECTOR: Don't keep saying yes. Just begin.

ACTOR: Yes.

DIRECTOR: Don't say yes. Begin.

[*The Director looks at his script.*]

DIRECTOR: Oh, I'm sorry. Of course. 'Yes.' That *is* the first word of your scene. I'd forgotten you began that way. I'll read the other part. You or rather Henry Hobbs enters door left. Comyns – that is Sir Ralph – says to you, 'You have been a long time gone,' and you reply quite correctly 'Yes.' All the same you really must study that Yes. It's a defiant Yes. Your Yes is literally the beginning of the end of your relationship with Sir Ralph – I mean Comyns of course. You disappear completely after Act One. All the more reason to seize your opportunity. Now throw that Yes right up to the gallery. They must hear it distinctly in the last row. Try again.

ACTOR: Yes.

DIRECTOR: That's a little better. Go on.

ACTOR: No.

DIRECTOR: What d'you mean 'No'? Go on with the scene.

ACTOR: No.

DIRECTOR: Young man, I am the Director – I order you to go on. Are you really refusing to go on? If you do it will lose you your job of acting in a play with Sir Ralph and Sir John. I'll give you one more chance. Do you refuse to go on?

ACTOR: No.

DIRECTOR: I'm very glad for your sake. I don't like to see a young actor throwing away a great chance. Who knows, you might well one day be a theatrical knight yourself? You'd like that, wouldn't you?

ACTOR: Yes.

DIRECTOR: Good. Then we'll forget this little dispute. Go on with your part.

ACTOR: No.

DIRECTOR: I've never in thirty years as a director heard such impertinence. Are you ready to rehearse or not?

ACTOR: Yes.

DIRECTOR: Then go ahead or leave the theatre.

[*The Actor looks at his script.*]

ACTOR: No.

[*The Director looks at his script.*]

DIRECTOR: Yes. I see you do say 'No'. I'm sorry. Sir Ralph says to you, 'I suppose you never thought of the anxiety you were giving me when you didn't return in time for dinner,' and you reply, 'No,' that's quite correct – I misunderstood – but all the same I'd like you to practise that No. It's got to reach the gallery too. You are still defying Sir Ralph, and now Sir John – of course I mean Edward Cruikshank – emerges slyly from the door right, happy to see that once again he has broken up the relationship of his old friend Sir Ralph – that is to say Comyns. You follow me?

ACTOR: Yes.

DIRECTOR: It's a very daring play. When I was young nobody would have produced it. We could never have hoped to cast Sir John and Sir Ralph in a play of this kind thirty years ago. It would have been forbidden by the Lord Chamberlain. I don't suppose you've even heard of the Lord Chamberlain.

ACTOR: No.

DIRECTOR: I never met him myself. We always had to talk to a Colonel in the Guards. Oh well, *autre temps, autres moeurs*. Do you speak French?

ACTOR: Yes.

DIRECTOR: It's always a good thing for an actor to talk French – not that it's much help in this play. Except that it might prove useful in Act Two when Comyns – Sir Ralph – has become attached to a French acrobat called René. Surely you've read the play that far?

ACTOR: No.

DIRECTOR: René has a much better part than yours. The beginning of an affair always contains more dialogue than the end. Perhaps I might get you to understudy René. If anything happens, anyone would be able to take *your* part. If René fell ill you would have a great opportunity. There is one scene of tremendous passion when Sir John discovers René with Sir Ralph – I mean of course when Comyns discovers René with Cruikshank. As you were, Cruikshank discovers René with Comyns? Do you mean to say you haven't even glanced at Act Two?

ACTOR: No.

DIRECTOR: You must realize if you're ever going to be a good actor the importance of understanding a play as a whole. However few words you have to speak in Act One they have to fit into the frame of the whole play. You haven't read Act Two or Act Three and that is why your Yes was so feeble, and your No lacked all authority. Don't let's get angry with each other. I want to help you. Now let's sit down and relax.

[*They sit on two chairs.*]

DIRECTOR: Have you seen *this* play of Privett's?

ACTOR: No.

DIRECTOR: I'll get you house seats. It's important you should realize what Privett is after. Now in this play – in his *staccato* style – he is making a great satirical statement about the heterosexual world we most of us live in without realizing its falsity. In our play – the play of long pauses – he is making a great satirical statement about the homosexual world we most of us live in – do you follow me?

ACTOR: No-o-o.

DIRECTOR: Let me put it more simply. In this play at this theatre he expresses the betrayal inherent in any homosexual relationship . . . as you were, in any heterosexual relationship, and in our play he exposes the betrayal at the heart of any homosexual relationship. You do follow?

ACTOR: Ye-e-s.

DIRECTOR: You've got to bear all that in mind when you say Yes and No in this opening scene. Your Yes has to be abrasive and your No a little scornful. It was suggested at one time that Privett should write in a part for Sir Michael in Act Three, but I argued that two theatrical knights would give the play dignity, but three knights might easily turn it into a sort of tournament. Tournaments were pretty rough. If one of the knights got knocked out it would be very difficult to find a replacement. No one can really understudy one of the knights, not you and certainly not the French acrobat. Don't you agree?

ACTOR: Yes.

DIRECTOR: Not that I underrate the importance of your minor role in this play. You know the old rhyme about the Battle of Waterloo – 'For want of a nail the battle was lost.' Think that you are a nail, an important, a vital nail . . . Now with all this in mind . . . let's look at the scene again. Sir John – I mean Comyns – no, Cruikshank – interrupts. In his sly trouble-making way he says, 'You have better things to think about, I suspect,' and you reply?

ACTOR: Yes.

DIRECTOR: No, no, here you have to make a long pause. You are deliberately insulting Sir Ralph – I mean Comyns . . . It's the end of the affair. Try it again.

ACTOR: No.

DIRECTOR: Not No. Yes. Yes. Damn it all, I can't understand why you aren't word perfect. You only have to say Yes and No in the right order. Imagine the disaster if on a single occasion you say No instead of Yes – or indeed Yes instead of No. The whole meaning of the play is altered in a flash. An actor can trip up on a long speech and recover. He gains support from the context. But Yes and No, these words have no context. They stand in

their dignity and certitude alone. Sir Ralph is expecting Yes and
you say No. Sir John waits for his cue and you say No instead of
Yes. What can they do? They will need time to recover: there
will be a sickening pause – not one of Privett's pauses. Now, try
again and get it right. Remember it's the end of the affair. Sir
John says, 'You have better things to think about, I suspect,'
and you reply . . .

ACTOR: Yes.

DIRECTOR: More boldly.

ACTOR: Yes.

DIRECTOR: Better. You do understand, don't you, that I only
want to help you? You have a lot of promise. If I'd known you
spoke French I might have given you the part of René. French
actors are so unreliable. Now, what happens after Yes? Sir
Ralph – I mean Comyns – is touched by jealousy as Sir John –
Cruikshank – intended and he asks, 'What better things?' Of
course, you don't answer. You stand silent. Better stand up and
we'll act this out together. We must get this scene right. A lot
depends on it. I'll take Sir John's part and Sir Ralph's. 'I think he
has been at the circus.' 'The circus, why the circus?' 'There's a
young French acrobat there called René. You have been to the
circus, haven't you, Hobbs?'

ACTOR: Yes.

DIRECTOR: A little bit more incisive.

ACTOR: Yes.

DIRECTOR: Bravo! We're getting somewhere. Now Sir John – I
mean Comyns, no, it's Cruikshank: 'You can't keep a young
man in chains, Cyril.' Sir Ralph – that's to say Cyril – 'Have
you ever felt in chains, Henry?'

ACTOR: Yes.

DIRECTOR: Isn't it No?

[He looks at the script.]

ACTOR: No.

DIRECTOR: You are right. It's Yes. I see it's Yes. Say it quite
calmly this time – perhaps a touch of irony? Just a touch. No
more. And cold, cold as ice. 'Have you ever felt in chains,
Henry?'

ACTOR: Yes.

DIRECTOR: Not half bad, but I have an idea. I think this is the moment for a Pause. Privett hasn't mentioned a Pause. It will be a surprise for him. You see, you want to keep Sir Ralph on tenterhooks. He still wants you to stay. He hasn't yet met René. That plot has been laid in devilish secrecy by Sir John. It was he who sent you the circus tickets anonymously. Tomorrow he will take Sir Ralph to the circus and your reign will be over, and René's will begin. But not for long. Oh no, not for long. In Act Three Sir John, that's Cruikshank, disposes of René in his turn. There is something quite Shakespearian about Privett. Aren't you reminded a little of *Richard III*?

ACTOR: No-o-o.

DIRECTOR: That's because you haven't read the whole play. You don't begin to understand why Sir John is intent on breaking up every relationship Sir Ralph has. And yet it's explained quite clearly in Act One. Surely you've read the beginning of Act One? Why, it comes just before your first scene. You must have read it.

ACTOR: No.

DIRECTOR: Incredible. You've simply read the parts where you have something to say?

ACTOR: Yes.

DIRECTOR: By God, I'd replace you – but it would upset Sir Ralph. He hates changes. Now, do listen carefully – what happens after Yes? [*He consults the script*] You move slowly across stage to door right. Sir Ralph says, 'Where are you going?' You don't answer. Go on. Move slowly. Sir John [*teasingly*]: 'He's only going to wash his paws – aren't you, Hobbs?' Now you stop in the doorway where you are now. You are about to speak the most dramatic line Privett has given you. You must milk it for all it's worth. You turn back to the room and the two old men. Everyone wonders what you are going to say. Privett indicates 'Long Pause'. That's where you went wrong yesterday. You hardly paused at all. You've got to develop an actor's sixth sense here. You must feel the suspense in the audience, you are the centre of attention, you must break the silence and speak only just before they grow impatient. Now. Go on. You feel the moment has come. Speak.

ACTOR: Yes.

DIRECTOR: No, no, damn you. It's No.

ACTOR: No?

    [*Both consult their scripts.*]

DIRECTOR: Oh, I'm sorry. My mistake. It was No originally, but I remember now Privett altered it. He said No was too obvious and it spoilt your re-entrance when you come in wearing a bowler hat and carrying your suitcase and Sir John says in his silky sneery way, 'I think you're seeing the last of Hobbs.' And Cyril says, 'You aren't leaving?'

ACTOR: Yes.

DIRECTOR: No, no. You say nothing. You walk out. You don't say Yes. You don't say No. Surely you can remember that.

ACTOR: Yes.

DIRECTOR: I hope to God you remember on the first night. Look, young man, I still believe I can make an actor out of you. Sit down in that chair and I'll try to explain to you what Privett's play is about.

    [*They take their seats.*]

DIRECTOR: You don't understand Sir John's motivation?

ACTOR: No.

DIRECTOR: Or his relationship with Sir Ralph?

ACTOR: No.

DIRECTOR: Just before you return from the circus the two old men have a very moving scene together. They are sitting as we are sitting now when they are remembering the past – their first meeting at school when Sir Ralph was Sir John's fag – as you were, it was Sir John who was Sir Ralph's fag. Their love for each other dates from that time – and Sir John's jealousy. He couldn't bear Sir Ralph's friendship with any other boy. They can both laugh at it now, of course, but we detect behind Comyns's laughter – I mean Cruikshank's – that is Sir John's – the jealousy which still lurks there. Sir John plays on the fact that Hobbs has not returned to dinner – he makes Sir Ralph uneasy, for Sir Ralph is deeply attached to you, of course. I mean Comyns is. Well, perhaps not so very deeply, for in the next act we see him in love with René, the French acrobat, and the French acrobat then deceives him with Sir John for money.

It all comes out because of a handkerchief with Guerlain scent on it. Like in *Othello*. The handkerchief betrays all. I told you Privett is quite Shakespearian in his ideas. Have you followed me this far?

ACTOR: Ye-e-es.

DIRECTOR: The last act is very very bleak indeed. Sir Ralph has quarrelled with Sir John, as we all of us think, irrevocably. Sir Ralph is alone as it were in the desert created around him by Sir John. The window-cleaner comes to the house. A young good-looking man with manners above his station. He breaks a pane of glass and cuts his hand. Sir Ralph bandages it with the very handkerchief that had belonged to the French acrobat. He says very tenderly – I can't tell you how very, very moving Sir Ralph is at this moment – 'Poor boy.' There is a long, long pause – perhaps the longest pause Privett has ever given us – Sir Ralph's eyes were full of unshed tears – I can assure you they will be there unshed every night and every matinée even if we play for a year – wonderful, wonderful Sir Ralph. The door left opens – who is it? Sir Ralph is bent over the bandage, he raises the window-cleaner's wounded hand to his lips – we see that it is Sir John who has returned. Sir John sees the window-cleaner – he says only one word 'Ralph' – I mean 'Cyril' – and the curtain *falls*. What a play! What an author! What actors! To think, young man, that you can be one of them if only you'll learn your lines. You will be on the stage taking the applause with them – between the window-cleaner and the French acrobat. Young man, can't you realize now that the whole success of the play may depend on your getting your Yes and No right?

[*The Actor listens to the Director's speech with bowed head.*]

Can't you see how important your part is?

[*The Actor raises his head. A Pause – one of Privett's longer Pauses.*]

ACTOR: Yes – and no.

[*Actor walks off.*]

CURTAIN

FOR WHOM THE BELL CHIMES

CAST LIST

For Whom the Bell Chimes was first performed at The Haymarket Studio Theatre, Leicester, on 20 March 1980, with the following cast:

X	*Phil Bowen*
MASTERMAN	*Roy Macready*
COLONEL FENWICK	*Derek Smith*
SERGEANT	*Alan Starkey*
NEIGHBOUR	*Malcolm Rennie*
INSPECTOR	*Carolyn Moody*
RSPCA MAN	*William Hope*

Directed by Robin Midgley
Designed by Terry Parsons
Lighting by Chris Ellis
Studio Stage Manager, Michael Halbert
Assistant Stage Managers,
Howard Harrison *and* Roger Troup
Company Stage Manager, P. M. Davies

Act One

The curtain rises on a very clean, very neat one-room apartment where everything has its place, though as we shall see before long the places are sometimes hidden places. A man in his forties with a great shock of dark hair lounges in an uncomfortable armchair biting his nails. He examines each nail with care after it has been bitten. The remains of a breakfast, two cups and two plates and a cardboard packet of cereal, lie on a long table in the centre of the room, with a cloth that extends to the floor. A picture hangs a little askew on the back wall. A scarlet telephone on the table remains conspicuously useless until the last act. The man, whom it is easiest for us to call X, looks from time to time over his nail at the picture. He gets up and examines it closer. He puts his hand on the frame, but instead of straightening it, he drags it even more askew and gives a grunt of satisfaction. Perhaps because it now disguises a button on the wall. He starts on another nail. The table next attracts his attention. He picks up the cardboard packet and begins to read aloud with evident distaste the description of the contents.

X: 'The Old World and the New World have joined forces to create a luscious novelty cereal of scrumptious flavour called Honey Crisps to tickle your taste buds . . .

[*The front door bell chimes a gentle melancholy tune and stops.* X *glances at the door in the right wall and goes on reading.*]

Honey culled from Alpine flowers . . .'

[*The bell plays its little tune again.* X, *carrying the cereal packet, goes to the door and opens it. A man stands in the doorway in a very shabby grey suit. When he takes off his hat he discloses a completely bald head. He carries an ancient attaché case and he wears a pair of rimless glasses.*]

MAN: Excuse me for disturbing you, sir. I see you are at breakfast.

X: Oh, no, I was just reading. What do you want?

MAN: I'm a representative of the Anti-Child-Polio Campaign.

X: Oh, yes? A worthy cause, no doubt, but what . . . ?

MAN: I'm glad you feel that, sir. May I step in for a moment and explain our objects?

X: I'm not a child and I haven't polio. But come in. Come in. I'm glad to have someone to talk to. I'm alone. I'm not used to being alone. [*He looks closely at the man*] I can see it's been raining.

MAN: We work in all weathers, rain or shine, for the poor little sufferers.

X: You'll excuse me saying – judging from your clothes you must be very badly paid. Even your shoes need repair.

MAN: Well, sir, we try to make our overheads as small as possible. So that there's more for the Campaign and the little ones.

X: You want to get money out of me, I suppose?

MAN: Not for me, sir. For these poor children. Here, for example, [*he has opened his attaché case*] is a photograph to touch the hardest heart. A little boy of six, sir. Think of it. Six.

X [*looking at the photograph*]: He seems very comfortable in his wheeled chair.

MAN: Supplied by the Campaign, sir, thanks to generous donors like yourself.

X: I've given you nothing yet.

MAN: Your neighbours on the floor below have been very kind. You can see for yourself. [*He takes an untidy scrap of paper out of his pocket*] Look at that now. Three five pounds and one tenner. The tenner's an old lady past ninety years. She told me so herself.

X [*looking at the list*]: So the old hag's called Marbles. I never knew that. She complained once at the noise we made up here.

MAN: In the next block a gentleman called Mr Hargreaves gave four silver spoons – he hadn't the ready.

X [*sharply*]: Where are your credentials?

MAN [*fumbling in the attaché case*]: I have them here, sir. Somewhere. No, that's the driving licence. Here, sir.

X [*examining the card*]: But in this photo you have as good a head of hair as me.

MAN: Yes, sir, almost as good, sir. But two months ago a severe Rash – of nervous origin the doctor said, a sort of melancholy induced by the sadness of my work for these poor children stricken down before they could even enjoy the joys of sport . . .

x: Lucky them! I always hated sports. What became of all your hair?

MAN: The doctors told me I had to have my head shaved. Because of the Rash.

x: You did it very thoroughly.

MAN: I thought it best, sir, while I was at it, to go the whole hog.

x: Hog is certainly the right expressive term. You're even pink on top. [*He moves restlessly around the* MAN *examining him from all angles*] What did my neighbours say about this photograph? Why don't you have an up-to-date one made?

MAN: We try to save even little expenses. Besides, it's seldom anyone asks for my credentials. The photos of the poor child are usually enough. And then – the Campaign manager has always said that my face carries conviction.

x: Conviction? I hope he meant it well! Come, make yourself comfortable. Sit down and tell me more about yourself. And the Rash. Did your hair come out in clumps – or slowly, hair by hair?

MAN [*uneasy*]: I don't want to take up your time, sir. Not with my poor self. You were reading when I came in. I hate to be interrupted in a good read myself.

x: You mean pay up and let me go?

MAN: Any contribution above a pound is welcome and enables you to receive our monthly magazine gratis. [*He searches for it in the attaché case*] Let me leave you a sample copy. You'll see – there are a lot of lovely photos.

x [*turning the pages*]: What a wonderful life of ease they all seem to have in their wheeled chairs.

MAN: Condemned to them for life. Poor little things. Turn to page 25, sir. There's a beautiful child for you. And what a glad brave smile she's giving to Princess Anne.

x: The Princess doesn't return it.

MAN: Only four years old. No happy future for that little girl. No marriage, no children, no happy future.

x: No horses either. You have a compassionate heart, I can tell that, but marriage doesn't necessarily mean a happy future, does it? I've had a good few fiancées myself, but we've always preferred to stay that way. An engagement can be broken so much more economically than a marriage. A few tears, perhaps, but no lawyers. Would you like a cup of tea?

MAN: Well – you are very kind, sir, really you are. The cup that cheers.

X: Something to eat with it? How about some of these? [*He picks up the packet of cereal*] 'The Old World and the New World have joined forces to create a luscious novelty cereal of scrumptious flavour called Honey Crisps to tickle your taste buds.'

MAN: I wouldn't say no, sir. I came out without my breakfast. For the Campaign, sir, you'll understand. For the Campaign.

X: 'Honey culled from Alpine flowers.'

MAN: You don't say. Fancy that.

X: 'Whole wheat from the vast prairies of the Middle West.'

MAN: It certainly sounds good.

X: 'Brown sugar from the storied Caribbean famous for buccaneers and rum. Crispy, crackly . . .'

MAN: It's real poetry, isn't it, sir?

X: Just boil a kettle while I find the tea. And wash the cups while you're at it.

[*The* MAN *looks round with bewilderment.*]

MAN: I don't see any door.

X: What door?

MAN: The door of the kitchen.

X: Oh, this is a very compact little apartment. You just press that button on the wall there.

[*He indicates a button on the left-hand wall. The* MAN *presses it and the wall slides back disclosing a tiny kitchenette with an electric stove and a basin.*]

MAN: How very clever, sir.

X: They call them Omni-Studios. A place for everything and everything in its place.

MAN: Will you be taking a cup, sir?

X: No, no. I've had mine. [*He goes to a small cupboard by the door in the right-hand wall and takes out a tin*] Here's the tea.

[*The* MAN *puts on the kettle and begins to wash the cups.* X *starts leafing through the polio magazine.*]

MAN: I've seen ladies weeping when they look at that.

x: Ah, but there's a silver lining, isn't there? They don't have to work like you. In all weathers. Rain or shine. And then – who knows? – the door of their little room opens and there's Princess Anne.

MAN: Very true, sir, but we have our health.

x: It's not a constant factor. I suffer very badly from hay fever every summer. It starts on Derby Day, reaches a horrible climax at Ascot. And fades away with Goodwood.

MAN: You could stay indoors.

x: My fiancée – this is her apartment – is too mean to buy a television. So you really got twenty-five pounds out of my neighbours? Not to speak of four silver spoons. You are quite a remarkable man. I never got so much as a smile out of one of them. [*Sharply*] You gave them a receipt, of course?

MAN: Of course, sir. I always give receipts. And the Head Office will send them a letter of thanks, signed by Mrs Falconbridge herself.

x: Should I know the name?

MAN: Our chairman, sir. Or should I say chairwoman? She's a personal friend of Princess Anne.

x: I might be able to let you have five pounds.

[*He opens the tin in the cupboard from which he took the tea and takes some pound notes from it – and then closes the cupboard.*]

MAN: Oh, thank you, sir.

x: The trouble is it's not *my* money. It's my fiancée's. I have none. I'm unemployable.

MAN: I'm sorry to hear it, sir. Perhaps an opening like mine . . .

x: I said unemployable not unemployed. To be unemployable has at least a certain dignity about it. Now, would my fiancée have agreed to give you the five pounds?

MAN: I'm sure when she hears about the cause and sees those pictures . . .

x: The trouble is she's of a very suspicious nature, unlike me. She would ask for credentials. She would want an up-to-date photo. Why, if she were here now you wouldn't be making that tea . . .

MAN: I'm sure she wouldn't grudge it me?

x: Don't be sure of that. She's a great grudger. [*Pause*] She has very small and pretty ears. They are the only pretty thing about her.

MAN: Ears?

x: But they hear the hell of a lot. She can hear me kissing a girl all across town. Avoid a girl with very small ears – they are very powerful electronic appliances, like the small transistors in a pocket computer. She computes all the time. What's your name by the way?

MAN: Masterman, sir.

x: May I call you Masterman?

MASTERMAN: Of course, sir.

x: And the Christian name? In case our friendship deepens.

MASTERMAN: Well, sir, I was christened Ambrose. But I prefer my friends to call me Chips.

   [*The kettle is boiling. He makes the tea.*]

x: The trouble is, Masterman, that I shall feel very guilty if I give you five of her pounds, intended for the housekeeping, and contribute nothing myself. [*Pause*] There are no silver spoons here and even the nickel ones belong to her. Sit down, sit down. Make yourself comfortable. Tickle your taste buds with the scrumptious flavour of Honey Crisps.

   [MASTERMAN *sits down and pours out the tea. A pause.* x *bites his nails and stares at* MASTERMAN'*s feet.*]

Your shoes are in a really shocking state. Your tootsies will soon be breaking through their prison bars.

MASTERMAN: I've got another pair at home. But I like to keep 'em for a special occasion.

x: What sort of special occasion?

MASTERMAN: Well, sometimes we hold little parties in a hospital when funds allow it for the poor young victims. Chocolate éclairs, bonbons, orangeade . . .

x: I'd be glad to contribute some Honey Crisps.

MASTERMAN: And at Christmas – oh, it's very moving to see all the little sufferers sitting in their little chairs around the festive tree.

x: And you wearing your best shoes?

MASTERMAN: Yes, sir.

x: And who knows? Perhaps Princess Anne might drop in.

MASTERMAN: It's always a possibility, sir.

x: And it wouldn't do for you to be wearing those shoes if she came in.

MASTERMAN: It would let the side down, as they say.

x: What size do you take, Masterman?

MASTERMAN: Nines, sir, though I can squeeze into an eight and a half without undue discomfort.

x: What will happen when those working shoes of yours collapse?

MASTERMAN: I'll have to wear my specials, I suppose.

x: I have an idea, Masterman. Personally I have no money to contribute to the Campaign, no spoons, only my fiancée's five pounds, but at least I could give you my shoes.

MASTERMAN: No, no, sir. What would you do without them?

x: Wear yours.

MASTERMAN: But, sir, you said yourself . . . a shocking state.

x: Perhaps they'll shock my fiancée and she'll buy me a new pair. Come along. Off with them. [x *slips off his shoes*] Go on. Try them. See if the little tootsies fit their new home.

[MASTERMAN *tries on the shoes*.]

MASTERMAN: Like a glove. It's really too, too kind of you, sir. [*He takes out the list*] Let me write your name on my list. Pair of shoes. What name, sir?

x: Just put Anon.

MASTERMAN: And the donor of the five pounds, sir?

x: My fiancée's name is Felicity Harwich.

[MASTERMAN *writes*.]

MASTERMAN: If you wouldn't mind spelling the last name, sir.

x: H-A-R-W-I-C-H. And now you must give me your shoes, Masterman, for I have to go out and post a letter.

MASTERMAN: I'm afraid it's a bit wet underfoot, sir, with the rain.

x: Never mind. Now that we've settled my contribution to the Campaign what about some more Honey Crisps?

MASTERMAN: I won't say no. They are very succulent.

x: Scrumptious is the correct term. Now, that jacket of yours . . . the right elbow is in need of repair and the sleeves are frayed. I wouldn't be surprised if you had a hole in your pocket.

MASTERMAN: In the left-hand one, yes.

x: Suppose the money for the little victims dropped through.

MASTERMAN: Oh, no, sir, I'd never risk that. It all goes straight into my attaché case. Anyway, it's generally in notes.

x: Have you a special suit too in reserve? I mean in case Princess Anne comes riding by?

MASTERMAN: This is my only one, sir. I can't afford another, even Burton's.

x: I feel ashamed, Masterman. At home I have two new suits from Simpson's. I'll tell you what – we must exchange jackets.

MASTERMAN: Oh, no sir, I couldn't accept . . . You've been generous enough . . .

x [*taking off his jacket*]: I'm not giving it to you, I'm giving it to the Anti-Child-Polio Campaign. You will work a lot better for it if you wear this.

MASTERMAN: I little thought, sir, when I rang at your door . . .
[*They exchange jackets.*]

x: An excellent fit. Perhaps a little large about the shoulders.

MASTERMAN: It's many a long year since I had a jacket as good. This is a red letter day for me, sir, meeting you like this. Can I finish the washing up before I go?

x: No, no, Masterman. I never wash up. My fiancée would think it very odd.

MASTERMAN: She's a lucky girl, that one.

x: You think so? I'm not sure that she would agree with you, but then tastes differ.

MASTERMAN: It's not for every girl to meet a gentleman as generous as you are. Would you mind, sir, if I put that picture straight? It worries me.

x: I can see you are a tidy soul. [*Sharply*] Don't touch that button or you'll bring the bed down on top of you.

MASTERMAN: The bed?

x: Didn't I tell you this is an Omni-Studio? Everything has its place.

MASTERMAN: I had wondered a bit – not even a sofa . . .

x: Well reasoned. A fiancée does require at least a sofa.

MASTERMAN: It's usual, sir. [*Looking round the bare room*] And then a girl requires somewhere to put her little pieces.

x: There are drawers under the bed. Perhaps you'd like to see. [*His hand hovers over the button*] Perhaps not. A girl has secrets.

MASTERMAN: Yes, sir. I wouldn't be one to intrude.

[*Pause.*]

x: You know, you make me very curious, Masterman. I liked you immediately I saw you. My shoes obviously like you. And my jacket likes you. What did you do before you became engaged in this door-to-door racket?

MASTERMAN: I worked, sir, on this and that. I laboured very hard for many years for little pay.

x: An indoors job?

MASTERMAN: An indoors job, sir, yes.

x: A desk job?

MASTERMAN: Not exactly.

x: Married?

MASTERMAN: I never had the time, sir.

x: Perhaps you have a little room somewhere rather like this?

MASTERMAN: Not like this, sir. Nothing so modern. No kitchenette. Only a gas ring. A bed, of course. But not stowed happily away like you have it here.

x: A bath?

MASTERMAN: Oh, dear me, no. I go to the Public once a week.

x: How would you like to take a nice hot bath here? It's cold and wet outside. You'd go to work with a lot more vigour after a hot bath.

MASTERMAN [*looking round*]: Well, sir, it's what they call a tempting proposition, but there doesn't seem to be any bath here that I can see.

x: Ah, but there is. Trust Omni-Studios Limited. Everything in place and a place for everything.

[*He lifts the cloth over the table and pulls out a plastic bath which he positions over an exit hole in the floor. Going to the kitchenette he fixes a rubber tube to a tap of the sink and fixes it to a tap on the bath. He then turns on the water and lets a little flow into the bath as a demonstration.*]

MASTERMAN: Well, well, what will they think of next? And where will they have found a place for the WC? If you'll forgive the vulgarity.

x: I'll show you if you want it.

MASTERMAN: No, no, sir. Quite unnecessary. Only curiosity.

x: Now what about your bath, Masterman?

MASTERMAN: Really not, sir. It would be infringing on your kindness. I couldn't possibly. Besides I have a lot of ground to cover before night.

x: Just take a feel for curiosity and see if it's the right temperature.
   [*As there is only a little water in the bottom of the bath* MASTERMAN *has to lean rather far over, disclosing a patch on the seat of his trousers.*]

MASTERMAN: Very nice and warm, sir.

x: My goodness, Masterman, your trousers.

MASTERMAN: What about my trousers?

x: You can't go about like that. Princess Anne or no Princess Anne.

MASTERMAN: How do you mean, sir? What's wrong?

x: The patch!

MASTERMAN: Oh, just a little tear, sir. Getting through a hedge.

x: What on earth were you doing in a hedge?

MASTERMAN: I like to take a country walk on Sundays.

x: But a patch like that doesn't go at all with my jacket.

MASTERMAN: You mean it sort of lets it down?

x: It certainly does. There's only one thing to do, Masterman. I'll have to give you my trousers.

MASTERMAN: Oh, no, no, sir. I couldn't think of such a thing.
   [*But* x *has already begun to take off his trousers.*]

x: Come on, man. Don't be shy. I'm not doing this for you. I'm doing it for those poor paralysed children.

MASTERMAN: My underpants, sir. I haven't had the time to go to the laundry this week. And they are a bit patchy too.

x: Never mind that. Nobody sees them. It's the outer appearance that matters.

MASTERMAN: Very true.

x: How long have you been doing this noble work of yours, Masterman?

MASTERMAN: Two years come November.

x: In all weathers, you say?

MASTERMAN: In all weathers, sir.

x: Snow and hail and heatwaves. Do you know, I am as much moved by your devotion to your work as I am by all those little children in their wheeled chairs? It would be so much easier for you in a wheeled chair. Perhaps a motorized one. Don't you sometimes envy them the comfort of their lives? When they are gathered round the lighted tree in their well-heated hospital ward you, Masterman, may be trudging through the snow begging from door to door.

> [*Reluctantly* MASTERMAN *takes off his trousers. He keeps his face to* x *because of the torn seat of the underpants. They exchange trousers. A long embarrassed pause.*]

x: Why now, you're quite a changed man.

MASTERMAN: That's exactly how I feel, sir. If you'd told me a quarter of an hour ago . . .

x: I feel rather changed myself. But my change started earlier. [*He looks at his watch*] Three quarters of an hour ago to be exact. [*Pause*] I tell you, Masterman, before you came I passed through a period of deep despair.

MASTERMAN: Something to do with your girl?

x: Yes.

MASTERMAN: A bad quarrel?

x: A final quarrel, Masterman.

MASTERMAN: Believe me, sir, you shouldn't take a lovers' tiff all that seriously. Hard words break no bones.

x: Oh, no bones were broken. And she was an awful bitch. Very fat with a squint. The ugly ones are the easiest to acquire and the most difficult to lose. Especially when they are employed and you are unemployable. It gives them an unbearable sense of superiority.

MASTERMAN: Remember the old saying, sir, there are as many fish in the sea . . . As long as a man's rod is not broken . . . If there was something I could do to *help* . . .

x: You've helped me already, Masterman. I little knew, when that bell chimed, that my good angel was there waiting at the door. Are you sure you won't take a bath?

MASTERMAN: I'd rather not, sir, if you don't mind. I have my little habits. The Public on Thursdays.

x: You needn't be shy of me. I have to go out to post that letter, Masterman.

MASTERMAN: No, no, really, thank you, sir.

[x *goes to the fourth wall and looks through an imaginary window.*]

x: The sun's come out again. The rain's over. You brought the sun with you. I won't be gone for more than five minutes. Stay till I come back. I want more of your company – it cheers me up. Give yourself another helping of Honey Crisps.

MASTERMAN: I really ought to be getting on with my work, sir.

x: But I haven't given you the five pounds yet, belonging to my fiancée. I'll do it when I come back. [*He takes* MASTERMAN's *spectacles from* MASTERMAN *and puts them on*] Why, they're plain glass, Masterman.

MASTERMAN [*with a look of shame*]: Well . . . as a matter of fact . . .

x: So they suit me just as well as they suit you.

MASTERMAN: I use them for my work, sir. You see, when your clothes are a bit shabby like mine are, the spectacles give you bit of class. They carry conviction.

x: Conviction again. That ugly word.

MASTERMAN: I'd like them back, sir, if you wouldn't mind. I've grown accustomed to wear them.

x: But you don't need them any more. It's *my* clothes which are shabby now.

MASTERMAN: Please, sir.

[x *goes towards the door.*]

x: You don't trust me, Masterman. Look – I'll tell you what I'll do. It's a fine day now and the sun's shining, so I'll leave you with my head of hair until I get back.

[*He quickly slips off his abundant hair, leaving himself as bald as* MASTERMAN, *and slaps the wig on* MASTERMAN's *bald skull. Then he snatches* MASTERMAN's *attaché case and whisks through the door.*]

Au revoir, Chips.

[*He slams the door to while* MASTERMAN *is still feeling his head with amazement. Pause of dismay.*]

MASTERMAN: Hey!

[*Followed by sound of door slamming.*]

[*Aloud to himself*] By God, you've been conned, Chips. Conned by a bloody amateur. [*He goes to the door, opens it and looks down the passage*] Twenty-five nicker blown. And four silver spoons.

[*He comes back into the room, leaving the door ajar. He sinks despairingly into the easy chair and begins to bite his nails as x had done. Between bites he ruminates.*]

You've lost your touch, Chips. What would Spike say if he could see me now? And Ginger. Dear old Ginger. Ginger'd die laughing if he wasn't dead already. [*Pause*] Ginger, old sod, wherever you are, think of me, pray for me, Ginger. Twenty-five nicker and four silver spoons. And those photos, Ginger. What will I do without those photos? And my credentials – with Spike's moniker on them to bring me luck. Ginger, help me, wherever you are, think of me, pray for me, Ginger. [*Long pause*] Yes, by God, Ginger, you were always the bright one. You always had the answer. He took that five nicker out of the cupboard. It won't be all there is.

[*He begins to search the cupboard thoroughly without finding anything. He drops an unopened packet of Honey Crisps on the floor with disgust.*]

Do they live on those bloody crisps? Ah!

[*He remembers the picture which was askew and takes it off the wall. Nothing there.*]

Ginger, old friend. [*Pause*] Yes, Ginger, I'm a bloody fool. You're right. The bed. Under the bloody old mattress. They never learn better.

[*He looks around for the button, finds it, presses it and that part of the wall begins slowly to fold down. Only when it reaches the floor do we see the body of a very fat girl in a nightdress with long blonde hair and a squint. For psychological as well as for economic reasons a wax model should be used – the caricature of an ugly girl.*]

[*Staring paralysed*] Oh, my God. Dead as doornails. Ginger!

[*The front door bell chimes its melancholy little melody.* MASTERMAN *struggles to lift the bed back into place, but the weight of the body makes it too heavy for him. The bell begins to chime again. In desperation he tries the button and the bed lifts slowly as the bell starts to chime for the third time. There is a click as the bed falls into place.* MASTERMAN *turns to face the door with his back defiantly*] *pressed against the concealed bed. A cheery male voice from outside calls, 'Anybody at home?' and the door is pushed open.*]

SLOW CURTAIN

[In the Haymarket Studio Theatre, Leicester, production no interval was taken at this point]

Act Two

We go back for the opening of Act II to the close of the previous act.
MASTERMAN *is pressed against the wall that conceals the bed. The last
chimes of the bell are sounding and a cheery voice calls outside the door,
'Anybody at home?' The door is pushed open and a tall elderly man in a
soft hat and a smart raincoat, with an umbrella hooked on his arm and
carrying a briefcase, stands in the doorway. He has a grey moustache and
a straight military carriage.*]

STRANGER: Good morning. I found the door open. Is Miss
Harwich at home?
   [MASTERMAN *for a moment is too frightened to reply.*]
Miss Felicity Harwich.
MASTERMAN: She went out to post a letter.
   [*The* STRANGER *takes off his hat.*]
STRANGER: May I come in? [*He doesn't wait for an answer*] If you
don't mind, I'll wait for her return.
MASTERMAN: She may be away some time. She has a lot of
shopping to do.
STRANGER: Have you been here long yourself by any chance?
MASTERMAN: What's that to you?
STRANGER: Oh, you mustn't take umbrage. Surely you are Miss
Harwich's fiancé, aren't you? The old lady on the floor below
told me you would probably be here. Miss Marbles is her
name. A rather curious name for a lady. May I sit down? I've
been walking rather rapidly.
   [*He sits on the chair by the table.* MASTERMAN *remains with his
   back to the wall.*]
Age tells. Age tells. Let me introduce myself. Colonel
Fenwick.
   [*He extracts a card from his waistcoat pocket and hands it to*

Masterman who leaves the wall. He picks up the cereal packet. ★]

FENWICK: Honey Crisps! My favourite cereal. I collect the lids. For twenty lids you get a box of Scrabble post free, but I'm holding on for thirty. A model Centurion tank in a Make-It-Yourself kit.

MASTERMAN: It says here you're an inspector. Are you a bogey?

FENWICK: Bogey?

MASTERMAN: Copper.

FENWICK: Dear me, no. Though I *am* hunting a man. [*He turns over the Honey Crisps packet*] You don't know, do you, whether Miss Harwich keeps the lids? If she doesn't, perhaps she'd let me take this one. It would make my twenty-fifth. Of course the Centurion, as tanks go, is rather a historic relic like the Spitfire. But they were names that struck the imagination of us all. I was in the Western Desert myself. In the Long Range Desert Group. We nearly snaffled Rommel.

MASTERMAN [*suspicious and nervous*]: What does it mean – inspector?

FENWICK: I work for the Anti-Child-Polio Campaign. A man can't just retire on his pension.

MASTERMAN: Who's this you're hunting?

FENWICK: A scoundrelly fellow. Bit of a come-down after Rommel.

MASTERMAN: What's he done?

FENWICK: Worse than murder, I'd call it.

MASTERMAN: Worse than murder?

FENWICK: The fellow goes round with phoney credentials pretending to collect money for the Anti-Child-Polio Campaign. I'm hot on *his* tracks, though.

MASTERMAN [*with astonishment*]: Do you call that worse than murder?

FENWICK: Much, much *worse*. Betrayal of trust. Stealing from these poor children we are trying to help. People are very generous. That old lady downstairs – Miss Marbles – tells me she gave the fellow fifty pounds she could ill afford.

★ In the Haymarket Studio Theatre, Leicester, production, to add to the element of farce, the bed, of its own accord, descended a number of times during this act without Fenwick noticing – Masterman having to push it back up.

MASTERMAN: Fifty pounds!

FENWICK: I'll try to get the Committee to reimburse her. They are a fine group. Energetic, imaginative, bold – we didn't have a better lot in the Western Desert. Princess Anne is one of our patrons.

MASTERMAN: All the same, sir. Worse than murder?

FENWICK: Yes, of course. Murder, after all, is only a form of killing. I have been responsible for two deaths myself.

MASTERMAN: Two?

FENWICK: In the Western Desert.

MASTERMAN: That was war.

FENWICK: My dear fellow, when are we not at war? Even cold war should have its victims if efficiently carried out. Unfortunately it very seldom is.

MASTERMAN: But this poor sod you're hunting – he needs the money probably.

FENWICK: Then let him kill for it like a gentleman. I can sympathize with a crime of violence, even of passion, but to tell lies and show phoney credentials – that's simply not on the cards.

MASTERMAN: You're getting me confused, sir.

FENWICK: Of course, I regret that those fellows in Parliament – trade unionists most of them – have abolished the death penalty. The death penalty made the whole business of killing more worthwhile. You risked your life when you killed.

MASTERMAN: Not when it was some poor innocent girl.

FENWICK: One mustn't be sentimental, my dear fellow. Innocent girls are rare, innocent girls who get murdered very rare indeed. Anyway, they belong to the stronger sex. You know Kipling's fine poem. 'The female of the species is more deadly than the male.' I'm all for women's lib, of course. Do you think Miss Harwich would mind if I smoked?

MASTERMAN: No. It won't affect her where she is now. I mean at Marks and Sparks.

[FENWICK *takes out a cigarette case.*]

FENWICK: Will you keep me company?

MASTERMAN: I've given them up. All those health scares scared me all right.

FENWICK: They've given me an added pleasure. I always buy

cigarettes with the biggest possible tar content. It's a sort of challenge. It or me. War to the death. [*Pause*] By the way, you've a very fine head of hair. Alas! Mine's all gone on top. How do you keep it?

MASTERMAN: I nearly lost all mine once.

FENWICK: Did you have it replanted? I read an advertisement – but the idea rather revolted me – all those little seedlings growing up there in my skull out of sight. I suppose one has to water them every day.

MASTERMAN: Mine just returned.

FENWICK: I believe my hair was a war casualty. I was always getting a lot of sand in it in the desert. Sometimes I'd be scratching half the night. People used to say it was the only thing they could hear for miles around.

MASTERMAN: I had a Rash once. But that was nervous.

FENWICK: Ah, war's a wonderful thing for calming the nerves.

MASTERMAN: Would you like a cup of tea? While you're waiting.

FENWICK: No, no, thank you. I'm a whisky-at-six man.

MASTERMAN: Some Honey Crisps?

FENWICK: No, no. I don't actually eat the things. I only collect the lids.

MASTERMAN: What do you do with the crisps?

FENWICK: Give them to my feathered friends.

MASTERMAN: They like them?

FENWICK: They disappear in a flash. I sprinkle them by my bird bath. I have a little garden in Wimbledon, you see, with a bird bath. That was a thing I missed in the desert. Birds. Such a waste. I could have done a lot of watching with my binoculars. Of course, there were other things to watch. That's another great thing about war. Killing and having time to watch. And the gossip of comrades while you wait. The kind of gossip we're having now. Waiting for Miss Harwich.

MASTERMAN: Like you used to wait for Rommel.

FENWICK: Exactly.

MASTERMAN: And do you find many interesting birds to watch in Wimbledon?

FENWICK: I still have my good Army binoculars and I once identified from a distance, on the Common, a long-tailed tit. I suppose it was watching birds which gave me the idea of volunteering as an inspector for the Campaign. So here you find me . . . At the old game of hunting.

MASTERMAN: Hot on the trail.

FENWICK: Of course, I have no legal power of arrest, but a scoundrel, like the one I'm looking for, I wouldn't have hesitated to strangle with my bare hands. In the good old days.

[*He makes a gesture with his hands, flexing the fingers, and* MASTERMAN *watches with apprehension.*]

Unfortunately, I suffer from gout now and I can't trust the thumbs. When you strangle the hard work is done with the thumbs. We had courses, you know, in silent killing. It's the kind of thing one always remembers. Like riding a bicycle. Of course, when silence is not essential you can do a lot of damage with the old knee jerk. Very painful it is too, even if it doesn't kill, and the effect can be lasting. Unfortunately I have gout in my right knee too now. I take Butazolidin – but in a sudden emergency the scoundrel could easily get away. All those splendid ways of killing – I remember them all, but they count for little now. I am an old man, all I have to rely on is a police whistle. [*He feels in his pockets*] To summon a constable to do the really interesting work. [*Pause*] By God, I've come out *without* it. I must have left it in my pyjamas.

MASTERMAN: You carry it in your pyjamas?

FENWICK: I'm never without it. I *would* forget it – just today of all days when I'm within smelling distance.

[*Stubs out cigarette.*]

MASTERMAN: Smelling?

[*He sniffs himself and casts an uneasy look towards the concealed bed.*]

FENWICK: How long did you say you'd been here?

MASTERMAN: About half an hour.

FENWICK: No callers? Not an ugly fellow with a completely bald head, shabbily dressed, wearing spectacles and carrying an attaché case? Pretends to sell copies of our magazine. Shoes almost falling apart. I telephoned the description just now to the local police. Can't be far away. Miss Marbles gave me a remarkably good description for a lady of her age. Said she knew at once there was something wrong.

MASTERMAN: Why did she give him fifty nicker then?

FENWICK: Nicker?

MASTERMAN: Pounds, I mean.

FENWICK: Ah, he appealed to her pity. You know how these men work. Sob stuff. Said the Campaign would sack him if he didn't show better results.

MASTERMAN: It's a bloody lie.

FENWICK: Of course it is. A man like that will stop at nothing. She said there was a veiled note of menace when he appealed to her pity.

MASTERMAN: He ought to have knifed the old cat.

FENWICK: Of course he should, if he had any gumption. I would have respected him if he *had*. She said when he left her he mounted the stairs in this direction.

MASTERMAN: Someone did ring the bell about twenty minutes ago.

FENWICK: What?!

MASTERMAN: But I was having a bath.

FENWICK: Did he come in?

MASTERMAN: He just opened the door and I told him to be off.

FENWICK: You saw him though?

MASTERMAN: Well, I had soap in my eyes. I didn't see clearly.

FENWICK: Could he have slipped in and be hiding in another room? I found your door unlocked myself.

MASTERMAN: There isn't another room. This is all there is.

FENWICK: But you mentioned taking a bath.

MASTERMAN: There it is. Under the table. [*He lifts the table cloth*] You just pull back the table.

FENWICK: How very ingenious.

MASTERMAN: This is an omnibus studio.

FENWICK: But I suppose there's at least a kitchen. He could be lurking there.

　　[MASTERMAN *slides back the wall to show the kitchenette, then closes it again.*]

Wonderful what these backroom boys do think up. I met a boffin once in Cairo who was working out a system for sending liquid fire by mail in what looked like an ordinary envelope. Asbestos lined, of course. Tear open the envelope and you were ablaze before you could count two. Imagine the kind of scene when the post turned up at Rommel's HQ. The idea was good, but there were a lot of practical difficulties. You couldn't post to Rommel from Cairo. Now, where do you keep the bed? No, don't tell me. I like to find out things for myself. I suppose the wall with the bed works the same way as the kitchen.

[*He begins to roam the room, to* MASTERMAN'*s consternation. He taps the walls in one place and then another.*]

Ha ha, you can't beat an old hand. Sounds hollow here. I bet you he hid in the bed while you were taking your bath. Knew I was after him probably.

[FENWICK *slides his hand over the wall. To* MASTERMAN'*s relief it's not the wall where the bed is.*]

We ought to call in the Sappers. They'd soon winkle him out.

MASTERMAN: But how could he get in there without my seeing him?

FENWICK: Perhaps while you were soaping your backside. Miss Marbles said he was a mean cunning type up to any tricks. Wheedling she said he was.

MASTERMAN: You can't trust an old cat like that. She's pretty mean herself. You shouldn't take that fifty pounds on trust, either. I bet it was nearer a tenner – if that.

FENWICK: This is it all right. Come on, my dear chap. Show me how the bed works.

MASTERMAN: It's stuck. It often sticks.

FENWICK [*knocking on the wrong wall*]: Get a chisel and a hammer from my bag. I'll soon open it up for you. [*His ear to the wall*] I think I can hear him breathing. Hurry up with that chisel.

MASTERMAN: There's nobody there. It's just wall all the way through.

[FENWICK *raps his hand on the wall and this time a rap comes in reply.*]

FENWICK: There. You heard that. I expect he's scared stiff. Stuck in the wall like one of those naughty nuns.

[*He raps again. Another rap in reply.*]

You heard him.

MASTERMAN: It's only the neighbours. You rap, they rap back. If you turn on the television they turn theirs louder. It's always dog eats dog in an apartment.

FENWICK [*with his ear to the wall*]: The breathing's stopped. The bugger may be dying. From lack of air. Bring the chisel. He'll escape justice yet.

MASTERMAN: If he's dying . . .

FENWICK: We can't leave a dead body in Miss Harwich's wall. Think of the smell, man. It would attract rats too. We must get it out before she returns.

> [MASTERMAN *brings hammer and chisel – anything to keep the Colonel safely occupied and make good his own escape.*]

Bring a bread knife too in case he's still alive.

MASTERMAN [*from the kitchenette*]: There isn't one.

FENWICK [*peeling panel off wall*]: There must be. Don't you have toast for breakfast?

MASTERMAN: Miss Harwich only eats Honey Crisps.

FENWICK: Good God. [*Uncovering plaster wall*]

MASTERMAN: Will a carving knife do?

FENWICK: Yes – more classical but makes a less interesting wound.

> [MASTERMAN *brings a carving knife.*]

MASTERMAN: While you're opening the wall, I'll go and get the police.

FENWICK: You'll do no such thing. Why should the police have all the fun? You stand beside me with a knife and, if the body falls out, give it a sharp stab through the throat below the Adam's apple in case it's still alive.

MASTERMAN: Suppose it comes out backwards.

FENWICK: Good chap. Good question. Stick the knife in between the shoulder blades, but a little towards the left-hand side.

> [FENWICK *begins to work on the wall. A lot of plaster falls. The rapping from the other side starts again with a certain frenzy.*]

Out of breath. Out of condition. [*He sits down and wipes his brow*] I go jogging every morning on the Common, but it's not enough when you've been used to the Western Desert. Anyway, you can tell the fellow's still alive.

MASTERMAN: Let me go and get the police. It's their job.

FENWICK: Not on your life. Never call on the Civil Arm if I can help it. Always carry a small flask of whisky. [*He takes a swill*] Not a drinker, mind. Strictly a six-o'clock man except in an emergency. This is an emergency. Only thing that makes life worth living.

MASTERMAN: Whisky?

FENWICK: No, no, emergencies, of course. [*He wipes his brow*] To work again. Got to get the bugger out even if it's only to bury him.

> [*He prises out a brick. An arm shoots through the hole and grasps his wrist.*]

VOICE: What the hell are you doing to my wall?

FENWICK: Here he is, by God. Help me pull him out.

MASTERMAN: The hole's not big enough.

FENWICK: Then cut through his fingers, man. Never mind my wrist. If we can't pull him out, maim him.

VOICE: Mona, ring the police and hurry. He's dangerous.

FENWICK: No point in bluffing, my man. Better come quietly.

VOICE: Who the hell are you?

FENWICK: I'm going to hold you till the police come.

VOICE: You're not holding me. I'm holding you.

FENWICK: Who are *you*? State name, rank and number. What are you doing in Miss Harwich's apartment?

VOICE: I'm not in Miss Harwich's apartment. I'm in my own. You've been destroying my wall.

FENWICK: On the contrary, this is Miss Harwich's wall.

> [MASTERMAN *goes to the door to sneak out.*]

You stay where you are. I need your help with this bugger.

VOICE: Don't use obscene words in front of my wife.

FENWICK: By God, he's got a bitch in the bed.

> [*The front door bell chimes its melody. The Colonel gets his arm free with a final tug. The door opens and a uniformed Police Sergeant enters, dragging in the bald-headed spectacled x with his attaché case.*]

SERGEANT: Can either of you two gentlemen identify this man?

CURTAIN

Act Three

Tableau. Colonel Fenwick stands beside the hole in the wall. Masterman stands in front of the picture and the button which opens the bed. X stands behind the Police Sergeant with his head bent in a parody of shame. A pause while everybody looks at everybody. Colonel Fenwick takes out his card case and proffers his card to the Police Sergeant.

FENWICK: Well done, Sergeant. Here's my card. Colonel Fenwick. It was I who telephoned to the station. Very smart work. I was close on the trail of the scoundrel myself.

SERGEANT: It was the good description that did it, sir. Found him not half a mile from here drinking coffee and eating cereals in a café as happy as Punch. Completely bald, shabby suit, shoes near falling apart, attaché case containing twenty-five nicker – pardon me, sir, pounds – and four silver spoons. Asked him for his papers. Photo didn't correspond to his face. Brought him here, came like a lamb. I thought I'd tie the whole case up before taking him to the station. Identified by old lady, Miss Marbles, who said that she'd seen him go up to this flat. Owner Miss Felicity Harwich. Two identifications always better than one. Old lady short-sighted. Vulnerable if cross-examined.

FENWICK: Miss Harwich is out shopping, Sergeant. This gentleman here is her fiancé. He tells me was having a bath when the fellow rang. Didn't get a clear look because there was soap in his eyes.

SERGEANT: Bath, sir? Was the bathroom door open?

FENWICK: No door. The bath's kept under the table. This is an omnibus studio. Very compact. Wouldn't mind having one myself.

SERGEANT: What's happened to the wall? Looks as if there had been an explosion.

FENWICK: Just a misunderstanding.

VOICE FROM BEYOND THE WALL: Misunderstanding your bloody eye.

SERGEANT: Who's that?

FENWICK: Seems to be one of Miss Harwich's neighbours.

SERGEANT [*to* MASTERMAN]: Take a look at the man all the same, sir. You might have noticed his bald head – or those shoes of his or the spectacles, or the attaché case.

MASTERMAN [*reluctantly*]: The shoes do seem sort of familiar.

SERGEANT: And the bald head? He hadn't a hat on when I found him.

MASTERMAN: I don't want to get the poor geezer into trouble.

FENWICK: A man like that is beyond pity. Breach of trust. False papers. Robbing a charity. It's worse than murder.

X: May I speak?

MASTERMAN [*to* FENWICK]: I think, if you don't mind, sir, I ought to go and look for Miss Harwich.

SERGEANT: I'd like you to stay here, sir, for the time being. I'll want to take your statement.

X: Gentlemen, please listen to me. I want to unburden my conscience. I want to tell you the whole truth and nothing but the truth, so help me God.

   [SERGEANT *gets out his notebook.*]

SERGEANT: Don't go too fast then. I don't know shorthand. Name first.

X: My name is Ambrose Masterman.

   [MASTERMAN *makes a movement of protest and then thinks better of it.*]

SERGEANT [*writing*]: Ambrose Masterman. What age? [*Delayed reaction*] Masterman?

   [The SERGEANT *comes close to the man and takes a long look at him. He snatches off his spectacles.*]

SERGEANT: Why, if it isn't old Chips? But you've changed a lot, Chips.

X: It's age, it creeps up on all of us, Sergeant, and privation. I've known a lot of privation.

FENWICK: You know this man?

SERGEANT: Why, he was one of our regulars five years ago. In and out of the Scrubs he used to be. He and his friend Ginger. Never anything very serious, mind. A bit of false pretences. Ginger was a – trans – trans – he used to dress up as a woman. What's become of old Ginger, Chips?

x: I wish I knew. Gone, I suppose, where we all have to go.

SERGEANT: Don't think you ever copped more than two years, did you, Chips?

x: Never, so help me God.

FENWICK: I hope they'll give him a life-term now. People used to be hanged for stealing a handkerchief. It's these persistent petty criminals who are the real threat to the State.

SERGEANT: Oh, sir, Chips never did anything violent.

FENWICK: A beetle can destroy a cathedral, Sergeant. And think of the expense – lawyers and the like. It all goes on our income tax. There's a great deal to be said for the Mexican way of dealing with them. Prisoner tries to escape. Shoot him down. Law of flight. No one asks questions.

SERGEANT [*shocked*]: That's murder, sir.

FENWICK: People take a very exaggerated view of murder, Sergeant.

SERGEANT: Chips never cost us much, sir. Not even lawyers' fees. Always defended himself, he did. And a real artist he was at that. He'd begin with his birth in an orphanage and go on to a broken marriage and a nervous breakdown. He could wring tears even out of a magistrate.

FENWICK: Pack of lies. If I were on the Bench I'd have no mercy on men like him. Put 'em away. Put 'em away for life.

SERGEANT: After all, sir, when you think of it, what's he done? It's only a matter of twenty-five nick – pounds, sir, and four silver spoons. And then there's all this inflation, sir, to take into account. Ten years ago what he's stolen wouldn't have been worth a couple of quid. Poor fellow has to live somehow.

[MASTERMAN *is making for the door. The telephone rings for the first time. Everyone looks at* MASTERMAN. FENWICK *answers – hands it to* MASTERMAN.]

MASTERMAN [*into the telephone*]: Hello. Hello. You've got the wrong number. [*He adds gloomily*] Someone wants the RSPCA.

VOICE FROM THE DOORWAY: Sergeant, put that man in charge.

[*It is the* NEIGHBOUR *from next door. A burly man in his shirt-sleeves.*]

SERGEANT: He is in charge.

NEIGHBOUR: Not him, I don't mean. Him. [*He points at the Colonel*] He's made a hole in my wall.

FENWICK: It's not your wall. It's Miss Harwich's.

NEIGHBOUR: He threatened my life.

FENWICK: Nonsense. I don't even know you.

NEIGHBOUR: He used obscene language about my wife.

FENWICK: I don't even know if you've got a wife.

SERGEANT: Come, come, my man. We'll go into all that later. We've got more important things on hand. Have you seen this man before? [*Indicating* X]

NEIGHBOUR: Him? Yes. I think so.

SERGEANT: Did he ask you for money?

NEIGHBOUR: I just saw him pass the door, that's all. I don't talk to strangers.

SERGEANT: What was he doing?

NEIGHBOUR [*indicating* MASTERMAN]: Closing that bugger's door.

SERGEANT: You're using obscene language yourself now. In the presence of the law. That makes it worse.

NEIGHBOUR: It's not obscene language. It's a description. [*Indicating* MASTERMAN] He *is* a bugger. He lives on girls.

FENWICK: The two things are incompatible, my man.

NEIGHBOUR: Miss Harwich is no beauty, but she deserves better than she's got. Fat she may be. Squinting she may be, bandy-legged she may be, but . . .

FENWICK: Aren't we straying rather far from the subject, Sergeant?

NEIGHBOUR: He spends her money on other women as soon as her back's turned. Always fat women they are. He has a fancy for fat women.

MASTERMAN: I've never known a fat woman in my life. I've no time for fat women. Or lean ones, either.

NEIGHBOUR: You are a bloody liar. I've got eyes in my head. My wife's got eyes in her head. Don't you call Miss Harwich fat? And that one a week ago. Came to see you as soon as Miss Harwich went shopping. Fat as a pregnant cow. Why, if my wife hadn't lost all her weight with the shingles I wouldn't have felt safe having you next door. As it is, poor woman, she's insulted with obscene language by this – calls himself a colonel.

FENWICK: I wouldn't know your wife if I passed her in the street.

NEIGHBOUR: Colonel Nose-in-the-Air – you'd know her fast enough if she was a general's wife.

FENWICK: I only meant I wouldn't recognize her because I've never seen her. I'm sure she's a very good woman.

NEIGHBOUR: Good woman's right. Even though she's a mere skeleton after the shingles. She wouldn't want to know *your* wife.

FENWICK: I haven't got a wife. This is absurd, Sergeant. We were supposed to be investigating a crime.

NEIGHBOUR: Destroying my wall; that's right.

FENWICK: Stealing money from a charity. False papers . . .

NEIGHBOUR: I bet the papers you have are as false as Judas. Call yourself a colonel!

FENWICK [*stung at last*]: I don't know what you did in the war, my man. I fought Rommel in the Western Desert.

NEIGHBOUR: I was an air-raid warden when you were tucked up safe in the Army. Fought Rommel. Fought your bleeding arse.

X: Might I speak a word?

[*The telephone rings.* MASTERMAN *takes the receiver.*]

MASTERMAN: Hello. No, madam, this is *not* the RSPCA. I can't help it. You've got the wrong number. No, I can't do a damn thing about your Peke. She probably asked for it.

[*General outburst*]

SERGEANT: Please, gentlemen. If we could get things sorted out in the right order of importance . . .

MASTERMAN: You've no right to keep *me* here, Sergeant.

SERGEANT: It's the duty of every man to help the police in their inquiries. Why do you want to get away so bad, anyway?

X: Are you or are you not going to take my statement, Sergeant? I tell you I admit everything. After all this bedlam I would like to get into the comparative quiet of a prison cell.

MASTERMAN: You don't need me. I saw nothing. I heard nothing. I want to go and look for Miss Harwich. I want to tell her what's happened to her wall. She ought to know.

SERGEANT: All in good time, all in good time. I'm going to take your statement after the prisoner's given his, Mr . . . I'm afraid I don't know your name, sir.

NEIGHBOUR: No one here knows his name. He was just Miss Harwich's fiancé. Fiancé, I ask you!

X: I confess everything. I've been taking money on false pretences. I have forged credentials. I . . .

SERGEANT: How do you spell credentials? Since I knew you last, Chips, you've begun to talk very fancy.

X: I've been attending night school. Put papers if that's easier.

SERGEANT: What age are you now, Chips? We have to write things down in proper order. Ambrose Masterman, commonly known as Chips, aged –?

X: Forty-one-and-a-half.

SERGEANT: What do you mean – half?

X: Forty-one plus one hundred and eighty-two and a half days – I may be a few hours out. My mother was never very accurate.

SERGEANT: Past employment?

X: I can't remember.

SERGEANT [*writing*]: Unemployed then.

X: No. Unemployable. There's a great difference.

FENWICK: There's an awful smell of cooking in this room.

NEIGHBOUR: That's your bloody fault. You made a hole in the wall, didn't you? My old woman's cooking a stew. [*He smells at the hole*] My God, she's letting it burn. MONA! [*He peers through the hole*] Look after that stew, Mona, it's burning. Don't hang around there listening to what doesn't concern you. [*He turns back*] Fat or thin, you can't trust them. Curiosity never kills those cats.

SERGEANT [*to* MASTERMAN]: You said, sir, you could identify this man's shoes?

MASTERMAN: I said I had soap in my eyes. I can't be sure. I don't make no charge.

SERGEANT [*to* X]: Well, there's sufficient witnesses without *him*, Chips. Miss Marbles and the gentleman with the spoons. We'd better be off to the station. I'll take your statement there.

X: What are we waiting for then? I'll go quietly. I told you. I want to unburden my conscience.

SERGEANT: You *did* learn a lot at night school.

FENWICK: Don't trust him. As soon as he's released he'll start again.

X: I want to atone for my offence. Before Society and Princess Anne.

SERGEANT [*quickly*]: Princess Anne? What's she got to do with this affair?

NEIGHBOUR: What about my wall?

SERGEANT: Nothing to do with me. That's a case for a civil action.

NEIGHBOUR: Civil action be buggered. How do you know he wasn't trying to rob my flat?

SERGEANT: It's not likely the Colonel . . .

NEIGHBOUR: Calls himself a colonel.

FENWICK: My dear fellow . . .

NEIGHBOUR: What does it signify, anyway? The Army teaches you to steal. Half the bank robbers were colonels once. Theft, murder, rapine.

FENWICK: I don't know what went on in your warden's post . . .

NEIGHBOUR: Darts. That's what went on. Darts. We used to play darts when we weren't in action. What did you do when you weren't in action? Not sit on your arse in the sand, I bet. Oh, I've heard stories of Cairo. Girls, donkeys . . .

FENWICK: What on earth would I want to steal from your flat?

NEIGHBOUR: Look at the two of them, Sergeant. In cahoots, they were. Ready to murder me, they were. 'Stick him in the neck below the Adam's apple.' I heard him with my own ears. Look at the table, Sergeant. There's the knife. [*Pause*] Makes a less 'interesting' wound than a bread knife, he said. Interesting! I ask you.

[*The* SERGEANT *takes up the knife.*]

SERGEANT [*to* FENWICK]: What were you doing with this, sir? It *is* an offensive weapon. In the eyes of the law. Possession of an offensive weapon . . .

FENWICK: Offensive weapon! It's only a kitchen knife.

SERGEANT: That's right, sir. But the emphasis in law is on knife, not kitchen.

FENWICK: Then how the hell do you carve a chicken without an offensive weapon?

SERGEANT: It's the intention that counts, sir.

NEIGHBOUR [*suddenly enlightened*]: Intention? That's it, Sergeant. Kidnapping and violation. My Mona.

FENWICK: I've no doubt at all that your Mona is an admirable woman, but I've never even had the pleasure of . . .

NEIGHBOUR: Pleasure! You heard him, Sergeant. You may be a bloody colonel, but I tell you she keeps her pleasure for her husband.

FENWICK: Sergeant, can't we please get back to facts? You've caught the scoundrel . . .

NEIGHBOUR: A pair of scoundrels – him and that fellow there [*pointing at* MASTERMAN]. Breaking down the wall, threatening me with a knife – what chance would poor Mona have had against the two of them? It's enough to give her hysterics. She's liable to hysterics.

FENWICK: From the smell in here she's quite happily occupied with the stew.

X: Sergeant, are you or are you not going to charge me?

SERGEANT: You oughter know by this time, Chips, you can only be charged at the station.

NEIGHBOUR [*to* SERGEANT]: You take the bloody Colonel and his friend to the station too. You have the evidence. You aren't blind, are you? That hole in the wall. You can see that, can't you?

SERGEANT: From where I'm standing it's Miss Harwich's wall.

X [*as though chanting a litany*]: Will all of you please note that I have been receiving money on false pretences, that I have carried forged identity papers and that I wish to purge my offence in some quiet cell at the Scrubs, preferably in solitary.

SERGEANT: Night school again. It's made another man of you, Chips. [*To the Colonel*] That hole, sir. I do think it needs an explanation.

FENWICK: I was looking for the bed. I thought that man [*indicating* X] might be hiding in the bed.

NEIGHBOUR [*indicating* MASTERMAN]: And him? He was helping you, wasn't he? Looking for the bed! Don't tell me he doesn't know where he keeps the bed. He uses it often enough. At disgusting times of the day too. Often when Mona's washing up the breakfast she hears things.

SERGEANT: What sort of things?

NEIGHBOUR: Screams that curdle the blood. She knocked on the door once, thinking it was murder, and all she got was a giggle. I'm asking you. At ten o'clock in the morning when any honest man is at work.

SERGEANT: Where *is* the bed?

MASTERMAN [*unwillingly*]: It's the wall, but the machinery got stuck.

NEIGHBOUR: I'll show you, Sergeant. We've got the same contraption ourselves. [*He moves towards the wall where the picture is.*]

MASTERMAN [*getting between*]: You aren't going to touch anything in my flat.

NEIGHBOUR: It's not your flat. It's Miss Harwich's. You're only a lodger – and that's a polite word for what you are.

MASTERMAN: Only Miss Harwich has the right . . .

SERGEANT: I don't know what the bed's got to do with it. Chips is here. He's not in any bed. It's a simple case of false pretences and forged papers.

NEIGHBOUR: It's a case of attempted robbery, destroying my wall, trying to rape Mona.

SERGEANT: But what's the bed . . . ?

NEIGHBOUR: That's his alibi, isn't it? The bloody Colonel's alibi. Said he was trying to find the bed . . . Why, he wasn't even trying the right wall. That's the right wall [*pointing*].

SERGEANT: Why did you pick on this wall, sir?

FENWICK: It sounded hollow.

SERGEANT [*to* MASTERMAN]: Why didn't you tell him it was the wrong wall?

MASTERMAN: I didn't want him interfering with Miss Harwich's bed.

SERGEANT: He's interfered with her all right.

MASTERMAN: That's different. A girl's bed's sort of sacred.

[*An angry snort from the* NEIGHBOUR.]

NEIGHBOUR: Sacred! What were you doing in it an hour ago? Praying?

MASTERMAN: Me? What do you mean? I wasn't in no bloody bed.

NEIGHBOUR: A disgusting time to do things. Half past ten by my watch. Wife was cutting up the carrots for the stew. She nearly cut herself when your tart started screaming. Disgusting it was. I wanted to knock on the door, but Mona said 'You'll only get a giggle.'

SERGEANT: So that's why you were having a bath, eh? Well, the law's not concerned with what goes on in private between consulting adults.

NEIGHBOUR: You call it private? When you can hear them in the kitchen going at it like a pair of cats?

SERGEANT: You might take a civil action. A case against the builders. Nothing criminal.

[General outburst.]

Now let me get the story straight. [To MASTERMAN] You were in the bath when this man arrived. You had soap in your eyes. You saw his shoes, but you are unwilling to swear to them. Was Miss Harwich still here? [Pause] Did she get a sight of him?

MASTERMAN: No. She'd gone shopping. I told you that. Marks and Spencers. And I want to go and find her. She ought to know what's going on here. It's her flat. She won't be far off.

SERGEANT: I don't want any one of you to leave. We can wait till she comes.

X: But I've made a full confession. You don't need more than that.

SERGEANT: Come off it, Chips. You know how often your friend Ginger confessed to the police and then denied it in court. Even when he was dressed up to the nines. Said he was going to a fancy dress party.

NEIGHBOUR: If you want to know what I think – she's not gone out, not Miss Harwich. She's in here hiding.

SERGEANT: Why do you think she's here?

NEIGHBOUR: I told you, didn't I, I saw that man going off [indicating X]. When I went to see if Mona was doing the stew right. We were having a bit of an argument when I heard steps again and I thought it was Miss Harwich off to shop and I wanted to give her a bit of my mind. Yelling like that at ten thirty in the morning. But it wasn't her. It was Colonel Nose-in-the-Air arriving and then all the hammering and swearing started. Oh, she's here somewhere. Ashamed to show her face. A great fat girl – you'd think she'd have more self-respect. Three of them at it, I thought, and now they want Mona. Perverts. Anyway, Miss Harwich knows what I think of her now. Wherever she's hiding.

SERGEANT: Hiding where?

NEIGHBOUR: In the kitchen like as not.

[*The* NEIGHBOUR *goes to the wall and operates the sliding door. The* SERGEANT *and the* COLONEL *look in the kitchen.*]

SERGEANT: You couldn't hide a cat in here.

NEIGHBOUR: Let's try the bath.

[*The* NEIGHBOUR *pulls out the bath from under the table. As the* SERGEANT *looks at it* MASTERMAN *moves towards the door.*]

SERGEANT [*to* FENWICK]: Just a minute, sir.

[*The* SERGEANT *puts his hand in the bath and licks his fingers.*]

SERGEANT: No one there. [*To* MASTERMAN] You took no bath. There's no soap in this water.

NEIGHBOUR: All bloody lies.

SERGEANT: Here you – I told you not to leave. [*He grabs* MASTERMAN *by the arm*]

NEIGHBOUR: Let's try the bed.

MASTERMAN: She can't be there. She'd suffocate. I tell you, she's out shopping.

NEIGHBOUR: Suffocate my eye. You know there's *ventilation*.

[*He goes to the correct wall and presses the button. A grinding noise and the bed descends and the body of Miss Harwich is disclosed. A pause of consternation. The* SERGEANT, *the* COLONEL *and the* NEIGHBOUR *approach the bed.* MASTERMAN *moves towards* X.]

X: Oh dear, oh dear. What a terrible thing to happen. She *has* suffocated.

NEIGHBOUR: Murder more like. I tell you these beds are ventilated.

SERGEANT: Alleged murder. No signs of violence.

FENWICK: Yes, there are, Sergeant. Look at the neck. A very skilful karate blow, I would say. I couldn't have done it better myself – thirty years ago.

[*The* SERGEANT *looks again at the body, then goes to the telephone and dials.*]

SERGEANT: Sergeant Russell speaking. That you, Bob? Tell the Chief Inspector . . . Having a shit? What do I care? I've got a case of murder here. What you mean where? Here. Those new Omni–Studios in Belcham Place. Third floor. Middle one. Get them to send the doctor, ambulance, all the works. Knock on the door, you fool, knock on the door. I know the Inspector. Reading the *Guardian*, that's all.

[*He puts down the receiver.*]

Did nobody hear anything?

NEIGHBOUR: That scream. It wasn't no giggle. That's when he done her in.

MASTERMAN: Not me, Sergeant. Him (*indicating* x). He's her fiancé. Not me. You know me. Old Chips. You can't have forgotten Old Chips.

[*He remembers the wig he is wearing and pulls it off. He plants it on x's head.*]

FENWICK: Nothing to be ashamed of, my man. Clean, quick blow. She won't have suffered at all.

[*The* SERGEANT *is gazing from* x *to* MASTERMAN *in bewilderment.*]

SERGEANT: You *sound* like Chips.

MASTERMAN: I *am* Chips, Sergeant. I was only at the old game. Money on false pretences. Forged papers. Nothing serious, Sergeant. *He's* her fiancé – he's the murderer [*pointing at* x].

x: I can see you are a bit confused, Sergeant. My fault entirely. I think it is time to admit that – well, that I've lied a little bit. It's my damn sense of humour. Always getting me into trouble.

SERGEANT: Someone's in real trouble.

x: Yes. Poor, dear Felicity. To think she was lying there all the time while I joked with her murderer. You see, I had to go out earlier than usual this morning. I left Felicity sound asleep and when I returned she wasn't there. But *he* was. Said that she'd gone shopping. Said that she'd given him a cup of tea and some Honey Crisps and promised him five pounds – an obvious lie. She wasn't that sort of girl. Look out for fingerprints, Sergeant, on the teacup there and the spoon. You will soon find they are his, not mine. Then he started his spiel about the poor children suffering from polio, so I played a naughty little trick on him. He had tried to con me, so I conned him. Got him to exchange clothes, said I was giving them for the cause, even took his case. Of course I would have returned his money and all the rest if you hadn't happened to find me. I was having a cup of coffee while I waited to intercept Felicity. I wanted to tell her about my little joke. To think that all the time she was lying there, murdered. I bet you'll find his fingerprints all over the bed and the studio.

FENWICK: Careless thing to do!

SERGEANT: Why didn't you speak up when I brought you here?

X: I was sorry for the poor devil, Sergeant. He was such an inefficient con man. Of course I would have told you all when we got to the station, but I was giving him a chance to get away. If I'd known he had killed poor Felicity . . .

MASTERMAN: It's a bloody pack of lies. You can't believe him, Sergeant. You know I've never been one for violence. It's not in my nature. You know me.

SERGEANT: I know all that, Chips. I wouldn't have believed it of you. But everyone has to begin some time. Perhaps you learnt all that at night school . . .

MASTERMAN: That was him, Sergeant. Not me. I've never been to night school.

SERGEANT: Christ, I'm getting muddled.

FENWICK: I would like to make an offer, Sergeant. Two crimes have been committed. One murder, one a good deal worse than murder. When you have decided which is the murderer I will undertake to pay a good lawyer for his defence.

[*The* NEIGHBOUR *begins to leave.*]

SERGEANT: Where are you going?

NEIGHBOUR: I want to tell Mona there's been a murder next door. She's a right to know.

SERGEANT: No one leaves here. No one. No one touches anything. When the doctor's examined the deceased – time of death, semen tests – all the works, and the fingerprint men have put their powder on everything touchable, and the photographers have taken pictures of the body – then maybe things will look a bit clearer. I hope to God they do, because it's a proper muddle now.

[MASTERMAN *has begun to mutter to himself.*]

SERGEANT: What's that you're saying, Chips – if you are Chips.

MASTERMAN: I was only talking to Ginger, Sergeant.

[*The* SERGEANT *looks wildly around.*]

SERGEANT: Ginger? Ginger? Where the hell is Ginger?

MASTERMAN: He's where Miss Harris is now.

SERGEANT: Harris?

X: Harwich.

[*As the telephone begins to ring,* X *goes to it as by right and is about to lift the receiver.* FENWICK *takes receiver – hands it to* MASTERMAN *–* SERGEANT *snatches it, hands it to* X.]

X: Hello.

SERGEANT: Use a handkerchief, man. I told you not to touch anything.

X: No, madam, you can't. I regret to tell you that the offices of the RSPCA are closed – for an indefinite period. The RSPCA is bankrupt.

[*The* SERGEANT *has sat down wearily at the table. Absentmindedly he picks up the teacup and looks in it.*]

X: Sergeant, you are destroying the fingerprints.

[*The* SERGEANT *wakes from his muse and drops the cup which breaks on the floor.*]

SERGEANT: Damn, damn, damn. Damn everything.

[COLONEL FENWICK *is peering at the corpse.*]

X: Taking a close look, Colonel?

FENWICK: These police doctors know nothing about karate. To them a bruise is just a bruise. I want my evidence to be precise. Isn't there a light we can put on? [*Finds button*] Ah!

[*At this moment the front door bell chimes again. The* SERGEANT *is on his knees gathering up the scraps of broken cup with a handkerchief. The* COLONEL *has touched a button on the wall, hoping that it is a light switch, the bed swings up against the wall.*

The INSPECTOR, *a woman with a deep voice, enters.*]

INSPECTOR: What the hell are you up to, Sergeant?

SERGEANT [*scrambling to his feet*]: Just a little accident.

INSPECTOR: Accident? You said it was a murder.

SERGEANT: Yes, yes, Inspector, it is a murder.

INSPECTOR: Where's the cadaver?

SERGEANT: Cadaver?

INSPECTOR: The body, Sergeant, the body.

SERGEANT [*looking wildly around*]: Oh, my God, it's gone.

FENWICK: I am really very sorry. I thought I was touching a light switch.

[*He presses the button again and again and nothing happens. The* SERGEANT *desperately tries to find the edge of the bed to pull it down, helped by the* NEIGHBOUR.]

X: These modern mini-studios are very badly built. Something always goes wrong. [MASTERMAN *has slowly approached the* INSPECTOR, *scrutinizing her closely. Suddenly he makes a grab and knocks off her cap, disclosing her red hair.*]

MASTERMAN: Ginger!

INSPECTOR: Chips!

MASTERMAN: I thought you were dead.

INSPECTOR: What are you doing here? Not up to the old game?

MASTERMAN: I was never any good at it without you, Ginger.

INSPECTOR: But not *murder*, Chips?

MASTERMAN: Of course not murder, Ginger. The Sergeant here – he's got everything screwed up the wrong way round. But you, you a policeman – I mean a policewoman . . . How did it happen?

SERGEANT: By God – Ginger!

INSPECTOR: It's a strange story, Chips, which redounds as much to the credit of the Metropolitan Police as to myself.

[*The* SERGEANT, FENWICK *and the* NEIGHBOUR *gather to listen.*]

MASTERMAN: You still have a fancy way of talking, Ginger.

INSPECTOR: Yes, perhaps it helped me. I have risen very quick. They say at Scotland Yard that I combine the intellect of a man with the intuition of a woman. I'll tell you how it all began. I was in hospital for my little operation. I met someone high up in the Crime Squad. She was in the next bed and we had the same surgeon and the same operation – only she was, as it were, going the other way.

MASTERMAN: You didn't love him – her –?

INSPECTOR: No need for jealousy, Chips. It was just friendship at first sight like women have. You see, there was a moment, before she was operated, when we were the same . . . like ships that pass in the night.

[*The bed descends.* x *exits unseen.*]

SERGEANT: Ginger, I mean sir, the body!

INSPECTOR: Don't be so carnal, Sergeant.

SERGEANT: The body, sir, the body's here. You ought to take a look.

[*The* INSPECTOR *goes reluctantly to the bed.*]

INSPECTOR: What a very ugly girl. I'm not surprised she came to a bad end.

FENWICK: Killed by a karate blow, Inspector.

INSPECTOR: You don't suspect Chips, surely?

SERGEANT: Well, it looks like it was him or this one.

[*Indicating where he last saw* x. *He panics, as he realizes* x *has gone, and exits.*]

INSPECTOR: Sergeant! [*To* FENWICK] Who are you and what are you doing here?

FENWICK: My name is Colonel Fenwick. Here's my card. Formerly of the Long Range Desert Group. We fought Rommel, you know, in the Western Desert.

INSPECTOR: Then you know all about karate?

FENWICK: Naturally.

INSPECTOR: Unarmed combat?

FENWICK: Of course. It was our speciality.

INSPECTOR: And this girl – she died in unarmed combat?

[*Pause. The* NEIGHBOUR *turns to listen.*]

FENWICK: What you are suggesting is absurd, Inspector. I am a Security Officer for the Anti-Child-Polio Campaign. I came here looking for a con man, who has been posing as a representative, getting money under false pretences.

INSPECTOR: And you found the girl in bed. I wouldn't be surprised if there were your fingerprints all over the bed.

FENWICK: I was examining the corpse to see how she was killed.

INSPECTOR: You Commandos get a taste for blood, don't you?

FENWICK: Blood, no. We always prefer to do it quietly with the hands.

NEIGHBOUR: This wasn't so quiet. Me and Mona heard a scream.

INSPECTOR: And what did you do?

NEIGHBOUR: Nothing. I thought they were just at it again. Disgusting!

INSPECTOR: As a military man, Colonel, I dare say you are well accustomed to rape.

FENWICK: I certainly am not. I am not even married.

NEIGHBOUR: He tried to cut off my arm.

FENWICK: He put his arm through the wall.

NEIGHBOUR: He was knocking down the wall.

FENWICK: I was looking for the con man. I thought he was hiding in the wall.

INSPECTOR: How can you hide in a wall?

[SERGEANT *re-enters*.]

Sergeant, you had better take the Colonel – if he *is* a colonel – to the station and let him make a statement. [*To* FENWICK] You are not under arrest. You are merely helping the police in their inquiries. Sergeant, I'll stay here for the doctor and the rest to arrive. Keep him at the station till I come.

FENWICK: On what possible evidence . . .

INSPECTOR: My intelligence as a man and my intuition as a woman.

FENWICK: You are a bloody transvestite.

INSPECTOR: I was once, but as you see I have made up my mind which sex to be. Sergeant, take him away.

FENWICK: I'll go. But this is monstrous. Ring up the Anti-Child-Polio Campaign. Speak to Mrs Falconbridge. Princess Anne is one of our patrons.

[*He goes away with the* SERGEANT, *followed by the* NEIGHBOUR, *shouting* 'Murderer! I knew it. I could tell. Murderer! Murderer!' *Romantic music*.]

INSPECTOR: At last, after all these years, Chips, we are alone – except for the body of course.

MASTERMAN: Why did you ever leave me, Ginger?

INSPECTOR: It wasn't good for your morale, Chips, waking up every morning, not knowing whether I'd be a man or a woman.

MASTERMAN: You look beautiful, Ginger. That blue uniform just goes with your hair and eyes.

INSPECTOR: I am glad you like me still, Chips. [*She pats her hair and looks round for a looking-glass*] My hair is all mussed up and there's not a mirror in the flat. How can anybody live without a mirror?

MASTERMAN: She was a very ugly girl, Ginger.

INSPECTOR: All the same, she had her man – and a colonel at that if he's telling the truth.

MASTERMAN: *You* could have any man you wanted, Ginger.

INSPECTOR: I don't want *any* man.

MASTERMAN: Ginger, what about me and you . . .

INSPECTOR: Yes?

MASTERMAN: I mean – now you've settled to be a woman . . .

[*The bell chimes. Romantic music stops.* INSPECTOR *collects hat from table.*]

MASTERMAN: Don't answer, Ginger.

INSPECTOR: I must. It's the doctor.

[*She opens the door. A* STRANGER *stands on the threshold. A timid figure in glasses.*]

INSPECTOR: Who the hell are you?

STRANGER: Miss Harwich?

INSPECTOR: Of course I'm not Miss Harwich.

STRANGER: Is she in?

INSPECTOR: It depends what you mean by in.

STRANGER: Can I speak to her?

INSPECTOR: Who are you?

STRANGER: I'm the Assistant Honorary Secretary of the local branch of the RSPCA.

INSPECTOR: Why do you want Miss Harwich?

STRANGER: She is our Branch Secretary. We have been telephoning her and receiving very odd replies. I must really speak to her.

INSPECTOR: What about?

STRANGER: About a dead bitch she's reported. Killed by someone unknown in what seem terrible circumstances.

INSPECTOR: Come in. Come in.

[*He enters tentatively, puts out his hand to* MASTERMAN *but drops it.*]

INSPECTOR [*pointing at the bed*]: There's the only dead bitch I know of round here.

STRANGER [*to* MASTERMAN]: How do you do?

MASTERMAN [*to* INSPECTOR]: Ginger?!

INSPECTOR: Yes, Chips, yes. [*She kisses him*] Yes, yes, yes.

    [*She kisses him again and tears off her uniform cap.*]

  Enough of this bloody uniform. Let's go, Chips.

    [*They leave, shutting the door behind them, just as the* STRANGER *reaches the bed.*]

STRANGER: That's not a Pekinese.

    [*Bell chimes again. He turns with a look of dismay. The door has closed and he is alone with the corpse.*]

CURTAIN